The Face of Crazy Horse

The Case for a Tintype Photograph of the Great Lakota Patriot

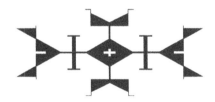

Cesare Marino and Pietro Abiuso

Foreword by Francis White Lance

Venerable Press®

Published in the United States by
Venerable Press®, a division of Surrogate Press®, LLC
and an imprint of Faceted Press®.

www.SurrogatePress.com

ISBN: 978-1-947459-08-3

Library of Congress Control Number: 2017961579

Photo restoration by: Doug Jepperson

Book cover design by: Katie Mullaly, Surrogate Press®

Interior design by: Katie Mullaly, Surrogate Press®

Dedicated to

Tašunke Witko (Crazy Horse)
whose true likeness long eluded us

and

Stephen E. Feraca (Wačiyapi)
who searched before we did.

"Tašunke Witko emaciyapilo!"

"He was a very handsome young man of about thirty-six years or so. He was not so dark; he had hazel eyes, nice long light brown hair. [...] his braids were wrapped in fur. He was partly wrapped in a broad cloth blanket, his leggings were also navy blue broad cloth, and his moccasins were beaded."

Susan Bordeaux Bettelyoun, daughter of James Bordeaux, 1936

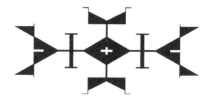

The Face of Crazy Horse

Tašunke Witko Taité

The tintype, attributed to James H. Hamilton, 1877.

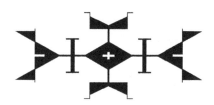

Table of Contents

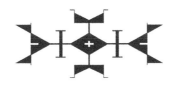

Crazy Horse, painting by Thom Little Moon (2014).

Acknowledgments

This book was made possible first and foremost by the unwavering determination of my friend Pietro Abiuso who, during much of his adult life,
relentlessly pursued his research on Crazy Horse's photographic portrait,
even though he was often confronted by nearly insurmountable obstacles,
skepticism, even hostility. My own interest in Crazy Horse led me to cross
paths with Pietro, discuss with him at length the tintype issue, and assume
the responsibility of articulating our joint effort into these written pages.
During the many years that our book was in the making, family and closest
friends showed patience and understanding towards our obstinate search
and seemingly endless project – I thank them all. I am indebted to those
who searched before we did, especially the late Steve Feraca (1934-1999),
and the authors, artists, and photographers whose works we cited or reproduced herein. Paula Fleming was always forthcoming anytime we asked
for her advice. Wopila tanka to Francis White Lance for his Foreword, the
information he shared with us, and his and wife Suzanne's hospitality. A
special thanks to Francis's nephew, Thom Little Moon, for his Crazy Horse
painting featured in our book.

Cesare Marino
Alexandria, Virginia

I wish to thank my friend Cesare Marino for trusting my original research, adding his own information and knowledge, and carrying the burden of writing this book. Of course, I also thank my wife Teresa and my children, Nicolina and Pasquale, for their support during these many years. My gratitude goes to the Connetquot Public Library, Bohemia, New York, for their help and cooperation. While today much information is readily available at the click of a mouse, thanks to the power of internet, when I first began my research over thirty years ago everything had to be done either in person or by paper correspondence. The Library's help was even more critical as I could not always afford traveling to distant locations out West. I also thank Francis White Lance for his friendship, the honor of having him as a special guest in my house, and his Foreword. Last but not least, I would like to remember with gratitude my late friend Richard Jepperson (1931-2003) from AuthorsDen who greatly inspired me and made me notice the wotawe clearly visible in Crazy Horse's left arm; a crucial detail that, initially, had not caught my attention.
Pietro Abiuso
West Palm Beach, Florida
In memory of my mother.

We wish to thank Katie Mullaly and Doug Jepperson for their crucial help with the editorial, design, and publishing process that made possible the publication of our book.
The Authors

Foreword by Francis White Lance

My introduction to the tintype photograph of Crazy Horse took place several years ago during a trip home from school in Evanston, Illinois. While visiting at my father-in-law's, Edgar Fire Thunder, he was showing my wife Suzanne some of their family pictures and other heirlooms that he kept in an old trunk. Among the things he was showing Suzanne, there was also an old newsletter of the Oglala Sioux Tribe written by Jake Herman in 1952. The newsletter contained a note about the tintype in which Herman said it was a supposed photograph of Crazy Horse. I asked my father-in-law about the old tintype and he mentioned that people there had been circulating the copy of the photograph for some time as a picture of Crazy Horse.

In early 1990, I began researching the history of my family and my tribe. My paternal grandmother was Susie White Lance, the daughter of Daniel White Lance. Daniel had two brothers, Joseph Horn Cloud and Iron Hail, who later took the name of Dewey Beard. Their father was Horn Cloud.

Horn Cloud's mother was the sister of the mother of Big Foot, the Mnicojou chief also known as Spotted Elk. Big Foot's father was One Horn who was the brother of Rattling Blanket, the mother of Crazy Horse. Rattling Blanket died when her son, who was then called Curly Hair, was still a boy. Big Foot and Horn Cloud were killed at Wounded Knee in 1890. Joseph Horn Cloud, Iron Hail, and my great-grandfather Daniel White Lance were among the survivors. They were all Crazy Horse's descendants, and it was my Grandpa/Uncle Dewey Beard, a relative of his, who shortly before his death in 1955, authenticated the old tintype as a photograph of Crazy Horse.

Further research on my tribe brought me across the book *The Killing of Chief Crazy Horse,* where there is a quote from a letter that was written to Billy Hunter Garnett from Dr. V.T. McGillycuddy (pages 115-116), about this photograph. McGillycuddy wrote, April 26, 1926, to his friend Garnett, "Many thanks for your letter of the 21st, and the information contained therein for it clears several matters of which I have been in doubt. I am surprised at the names of several of the old timers still alive, particularly He Dog. I enclose that alleged picture of Crazy Horse recently published, I made up my mind that it [referring to the photo of Greasy Hand] was a fake.

He [meaning Crazy Horse] evidently posed [referring to the tintype]. Crazy Horse was a strange looking man, and I would have known him anywhere.

You can return the picture anytime. Some of these days I intend to write up what I know about the killing of Crazy Horse, he was a good man, and I would trust him anywhere. Gen. Jesse Lee who was Lieut. Lee in those days died a few days ago in Washington, he was completely out of his head for past year. Yours truly, V.T. M'Gillycuddy." This is a statement by someone who had known Crazy Horse and what he looked like and who validated the photograph.

I have since used the photograph in my classroom as a teaching tool for the students of my tribe to learn about our history and our tribal chiefs. As a Lakota teacher and historian, it became important for me to tell my students about the life of Crazy Horse, and to show them how their own ancestors were connected to him. I teach our language, traditions, and songs, and I explain to our children the winter counts to connect them to their history and their ancestors.

We have many old photographs of our chiefs and spiritual leaders, including that of Crazy Horse reproduced from the tintype. The photographs are not stored away, but in full view on the classroom wall so that our students can always see and relate to them. As for the photograph of

Crazy Horse, I have also published it in my books, and I refer to it in my classroom as a teaching tool for the students of my tribe to show them the true likeness of our great chief. Many people still believe an old myth initiated mostly by White men who said that Crazy Horse did not have a picture taken, that he was never photographed. But after careful research and consideration I came to the conclusion that the tintype is a true representation of him. My conviction is also based on the oral history that has been passed on to me by my tribal elders.

There are details in the tintype photograph that match our family knowledge of Crazy Horse. Like I have written in one of my books, Crazy Horse had seven sacred stones. One stone, which was part of his medicine bundle, shows clearly in the tintype held together with his eagle feather by a lanyard, just by his left knee: that is Crazy Horse's Heartstone which he wore in battle on the side of his heart. The tintype also clearly shows the other stone, the smaller one he wore around his ear. It is visibly resting on the otter-skin, near the eagle-bone whistle Crazy Horse always carried with him, as it was part of his *wotawe*. According to oral history passed on to me by my grandparents, as a young boy Crazy Horse changed his name from *Pehin Yuhaha*, meaning "Curly," to *Tašunke Isakib Wanka Najin*, Horse Stands in Sight. When his name was changed, he was given a white eagle plume, a trademark of his Mnicojou family, to honor his mother's family. This is the same white plume so noticeable in the tintype. Then he took his father's family name, and from then on he was called *Tašunke Witko*, Crazy Horse. As he grew up and became a skilled hunter and an accomplished warrior, the People gave him also an eagle feather. No Oglala or any other tribe wore a plume for a man's name. The only exception were the Mnicojou, who could keep the same plume as old men if they wanted to. Crazy Horse was no exception and kept wearing the same white plume for the rest of his life as a sign of honor and respect for his mother's people, with the sole exception of when he dressed for battle.

As a Lakota, when you are born, people always look for any physical trademark that can tell which family you belong to. Crazy Horse's family physical trademark was the prominent wrist bone that is also clearly visible in the tintype photo. Sonya Holy Eagle, Minicojou from Cheyenne River and a relative to Crazy Horse, has the same prominent bone protruding from the wrist as Crazy Horse did. When I was born, my grandma looked at me for the family trademark that my grandfather Daniel White Lance had passed on, and as soon as she recognized it she said, "White Lance came back!"

I met Pietro Abiuso through a visit to the Custer Battlefield Museum, Garryowen, Montana. I was given his contact information by the owners and was told briefly about the research he was doing in connection with the tintype photograph. We later met during a visit to New York City that I made to have a prayer ceremony with some of the men who help us as firekeepers during our annual Sundance ceremony. Pietro attended the prayer ceremony and we had the opportunity to visit and talk about his research. I shared with him what I knew from my elders and other information I had discovered through my own research on Crazy Horse. Pietro introduced me to Cesare Marino when they visited me in Allen, Pine Ridge Reservation, South Dakota, to discuss their findings and deliver to me the final draft of their work. It was a pleasure reading this book, and I believe it makes an important contribution to the history of Crazy Horse. Pietro and Cesare did their research and writing with an open mind and a true heart for the People.

I recommend this book to anyone who has seen the tintype photograph and has questions and doubts about its authenticity as a picture of Crazy Horse. I also recommend it to all those who have a general interest in the life of Crazy Horse.

I want to thank Pietro and Cesare for their friendship and respect. I applaud their effort to present with honesty and objectivity to the Lakota People and the world their case for a tintype portrait of our chief Crazy Horse.

Wopila tanka, kola –
Dr. Francis White Lance
Allen, South Dakota

The Genealogy of
Chief Crazy Horse

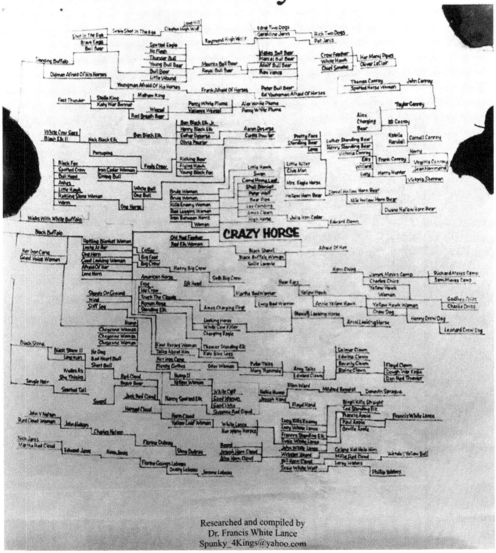

Crazy Horse's Genealogy, researched and compiled
by Dr. Francis White Lance (2013).

Crazy Horse's war shirt. The white plume represented Crazy Horse's Mnicojou lineage and kola pledge. It was originally published as color plate with caption "Scalp Shirt of Little Big Man (Sioux)" by Capt. John G. Bourke in Ninth Annual Report of the Bureau of Ethnology for 1887-88 (1892).

A Crazy Horse Timeline

c. 1840-1842 Crazy Horse is born in the Black Hills, the son of the elder Crazy Horse (also known as Worm, ca. 1810-1881) and Rattling Blanket Woman (1814-1844); his childhood name is Curly Hair / Light Hair Boy.

1844 Curly's mother, Rattling Blanket Woman, commits suicide.

1851 Treaty of Fort Laramie (I), defines Lakota treaty lands, from the Missouri River to the Bighorn Mountains, and the exclusive right to the Black Hills.

1854 Killing of Mnicojou Chief Conquering Bear; death of Lieut. John L. Grattan and his men in the "Grattan Fight" east of Fort Laramie. The young Lakota boy has a vision of a warrior struck by lightning on his face and hailstone marks on his body, and receives his protective medicine from the red-tail hawk and the Thunder Beings.

1855-1863 Curly becomes a warrior and is given his father's name, Crazy Horse.

1864 Black Kettle's Cheyenne village destroyed at Sand Creek, Colorado, by Col. John Chivington.

1865 Crazy Horse fights alongside Red Cloud, Roman Nose, and Dull Knife in the battles of North Platte River Bridge Station and Red Buttes, Wyoming.

1866-1868 Red Cloud War; in December 1866, Crazy Horse leads a decoy of Lakota and Cheyenne warriors who lure Capt. William Fetterman and Lieut. George W. Grummond out of Fort Phil Kearny, northern Wyoming, in an attempt to rescue a wood train; all soldiers are killed.

1867 Crazy Horse participates in the Wagon Box Fight, also near Fort Phil Kearny; Lakota warriors are outgunned by the soldiers armed with new breech-loading rifles.

1868 Crazy Horse is selected a Shirt Wearer (Ogletanka Un) along with American Horse, Young Man Afraid of His Horse, and Sword Owner; Treaty of Fort Laramie (II) with recognition of the Black Hills to the Lakota and establishment of the Great Sioux Reservation; Lt. Col. George A. Custer destroys Cheyenne chief Black Kettle's village on the Washita River, western Oklahoma.

1870 Crazy Horse takes Black Buffalo Woman on a buffalo hunt; her husband No Water shoots Crazy Horse in the face and reclaims his wife; Crazy Horse is stripped of his Shirt Wearer status; his younger step-brother Little Hawk is killed by either Shoshone or Ute warriors, or perhaps by American settlers; his older Mnicojou kinsman and kola High Backbone also killed by Shoshone.

1871-1873 Crazy Horse marries Black Shawl who gives birth to their only daughter, They Are Afraid of Her; the child dies in 1873; Crazy Horse is heart-broken.

1874 Crazy Horse joins Sitting Bull and the Northern Cheyenne against the Yellowstone Wagon Road and Prospecting Expedition in the Battle of Lodge Grass Creek, Montana.

1876 Crazy Horse leads Lakota and Cheyenne warriors in the Battle of the Rosebud, Montana, forcing Brig. Gen. George Crook to retreat; a week later, he leads the same coalition in the victory over Lieut. Col. George A.

Custer in the Battle of the Little Bighorn; fights Capt. Anson Mills in the Battle of Slim Buttes, South Dakota.

1877 January: Crazy Horse fights against Col. Nelson Miles in the Battle of Wolf Mountain (also known as Battle of the Tongue River), Montana. Early May: Crazy Horse agrees to peace and leads his People to Red Cloud Agency, Camp Robinson, Nebraska. Enlists as a U.S. Army scout and waits for his own separate agency to be assigned in the North Country. July-August: the agency chiefs and the military turn against him. September 5th: Crazy Horse is mortally wounded in the attempt to avoid imprisonment; he dies later that night.

A Wakinyan / Thunderbird shield given to author Cesare Marino
by Randy Emery and Steve Feraca.

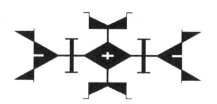

Introduction: Steve says no![1]

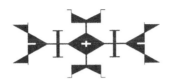

"Crazy Horse was a nice-looking man."
Red Feather, Mrs. Annie Rowland interpreter, 1930

"Jake Herman, a mixed blood [...] will show any interested party a tintype of a good looking young warrior with typical Sioux features."
Stephen Feraca, 1964

Many years have passed, the pleasant memories are still fresh in my mind. I always looked forward to my end-of-the-work-week lunch breaks with zu' Stefano, as we called him in the Calabrese dialect. Fridays, by mid-day, things slowed down in Washington, D.C. as happy hour rapidly approached. Deadlines and weather permitting, and after a quick phone call to confirm, I hopped on my bicycle and in a matter of minutes I covered the short distance separating my office at the National Museum of Natural History and the Bureau of Indian Affairs (BIA) where Steve, then nearing retirement, worked.

Stephen E. Feraca was an articulate and controversial man, passionate and contradictory.[2] Both a protagonist and a by-product, so to speak, of a critical transitional period in modern American Indian history and federal–Indian relations, Feraca witnessed first-hand the birth of Red Power, the affirmation of tribal self-determination, and what he regarded as the mixed-blessings of tribal sovereignty.

Stephen was an avid smoker. He was known both inside and out of the BIA for his strong views and uncompromising ways. He had a bright mind and a short temper. Back in the 1970s and 1980s, Steve expressed disdain for those whom he referred to as "fake Indians," individuals who made a business of their often minimal "Indian blood" to become, in his words, "professional Indians" rather than Indian professionals. A provocateur, Steve arguably admitted of being, again in his own words, "a benevolent Fascist" (a label, minus the "benevolent," also facetiously applied to Feraca by academic activist Ward Churchill). He was the epitome of political incorrectness. True to his nature, Steve took his BIA work very seriously and was generally liked by those who got to know him intimately. That is, after he shed his official role as "the Washington man."

At Pine Ridge Reservation, Steve earned the respect of many Lakota and was adopted as her son by the late Mary Fast Horse (Winyan Waštewin, 1888-1970), a revered tribal elder and herbalist of the Wounded Knee (Čankpe Opi Wahkpala) District. Less amicable were Feraca's relations with the American Indian Movement (AIM) militants involved in the historic 1973 take-over during which the Wounded Knee Trading Post and private museum, run by Steve's in-laws Clive and Agnes Gildersleeve, were occupied and wrecked.[3] Steve was uncompromising in his condemnation, no matter how hard I tried to play devil's advocate.

We found more common grounds when we talked about old Calabria and Sicilia during the tasty pasta dinners he and wife JoAnn hosted at their home in Reston, Virginia. Steve's hospitality was proverbial. Likewise, was his craftsmanship in making Sioux-style, double-curve bows and properly notched, fletched, and tipped arrows. He called himself an "artifaker" and patiently carved catlinite and other soft stone pipe bowls, ash-wood pipe stems, and intricate tampers, which he gave away as gifts. I am one of the lucky recipients. The thin blade of his inseparable old small pocket knife saw much sharpening over time, and it showed.

Feraca authored important official BIA reports and seminal anthropological works on the Teton Sioux in whose language he was conversant. I vividly remember one occasion in particular, when Steve and Pete Catches,

Sr. (Petage Yuha Mani, 1912-1993) carried on a lively conversation, occasionally laughing at something they had shared in Lakota, which I did not understand.

It was Chuck Emery, one of Feraca's Lakota relatives who introduced me to Steve. It was more than thirty years ago while I was doing research on bilingual education for the National Congress of American Indians during Ron Andrade's tenure as Executive Director. I visited Mr. Emery at the Department of Education, and my foreign accent and interest in Native American history and contemporary issues sparked his curiosity. When I told him I was born in Southern Italy, the island of Sicily to be precise, his imposing physique rose from his office chair, his face lit up with a big smile and, to my great surprise, he exclaimed, "Well, then we're relatives!" while giving me a strong handshake. "You ought to meet my compadre Steve Feraca at the BIA," he continued, "I'm sure he'd love to talk to you." Mr. Emery explained that Feraca too, had Southern Italian roots, and that Steve had adopted Randy, one of his sons, as his godson. Therefore, in the Lakota way, he considered me also a relative as Steve and I had a common ancestry. He was certain I would get along well with both Steve and Randy. We then discussed topics relating to the original purpose of my visit.

As I was about to leave, Mr. Emery encouraged me to continue my graduate work in anthropology. He again surprised me, giving me yet another lesson in Lakota hospitality and generosity, when he spontaneously removed from his office wall, the framed drawing of a sun dancer that had earlier caught my attention. Sketched in ink on cardboard paper by his other son Richard, a gifted artist, Chuck Emery presented it to me as his personal gift. I was moved. I have cherished "the sun dancer" ever since, together with the memory of the gentleman who had never seen me before and yet treated me so kindly.[4]

The very next day I went to the BIA where I introduced myself to Mr. Feraca. My first encounter with Steve Feraca, whose name was already familiar to me from his controversial reputation and writings,[5] was as cordial and instructive as the meeting I had with Chuck Emery. Steve and I soon established a friendship that lasted until his premature passing on the eve of the new millennium. He was engaging, witty, at times abrasive, polemic, and sarcastic to the limit, yet sincere, never motivated by selfish interests. Although I strongly disagreed with him on many issues, especially his opposition to tribal sovereignty, I respected his knowledge and passionate character.

Feraca thought the federal government should not continue dealing with tribes as sovereign nations because their members had, as individual American Indians, long accepted U.S. citizenship. Paternalistic, he feared this state of affairs perpetuated a culture of "hostile dependency" and entitlement, fostering new generations of socially dysfunctional Indians. He also disliked those individuals with minimal or questionable Indian "blood" who, often with equally minimal qualifications, occupied privileged "Indian desks" throughout the federal system and Indian Country.

I made a point of stopping by Feraca's office whenever I conducted research at the BIA and the Department of Interior Library. In the course of these years, Steve introduced me to tribal officials who routinely came to discuss with him issues relating to land claims awards. One was Dr. Kenneth Ryan (Tašunga Saba, His Black Horse), at the time Chairman of the Fort Peck Assiniboine and Sioux Tribes, who, like Chuck Emery, championed American Indian higher education. Ken and I became good friends, even traveled together to Italy, and on many occasions we talked about my interest in Crazy Horse, as I did with Feraca.

In good weather, I often joined Steve for lunch at the BIA. We had our routine well established. By the time I arrived on my bike at Rawlins Park, on the north side of the Interior Building, Steve had made his stop at a small deli across the street to pick up our sandwiches. Since both he and I refused to corrode our "Italic" digestive tract with artificially sweetened and colored soda-pop, zu' Stefano also purchased a couple of Buds, his favorite "foamy water," each can concealed, so to speak, in a brown paper bag. "The problem with Indians," would be his habitual opening statement accompanying our salute, "is that they do not know how to drink. For us paesani, a glass of wine or a beer, is just part of the meal, you know, we grew up with it, isn't so Cesarino mio?" "Yup, Steve," would be my condescending reply, "on top of everything else, Indians got cheated with the worst alcohol, pure poison, those greedy wašiču could pour down their throats!"[6]

On a warm late-summer noon we were joined by Chuck Emery's son Randy (Tokàla Sapa, Black Fox)[7] whom Steve, as I said, had adopted as his figlioccio. A handsome and engaging young man, Randy too enjoyed Steve's company, along with a cold beer (also concealed in a brown bag). And talking, well, at times actually arguing, about the cultural parallels Steve drew between traditional Sioux cultural traits and those of Southern Italy: tightness of the family, extended network of blood and affine relatives bound together by strong reciprocal obligations (or sharply divided by equally strong feuds, jealousies and gossip), a code of honor requiring revenge and omertà, religious mysticism and belief in immanent justice, male aggressiveness (machismo), the seemingly submissive yet central role of women, generosity and hospitality, and so on. Being early September, our chatter turned to Tašunke Witko, the legendary war chief of the non-agency Oglala, killed at a military outpost in northwestern Nebraska, on the fifth day of that month in 1877.

As we thumbed through an issue of the Crazy Horse Monument Newsletter I had recently received in the mail, Steve commented with his usual wit on what he anticipated would be, one day, the unlikely result of the Herculean efforts by Polish-American artist Korczak Ziolkowski (1908-1982) – who had recently passed away and whose work was then carried on by his wife Ruth (who died in 2014) and their children – to blast off and carve out of a mountain in the Black Hills of South Dakota a huge memorial to Crazy Horse. When finished, the gigantic figure would be some 563 feet tall; higher than the Washington Monument (555 ft.), the Great Pyramid of Giza (481 ft.), and the famous Statue of Liberty (305 ft.).[8] The magnitude of the great endeavor did not impress Feraca, who insisted that Crazy Horse would not have liked it either. On this very point, Steve agreed with noted AIM leader and Lakota nationalist, the late Russell Means (1939-2012), also a harsh critic of the project who did not spare his vitriolic rhetoric against it. "The Crazy Horse Monument is a farce," Means often stated. "Once it is completed lightning is going to strike and destroy the whole thing. There was never a picture of Crazy Horse. Ziolkowski gathered up all those old chiefs and gave them each $100 and asked them to pose and smoke the pipe with him, so later he could claim that he got their approval."[9]

Ziolkowki had done more than that. The year before J.W. Vaughn published the "Crazy Horse" tintype (that has since been the subject of controversy and is now addressed in these pages), the sculptor expressed interest in an alleged "photograph" that might have been a true likeness of Crazy Horse in an early October 1955 letter to Charles Dettborn of Tacoma, Washington. "Since the inception of the Crazy Horse project," Ziolkowski wrote, "I have done extensive research into the life of the man and have looked far and wide for a picture of the great Sioux chief. None have come to light. However, from the description of the photograph which you have in your possession, you may have the picture for which so many persons have searched for so many years."[10]

The description of the alleged photographic portrait was provided by Dettborn in an August 1955 letter to the sculptor: "I have been wanting to write you for some time on a matter that may be of great interest to you. Myself being a great admirer of Chief Crazy Horse, I find there are no known pictures of the great warrior. I came into possession of two pictures years ago at an eastside shop in New York City they came from an old Indian collection / the picture I refer to is named the war chief, and is Sioux. I've made extensive study of Crazy Horse [...] and the picture fits the discription [sic] exactly even to the scar under the left eye a man in his early 30th expression of quiet dignity – blanket and standing. In the book Crazy Horse [by Sandoz] they refer to him as the war chief and always wearing one feather could it be possible that I have a picture of the great chief?"[11]

The issue was further confused by a subsequent letter Dettborn sent Ziolkowski in October of the same year in which he wrote, "I trust this might be the picture you are looking for. I had a print made of the large picture which is named the war chief its [sic] 21 by 26 inches. Bert Phillips is the artist [...] The picture is copyrighted 1910 by the Gray Lith Co. N.Y."[12] Of course, Bert Geer Phillips (1868-1956), one of the founders in 1912 of the Taos Society of Artists, was a painter, not a photographer.[13] The Dettborn-Ziolkowski exchanges were evidently based on a liberal use of the word "picture," Dettborn having sent Ziolkowski photographs of the portrait painting by Phillips. A few days later, Ziolkowski acknowledged receiving "the pictures of the War Chief" and he thanked Dettborn "for the opportunity to see and examine them."[14]

Ziolkowski, meanwhile, was busy blasting, carving, and sculpting. Whether one agrees or not with the megaproject, no doubt Ziolkowski was sincerely motivated when he began his colossal endeavor in the late 1940s. After meeting with Oglala Chief Henry Standing Bear, a maternal second cousin of Crazy Horse, and other elders at Pine Ridge, the artist sculpted a marble 1/300th scale model of Tašunke Witko on his war horse, his left arm outstretched, upon which the mountain was to be carved.

In the ensuing years, as news spread, the project became internationally known. Between 1987 and 1998 progress continued. Blasting the top of the rock and sculpting the face were completed on the fiftieth anniversary of the first explosion. Seen now from the front, the gigantic facial features are still somewhat reminiscent of the thirteen-cent U.S. postage "Crazy Horse" stamp of the Great Americans Series. Issued on January 15, 1982, at the Crazy Horse Memorial Post Office, the neck in particular appears disproportionately thick and the nose and chin equally big; not surprisingly, as the stamp itself "was sketched from Korczak's scale model for the mountain carving."[15]

Crazy Horse, by Brad Holland; USA 13c stamp, Great Americans Series (1982).

The present monument's nose-eye features seem to resemble those of Chief Standing Bear, and opinions differ on the similarities between the monumental face and the features of any known historic or contemporary Lakota.[16]

Crazy Horse Monument, Thunder Mountain,
South Dakota; the face (2017).

The key question, "What did Crazy Horse look like?" was addressed by Charles E. Trimble, Oglala, in an article featured in *Indian Country Today* in summer 2005. Trimble noted that "modern depictions of Crazy Horse in movies, paintings, and monuments continue to be stereotypical caricatures of what an Indian man is 'supposed to look like.' Take, for example, the massive sculpture transforming a granite mountain in the Black Hills." He continued, "The face on that mountain doesn't portray the chief's fine featured countenance described in so many reliable sources: for one thing, the nose is a feature that would be more like of the ancient Red Cloud in his final days than that of Crazy Horse. However, this does not demean the good intentions on the part of the Ziolkowki family and foundation of honoring so great a leader."[17] When Korczak Ziolkowski died in 1982, his funeral drew over 1,500 people. On the occasion, Robert Fast Horse, Executive Director of the Oglala Sioux Tribe, eulogized the artist with these befitting words: "Let it be said today that this image of a great man, Crazy Horse, is matched by a great inspiration, of a man who had a great heart, Korczak Ziolkowski."[18]

Still, many of us wonder why not honor Crazy Horse and his propensity for modesty by carving instead, let's say, a life-size Indian pony inspired by the chief's war horse, and place it in a prominent location on the same mountain, without blasting the latter out. The Lakota hero was a Thunder Dreamer, but the White man's dynamite does not seem to fit well with his spirit, and all that Crazy Horse stood for, including the sacredness of the Black Hills. Crazy Horse's greatness stands on his own merit and need not compete in statuary granitic terms with neighboring Mount Rushmore (itself not without a controversial history), nor with any other man-made gigantic structure. On this, Feraca and I agreed, and during our lunch with Randy, Steve reiterated his opposition. Ever a skeptic and intolerant of what he considered the incongruous assertion that the huge "thing," the face alone is nine-stories high, was not meant to reproduce Crazy Horse's true likeness, but rather his "spirit." In a crescendo of disdain for the cyclopean carving Steve remarked that, whatever the final product may look like, it would fall short. Especially because contemporary eyewitness accounts were not at all consistent about Crazy Horse's facial features.

Since the monumental face was to be (and now actually is) so prominent, all other considerations notwithstanding, in Feraca's view the overall effort was fundamentally flawed. Steve recognized there was general agreement on the war chief's long hair being unusually light for a Lakota. But opinions differed sharply on some specific characteristics, including the famous scar on his face. "It remains to be seen," he commented, "how the scar will show [on the monument]." Steve then took another sip and assumed a mischievous look. "Well, if those folks up there in the Hills need a real model, they might as well use my godson here whose features are as Sioux as those of the Indian on the buffalo nickel!" he blasted, while affectionately grabbing Randy's face with his hand. As we all laughed, after a brief pause Steve turned serious and added, "Besides, what we really know for sure about Crazy Horse would barely fill a chapter in a book!" Novelist Larry McMurtry echoed this same view almost verbatim nearly two decades later in the opening pages of his concise biography of the Lakota chief.[19] Steve's "we" referred not only to us "White folks" interested in Crazy Horse, but also to most Sioux and Indians in general. As for Mari Sandoz's classic, *Crazy Horse: Strange Man of the Oglala*, he disagreed with the critical acclaim that welcomed the book since it was first published in 1942 and expressed dismay at writers like Stephen B. Oates who ranked Sandoz's *Crazy Horse* "among the best biographies ever written."[20] He regarded Sandoz's a good historical novel, certainly not a sound and accurate biography.

The "silent killer" did not let Steve live long enough to read Kingsley Bray's *Crazy Horse*, and Thomas Powers's *The Killing of Crazy Horse*, two thoroughly researched works that overcome the elegiac tone of Sandoz's prose. Knowing Steve, he would have most likely approved of both, perhaps with some reservations. To their credit, both Bray and Powers contain a wealth of sound historical and biographical information, with a caveat. Bray says practically nothing of a possible Crazy Horse photograph, reinforcing the entrenched view against any existing authentic portrait of the great Lakota. Powers, on the other hand, does spend a few words on the photo question, recalling that when sculptor Ziolkowski began his work in 1948: "Few survived who still remembered Crazy Horse, and despite much searching no one had found a photograph of him. One of the first to look was John Gregory Bourke, who wrote [Gen.] Crook's widow [...] to ask if a Crazy Horse photograph was among his papers. Mary Crook said there was not, and suggested that Bourke contact the old Fort Laramie sutler, John Collins [... who] did not have one either, and told Bourke to ask Ben Paddock, a trader at Fort Robinson. So it went for fifty years. Many photographs were touted for a time but all proved to be of someone else." Ziolkowski, Powers continued, "admitted he could get no closer than a likeness of the 'spirit' of Crazy Horse, which in his sketches, and later as he carved into the mountain itself, gave the chief a noticeably Slavic [!] cast." In a brief endnote, Powers further concedes that a photographer was "operating a studio at the agency at the time Crazy Horse was killed; [...] If a photograph of Crazy Horse was ever taken," he concluded, "it is likely that James Hamilton was the man who did it." [21]

As Steve, Randy, and I debated what Crazy Horse might have looked like, I tried to argue that, after all, there was an alleged black and white photograph of the famous Lakota published by Jesse Wendell Vaughn in his classic on the Rosebud fight of June 17, 1876 (of which I owned a first edition).[22] Steve, who knew both the book and the tintype reproduced therein, ever impatient on such matters, cut me short with his trademark exclamation "nonsense!" Randy, too, shared Steve's view, but in a more diplomatic and friendly way. In fact, Steve reminded me that in the summer of 1954, two years before Vaughn's book with the tintype appeared in print, he had himself looked into the Crazy Horse picture story at Pine Ridge. Feraca had spoken with Indian old timers, including Jacob "Jake" Herman, the Oglala Sioux tribal councilman later cited by Vaughn as one of the authoritative sources for the authenticity of the tintype. Feraca recalled that Herman was positive about the identification of a tintype depicting what he and a few other Lakota believed to be a true likeness of Crazy Horse. Still, based on his own readings and additional interviews he conducted at Pine Ridge, Steve remained skeptical and later published the inconclusive results of his inquiry. In 1964, Feraca stated that "Crazy Horse remains an enigma for one good reason. He didn't live long enough. Unlike Sitting Bull, Red Cloud, and Geronimo who were finally herded onto reservations to languish for years, Crazy Horse was in the company of his conquerors for a comparatively short time. While many other Indian leaders lasted long enough to satisfy countless interviewers, photographers, and portrait painters, the young Oglala was visited by none of these after his surrender. His battle prowess is unchallenged but hardly a recorded word of his remains. Worse, considering the unjustified honors given to chiefs of lesser ability, we have not one authentic photograph of him and the location of his grave is unknown.[23] No picture! And no headstone!" was Feraca's lapidary conclusion.

Knowing the thoroughness of Steve Feraca's research, after reading his article I too was convinced. After all, that was also what a wrinkled, elderly Oglala named John Y. Nelson "Yellow Plume" had told Feraca when, čanli and minipiha in hand, he visited the elder in a log cabin on Pine Ridge, on the seventy-eighth anniversary of the Custer battle. Actually, John Yellow Plume related an old tell-tale and admitted that one picture of Crazy Horse had been taken, but turned out to be unusable. "The only photo known to him," wrote Feraca retelling the old Indian's story, "was that taken by Doctor McGillycuddy who attended the war chief as he lay dying in the jailhouse. Crazy Horse, says old John, turned to the wall as the picture was being taken and the resulting photo or tintype was worthless."[24] We know that after Crazy Horse was mortally wounded by a soldier's bayonet and his own knife during the scuffle that ensued outside the Camp Robinson guardhouse, the dying chief was taken to the Adjutant's Office nearby, not back to the jailhouse whence he had rushed out.[25] On the conflicting accounts of Crazy Horse's death, and the absurdity of Dr. McGillycuddy's purported on the spot, middle of the night photo session with a dying man, who happened to be no less than Crazy Horse, we shall return in detail later.

Brief Excitement

In 1976, bicentennial of the United States and centennial of the Lakota-Cheyenne victory over Custer, the same Crazy Horse photograph, published two decades earlier by Vaughn but rejected by Feraca and practically all others who had a strong opinion about it, appeared again in Carroll Friswold's, *The Killing of Chief Crazy Horse*, released posthumously by Robert A. Clark.[26] In addition to a clearer, full-page print of the purported picture of "Chief Crazy Horse," Friswold corrected Vaughn's location and date of the photographic sitting not "about 1870 at Fort Laramie" as Vaughn had written, but at Camp Robinson in 1877. Friswold also provided a second affidavit signed by Mrs. Ellen Garnier Howard retracing what he called the "line of ownership" of the original small tintype to its first owner, Ellen's father, mixed-blood scout Baptiste "Little Bat" Garnier (1847-1900). Little Bat, whose photographic portrait was also reproduced in *The Killing*, was then married to Julie Mousseau (1855 [or 1861] – after 1896), a mixed-blood relative of Crazy Horse himself. Through this kinship, Friswold pointed out, Little Bat befriended Tašunke Witko during the four months the war chief was at Red Cloud Agency. There was a photographer at the agency, and one day Little Bat convinced Crazy Horse to have his picture taken for his own keepsake.

After Little Bat's death (tragic parallel: he too was murdered), the small image remained in the possession of the Garnier family until Mrs. Ellen Howard, Oglala tribal member, through fellow tribesman Jake Herman who had secured Dewey Beard's authentication, made the image available to J.W. Vaughn. The tintype was shortly thereafter acquired by Fred B. Hackett, adopted son of Iron Tail and a friend and benefactor of Ellen Howard's impoverished family. From Hackett, the ownership of the original tintype passed to Carroll Friswold, who reiterated its authenticity as a photographic portrait of Crazy Horse: "Crazy Horse liked Bat, and Mrs. Bat was a cousin of his, so he was at ease and relaxed, being with friends. [...] Bat dared Crazy Horse to have his picture taken, and he finally consented. According to the story, he even borrowed the [beaded] moccasins to make a good appearance. [...] The picture shows an Indian of medium stature, lighter-haired than the average Indian, with a rounded face rather than one with high, wide cheekbones. His hair is in braids to his waist [...]. Also the picture shows clearly the scar in the left corner of his mouth where he was shot some years before by No Water, after he had ridden away with No Water's wife. [...] From the people involved and my searches I firmly believe this is an authentic likeness of Crazy Horse."[27] Friswold omitted to say that the picture also showed an Indian of lighter complexion.

The new evidence and Friswold's passionate harangue did not seem to matter and, with a very few exceptions, the verdict of historians, American Indians, and the general public remained the same: no picture![28] A few years later in 1981, the interviews on Crazy Horse that were collected in the 1960s at Pine Ridge by Edward and Mabell Kadlececk were released with the telling title, *To Kill an Eagle*. Still without a positive answer on the tintype or any other possible photograph of the war chief.[29] In 1989, Jason Hook published a chapter on Crazy Horse in his collection of biographical sketches of great Indian leaders.[30] Hook was apparently unaware of

Friswold's book and reproduced the old tintype from J.W. Vaughn's work. The British author repeated the story that Crazy Horse had a profound distrust of "shadow catchers," but also admitted that the tintype could actually be the real thing. "Crazy Horse," wrote Hook, "boasted that he would never allow the white man's camera to 'steal his shadow.' No fully authenticated image of him exists, although several photographs have been published purporting to be him. Of these, this old tintype is the most likely to be authentic. [...] It bears a fascinating resemblance to written descriptions of Crazy Horse, and it was authenticated as being him by Jake Herman [...] after consultation with the Lakota elders."[31]

In the summer of 1996, yet another American Indian photograph purported to be that of Crazy Horse was featured in the editorial "Is This Crazy Horse?" in *Indian Country Today*. It showed the studio portrait of an Indian with a round face, prominent check-bones, large nose and thick lips, wearing a single eagle feather, a dentalium shell choker and long dentalium and mother of pearl pendant earrings, one of his braids wrapped in trade cloth. The subject is seated, partly wrapped in a trade blanket ornate with a large beaded strip. His white shirt under a dark vest is typical of many 1870s-1880s Sioux portrait photographs, and similar to that of the Indian in the tintype.[32] It was later ascertained that the subject was Stabber (Wačepe), a member of the large 1872 Oglala delegation to Washington. In the Capital City, at the request of William Blackmore, an English philanthropist friend of the Indians, Stabber, Red Cloud, Red Dog, and other Sioux leaders agreed to have their picture taken in Alexander Gardner's popular photographic studio on Pennsylvania Avenue. [33]

Crossing Paths

The new millennium began without the global meltdown most feared the computer "bug" would bring. Later that year, the "picture story" broke-up again with greater coverage and controversy in the press and the new super-fast "moccasin telegraph news," the internet. The very old 2.5 x 3.5-inch original (quarter) tintype that had been inherited by Carroll L. Friswold resurfaced as part of his father Carroll Friswold, Sr.'s estate and was sold at auction in Los Angeles in December 2000.[34] The tintype was acquired by James "Putt" Thompson, owner of the Custer Battlefield Trading Post on the Crow Indian Reservation, Montana. Symbolically, perhaps, not far from where Crazy Horse's own lodge once stood on the western bank of Pejisla (Pejislusluta) Wahkpa, the Slippery (Greasy) Grass River that saw Tašunke Witko victorious over George Armstrong Custer.

I would have remained on the sidelines, weighing the evidence, some new, some old, set forth by the opposite camps in favor of, or against this re-discovered "true likeness" of Crazy Horse, were it not for the fact that the main supporter of the authenticity of the tintype as a photographic portrait of the great Lakota patriot was a fellow Italian named Peter (Pietro) Abiuso from Ronkonkoma, Long Island, New York. Coincidentally, I had just finished reading a new biography of Crazy Horse written in Italian by Vittorio Zucconi, one of Italy's foremost journalists who at the time was a news correspondent in Washington. Accompanied by his wife, Zucconi visited the Pine Ridge Reservation and met with tribal members including a descendant of No Water who, after learning of his interest in Crazy Horse, gave the journalist the cold shoulder. Zucconi was later invited to a yuwipi ceremony conducted by Marvin Helper (1951-2017). Marvin, related on his father's side to Hump and Big Foot, hence also to Crazy Horse, is the grandson of Simon Helper, a survivor of Wounded Knee. According to Zucconi, during Marvin's yuwipi, contact was briefly established with the spirit of Crazy Horse, a sign of consent to his book project. As for a photograph of Crazy Horse, Zucconi echoed the common view that the Oglala war chief had always refused to have his picture taken.[35]

I reached Pietro on the phone and we talked eagerly, glad our paths had crossed because of our shared interest in Crazy Horse. I was impressed with Pietro's knowledge of what, just a few years earlier had been lesser known facts about Tašunke Witko's life. Although Pietro was not a professional historian, he had spent endless hours reading, searching, and gathering often obscure yet crucial information on Crazy Horse. Like many of us, Pietro too had been struck by the greatness of the legendary war chief of the Lakota hunting bands. Pietro had also focused on the possibility that – contrary to what not only Sandoz and nearly every other authority, but also most of the Lakota hero's descendants and Indians in general long maintained – the image reproduced by Vaughn and Friswold from the original tintype recently auctioned in California, was indeed an authentic, true likeness of Crazy Horse.[36] I shared the new developments with friend and colleague Paula Fleming who at the time was approaching retirement from the National Anthropological Archives. With a thirty-year experience on North American Indian photography,[37] Paula was very familiar with the Crazy Horse photo question but leaned towards the "no picture" camp. Still, as an open-minded scholar, she was willing to take yet another closer look at the whole issue, including the material gathered by Pietro.

On a sunny mid-fall weekend in 2003, Paula, Pietro, and I met at my red-brick rambler in Virginia, and together we reviewed the old and new documentation spread out on the kitchen table. Even though some key diagnostic questions remained, including the studio setting, the ornate backdrop, and the long breastplate, Paula and I agreed with Pietro that the case was strong enough to justify a new reading of all the contextual and documentary evidence assembled so far. Due to prior obligations, Paula eventually ended her active collaboration, but remained interested in our progress. Pietro and I plowed along, motivated by our passion for the subject and our respect for the memory of the Lakota hero. But also the conviction that, if indeed Crazy Horse had finally agreed to have his picture taken while at Red Cloud Agency in the summer 1877, he would want, now that a whole mountain is being carved out in his honor, to have his true likeness finally acknowledged. After I retired from the Handbook, I devoted greater attention to the Crazy Horse tintype and I began writing. I worked closely with Pietro every step of the way, until the last draft page was typed. In 2013, Pietro and I visited Francis White Lance in Allen, South Dakota, to discuss our findings and hand deliver to him our final draft. Francis took the time to review the book and endorsed it with his Foreword.

New Books and DVDs

Our effort was not intended as or pretended to be a new biography of Crazy Horse, much less a critique of the complex historiography associated with his charismatic figure. In fact, the recent decades have seen a resurgence of interest in the great Lakota, with a wealth of new publications revisiting with a critical eye, the romanticized story, good for the time, originally told by Mari Sandoz. The posthumous publication in 1976 of Friswold's *The Killing*, and of the *Oglala Sources on the Life of Crazy Horse*, originally compiled by Eleanor H. Hinman in 1930, were prelude to a new wave of publications inaugurated by Richard G. Hardorff with *The Oglala Lakota Crazy Horse* (1985), followed by *The Crazy Horse Surrender Ledger* [1877] (1994) edited by Thomas R. Buecker and R. Eli Paul, and again Hardorff with *The Surrender and Death of Crazy Horse* (1998), reprinted as *The Death of Crazy Horse* (2001). These works paved the way to the Crazy Horse biographies by Bray and Powers, mentioned earlier. Then came Cleve Walstrom's *Search for the Lost Trail of Crazy Horse* (2003), Joseph Marshall, III, (Sičangu) with *The Journey of Crazy Horse* (2004), and finally the new DVD series *The Authorized Biography of Crazy Horse and His Family*, produced by Bill Matson and Mark Frethem in cooperation with Crazy Horse's Mnicojou descendants Don Red Thunder (Crazy Horse III), Floyd Clown, and Doug War Eagle. The Crazy Horse Family oral history interviews comprise four DVDs: *Part One: Creation, Spirituality, and The Family Tree* (2006); *Part Two: Defending the Homeland* (2007); *Part Three: The Battle of the Little Bighorn* (2007); and *Part Four: Surrender, Death, and The Family Survives* (2008). The content of the DVDs was later edited in book form with the tile *Crazy Horse: The Lakota Warrior's Life & Legacy* (2016).[38]

Thoroughly researched and meticulously documented, the works cited above do not always provide definitive answers to all the fundamental questions about Crazy Horse. At times, they even present conflicting information and interpretations that have resonated through acrimonious exchanges on the web and the American Indian press. Take, for example, the claim in the first DVD of an exclusively Mnicojou ancestry of

Crazy Horse, on both his father's and mother's side. It not only contradicts Hardorff and Bray (and Sandoz and others) on the paternal issue, but it has been challenged by the Oglala descendants of the war chief, as reported in 2007 by *Indian Country Today*: "Floyd Clown pointed out in the DVD that Crazy Horse was Minneconjou, not Oglala, as most historians and many Lakota claim. Yvonne Kay Clown, granddaughter of Amos Clown, verified that Crazy Horse's father was Oglala. According to court documents, lineage in the Lakota culture is patriarchal. She also said that historians will 'tear the DVD apart and other medicine men will denounce it.'"[39] The Edward Clown Family insisted on the accuracy of the biographical and historical information based on a long standing and carefully guarded oral tradition, including the absolute certainty that no photographic portrait of Crazy Horse was ever made. A different view was held by Francis White Lance who gave what he then called "the alleged photo of Crazy Horse" the benefit of the doubt. In his *Tasunke Witko Woihanble: The Vision of Crazy Horse* (2007), White Lance published a copy of the tintype and a computer color-enhanced version of the same, with notations in support of its positive identification as a portrait of Tašunke Witko.[40] As he stated now in the Foreword, White Lance is positive the tintype is a photograph of Crazy Horse.

All of the above considerations, the new publications, and on-line discussions of Crazy Horse, convinced Pietro and I that our work should remain focused on the controversial tintype. Rather than retracing once again, chronologically, the life of Crazy Horse, now reconstructed by competent authors and the DVDs, we followed the complex trail that we hoped would lead us to the positive identification of at least one image of the noted Indian leader. Specifically, the tintype, whose validity as a genuine image of the Lakota patriot has long been debated.[41]

Context and Content: 'Nay' or What?

"Crazy Horse was a man not very tall not very short, neither broad nor thin [...] had a very light complexion, much lighter than the other Indians. His features were not like those of the rest of us."

Short Bull, John Colhoff, interpreter, 1930.

The great Lakota hero did not live in a historical and cultural vacuum. In fact, he was profoundly affected by his times. Since photography had recently asserted itself as the new technological wonder for reproducing likenesses, contextualization was critically important in approaching the picture question. Our research, therefore, was as much about the contextual history of American Indian photography, Sioux in particular, as it was specifically about the case in favor of the tintype portrait of Crazy Horse. To begin with, we questioned the fact that the "nay" supporters long based their opposition on not-so-settled arguments, including clothing and accessories, spurious attributions of fear and hate, and the incongruity that Crazy Horse was never in the presence of a photographer and yet, conversely, he always refused to have his picture taken. Such views dominated the scene by the time Ziolkowski began his monumental work. Yet, almost concomitant with Ziolkowski's first blast in the heart of the sacred Black Hills, it looked as if the photograph question was to be finally answered – to everyone's surprise – with a positive identification. On September 1, 1947, *Wi'iyohi* ("each moon" in Lakota, that is, monthly), the bulletin of the South Dakota Historical Society, featured on the front page photographic portraits of two American Indians. The close-ups were cropped from two full stereoscopic portraits and were introduced to the readers by an editorial titled "Is There a Picture of Crazy Horse?" It read, "What started out to be a fishing expedition, originated by Joe Koller, west river historian, has become a first class controversy with the non-picture fans having a bit the best of it. The pictures [...] were sent in by Miss Blanche M. Lewis of Sioux City, [Iowa]. Her brother got them years ago and wrote 'Crazy Horse and his squaw' on the back of them. They are our best bet to date if there ever was a picture taken of this notable warrior."

The author of the editorial, Will G. Robinson, Secretary of the Society, however cautioned the readers: "Mr. E.A. Brinistool [sic] who published a purported picture of him in his book, *A Trooper with Custer*[42] now says (July 25 [1947]), 'I published a picture sent me by the War Department, that it was Crazy Horse. I now do not think it was. D.F. Barry the old time Indian photographer, told me he had repeatedly tried to bribe him to sit for a picture, but he always refused.'"[43] We address this outrageous statement by "the old time Indian photographer" in detail later. Here we focus on the two images that are of comparative relevance to our search for the true identity of the tintype Indian. In the *Wi'iyohi*, the close-up on the right shows the face of a young, pretty-looking, mixed-blood woman with a tree-trunk as background. As noted, she was identified as Helen "Nellie" Laravie (Larrabee, also Lavarie), the third wife – others say second, disregarding the brief affair with Black Buffalo Woman – of Crazy Horse. The portrait on the left is more intriguing, being the close-up of a handsome, "intelligent" looking, adult Indian male, not too young, not too old. His braids are wrapped in otter skin, and feather decorations (not a war-bonnet) are visible in his hair. The expression is firm, proud, resolute, yet relaxed and certainly not "hostile." Opinions do not agree with regard to his complexion, indeed hard to tell, but there is consensus on his pleasant features and possibly, the presence of a "mark" or scar on his face, just below the left nostril. This led Will G. Robinson, a month later, to write to fellow historian James C. Olson of the Nebraska State Historical Society saying that "the blow up shows a pronounced scar about the place Miss Sandoz places it in her book and I am very much of the present opinion that we have a picture of the noted Chief even though the whole past opinion has been that there was none."[44]

The two photos, especially the alleged Crazy Horse one, prompted many responses, a few actually in support of the identification of the Indian in the picture as the Oglala war chief. Such was the case of Ms. Eagle Feather, quoted in a November 29, 1947, letter to Will Robinson by Rudy White

Buffalo, of La Plant, South Dakota, identifying himself as a grandson of Sitting Bull: "I have spoke[n] to Ms. Eagle Feather relative to Chief Crazy Horse and she said Crazy Horse is her cousin and she remembers the scar on his face distinctively and also about wearing a few eagle feathers on the right side of his head occasionally, especially during gatherings – so she is positive you have an authentic picture of Crazy Horse and want to thank you again for the three dollars you trust me with and I shall wait patiently for a letter and a trip to Slim Buttes."[45] Noteworthy that, as a descendant of the Oglala war chief, Mrs. Eagle Feather made no reference to Crazy Horse's alleged fear of the camera, or hate of the White man, commonly attributed to him by "nay" advocates. And even though her identification was incorrect, it showed how open minded the elderly Lakota woman was, answering after so many years without preconceptions, such a controversial question. True, she must have been a teenager when Crazy Horse was killed, and therefore her recollections were vague at best. Still, she honestly thought she had recognized the very features of her famous elder cousin in the face of the Indian in the *Wi'iyohi* photograph.

There were also those who strongly disagreed. "Not him," wrote Henry Standing Bear (Mato Najen, 1874-1953) a few days later to Will Robinson from Tulsa, Oklahoma. Henry Standing Bear, another relative of Crazy Horse, was only three years old when Tašunke Witko was killed, and had no visual memory of what Crazy Horse looked like. Henry was the son of Brule chief George Standing Bear and his second wife Roaming Nation. She was the daughter of Rattling Stone Woman (also known as One Horse), a sister of Worm, Crazy Horse's father. Henry was a maternal second cousin of Crazy Horse and, according to those who had known the Oglala war chief, young Henry had features surprisingly reminiscent of those of his famous relative: "I made several trips to people who lived by Crazy Horse and his wife for years to verify my word that Crazy Horse never was photographed [and] that the pictures in the *Wi'iyohi* [...] are not Crazy Horse and his wife. I knew this as soon as I saw these pictures."[46] Clearly, within the very Lakota community opinions were not at all in agreement on the existence of a Crazy Horse photograph, as documented also in the extensive correspondence Will Robinson exchanged with both Indians and non-Indians on the identification of the *Wi'iyohi* man. Robinson was understandably cautious, and while he kept an open mind on the issue, a few years later in a letter to Oglala tribal councilwoman Ethel Merrival, he echoed the position that "the Indian tradition of course is that he [Crazy Horse] would never allow his picture to be taken."[47] Why of course, given that some, though mistakenly, thought the *Wi'iyohi* Indian was actually Crazy Horse?

This brings us back to the incongruity of two often repeated arguments against a likely photograph of Crazy Horse: that he was never in the vicinity of a photographer, and that he always refused to have his picture taken. For Crazy Horse to decline, repeatedly, to be photographed, it seems logical that there must have been a photographer to decline to. Documenting the presence of one "shadow catcher" at Camp Robinson and nearby Red Cloud Agency in 1877 was a crucial tassel in assembling the puzzle of a possible Crazy Horse photo-portrait. On this very issue, it is telling that long before recent photo historians uncovered a new wealth of visual information, some testimonies coming again from within the Lakota community did report the presence of at least one camera worker during the few months Crazy Horse was at Red Cloud Agency. Writing to Charles Dettborn in 1956, a persistent Will Robinson while reiterating that "the Indians have always claimed that there was no picture of Crazy Horse," left the door open to a possible reversal of the majority view. "I am satisfied," Robinson continued, "that there was NO painting of Crazy Horse. There however was a photographer at Ft. [Camp] Robinson according to Bill Larvie, a brother of Crazy Horse's second wife, at the time Crazy Horse was there in the summer of 1877. So that would indicate that a picture at least could have been taken." Still referring to what turned out to be a case of mistaken identity, that is, the *Wi'iyohi* portrait, Robinson concluded, "Personally I think that we have a pretty good identification but I am still trying for a negative angle to find somebody who can or will say that our picture is someone other than Crazy Horse. To date nobody has said it was other than he nor has anyone except Zoe Laravie and Mary Russell said it was Crazy Horse."[48]

Significantly, the positive identification of the mixed-blood young woman in the *Wi'iyohi* photograph as Nellie Larrabee had come from her closest relatives, as Robinson underscored in his closing response to William Bordeaux. William, in his October 25 letter, had stated that his late father Louis Bordeaux "was firm in his convictions that no photo was ever taken of [Crazy Horse]." To which Robinson wisely remarked, "The fact that your father did not know there was ever a picture of Crazy Horse taken would not mean much as would the testimony of any other person. Mrs. [Zoe Larrabee] Utterback had never seen a picture of her [older] sister [Helen/Nellie] and did not know there was one taken. Sophie White did not know there was a picture of her mother. Yet, both immediately identified it as a picture of Helen Larvie. You can see the negative testimony is of very small value [etc.]."[49]

Before we cry foul, we should consider the obvious that the mixed-blood woman and the Indian man in *Wi'iyohi* must have had a good degree of resemblance to the real Nellie and Crazy Horse, respectively. And indeed, both seem to have fairly attractive features even by today's standards. Feraca reproduced the Indian man in his 1964 article as "one of the several unauthenticated photos of Crazy Horse."[50] The same picture was subsequently discussed by Tom Buecker and Jack Heriard, who concurred he is not Crazy Horse.[51] The verdict on the alleged Nellie photograph is still open but Buecker suggested the young female in the picture was actually a mixed-blood Winnebago photographed by James H. Hamilton and listed as "No. 70. Winnebago Squaw" in his *Catalogue.* Again, whether they are right or wrong is not the point. What matters is that the Hochunk woman and Nellie must have looked much alike. Nellie's own sister and daughter thought the woman in the picture was actually their closest relative.

Many picture deniers embracing Sandoz's romantic portrayal of Crazy Horse as the irreconcilable warrior, continue to invoke the Oglala chief's profound hatred of the wašiču as the main reason why he could not possibly have had his picture taken. "According to ancestors of mine," wrote

Martin Knifechief, Hunkpapa, in response to Heriard's article on the tintype, "Crazy Horse would have never posed for a photograph, due to his hatred of the white man. [...] There are no known images of him but some descriptions from soldiers I have heard. The Indian people that I know are thankful that he cannot be marketed and his image sold."[52] We sympathize with Knifechief's latter point. We have already acknowledged the rightful stance against the commercial exploitation of anything relating to Crazy Horse, images included. Regarding our own work, we can only reiterate that we searched for proof of positive identification of the tintype strictly for historical reasons. As with the presence of one or even more photographers at Camp Robinson-Red Cloud Agency (until recently overlooked by those interested in Crazy Horse), the issue of the war chief's "hatred" had to be carefully scrutinized beyond the stereotype, again on the basis of the historical evidence. We shall see that on the question of continued "profound hatred" there is proof to the contrary, including the following. In late 1947, at the height of the debate over the purported "Crazy Horse and squaw" photographs featured in *Wi'iyohi*, Zoe Larrabee Utterback told Will Robinson that she herself had heard Crazy Horse declare "that as long as he had given up [fighting, and surrendered] that he might as well be like the White man."[53]

Susan Bordeaux Bettelyoun too, among others, maintained that when Crazy Horse agreed to report to Camp Robinson-Red Cloud Agency, he set aside much of his animosity towards the Whites. After interviewing several Indian old timers, Mari Sandoz implicitly contradicted herself, adding also a specific reference to photography, when she wrote that "soon the soldier chiefs were speaking well of the hostile Crazy Horse, calling him a fine, quiet, and modest man, one much concerned with the welfare of his people. Even his anger at the picture men, those with the black box who would catch his shadow as that of Red Cloud and others had been caught seemed good to them."[54] Sandoz used the plural, perhaps acknowledging there was more than one photographer operating at Red Cloud Agency during Crazy Horse's stay.

Equally important, and often downplayed if not altogether ignored, is the fact that during the few months he spent at the agency, Crazy Horse actually enlisted as a U.S. Army scout; not once, but twice. Writing in the early 1990s, Bob Lee, a reporter and a friend of the Lakota who in 1955 had received Dewey Beard's čannupa at the giveaway following the funeral of Crazy Horse's second cousin – who, as we shall see supported the authenticity of the tintype – wrote, "Crazy Horse, a Sioux warrior who spent much of his life fighting the U.S. Army, actually worked for the cavalry briefly as scout. And not once, but twice. While his brief service as an Army scout in no way diminishes Crazy Horse's remarkable record as a mighty Sioux warrior and patriot, it does somewhat tarnish the myths and legends that have sprouted up about him."[55] Precisely. It's not the name and spirit of Crazy Horse that were "tarnished," but the myths and made-up stories others had created around him. Modern purists who embrace an a-historical ideal of unrelenting Indian resistance have disingenuously brought up the "tarnished image" with regard to Sitting Bull's season in *Buffalo Bill's Wild West* as well. The Hunkpapa holy man's reasons for joining Col. Cody are well-known, and need not be repeated here. As for Crazy Horse, we shall return to his enlistments later.

Dr. Valentine T. McGillycuddy

One of the main "proofs" often cited by the "nay" supporters – that Crazy Horse always refused to be photographed – is actually a myth originated by the old frontier doctor and later Sioux Indian Agent Valentine T. McGillycuddy (1849-1939), assistant post surgeon at Camp Robinson at the time of Crazy Horse's surrender and death. Considered an authoritative source by historians, McGillycuddy's credentials as an objective and credible voice did not pass our scrutiny unfortunately, when it comes to Crazy Horse. More to the point, regarding his purported friendship with the Oglala war chief, the doctor was some kind of a braggart. McGillycuddy claimed he had a "kola" relationship with Tašunke Witko while at Camp Robinson. For the Lakota, the term kola defined a pledged, intimate mutual bond, and more. Hence, it would be safe to assume the doctor knew more than the basics about Crazy Horse. Yet, in a letter he sent to William 'Billy' Hunter Garnett (1855-1930), the famous mixed-blood interpreter and Army scout at Red Cloud Agency, dated February 28, 1922, the doctor actually asked, among other things, simple personal information he should have known well: "Hotel Claremont. Berkeley, California. Wm. Garnett, Dear Sir: I wonder if you are still alive or have 'gone over the range'. [...] If you receive this will you give me information on the following. [...] How did Crazy Horse get his name, was his father's name Crazy Horse, and was he a chief by birth, was he an Uncpapa and his wife an Oglala. [etc.]". Now, was the good doctor senile? The answer is no, as in the same letter he stated, "I am getting along in years myself, had my 73rd birthday [...] but am still active and in good health."[56] The sixty seven-year-old Garnett, who lived at Pine Ridge, replied on March 6, "Mr. V.T. McGillicuddy [sic] [...] My Dear Friend: I received your letter [...] asking information regarding several old Indians [...]. Crazy Horse is all Sioux but his father was an Oglala, and his mother was a Minni-ko-wo-jun (Cheyenne River Agency, So.Dak.). He took his name from his father who was also named Crazy Horse. He was not a chief by birth but was chosen chief in 1868, on account of his fighting ability. There is no question but that he was the bravest and best fighter in the Sioux Nation."[57]

On April 15, 1926, four years after Garnett had clearly explained the tribal identity of Crazy Horse's parents, the doctor asked again: "Was not his father an Oglala, and his mother an Huncpapa [sic]. At what agency was Crazy Horse located in 1875 and in the Spring of 1876, when the Indians were organizing the hostile camp [?]." Ever insistent and redundant, old Dr. Valentine continued boasting to having known Crazy Horse intimately, but on May 10, 1926, he again troubled poor Garnett, as he put it, with more questions. "Where did Crazy Horse get his name?" asked the doctor. "Was his fathers' [sic] name Crazy Horse, and was he a chief. Was not Crazy Horse rather queer in his head [...] What agency if any did he belong to."[58]

Should not the doctor have known that it was precisely because neither Crazy Horse nor Sitting Bull had reported to their respective agencies, as ordered by the Indian Bureau, that the historic Sioux Campaign of 1876 got underway, with the outcome we all know? That eventful year, as contract surgeon for the Army, McGillycuddy had been with Gen. Crook at the Rosebud on June 17, then in the Battle of Slim Buttes on September 9-10, and finally in the so-called Starvation or Horsemeat March during which he attended sick and starving troopers, and was himself photographed by Stanley J. Morrow.[59] As a participant observer in the midst of the Great Sioux War of '76, and a surgeon at Camp Robinson, the doctor – an educated man – must have read the newspaper dispatches on Crazy Horse, who was often referred to as the "Ogallalla" war chief.

McGillycuddy also claimed he often visited Crazy Horse's camp at Red Cloud Agency, and he must have known, to the very least that both Crazy Horse and his band were non-treaty Oglala. In the same letter to Garnett, Dr. McGillycuddy raised the photo issue, declaring he had unsuccessfully tried to photograph the war chief. "Did Crazy Horse ever have his picture taken?" he asked Garnett. "They claim to have one of him, but I hardly believe it, for I tried hard to have one taken of him in 1877."[60] The doctor, who knew basically nothing of the Oglala war chief, insisted on the negative claim. In a letter to Addison E. Sheldon, Superintendent of the Nebraska State Historical Society, McGillycuddy correctly rejected the photograph of Crazy in the Lodge, but, he attributed mysticism and superstition as motives of Crazy Horse's refusals: "Regarding the photograph [of Crazy in the Lodge] which I return herewith, I regret I have to state that it is not Crazy Horse, for he was much of a mystic and superstitious and positively refused to pose." He gratuitously added that since the Lakota war chief was "living before the days of the quick acting Kodak, it became impossible to snap one of him."[61]

McGillycuddy's biography written by his second wife Julia says nothing of the doctor as a photographer while stationed at Camp Robinson.[62] If the doctor had an interest in photography, wouldn't he have put it into practice? Like other "shadow catchers" who came through Camp

Robinson, wouldn't he have photographed, first and foremost Red Cloud and the other agency chiefs, let alone the officers and civilians at the post? Giving McGillycuddy the benefit of the doubt, we can even assume that, as there was a permanent photographic studio at Red Cloud Agency, perhaps he, through an interpreter, at some point did ask Crazy Horse to pose for a picture, with the request being declined. Only with this reasoning we can conceivably accept, without accusing him of lying, good old McGillycuddy's assertion to Brininstool. But we cannot accept, as for example Denis McLoughlin did in his otherwise worthy *Wild & Woolly: An Encyclopedia of the Old West*, the tale of the frontier surgeon tending to the dying war chief while attempting to take his picture. "When Crazy Horse was dying Dr. McGillicuddy [sic] tried to take his photograph (some doc!), but the war chief turned his head to the wall, remarking to the effect that 'no one must take away his shadow.' Writers have used this incident," comments McLoughlin, "to prove that Crazy Horse never allowed his photograph to be taken, but this of course is ridiculous." Incredibly, McLoughlin gives this invented tale the weight of history. Rather than seeing the absurdity of such an assertion, he continues, "Crazy Horse was dying, and to an Indian in extremis his shadow would be something tangible, a very hold on existence; therefore the McGillicuddy [sic] incident only proves that the war chief did not want his photograph taken under the circumstances related. If this assumption is correct, then one of the half-dozen or so photographs going the rounds that are alleged to be of Crazy Horse may be a likeness of him."[63] Though his premise was wrong, at least McLoughlin accepted that a photograph may exist.

Regarding McGillycuddy's credibility, Thomas Powers reported that Crazy Horse's father suspected the doctor might have even poisoned his son: "[Worm] saw the doctor fill his syringe and inject some stuff into his son's body. 'He died awful quick after that.'"[64] Others believe the doctor only injected morphine to ease the pain. Also Tom Bucker recognized the scarce credibility of the famous doctor overall, and more specifically in regard to his attempts to photograph Crazy Horse: "McGillycuddy, frequently sought out by later historians, unfortunately was not totally credible. Despite his status as an interesting historical figure, his recollections were sometimes greatly overblown."[65] "I never obtained his picture," wrote the doctor to Custer historian Earl A. Brininstool (1870-1957). "His invariable reply to my request was, 'My friend, why should you want to shorten my life by taking from me my shadow?'"[66]

Buecker commented the doctor's historic phrase with these powerful words: "Certainly a moving statement, but it is probably another piece of McGillycuddy folklore, manufactured to appeal to the preconceived notions about American Indians of later generations of Americans. Apparently this reticence to photography did not stop dozens of the other Sioux, including followers and close friends of CH from being photographed." Buecker went even further, stating that, "Will Robinson, who probably mulled over the photo question more than any other historian, believed this statement was the genesis for the notion that Crazy Horse never had his photo taken. Robinson could not understand how McGillycuddy could categorically deny a photo was ever taken." In a letter to Thomas W. Right, dated April 3, 1958, Robinson reasoned, "No man unless constantly with another can make a positive negative statement."

According to McGillycuddy, the last and more important refusal allegedly occurred the very night Crazy Horse was soon to die. Any reasonable person would wonder how could a young doctor attending a moribund Lakota war chief, who happened to be no less than Crazy Horse laying mortally wounded, in great pain, on the floor of a dimly-lit room, with the chief's own father, step-mother, and cousin Touch the Clouds weeping, really concern himself with photography? And what kind of a "night-camera" did the doctor have? For the sake of argument, if indeed a camera and tripod were taken into the crowded room in the middle of the night, Crazy Horse's own relatives would have stopped the doctor there and then. And, both they and the other witnesses to the chief's final hours would have later related that fact. They did not, as there was no camera! McGillycuddy himself recalled how potentially explosive the situation was: "We had a close call that day while Crazy Horse was lying on the ground writhing in agony, for had a single shot been fired on either side, there would have been a killing unequalled in this history of our Indian trouble. We all felt it, and each side held back."[67] No attempt was made at photographing Crazy Horse on his death bed. And it had nothing to do with the metaphysics of fear, loss of soul, or violation of tribal taboo.

David F. Barry, "Catcher of the Little Shadow"

Unfortunately, in time doctor McGillycuddy's story became historically true and convincingly significant. It was appropriated, among others, by noted Western photographer David F. Barry who, like the fake war paint inked on Indian portraits by some of his fellow "shadow catchers," added yet another twist to it. Worse, he inserted an utterly false bribery element into McGillycuddy's tell-tale. Barry's invented photo-op scenarios with Crazy Horse and the latter's purported refusals to be bribed are a total lie. David F. Barry's photo-portraits of the surviving Indian and White protagonists of the Battle of the Little Bighorn, and the battlefield itself, are an invaluable visual record of that most historic episode and of many participants. But when it came to Crazy Horse, D.F. Barry, too, fell victim of the mystique, stating the absurd and blatantly lying about it, that he himself had attempted repeatedly to photograph the great Oglala war chief, to no vale. In his Introduction to *Crazy Horse, The Invincible Ogalalla Sioux Chief*, a sympathetic collection of first hand-accounts by "actual observers" focusing on the "foul murder" of Tašunke Witko, Brininstool corroborated McGillycuddy's "no picture" myth with Barry's own "attempted bribery but no picture" testimony.[68] Brininstool insisted on this point. Writing years later to Will Robinson, in the summer of 1947, he reiterated that "D.F. Barry, who took pictures of most of the noted chiefs of the 1876 period, told me personally that he had repeatedly tried to bribe Crazy Horse to sit for his picture, but was always refused permission. If HE couldn't get one, I am sure nobody else could."[69] Assuming that Brininstool did not make up the story, and there is no reason to believe he did, the falsehood of Barry's claim is regrettable. Equally regrettable, this statement has never before been seriously challenged, except a brief mention by Tom Buecker in 1998.[70] Even the careful researcher and Western historian Thomas W. Wright, who in the 1950s-1960s reviewed several photographs allegedly identified as Crazy Horse, did not seem bothered by the outrageous claim. "David F. Barry," Wright wrote, "tried on a number of occasions at Fort [sic] Robinson in the summer 1877 to persuade the Oglala chief into having his picture taken, but he found that Crazy Horse was unmovable on this matter."[71]

There is no record of Barry, at the time barely a twenty-year-old apprentice in the photographic studio of Orlando Scott Goff in Bismarck, being anywhere in northwestern Nebraska. Barry's own date of birth is uncertain; 1854, 1855, or even 1858, but we do know he began his Western photographic career after Crazy Horse's death. The research conducted years ago by John S. Gray was indirect proof to that. Although Gray was not specifically concerned with the Crazy Horse picture question, in his reconstruction of Barry's life he noted that "the most crucial item in Barry's career is the date of his arrival in Bismarck. Mrs. Holley, a local historian who knew him at the time, wrote that 'D.F. Barry has been in Montana and Dakota most of the time since 1878.' The local paper, so lavish in its notices on Goff, and later Barry as well, does not mention the latter until the fall of 1879. [...] Finally, Goff's daughter wrote that soon after her father built his first Bismarck studio [...] in June 1878, he 'took a young man, D.F. Barry, under his wing and taught him the photography business from time exposures to burnishing pictures.' This evidence forces us to conclude," says Gray, "that David Barry came to Bismarck, not fully trained and independent in 1874, but as a beginning protégé of Goff no earlier than the fall of 1878 – long after Custer's day." And, we may add, a whole year after the death of Crazy Horse.[72]

Barry's biographer Thomas Heski also admitted that "D.F. Barry entered the photographic profession during the wet plate days in 1878 as a protégé of frontier photographer Orlando Goff," and that a research on Barry's alleged photographic activities "from 1870 until 1878, proved futile."[73] We have to wonder why did he, "noted photographer of Indian life" lie so blatantly about Crazy Horse. Barry could have simply stated the truth that Crazy Horse was already dead when he began his career. Instead, with the made-up story of Crazy Horse's "repeated refusals," he perpetuated and reinforced the "no picture" tale. Although not a plausible reason for lying about it, after the tragic death of General Custer, both Goff and Barry had become close friends of the late General's widow, Elizabeth "Libby" Custer. Like other Custer sympathizers, Barry supported Libby's crusade in defense of her "hero" husband's memory, and he provided her with images of the participants in the battle. Given the key role Crazy Horse had played in Custer's defeat, Barry endeavored to secure from old sources an image of Tašunke Witko to accompany those of other famous Indian and White combatants he later produced himself. Unable to find an authenticated image of the Oglala war chief, Barry saw an opportunity to place himself in the spotlight and invented the story of his "repeated attempts" made directly to Crazy Horse. At the time, it made perfect sense. After all, it was common practice for American Indians, chiefs especially, to require compensation for having their picture taken. Crazy Horse, according to Barry's galloping fantasy, was a notable exception precisely because he repeatedly turned down both payments and photos. Furthermore, the refusals fit perfectly Crazy Horse's legendary aura. Historian Earl A. Brininstool took the McGillycudddy and Barry testimonies at face value. Both men's names and reputation carried much weight. He had no reason to doubt them and he, too, turned their "stories" into "history."

It did not end there. In a reply letter to William J. Bordeaux, author of *Custer's Conqueror*, Will G. Robinson further authenticated Barry's state-ment with the weight of his authoritative voice as Secretary of the South Dakota Historical Society. "As regards the picture of Crazy Horse," Robinson wrote in 1951, "there is a very long standing tradition that no picture was ever made of him and the photographer, Berry, [sic] stated Crazy Horse refused all his overtures to take a picture."[74] The "no picture" and "fear factor" themes were passed down across generations. In the 1950s, attor-ney and amateur historian Robert R. Wellington of Crawford, Nebraska, investigated the Crazy Horse picture question and concluded, "I am of the firm opinion that no picture was ever taken, or is extant [...] he never allowed a picture to be taken of himself for the reason that he thought that it would take away part of his soul and authority."[75]

White Man's Garb

Other "official" arguments against a possible photograph of the famed warrior border the ridiculous. In a reply comment to Jack Heriard's article, John L. Smith recalled that in the 1960s, as a young anthropology student he had several written exchanges with the very Mari Sandoz. "One of our discussions," he wrote, "concerned the photos of Crazy Horse. She was very adamant that no photo existed. Each time I would ask her about a particular one, including the one in your article [...] she would have several reasons why it could not possibly be her 'strange man.' Her contention was, regarding your photo, he [Crazy Horse] would never have submitted to wearing white man's clothing ... the shirt, metal arm bands, etc."

We strongly disagree and maintain without disrespect that whereas Mary Sandoz was a gifted writer, she knew very little about Lakota material culture, dress, and accessories in Crazy Horse's time. The same John L. Smith recognized that contrary to Sandoz's opinion, "some sources, including the ledger drawings of Bad Heart Bull, do indeed depict Crazy Horse in 'white man's garb.'"[76] Actually, this latter definition too is misleading, because the "basic" dress illustrated by Amos Bad Heart Bull, that is, long white (or color-patterned) muslin/cotton shirt over dark stroud trade cloth leggings, was common male Indian attire during the early agency period.[77]

In the parlance of at the time, "Indian dress" meant buckskin, beads, and feathers. Yet, cloth had already become prominent and widespread, individually embellished as it were with beads, brass tacks, buttons, representing the very common (post-buckskin) new-style "Indian garb." The 'new' Indian dress, in all of its individual and tribal variations, was obviously the syncretic product of tradition and innovation, and as such it was genuinely "Indian" regardless of the fact that the new materials and items of clothing came from the White man. Indian garb, certainly not "white man's garb." It can be seen in countless historic Sioux (and Cheyenne and Arapaho) photographs of the same period, ledger art drawings as the one just mentioned, and was described in actual eyewitness accounts, like that of Susan Bordeaux Bettelyoun, below. If that were not evidence enough, we have the official annuity records of the Sioux Agencies, and the inventories of local agency traders who stocked their shelves with rolls of cloth and manufactured cotton clothing, expressly for their Indian customers. Unfortunately, because of the savage Indian stereotype combined with the prejudicial smoke screen raised by McGillycuddy, Barry, Brininstool, and later Sandoz around the picture question, much distortion, mythologizing, and outright ignorance clouded the issue and hindered objective research.

A Close-Up Look

Distortions and exaggerations, some coming from the Indians themselves, perpetuate an idealized stereotype of a Lakota patriot who does not need additional fake feathers and war paint, as Crazy Horse stands tall on his own. They ignore the real, complex dynamics of tribal social interaction and political power-struggle at Red Cloud and Spotted Tail Agencies, especially after Crazy Horse's surrender. "Tasunke Witko was NEVER photographed," stated a proud Sioux response to the old picture conundrum posted recently on the web. "And, we as Lakota people know [that] for several reasons. The main one is that Crazy Horse said he would not allow his photo to be taken, though many tried [!?]. His family and his People protected him from the cameras. You must remember that during the time period we are talking about cameras were big bulky things and exposure times were fairly long." Again insisting on a unilateral reading of Crazy Horse, "To have such an image taken of himself was against what he stood for [...] and up until his death no one with a camera was allowed near him. We know this as Lakota."[78]

Crazy Horse's tipi circle stood about six miles from Camp Robinson, and many Agency Indians and some of his own friends and allies had come to regard the surrendered chief as a troublemaker. Protect him? Crazy

Horse's extreme attempt to seek refuge at Spotted Tail, his step-uncle's cold reception there, and the rude expulsion of the Oglala war chief from the Brule agency prove otherwise. The picture question cannot be objectively addressed without acknowledging that after the initial welcome and dog feasts, Agency chiefs and headmen at both Red Cloud and Spotted Tail increasingly resented the Northern "intruder" and openly opposed him. As sides polarized, those chiefs wanted Crazy Horse gone for good. In such unsettled times in tribal politics, "gone" could very well mean "dead," no matter how aberrant the thought could be to traditional Lakota values. And death it was. Unfortunately, these well documented historical facts have been sanitized by Indians and Whites alike.

We are obviously respectful of the opinion of others. But considering the iconic nature of the man and his continued impact on Lakota history and culture, not to mention his popular world-wide image, an objective case in favor of the tintype as a picture of Crazy Horse could not be pursued without a careful scrutiny of these and similar misconceptions. Therefore, we searched beyond the frozen image of the irreconcilable "hostile," the clichés of a quasi-superhuman, impassive, distant hero, his unrelenting intransigence and hate of the White man, and his alleged enmity towards the camera, that for so long shrouded the more complex, articulate, real nature of Crazy Horse. Many of the myths and sagas that flourished around him, often repeated today, proved to be just that. Equally important was the context of Lakota (and Cheyenne) historical photography during his lifetime.

Once it was documented that photographers did visit Red Cloud Agency and Camp Robinson starting when the post was established in 1874, and that there was even a permanent photographic studio at Red Cloud, we looked specifically at the known "shadow catchers" who operated their business among the thousands of Oglala, Cheyenne and Arapaho camped in northwestern Nebraska in the spring-summer-fall of 1877. We then focused on a contextual and comparative analysis of the tintype itself. On the basis of contemporary eyewitness testimonies, we tried to define Crazy Horse's features and overall physical appearance and the clothes he reportedly wore, those habitually worn by the Sioux at Red Cloud and Spotted Tail Agencies and on delegation trips in the mid-to-late 1870s, and compared them to those of the Indian in the tintype.

We also examined what turned out to be the not-so-settled issue of the scar on Crazy Horse's face from the small caliber bullet wound inflicted by fellow tribesman No Water. We looked at the warrior's most cherished personal possessions: the red blanket he habitually wore and also had at the time of his death, and his wotawe, the protective charms given to him by Ptehe Woptuha, Horn Chips (ca. 1830-1816), his Oglala elder cousin, religious mentor and powerful yuwipi man. We sorted out many, at times contradictory accounts of Crazy Horse's features and general appearance, and compared them with the tintype portrait. Finally, we profiled the key protagonists of the family history that originally linked the tintype to Little Bat Garnier and his wife Julie Mousseau, a Lakota. A history supported by written affidavits provided in the 1950s by their daughter Ellen Garnier Howard, herself a Sioux. Mrs. Howard's testimony was endorsed by Ethel Merrival, Jake Herman, and C. Bear Robe, all Oglala tribal members. And by Fred Hackett, adopted son of famed Oglala Iron Tail. Contemporary statements by other Lakota in support of the tintype have also been included.

Open Mind

Joseph Marshall, III, previously cited, expressed skepticism about the existence of a photograph of Crazy Horse. He also has a website that reads, "Misconceptions and stereotypes about us are a detriment to Indians and non-Indians alike. They have existed so long that some are regarded as truth. They obscure the reality of what and who we really were and are. [...] Stories as far as I'm concerned, are the best way for people to get to know about each other. [...] The more honest stories we know about one another the more realistic awareness we gain. The more awareness we have the more likely we are to think of and judge one another fairly. Then we are more likely to greet one another with an open hand and an open heart, rather than a closed fist and a closed mind."[79] On the issue of historical knowledge, Marshall also noted that "no individual or group is a single omniscient source when it comes to history. It is a composite, and we need the true voices from each part to tell a complete and realistic story. Anything less is an insult to all of the people who lived that story and contributed to the history we study and tell about in our times."[80]

Marshall's remarks were obviously directed principally at the presumptuous writings of White authors who often embraced ethnocentric, biased, even racist views, challenging, furthermore, the validity of Native Peoples' own oral traditions. Yet today, a similar absolutist presumption of knowledge characterizes some of the literary and media productions by American Indians themselves; a paradoxical reversal of roles that does not help intercultural dialogue, nor the search for objectivity and truth.

Those asserting to "know it all" about Crazy Horse fall into this very trap. Writing to Dr. McGillycuddy in mid-1920, Billy Garnett scorned both Whites and Indians alike who, already back then, pretended to speak authoritatively on things they knew little about: "I am like you [Dr. McGillycuddy], and am continually finding people who were not born when these events took place; who seem to know more about them than you and I do, who were actually there."[81] We shall return to McGillycuddy and Garnett. When it comes to the possibility that a photographic portrait of Crazy Horse may exist, partisan rhetoric, anger and even hate cloud up the debate creating unnecessary obstacles to anyone searching for the truth.

Short Bull (Tatanka Ptečela)

The absolutist thesis that Tašunke Witko "was never photographed" or, conversely, that "there is no picture of Crazy Horse,"[82] is an example of close-minded dogmatism. Yet, how many times have established historical and scientific "truths" been questioned, some even shattered by new evidence, discoveries, revelations? Regarding a possible Crazy Horse photo, we reported the opinion of Mrs. Eagle Feather. But it was a wrong identification, critics would say, missing the point. We suggest, then, that those who so vehemently deny Crazy Horse could have ever been photographed reflect on another important, credible testimony that he actually was. A testimony rendered long ago, again – like most of those in favor of the tintype – from within the Lakota Nation. Not the words of a wašiču, or an "Uncle tomahawk," but of a true Lakota, a full-blood Oglala named Short Bull (Tatanka Ptečela, ca. 1850-1935), younger brother of He Dog (Šunka Bloka, ca. 1840-1936). The Oglala Short Bull, later known as Grant Short Bull, should not be confused with his Brule contemporary Arnold Short Bull (ca. 1845-1923), author of an alleged 'Crazy Horse' sketch discussed below.

The Čankahuhan (Soreback) Oglala Short Bull was born near Fort Laramie about the time of the first treaty. He was handpicked by Tašunke Witko to be a member of the "Last Child" akičita society. Short Bull was with the Soreback band on Tongue River in January 1876 when the government's ultimatum to report to the agencies was delivered to the Northern bands. On March 17, 1876, while he was absent on a raiding party, his village was attacked by General George Crook's troops, under the direct command of Colonel Joseph J. Reynolds. Short Bull returned in time to help recapture part of the village's horse herd. He later explained that, had it not been for that attack by Crook on Powder River, the Sioux war would have been avoided. Short Bull participated in both the Rosebud and Little Bighorn fights under Crazy Horse, and he surrendered with him at Red Cloud Agency on May 5, 1877. After the killing of Crazy Horse, Short Bull fled to Canada and he surrendered again with other Oglala at Fort Keogh in 1881. He remained less than a year at Standing Rock, and was then transferred to Pine Ridge where he resided until his death, in a car crash. The year before the accident, in 1934, Short Bull attended the Crazy Horse monument dedication at Fort Robinson.

No one can doubt Short Bull knew Crazy Horse well and was a close friend of his. Interviewed in 1930 by Eleanor Hinman, Short Bull stated through interpreter John Colhoff something remarkable relating to the overall case for a Crazy Horse photograph: "I have seen two photographs of Crazy Horse that I think were really he, both showing him on horseback. One showed him on a buckskin horse he owned, one on a roan. I have seen a third photograph that I am sure was he, because he showed him on the pinto horse he rode in the Custer fight. I could not possibly make a mistake about that horse, and nobody rode it but Crazy Horse."[83]

These words were spoken before the picture question became the subject of intense speculation and debate, and are indicative of the objective and open-minded traditional Lakota. If Short Bull, a respected elder, expressed the possibility that a photographic image of Tašunke Witko may exist, he did so based not on speculation or personal gain, but his own recollections and firm belief. Short Bull was so familiar with the chief's distinctive features that he could easily recognize him, hence his certainty that the images he saw "were really he." Not only did Short Bull know Crazy Horse intimately but, in a horse culture like that of the Lakota, he also knew the chief's favorite war horse. Whatever one may think of the entire Crazy Horse picture controversy, Short Bull's testimony should be given the respect it deserves and, if nothing else, the benefit of the doubt. It is puzzling that while great historical value is now recognized by historians to Indian testimonies of the Custer fight, Short Bull's and other Lakota statements in favor of a Crazy Horse photograph are generally overlooked if not altogether ignored.

The same Korczak Ziolkowski family referred to Short Bull as a respected Lakota friend of Crazy Horse and the great-grandfather of Arthur Short Bull, contemporary Oglala Lakota artist. They posted with pride the photograph of Arthur Short Bull, who "designed our unique holiday ornament for 2015. He has painted a red-tailed hawk watercolor, reflected as a lithograph on a one-of-kind porcelain ornament [...]. We see these hawks often in the Black Hills as they soar near and around the Mountain."[84]

Pertaining to the photos mentioned by Short Bull, in 1957 Will G. Robinson sent a reply letter to Mrs. Helen A. Bowser in Los Angeles in which he acknowledged the following: "We have your letter [...] with the three pictures of the so called Crazy Horse bust. They are very interesting to me. [...] About the most positive thing we know about Crazy Horse was that he had a scar on his face near his nose. Your picture certainly looks more like the word picture we have of Crazy Horse, written by competent eyewitness reporters. We certainly thank you. I was at Crazy Horse Mountain just yesterday and talked with Ziolkowski, and your letter was mentioned. I will take the pictures out the first time I got out there again and certainly thank you for your cooperation and courtesy."[85] What happened after that, we do not know. Could these three pictures be the ones that Short Bull was referring to? Short Bull said that the officer who had these three pictures moved to California. Could this be a coincidence? Many people claimed to have a picture of Crazy Horse, but three? We strongly believe that these three photos are the photos Short Bull was referring to.

Coming Together

We concur with Marshall that knowledge is not exclusive but rather inclusive, complex, composite, at times contradictory, like the human hearts and minds producing it. Still, as for a photograph of Tašunke Witko specifically, in a feature article in *Native Peoples* magazine, while not rejecting the possibility that an image of the war chief might exist, Marshall relied on the negative judgment of the "experts" who, he wrote, "doubt any photographs were ever taken of the elusive Crazy Horse."[86]

We disagree with the experts and those of a likewise persuasion. We believe instead that the question of a possible Crazy Horse photographic portrait can be addressed objectively and answered with a degree of humble certainty. To this end, we approached the Crazy Horse picture conundrum from a holistic perspective, taking all sides into account.

Questioning both academic dogma and popular views, a somewhat analogous line of thinking guided Alice Kehoe in her provocative study of a very different yet conceptually similar and equally controversial subject. The Kensington rune stone, purportedly inscribed in 1632 by Vikings "lost" in the heart of North America and later found by a Minnesota farmer in 1898. Long discredited as a fake by historians and linguists, the inscription is still "thumbs down" for the experts. Yet, after looking at the whole picture and carefully examining the broader ethnographic, historical, linguistic, and contextual evidence of the highly debated stone, Kehoe concluded that "the weight of probability now favors [its] authenticity."[87] Whether one agrees with Kehoe's minority conclusion or not is not the point. What matters here is her open-minded, non-exclusive approach to and thorough research on a historical mystery that is still regarded by most an improbable case.

Similarly, with the Crazy Horse tintype, we pursued questions of possibility and plausibility without a priori, arbitrary, unsubstantiated assumptions, and exclusions. Contextually, we took an inclusive look at the broader issue of American Indian photographic portraiture in the second half of the nineteenth century, specifically the relationship between photography and the Sioux (also the Cheyenne), and the profound changes affecting Lakota life in the crucial decade from the Fort Laramie Treaty of 1868 to the surrender and death of Crazy Horse in 1877. What historian Paul Hedren called "loss and transformation in Sioux Country" reached a crucial climax after the Custer Battle.[88]

We took notice of Crazy Horse's transition from irreconcilable war leader of the Northern Indians to twice-enlisted U.S. Army scout and sincere, albeit disingenuous, seeker of peace. It was in this final stage of his earthly journey that in good faith and goodwill, Tašunke Witko agreed to have his picture taken. There was nothing contradictory on the part of Crazy Horse to sit for a photograph, also considering that he was now drawing a salary as a scout from the very Army he had until recently fought against. Like the other agency chiefs, Crazy Horse too raised his right hand and swore allegiance to the United States of America. Many Lakota have done that ever since, serving honorably in the U.S. Armed forces, and many still do.

This, too, reflects the warrior spirit of Crazy Horse. Both circumstantial and documentary evidence suggest the tintype portrait of Crazy Horse was taken at Red Cloud Agency in the summer of 1877 by traveling photographer James H. Hamilton. While we cannot relate the exact details of that historic sitting, the testimonies and documents cited in the pages of this book together with the thorough historical and comparative analysis of the image itself make a convincing case for the identification of the tintype as indeed "the face" and full portrait of Crazy Horse.

"The sun dancer" by Richard Emery (1970).
Presented by Charles 'Chuck' Emery to author Cesare Marino.

PART I

Faces of the Lakota (and Cheyenne)

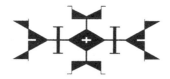

"[…] there were twenty or more of the different bands, each one with their chief at their head, over whom was a superior chief and leader, a middle-aged man, of middling stature, with a noble countenance, and a figure almost equaling the Apollo. […] This chief […] has risen rapidly to the highest honors in the tribe, from his own extraordinary merits, even at so early an age. […] he took the name 'One Horn' (or shell) from a single small shell that was hanging on his neck […]. He treated me with great kindness and attention, considering himself highly complimented by the signal and unprecedented honor I had conferred upon him by painting his portrait […]."

George Catlin, 1832

"Crazy Horse [… was] a light complexion man, medium height, light hair, handsome pleasant face, medium built."

Pugh Young Man Afraid of His Horse,
nephew of Young Man Afraid of His Horse, 1958

"Around his neck [Crazy Horse] wore a leather thong threaded through the end of a buffalo horn. In the buffalo horn he carried a small pebble."

Dr. Robert H. Ruby, 1955

Crazy Horse remains one of the most captivating and inspiring figures in American Indian history, and equally in the collective conscience of both Indians and Whites. Yet until fairly recently, much uncertainty surrounded our knowledge of the Oglala war chief. His true facial features in particular seemed to have defied accurate recording even by his own Indian and White contemporaries. Eyewitness testimonies on this very subject often disagree. This is odd, because Crazy Horse lived at a time when enterprising, daring, even reckless artists and photographers were documenting the Frontier, many focusing specifically on the American Indians. Yet, like the patriots of other tribal nations who before him had led the Native struggle for freedom and independence – King Philip (Wampanoag) in 1675 against the New England colonists, Po'pay (San Juan Pueblo) in 1680 against the Spaniards, Pontiac (Ottawa-Chippewa) in 1763 against the British, even the great Tecumseh (Shawnee) in 1810-1813 against the Americans, just to name a few – the Lakota war chief too seemed destined to remain a faceless, albeit powerful icon in the annals of history.[89]

We do not know whether Crazy Horse was aware of his Native predecessors who had attempted to stop the Euro-American invasion, but he certainly was spiritually and ideally linked to them. The connection was recognized by Santee medical doctor and author Charles A. Eastman (Ohiyesa, 1858-1939) who drew a sympathetic portrait of the Lakota mystic warrior: "Like Tecumseh, he was always impatient for battle; like Pontiac, he fought on while his allies where suing for peace."[90] And like those famous leaders, whose likenesses were later recreated mostly on a conjectural basis by non-Indian artists, also Crazy Horse's fame grew shrouded in the apparent lack of an authenticated portrait or photograph of him.

Unlike the aforementioned Indian patriots of pre-camera days, Crazy Horse represents an iconic anomaly, given that, as we just said, photography was very active in his lifetime. An anomaly also because practically all of Crazy Horse's Indian contemporaries, including his closest associates He Dog, Short Bull, Little Killer, Red Feather, Little Big Man, his spiritual mentor Horn Chips, along with those who had become his antagonists, notably Red Cloud, Spotted Tail, American Horse, Red Dog, Hunts the Enemy (Sword), Woman Dress, Three Bears, and many more, all had their pictures taken. Both friends and foes of Crazy Horse were willingly "captured" by the camera. Crazy Horse's own relatives Lone Horn, Iron Crow, Little Hawk, Touch the Clouds, and others were photographed before and after the Oglala war chief finally agreed to lead his followers to Red Cloud Agency - Camp Robinson that spring of 1877.

The impressive number of previously unknown American Indian photographs that have appeared in recent publications, auction catalogues, and posted on the web, remind us that what we know today of 19th-century American Indian photography may actually represent the proverbial tip of the iceberg. While old-fashion, tedious archival research will never be fully replaced, and constitutes the bedrock of sound scholarship, the internet has incredibly expanded our knowledge and revolutionized access to an unprecedented wealth of older images. Opening, so to speak, not just a new window, but a huge balcony on to the study of American Indian historical photographs. Crazy Horse, too, falls into this category. Leaving aside for a moment the question of the tintype, as we shall see other photographs have been found that relate directly to the famous Lakota chief. Unthinkable, only a few decades ago. As new historical images continue to surface, many American Indian photographs are being revisited and analyzed with greater accuracy.

Mistaken Identity

Good history and common sense call for caution with regard to the correct identification, date, location, tribal affiliation, and authorship of vintage American Indian photographs. This is a central issue in our search for positive answers in favor of the tintype, especially in light of the *Wi'iyohi* case and other images erroneously identified as Crazy Horse. Many historical photographs of American Indians often lack proper or complete documentation, and as a result they have been misidentified or misrepresented. It was also common among early photographers to purchase the works of other "shadow catchers" and market them under they own imprint. In the process, with the passing of time, key information could be misinterpreted, purposely manipulated, or lost altogether. Close to Crazy Horse, there are two famous photographic examples of mistaken identity. One pertains to Crazy Horse's kola He Dog (1840-1936), the Oglala shirt-wearer of the Smoke (Bad Faces) band often confused with a contemporary Brule by the same name. A photograph of "He Dog" was published as frontispiece in Eleanor Hinman's *Oglala Sources* relating to Crazy Horse, with the caption reading: "He Dog (Sunka Bloka), a sub chief, Cut Meat District, 1900."[91]

The image in question actually portrays the Brule headman He Dog, photographed by John A. Anderson on the Rosebud Sioux Indian Reservation with Cut Meat being one of that reservation's twenty Sičangu communities. Hinman should have published instead a photograph of the Oglala He Dog, the one she interviewed. If she or her editors did not have a recent portrait, they could have used the old photo of He Dog taken in Washington, in October 1877.[92] Hinman did include a photograph of the right "He Dog and wife, 1899" later in the text. This, of course, does not diminish the importance of Hinman's work as an indispensable source on Crazy Horse. The same mistake was made by Jason Hook who reproduced the photograph of the Brule He Dog with a caption that identified him, erroneously, as the Oglala life-long friend of Crazy Horse. Hook stated that it was the man in the picture, "who provided Eleanor Hinman with a remarkable history of his comrade the Oglala chief."[93]

Another case of misidentification connected to Crazy Horse is that of Si Tanka (Big Foot). Years ago, Big Foot was featured on the web with his wife *Četan Ska* (White Hawk), in a photographic portrait taken by Alexander Gardner in Washington in 1872. The cabinet card (advertised at a 2007 Cowan's Auction of Western Americana) had a caption that read, "Also known as Spotted Elk (Hehaka Gleska), this is the only portrait known to survive of this important image of the Mnicojou leader who died in the infamous Wounded Knee massacre, December 29, 1890. The photographs of his frozen corpse have haunted the American psyche for more than a century. Born circa 1820, he was son of the Mnicojou Head Chief One Horn, and a cousin of [...] Crazy Horse. Photographed by Gardner in his early fifties, Big Foot was a tall, imposing man wrapped in a wool blanket with a beaded strip probably made by his wife. His neckerchief is secured with a nickel-silver cross. The smaller, two-armed crosses hanging from either side represent dragonflies [sacred messengers]. White Hawk [?] wears a dress of printed calico and a striped wool shawl."

Contrary to the statement above, the Big Foot photographed by Gardner is most likely not the Mnicojou relative of Crazy Horse, but the Oglala signer of the 1868 Fort Laramie Treaty under the full name Big Wolf Foot; the "Wolf" later dropped in English and thus identified simply as Big Foot. As such, the Oglala Big Foot was a member of the 1872 Red Cloud delegation to Washington, where he was photographed by Gardner.[94] Big [Wolf] Foot's name appears along with that of Red Cloud (and Mr. Blackmore), Red Dog, Little Big Man, Slow Bull, Old and Young Man Afraid of His Horses, Little Wound, He Dog, Three Bears, Sword, Stabber, and other "Ogalalla" in W.H. Jackson's *Descriptive Catalogue* of American Indian photographs, a key early reference published the same year Crazy Horse was killed.[95] Relating to the debate over a photograph of the "mystic warrior," we can anticipate that the Stabber image by Gardner was long confused as Crazy Horse until the case was resolved by History Detectives. As for the misidentification in the auction ad, it was probably due to the fact that the Mnicojou Big Foot, too, touched the pen in 1868, but next to his other name Spotted Elk, along with band leaders One [Lone] Horn, The Elk That Bellows Walking, Young White Bull, Afraid of Shield, Slow Bull, Iron Horn and other "Minneconjon" (a Kappler misprint), some of them were indeed photographed by Gardner at Fort Laramie on that historic occasion.

There are numerous other cases arising from improper name translation, lacking or erroneous documentation on the original print, and a host of other reasons. The problem of correct identification does not alter the fact that so many tribesmen closely associated with, even related to Crazy Horse, were photographed during the pivotal 1868-1878 decade. It is legitimate then to ask why a picture of Crazy Horse may not exist, provided a photographer crossed paths with the war chief at the right time and the right place. And conversely, where does the absolute verdict that no image of Crazy Horse was ever made come from? Even assuming that Crazy Horse was never photographed, was it truly because, as the McGillicuddy's saga maintains of Crazy Horse's "fear" his soul be "stolen"? Or, as others have written, because of his deep hatred of the milahanska and the intrusive picture men? The historical evidence suggests otherwise to both assumptions. It is true that Crazy Horse never sat in front of a camera most of his entire life, having kept away from the wašiču and out of reach from a photographer. But things eventually changed when Crazy Horse ended his fighting and agreed to lead his people to the Oglala Agency in 1877.

He Dog's son Eagle Hawk, later baptized as Joseph, was a seven-year-old when Crazy Horse surrendered at Camp Robinson. Many years later, around 1940, he drew a number of pictographs accompanied by explanatory notes based on his father's recollections that are extremely revealing, especially of Crazy Horse's new attitude after he formally put an end to hostilities. "[Pictograph 3]. So Crazy Horse said he would [make peace], and the others who were sitting down on the ground were all in favor of it also. He said he would take the peace pipe and smoke, and he said the reasons [he] was at war was that he [had been] protecting the Black Hills [...]. But he said 'Now I will smoke and everything will be in peace henceforth. He Dog reported the same for Crazy Horse: that he would lay down his arms and be for peace henceforth."[96]

In the fall of that year, 1877, the same He Dog agreed for the first time to be photographed by D.S. Mitchell. As did other Crazy Horse's close friends and relatives, regardless of whether they retained their loyalty to the late war chief or had turned their back on him. Could it be, then, that towards the very end of his troubled journey on Mother Earth circumstances did temporarily change and Crazy Horse, too, allowed his likeness to be finally impressed on a small metal plate? If such an unprecedented act in Crazy Horse's life did occur, was it to show his new good disposition towards the Americans, as even a staunch "nay" supporter as Mari Sandoz hinted, or to satisfy the request of a friend, or relative, as the Little Bat Garnier story related by Ellen Howard suggests? Or a combination of both?

This is not to say that at some point at Red Cloud Agency, Crazy Horse may have not publicly declined, by sign language, expressly in Lakota through interpreter, or all of the above, to be photographed. A refusal dictated by reasons of his own, bad timing, distrust or dislike of the requestor, whatever. Thus giving credence, for good reason, that a picture of him was not taken. In the creation of the Crazy Horse myths, from an incidental "no" to an absolute "never," the distance was small. Others then added their own made-up stories, even lies. Considering Tašunke Witko's solitary personality and his aversion to drawing attention upon himself, a refusal based certainly not on fear but a temporary disposition or concern his image may be used against him makes sense. But what if on a given day, the request to stand in front of a friendly White man equipped with a "little shadow box" came at a more appropriate time, from or through someone he felt he could trust? The answer to this question may not be as improbable as it has generally been assumed. In Crazy Horse's own ancestry, there was a telling, famous antecedent.

Catlin's Magic

George Catlin (1796-1872) is perhaps the best known painter of American Indians of all time. His colorful, large Indian Gallery of over 500 paintings and sketches, included the striking portraits of chiefs such as Four Bears (Mah-tó-tóh-pa) of the Mandan, and Buffalo Bull's Back Fat (Stu-mick-o-súcks) of the Kainai (Blood) Blackfoot. Connected with Crazy Horse were the portraits of his Mnicojou (step-maternal) grandfather Corn (Wúk-mi-ser, ca. 1790-1846), and his maternal uncle One Horn (Ha-wan-je-lah, ca. 1795-ca.1835), both captured on canvas by Catlin in 1832 at the mouth of the Teton River on the Upper Missouri.

What Catlin wrote of One Horn (aka Lone Horn) in particular, whose long hair was also unusually light-brown for a Lakota, reads remarkably like a premonition of Crazy Horse himself: "I found here encamped, six hundred families of Sioux, living in tents covered with buffalo hides. Amongst these there were twenty or more of the different bands, each one with their chief at their head, over whom was a superior chief and leader, a middle-aged man, of middling stature, with a noble countenance, and a figure almost equaling the Apollo. [...] This chief [...] has risen rapidly to the highest honors in the tribe, from his own extraordinary merits, even at so early an age. He told me that he took the name 'One Horn' (or shell) from a single small shell that was hanging on his neck, which descended to him from his father, and which, he said, he valued more than anything he possessed. [...] He treated me with great kindness and attention, considering himself highly complimented by the signal and unprecedented honour I had conferred upon him by painting his portrait [...]. This extraordinary man [...] in the chase he was foremost [...] it was proverbial in his tribe, that Ha-won-je-tah's bow was never drawn in vain." For his portrait, One Horn, whose pleasant features in Catlin's painting border the feminine, put his hair up in the turban-like old-style Lakota fashion.[97]

One Horn, Mnicojou Shirt Wearer and formidable hunter, died prematurely in 1834 or 1835. His fame and status among the Lakota and the circumstances of his death warranted an entry in the winter count later drawn by Wounded Bear (Mato Opi, b.1842), Oglala, a contemporary of Crazy Horse. The Mato Opi pictograph for the winter 1835-36 shows a wounded buffalo bull, with knife and arrow(s) protruding from its back, captioned "Tatanka wan cepa opi," a fat bull was wounded. The cryptic entry was elaborated by Feraca, based on Catlin's writings: "Lone Horn (One Horn), a Minneconjou chief, deranged by his son's death, committed suicide by being gored and trumped by a buffalo bull that he had goaded with arrows and then a knife."[98]

Crazy Horse may have inherited One Horn's small shell wampum or horn if that is what Short Bull referred to years later to Eleanor Hinman: "[Tašunke] usually wore an Iroquois shell necklace; this was the only ornament he wore."[99] According to Dr. Robert H. Ruby (more on him later), "Around his neck [Crazy Horse] wore a leather thong threaded through the end of a buffalo horn. In the buffalo horn he carried a small pebble."[100] What that pendant looked like we do not know. If it was indeed the one inherited from One Horn, we can infer its shape and size from Catlin's painting, although the "small" perforated shell seems rather large. Perhaps the shell or bone original size and shape suffered from Catlin's artistic license to make it more visible. Had the subject in the tintype not worn a neckerchief, we might have had an additional clue of his positive identification as Crazy Horse.

One Horn, by George Catlin (1832).

The Sioux were impressed with Catlin's magic, "capturing" not just individual people but even putting "many of our buffalo in his book!" Some regarded the White artist a powerful wičaša wakan, potentially dangerous. Perhaps, Catlin was at the root of the initial Sioux debate over the "power" certain wašiču had to "steal" an Indian's image or soul on their flat canvas, and, later, on their glass or metal plates in a wooden box. Thus, early on not everyone showed the same positive attitude One Horn did. This was the case of a young Yankton warrior who publicly accused Mr. Catlin: "See what he has done! He looks at our chiefs and our women, and then makes them alive!! In this way he has taken our chiefs away, and he can trouble their spirits when they are dead! [...] You tell us that they are not alive – we see their eyes move! Their eyes follow us whenever we go, that is enough! I have no more to say!"

Others thought otherwise, like an older Yankton who replied, "These are young men that speak – I am not afraid! [the] white medicine-man painted my picture, and it was good [...] I am very glad to see that I shall live after I am dead! I am old and not afraid! [...] his medicine is great and I wish him well – we are friends!"[101] So, there was disagreement about having one's image taken also in pre-camera days.

Worm, too, a medicine man of the old generation, was likely suspicious of picture taking, both the colorful painted portraits and the new and more realistic small black and white images created inside a box. Waglula may have recalled the deadly strife unintentionally triggered by Catlin, when Shónka (The Dog) shot Mató-chega (Little Bear) after an altercation caused by the latter's profile sitting with the visiting painter. Since the three-quarter view did not show nearly half of Little Bear's face, Shónka insulted Mató-chega calling him "half a man." From strong words to bloody action, the sad outcome was that both were killed in a spiral of violence. Catlin too might have paid with his own life for this unintentional provocation, hadn't he soon traveled downriver to the safety of St. Louis.

Again close to Crazy Horse's family, chief Corn, too, some years after sitting for Catlin was touched by death. The revised genealogical information posted on the previously cited websites and Wikipedia says that about 1844, when Curly Hair was just a child, Corn's village was attacked by the Crow who killed the Mnicojou headman's wife. Greater slaughter would have occurred had not Curly Hair's own father Crazy Horse, then in his mid-thirties and out on a buffalo hunt, rushed to Corn's rescue. Grateful, chief Corn, about fifty-six years old, presented Waglula with his two daughters Iron Between Horns, age eighteen, and Kills Enemy, a year younger, as new brides. They were later joined also by their youngest sibling, fifteen-year-old Red Leggings. Worm's first wife Rattling (Rattle) Blanket Woman, Curly's biological mother, was about thirty-four years old but apparently no longer able to conceive. Understandably, Rattling Blanket might have felt pushed aside in a lodge now crowded with younger

Lakota women in their prime. Her unhappiness was possibly aggravated by other sorrowful circumstances. Oral histories mention the death of a relative, even an alleged love affair with Male Crow, Worm's younger brother killed by Shoshone and Crow warriors later that year. Gossip also hinted at the never fully resolved issue raised with Rattling Blanket Woman by Worm's relatives on the true paternity of Curly Hair, precisely because of the boy's light hair and complexion.[102] Whatever the reason, or combination of reasons, the sorrow in Rattling Blanket's heart must have been deep. Distraught, Curly's mother hung herself from a cottonwood tree along the White River. Was the death of Corn's wife indirectly, tragically linked to that of Rattling Blanket, and had it all started with Catlin's "bad paint medicine"?

Rare Finds

A reminder of what still remains to be uncovered about the Lakota hero, specifically in terms of visual documentation is a relatively recently new, previously unknown photograph of Crazy Horse's scaffold grave near Camp Sheridan that was added to a similar image, thanks to the skilled research efforts of Ephriam D. Dickson.[103] The two photographic views of Crazy Horse's grave were taken by Private Charles Howard, a "shadow catcher" who passed through Red Cloud and Spotted Tail agencies in early fall of 1877, after the killing of the Northern chief. Thomas Powers has written, apparently in error, that it was James H. Hamilton, "a civilian photographer who had been staying at the Spotted Tail Agency" who took the photographs: "He mounted the hill above the agency and took two stereoviews of the burial site."[104] We discuss Hamilton and Howard later. What matters here is the extraordinary nature of the two photos, regardless of who actually took them.

The first image, published by Hardorff in 1998 without the photographer's name, [105] was reprinted by Dickson in 2006 with detailed information on the maker and the context relating to the burial. This first photograph was a great surprise and provided rare documentation on the scaffold itself, partially visible, with the wooden plank fence around it. The photograph amended an artistic rendering of the same "elevated grave" published in *Frank Leslie's Illustrated Magazine*[106] about a month after Crazy Horse's death. The *Leslie's* drawing shows the grave without the surrounding fence erected by agency carpenter Jack Atkinson. Showing empathy for Crazy Horse's mourning relatives, Lieut. Jesse M. Lee (1843-1926), Acting Agent at Spotted Tail – whom Louis Bordeaux called as a sincere and warm friend of the Indians – accepted Worm's request that a temporary barrier be placed around the scaffold to protect it from hungry dogs or coyotes that may be attracted there by the dead horse or horses sacrificed during the Ghost Owing ceremony held one week after the chief's passing.

At the base of the scaffold grave covered with blankets, the drawing did show two dead horses. The fence was also somewhat of a deterrent for ill-intentioned individuals. It was not uncommon for enlisted men (occasionally officers, too) when coming across an Indian burial, to engage "in the pleasant occupation of tumbling an Indian body down to the ground and robbing the grave of its blankets and beadwork," as witnessed by Charles St. George Stanley, a "Bohemian of Frank Leslie's staff," who in May-June 1876 was with Gen. George Crook's command, including at the Rosebud where Crazy Horse had fought with his usual valor.[107]

Now, little over a year after the Rosebud and Little Bighorn victories, Crazy Horse's own lifeless body was laid to rest, with relatives and other mourners keeping watch. Eyewitness accounts indicate that on September 13, day of the funeral ceremony, the "planking that surrounded the scaffold was hung with red blankets." With hundreds of mourners present, "the coffin was lashed to the scaffold, and Crazy Horse's body placed inside. Beside the body were laid a pipe and tobacco, a bow and quiver of arrows, a carbine and a pistol with ample ammunition, and supplies from the agency warehouse of coffee, sugar, and hard bread. [...] Crazy Horse's favorite war pony was led up and slaughtered, to fall beside the grave. [...] At length the crowds broke up and drifted homeward. Eight chief mourners remained at the grave site."[108]

The same artistic drawing shows six of them on the viewer's side. We also have the testimony of Lieut. Henry R. Lemly, a veteran of the Rosebud fight who also later claimed to have seen a photo of Crazy Horse and was present when the chief was mortally wounded. Lemly visited Lieut. Jesse Lee at Spotted Tail and reported that Crazy Horse's grave had been left "in charge of the chief mourners [...] without food or drink, naked, and hideously blackened, eight figures lie around the corpse and howl [sic.; cry in grief]."[109]

The first Howard photograph (shown here) was taken three weeks later and captured a desolate and lonely setting devoid of human presence. The dead horse or horses shown in the etching are not visible either, having been removed as they began to decompose. A similar sense of loneliness and desolation pervades the second stereoview by Private Charles Howard. It shows the same fenced scaffold grave from a slightly different angle, and a panoramic view in the background. In the foreground, next to the big fence of wooden planks, is visible another, smaller white-fenced grave.[110]

Crazy Horse's scaffold grave near Camp Sheridan, Nebraska, by Pvt. Charles Howard (1877).

Recently, a new collection of American Indian photographs, several dealing specifically with Camp Robinson and Red Cloud Agency in the crucial years 1876-1877, has been made public. The rare stereo photographs were assembled by Peter T. Buckley who worked then at Camp Robinson, and were later acquired by Larry Ness of Yankton, South Dakota, who allowed Thomas R. Buecker to scan and publish them. We had seen some of the Buckley Collection images posted online, and in our original draft we had already made specific reference to their historically important content, including Indian clothing, the photographer's studio, and especially the studio's skylight, as it relates to the natural light projection in the Crazy Horse tintype. We also noted the height of the ceiling rafters visible in the tintype corresponding to that of that the roof planks of the picture gallery at Red Cloud Agency in two of the Buckley Collection photos.

We were very surprised that in *The Last Days of Red Cloud Agency*,[111] published posthumously in 2016, a seasoned historian like the late Tom Buecker (1948-2015) failed to connect the dots to the tintype, particularly in light of the fact that nearly thirty years ago he had himself labeled the tintype in question "the elusive and improbable" photo of Crazy Horse. Buecker had originally come down against the tintype because, he wrote, "If any photographer managed to have Crazy Horse sit for a photo, he would have certainly remembered it – and exploited it. Yet no existing period documents mention Crazy Horse being photographed. [...] Also, if photographer [J.H.] Hamilton did take one, he never advertised the fact." The opposite is true. Hamilton did advertise a photograph of the Oglala war chief as "No. 104. Crazy Horse" in his *Catalogue of Stereoscopic Views of the Northwest*, published in Sioux City, Iowa (ca. 1878). And, he did try to exploit it, having it for sale along with two hundred and twenty-nine other images of "Indian Scenes, Representing Distinguished Chiefs and Prominent Characters," etc.

Setting aside the difference of opinions over the tintype, the discovery of the Pvt. Charles Howard photographs and additional images and portraits taken at Red Cloud Agency between 1875 and 1878 by Howard himself, J.H. Hamilton, and yet other previously unknown photographer, W.C. Thomas from North Platte (also featured in the Peter T. Buckley Collection), all contradict what has been argued for years, that is that Crazy Horse was never in the presence or the vicinity of a photographer. He certainly was not for most of his life, but not never. Even Eleanor Hinman had admitted that during Crazy Horse's four-month stay, there was an officer and a serviceman who had cameras at Camp Robinson. This, in addition to the photographic studio in a log-house structure with skylight and large "Pictures" sign at Red Cloud Agency, now prominently featured on the front cover of Tom Buecker's book, the permanent studio, and the traveling "shadow catcher" James H. Hamilton who stopped there in the spring and summer of 1877 are irrefutable proof that photography and Crazy Horse did cross paths at Camp Robinson-Red Cloud Agency that fateful year 1877.

We do not know what other photographic surprises the future might bring us, but the Howard, Hamilton, Thomas, and Buckley Collection rare finds are cautionary against negative dogma and exclusive thinking. Even the rich photo album of the savvy and photogenic Red Cloud, thought to be complete thanks to the thorough research of photo-historian Frank H. Goodyear, has recently added a previously unknown image.[112] This latest Red Cloud surprise is an outdoors photograph of the old chief standing, wearing baggy dark trousers and beaded moccasins, fringed jacket, war-bonnet, long bear-claw necklace, and holding a long rifle. The barren landscape adds a dimension of emptiness and melancholic sadness to this staged portrait of the nearly octogenarian Mahpiya Luta. The image is undated, location and photographer unknown. Most likely it was taken at Pine Ridge, possibly by John Hauser who was a friend of the old chief. Cincinnati-born John Hauser (1859-1913) was a prolific artist. Grahamew

(Grahame Wood), author of the online *Hauser* threads, pointed out that a number of Hauser portraits of Indians "have clearly been painted from photographs – after all, some of the subjects were dead and the images are clearly recognizable to anyone with even a passing familiarity with 19th-century photographs of American Indians."[113]

Specifically, Grahamew referenced two leather-bound albums titled Sioux and Apache and Pueblos of New Mexico that were discovered in Indiana: "Each album page has four tipped-in-albumen images to a side, for a total of 564 images. In addition, there are four pages [...] containing a partial inventory of the photographs, labeled and numbered. These albums contain photographs that match Joseph Henry Sharp's [... and] many of John Hauser's extant works. [...] There is no question that many Western artists used photography as an alternative to live models. Knowing that Hauser could use a camera, it was always assumed that he also executed paintings from photographs [...] through comparison, we know that Hauser was using these very albums as a basis for numerous paintings." The picture is so far the only known photograph of Red Cloud holding a weapon, whereas in most portraits the famous Oglala chief holds instead his čannupa. The photograph was used by Hauser as a model for his theme paintings of an Indian "man standing/walking with rifle."[114]

Ephriam Dickson noted that "the heart of the photography business in the 19th century was portraiture [...] and portraits of Indians were particularly saleable."[115] Those familiar with the history of American Indian photography easily recognize the names of early camera trailblazers like Thomas M. Easterly (1809-1882),[116] James Earle McClees (1821-1887), Alexander Gardner (1821-1882), Antonio Zeno Shindler (1823-1899), Mathew Brady (1823-1896), Orloff R. Westman (active in the 1870s), William S. Soule (1836-1908), William A. Bell (1841-1921), John K. Hillers (1843-1925), William Henry Jackson (1843-1942),[117] and many others. Their studio and out in the field production was astounding.[118] We can only wish ALL of their images had been saved and positively identified. Only in recent decades we have begun to explore the true extent of American Indian historical photography, and the challenges thereof. Photo historian Elmo Scott Watson was right on target when he lamented, "How often have I had occasion to curse the individual or individuals who failed to title, date, or otherwise describe in writing what was apparently an important historical photograph! Even if the photographer who could not look farther than the lens of his camera and realize that he was an historian did not do it, the buyer of his photograph should have thought of it ... Such undocumented photographs are not always a total loss as historical fact, but their proper documentation in many cases becomes a laborious search to identify the original photographer."[119]

Bad Medicine and Good

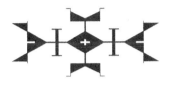

Much has been written about the negative reaction the camera elicited from the American Indians who, most claim, generally considered it "bad medicine." This very theme underlies the general view against any possible photographic image of Crazy Horse. On the broader issue of the American Indian relationship with the camera, the voluminous number of Indian individual and group photographs we know of speak clearly against the popular notion of nineteenth century Indian reluctance, even opposition to photography. Again, the static view of initial suspicion and selective avoidance projected on the remainder of the historic period is biased. Very quickly American Indians came to view photography as an intriguing and interesting experience. The photographs and writings by "shadow catchers" who attended treaty negotiations in the field, near where Indians were camped, shed new light on the issue of so-called "bad medicine" and purported fear of the camera.

Paula Fleming has researched the pioneering work of the talented Ridgway Glover (1831-1866).[120] While unfortunately most of Glover's photographs appear to have been lost, his correspondence to the *Philadelphia Photographer* contains companion information on the images themselves, the Indian reaction to the camera, and related matters that are extremely revealing. Glover was a New Jersey Quaker who left the bucolic life on the farm to embrace the exciting, uncertain, and for him prematurely tragic career of the camera worker. In the summer of 1866, Glover, as official photographer, accompanied a new Peace Commission bound for Fort Laramie where the old Treaty of 1851 with Sioux, Cheyenne, and Arapaho was to be renegotiated. The new 1866 Treaty, held at the mouth of Horse Creek some forty miles below Fort Laramie, was recorded in Lakota winter counts with the pictograph of a blanket, symbolizing Wakpamnipi tanka, the "Big Issue," the large distribution of goods by government negotiators.[121] Rendered obsolete by the post-Civil War flood of immigrant settlers, gold seekers, cattlemen, land speculators, and the new garrisons built to protect them, the 1851 Laramie Treaty made no explicit mention of separate "reservations." Conversely, the new treaty was to establish a single, large, bounded territory for the Sioux and other Plains tribes. The government was also to secure from the Sioux and their allies undisturbed passage for settlers and pioneers traveling along the Bozeman Trail, from Fort Laramie to Virginia City and the Montana goldfields.

While the six Peace Commissioners and the Indian chiefs were busy discussing the matter, Glover was "hard at work photographing the various activities."[122] In a June 30, 1866 letter to the *Philadelphia Photographer*, Glover detailed his work in the field: "I have been in this wild region nearly a month, taking scenes in connection with the Treaty that has just been made with the Sioux, Arapaho and Cheyenne, and have secured twenty-two good negatives [...] that will illustrate the life and character of the wild men of the prairie." But there were technical difficulties to be reckoned with, as Paula explained: "The complex photographic process of applying collodion to the glass plates, sensitizing and exposing them while still sticky, and then developing them was a challenge. The water was muddy, hard and full of sand [...] and of the 50 negatives he exposed, more than half were unusable." Technical problems aside, Glover also commented on the Indian reactions to the camera. We should keep in mind that like the treaty negotiators, Glover had no knowledge of Indian languages, hence both Commissioners and photographer had to rely on mixed-blood interpreters. He welcomed the negotiations as a constructive substitute to war, but could not shed his prejudice and misconceptions of Indian behavior and beliefs. Glover's first impression was precisely that: "I there saw the lazy, sleepy red man treating for peace and friendship." To his advantage, the photographer had the new instrument, and even the mixed reactions he evoked from the Indians could in turn be used to the benefit of his art.

Since the beginning of contact, American Indians been interested in the White man's technological novelties and out there on the Plains in 1866, the camera also intrigued them. Glover's first-hand reporting as a photographer is priceless. It relates not only the different moods American Indians themselves exhibited before the camera, but most importantly – in light of the "fear" and "superstition" popular stereotype – how quickly Indians recognized the innocuous nature of photography. Regarding the Sioux gathered at Laramie in '66, we do not know how much of what occasionally seemed to the photographer "frightened behavior," was instead an Indian practical joke. Even the ostensibly weird reaction of a Lakota clown and thunder dreamer, a heyoka or "contrary," or simply a reflection of that individual's less agreeable mood.

Such theatrical antics against the camera were indeed rare. Far more common was the composed body language exhibited by the Indians two years later again at Fort Laramie, at the historic Treaty of 1868. A large group photo taken by Alexander Gardner portrays "Dr. Mathews, Mountain Tail, Black Foot, Winking Eyes, Crane, Poor Elk, Pounded Meat, White Fawn, White Horse, Shot-in-the-Jaw, Pretty Young Bull." Only the third Indian from the right, White Horse, lowered his head, but we do not know why. In some old photographs, occasionally Lakota women are seen partially covering their face, or simply their mouth, a traditional behavior in the presence of unrelated men, especially strangers.

The myth of a generalized "fear of soul loss" attributed to the Indians was clarified by Glover himself, who reported that once the basic theory behind the photographic process was explained, the majority of the Indians "brightened up" and stood or sat willingly before the camera: "I had much difficulty in making pictures of the Indians at first, but now I am able to talk to them, yet I get pretty much all I want [...] Some of the Sioux think photography is 'pazutta zupa'[123] [...] Some of the Indians think they will die in three days, if they get their pictures taken [...] I pointed the instrument at one of that opinion. The poor fellow fell on the sand, and rolled himself in his blanket. The most of them know better, though, and some I have made understand that the light comes from the sun, strikes them, and then goes into the machine. I explained it to one yesterday, by means of his looking-glass, and showed him an image on the ground glass [of the camera]. When he caught the idea, he brightened up, and was willing to stand for me."

Glover also related his frustration at the distribution of presents to the Sioux assembled at Laramie. Because of the strong prairie wind, he could only make one "passable negative" of what his professional eye regarded as "some of the most interesting scenes imaginable. Here [...] some 1200 Sioux were arranged, squatting around the Commissioners in a large circle, three rows deep. The village embraces more than 200 tribes (lodges) led by 'Spotted Tail,' 'Standing Elk,' 'The Man that walks under the ground,' and 'Running Bear.'" All four were friendly to the photographer and had their individual picture taken. They were also photographed in group, again, along with other chiefs, a couple of days later on July 2 at the closing of negotiations. Glover wrote that he had the good fortune "to be present when Colonels [R.N.] McLean [McLaren, of Minnesota] and Thomas Wistar [a Philadelphia Quaker] were distributing the goods to the Chiefs, and although the interpreters were discouraged, and the Indians seemed unwilling, Thomas and McLean at last persuaded them to sit, and I got a stereoscopic group of six Ogholalla, and eight Brulie Sioux. The wind was blowing, and the sand flying. The negative is, therefore, not quite clean, but all the likeness are good, and they can be readily recognized. They are: BRULIES, 'Spotted Tail,' 'Dog Hawk,' 'Standing Elk,' Brave Hear[t],' 'Swift Bear, "Thunder Hawk,' Tall Mandan,' 'White Tail.' OGHALOLLAHS (They pronounce it), The Man that walks under the ground,' 'The Black War Bonnet,' 'Standing Cloud,' 'Big Mouth,' 'Blue Horse,' 'Big Head.' The Signers of the Treaty."[124]

Crazy Horse, already a proven akičita but still relatively young and lacking representative rank, did not attend the 1866 Fort Laramie negotiations. Red Cloud, elected tribal spokesman after his successful stand against the three-pronged military expedition brought in the summer 1865 by

Gen. Patrick E. Connor, Col. Nelson Cole, and Lieut. Col. Samuel Walker against the Lakota, Cheyenne and Arapaho hunting bands, finally made it to the "big issue" grounds, only to witness yet another provocation: the arrival of Col. Henry B. Carrington with some 2,000 troops. In violation of the agreement whose ink was still wet, Col. Carrington's mission was the fortification of the Bozeman Trail. The Fort Laramie Treaty of 1866, thus immediately broken, was obviously never ratified, and the so-called Red Cloud War begun.

Glover would soon become one of the innocent victims of this new failure of federal Indian policy. From Laramie, Glover traveled with a military convoy to Fort Phil Kearney on Little Piney Creek, Upper Powder River, and there, on September 14, his love of photography cost him his life. "He [had] left [the Fort] with a private as a companion, for the purpose of making some views. It was known that the hostile Sioux were lurking around, but, knowing no fear, and being ardent in the pursuit of his beloved profession, he risked everything, and alas! The result was that he was scalped, killed, and horribly mutilated."[125] Also the fruits of Ridgway Glover's passionate work, in particular his Fort Laramie negatives, seem to have fared the worst. Except for a few images, including a "poor quality stereo photograph of Standing Elk" reproduced by Fleming, "the main cache of Glover's photographs has not yet been located."[126] Still, it is possible that at least some of Glover's negatives were later acquired by Alexander Gardner and printed on his mounts. As Paula concluded, "the scholarly hunt continues."

Glover's tragic death was but one episode of the bloody struggle that enflamed the Great Plains. In December 1866, in a famous incident stemming from an Army attempt at rescuing a besieged wood-wagon train on the Tongue River, the entire command of 80 men under Captain William J. Fetterman was drawn into a deadly trap by a decoy of Cheyenne, Arapaho, and Lakota warriors led by the emerging Crazy Horse. Tašunke Witko, then in his early to mid-twenties, was closer "than they ever would be" to the older and still fiercely determined Red Cloud.[127]

The following summer, 1867, Cheyenne and Mnicojou warriors attacked Fort C.F. Smith while Red Cloud and Crazy Horse led the Oglala and Sans Arc in the Wagon Box Fight near Fort Phil Kearny. Both attacks this time were repulsed by new superior American fire power. Unknown to the Sioux and their allies, in the spring 1867 some 700 new breech-loading Springfield rifles, replacing the old single shot muzzle-loaders, and 100,000 rounds of ammunition had been delivered to the region's forts.[128] The Indians' determination, however, eventually prevailed. In the end, the Red Cloud War forced the Americans to vacate their military forts along the Bozeman Trail running along the eastern side of the Big Horn Mountains. But then again, it was only a temporary victory. Neither Red Cloud, who eventually gave in to compromise, nor Crazy Horse, who tried a while longer to resist militarily, would be able to stop indefinitely the influx of White settlers and soldiers on their homeland.

Glover's legacy was inherited by the burly, bearded Scottish-born, former Civil War photographer Alexander Gardner, who took rare stereoviews of the Fort Laramie Treaty Council in the spring 1868. Raymond DeMallie remarked that even though many negatives of Gardner's original set have been lost, and the surviving prints are not as sharp, "they are, nonetheless, of remarkable quality, and depict a wealth of details in ways only photographs can."[129] At the historic gathering of Lakota, Northern Cheyenne, Northern Arapaho, and Crow, Gardner assembled a most telling visual documentation of the Northern Plains Indians on the eve of the irreversible transition from the buffalo days to agency and reservation life. Some 200 glass plate negatives originally comprised Gardner's *Scenes in the Indian Country*, and nearly half of them were stereoscopic views. While in many instances Gardner indulged in posed photography, dictated by circumstances and the slow technology of the time, several of his images as again DeMallie pointed out, "Appear on the whole to be less formally posed than the larger views. Not only do they depict more details of camp life and more views of women and children, but they also depict Indians in their daily dress, rather than their finery."[130]

This is clearly the case of the group portrait Gardner took of Northern Cheyenne chiefs. All standing, the first two are simply wrapped in Army blankets while the latter wears a Confederate coat with cape, all items of clothing typically presented as gifts to Indian chiefs and headmen. Completely wrapped in blankets are also Brule chiefs Spotted Tail and Fast/Swift Bear, shown standing side by side in another classic Gardner photograph.[131] "We are fortunate," DeMallie wrote, "that Gardner left us such an intimate portrayal. Careful study of the photographs can help us immensely in any attempt to visualize the situation on the plains during the 1860s and reconstruct the feeling of Indian life at the very end of the buffalo-hunting days."[132] The relaxed poses of men, women, children, and ordinary camp life in many of Gardner's images indicate a degree of comfort before the camera that contradicts later assertions of widespread "fear," "suspicion," even "hostility."

Priceless for its context and content, a panoramic view titled by Gardner "Interior of Council Chamber. Man Afraid of His Horses Smoking," shows the elder Tašunke Kokipapi (His Horse They Fear, 1802-1887), hereditary chief of the Hunkpatila band of Oglala to which Crazy Horse belonged, smoking the peace pipe. The photograph is perhaps "the only one ever taken of the ritual smoking of the pipe at a solemn treaty council." Other companion images in Gardner's *Scenes* document the same gathering of Indians, mixed-bloods, Army officers, and U.S. Commissioners assembled in the tipi iyokiheya, the large council "talk" lodge made of tipi covers joined together. In these photographs as well, the dress seems to be rather "down" and practical, with a shirtless Old Man wrapped to his waist in a trade blanket.[133] A portrait of Old Man appears in another image where he is flanked by Fire Thunder (Wakinyan Pehtah) and Pipe (Čanupaiyah; Presents/Carries the Pipe), both also Oglala signers in 1868. Also of note, the several mixed-blood interpreters present, many of them – like Little Bat Garner visible in another group photo by Gardner – were closely associated through marriage with the Lakota.

More formal in dress, some wearing decorated scalp shirts, fully beaded moccasins, and leggings, are the subjects of another historic, large group photograph in which Gardner craftily alternated a standing Indian and a seated one. One in the group is Lone Horn (Hehwanjelah, ca. 1800-1875) who in 1835 or 1836 had taken his older brother One Horn's place as Mnicojou hereditary chief following the latter's death. In 1851, Lone Horn had made peace with the Mountain Crows,[135] and on May 26, 1868, he touched the pen at Fort Laramie, where he was photographed in at least

The Great Sioux Reservation, established by the Fort Laramie Treaty of 1868, minus the Black Hills, taken illegally with the "sell or starve" Agreement of 1877. Camp (here Ft.) Robinson in the lower left-hand corner, below Chadron. Map in *Annual Report of the Commissioner of Indian Affairs*, 1877.

two different sittings. In the Gardner image, often published,[136] Lone Horn wears a beautiful war shirt decorated with weasel tails. The other Lakota chiefs are, left to right: Spotted Tail (Brule), Roman Nose (Mnicojou, seated), the elder Man Afraid (Oglala), Hehwanjelah himself, seated, Whistling/Bellowing Elk (Mnicojou), Pipe (Oglala, seated), and Slow Bull (Mnicojou).

Roman Nose and White Bull

Some of the Gardner's Fort Laramie photos also present the old problem of correct individual identification and tribal affiliation. As with He Dog and Big Foot, we have a similar problem with the Roman Nose portrayed in the Gardner group photo, whereas the subject in question has been identified by some writers (and on Wikipedia), not as the Mnicojou headman, but as the famed Cheyenne warrior by that name.[137] The latter identification is most likely incorrect. The Cheyenne Roman Nose (Wookanay / Woqini / Vooxénéhe, "Arched / Hook Nose"), born about 1835, was a formidable fighter who embodied the same intransigent patriotism of Tašunke Witko. Not a tribal chief, but a member of the Crooked Lance warrior society, Vooxénéhe strongly opposed White encroachment and any compromise with the Americans. Crazy Horse and his half-brother Little Hawk had fought alongside this Cheyenne warrior in the Bozeman Trail war. In his youth, Curly himself had often visited the Cheyenne camp where he felt at ease as if among his own people.

Like the Lakota, the Cheyenne too recognized holy men endowed with special powers and strong medicine. White Bull, also known as Ice Bear, or simply Ice, was a prominent Cheyenne medicine man who routinely camped with the Lakota hunting bands. Ice had made Roman Nose a war bonnet that would make him bullet proof, but a breach of taboo rendered the protection vain. Roman Nose, regarded as the Cheyenne equivalent of Crazy Horse, was killed in his prime during a charge in the Battle of Beecher Island on the Republican River, northeastern Colorado, in September 1868.[138] The Cheyenne warrior was never photographed; he had died prematurely defending his homeland. We only have his idealized likeness in an anonymous Cheyenne ledger-book drawing that portrays Roman Nose on horseback with the profile of his distinctively big nose.[139]

By contrast, and again close to Crazy Horse, photography would not be rejected by Roman Nose's spiritual mentor. The Cheyenne fighting spirit and love of freedom impressed Crazy Horse, and he sought counsel and guidance from White Bull/Ice. Francis White Lance lists Ice (Čaga, in Lakota) as one of the seven medicine men who mentored Crazy Horse: "Ice was a Cheyenne Chief, a yuwipi man, and a mentor to Crazy Horse."[140] The name derived from his ability to produce ice from his mouth during trance, and like his tribesman Roman Nose, White Bull too was as determined in fighting off the Americans. Born circa 1834, as Hardorff put it, Ice "acquired the healing powers of the bear, the antelope, and the wild hog, and he was instructed by the Thunder Beings in the making of several protective war bonnets, including the one worn by the celebrated warrior, Roman Nose."[141] Ice fought at the Little Bighorn, and in January, 1877, he and Two Moon were again alongside Crazy Horse against Col. Nelson Miles in the Battle of Wolf Mountain, Montana.[142]

After his surrender shortly thereafter, in April, 1877 at Fort Keogh, Montana, like many other prominent Lakota and Cheyenne warriors, White Bull/Ice enlisted as a U.S. Indian scout. Unlike Crazy Horse, who later refused to go after the Nez Perce, Ice actually served under his former enemy Col. Miles in the spring 1877 campaigns against Lame Deer's Mnicojou, and later also in the pursuit of Chief Joseph's Nez Perce. That same year, Ice was photographed at Fort Keogh by Stanley J. Morrow (1843-1921). As with Crazy Horse's double enlistment as an Army scout, these biographical details (often ignored or downplayed) do not diminish the stature of the man, but reflect how the new balance of power and rapidly changing circumstances demanded adaptation and compromise. Even by the formerly most determined "hostiles." It has been said that Ice actually cut Lame Deer's head off after the Mnicojou chief was killed at Muddy Creek. No matter how disdainful to historical purist and sanitizers who read history through the revisionist glasses of political correctness, scouting for the Long Knives simply became a matter of survival and, contextually, it reflected the same compromising path Crazy Horse, with his surrender and enlistment in Lieut. W.P. Clark's scouts, intended to follow.

Returning to the problem of correct identification, the Roman Nose in the 1868 Gardner's photo was the hereditary chief of the Wakpakinyan (Fly By The River) band of Mnicojou. He was the father of Looking Horse who later in 1873, together with Short Bull, Kicking Bear, Eagle Elk and other young Sioux warriors joined Crazy Horse's Last-Born Child warrior society. Roman Nose himself did not fight alongside Crazy Horse in the Rosebud and Little Bighorn battles, but he left the agency in late September, 1876, for fear of gun and pony confiscation by the Army. He surrendered the following spring on April 14, 1877, at Spotted Tail Agency, along with Touch the Clouds, and Worm, Crazy Horse's father.

Like Roman Nose, it was later said that Touch the Clouds was not involved in the Custer fight, even though at the time, because of his absence from the agency, many thought he did. Now, this latter view is supported by his descendants, based on family oral tradition originally kept secret for fear of punishment by the government. The belief that Touch the Clouds fought at Greasy Grass was reflected in the James H. Hamilton's caption in his stereoscopic view No. 129, "Led principal charge, under Crazy Horse, in Custer Massacre."

Less than a month after surrender, on May 2, Roman Nose was sworn in as a Corporal in Lieut. Clark's scouts at Red Cloud Agency.[143] That same year, the Mnicojou chief was photographed by D.S. Mitchell who listed Roman Nose as No. 28 in his *Western Stereoscopic Gems*, published in 1878 by Mitchell in partnership with Joseph H. McGowan at Omaha, Nebraska. Mitchell was one of the photographers who in 1877 visited the two Lakota agencies and nearby military camps. Roman Nose's name also appears twice, as photos "No. 116. Roman Nose and War Pony" and "No. 171. Roman Nose, Sioux Chief," in James H. Hamilton's *Catalogue of Stereoscopic Views of the Northwest,* published in Iowa City (ca.1878). It is unclear whether at least the latter image is a new photo by Hamilton or one he obtained from D.S. Mitchell. As we shall see later in detail, J.H. Hamilton, too, was at Red Cloud Agency in 1877. Finally, the same subject is listed as number "76. Roman Nose, Sioux Chief," in Pvt. Charles Howard's *Views*, (ca. 1878), the previously mentioned collection of stereoscopic views and cabinet size portraits taken by the soldier with a camera. A sketchy pictographic profile of Roman Nose exhibiting his "large and aquiline nose" was included in the pictorial census known as *Red Cloud's Census* compiled in 1884 at Pine Ridge.[144]

Sitting Bull the Oglala

Neither Crazy Horse nor Sitting Bull were at Laramie in 1868. Yet, for a curious and quite common case of American Indian homonymy, the treaty does bear the names of Tahtonkah-heyotakah, "Sitting Bull," and Shunke-witko, rendered as "Fool Dog." These treaty signers were obviously not the two famous Northern chiefs. The names in Kappler's transcription refer, respectively, to an Oglala sub-chief and to a Hunkpapa headman.[145] Little is known of Fool Dog, also known as Mad Dog or Crazy Dog, and at times mistranslated as "Crazy Horse." He was with the Hunkpapa Sitting Bull at the Little Bighorn, and followed him to Canada. Crazy/Mad Dog surrendered at Fort Buford in 1881 with the remnants of the Sitting Bull and Four Horns band, comprising altogether 41 families and 195 people. He is listed as head of "family 5" with the Lakota name Sun-gna-skin-yan and the English equivalents of Crazy (crossed over) Mad Dog, age 45.[146] After imprisonment at Fort Randall in the spring of 1883 Crazy/Mad Dog was transferred with Sitting Bull's band to Standing Rock Agency.[147] These scanty details exclude that the Hunkpapa Crazy/Mad Dog might have been photographed and listed as "Crazy Horse" in the catalogues of stereoscopic views and Indian portraits by the photographers who visited Red Cloud and Spotted Tail agencies before 1878.

More is known about the Oglala Sitting Bull, a nephew of chief Little Wound. Born ca. 1841, he was also known as Young (or, Good) Sitting Bull, Sitting Bull of the South, Drum Carrier, or Packs the Drum. Although some ten years younger than the homonymous Hunkpapa chief, he had features strikingly reminiscent of his famous Northern contemporary. A respected headman of the Kiyuska band, Sitting Bull/Packs the Drum was photographed by Alexander Gardner at Fort Laramie in 1868, in a group portrait with other Indians and Whites. Of interest, with regards to a later discussion, is his clothing. The Oglala Sitting Bull is wearing a long sleeve white shirt and a large neckerchief. He is also holding a two knife-blade war club, symbol of his akičita rank. A few years later, Young Sitting Bull proved his authority and courage brandishing a similar club, this one with three Green River knife-blades, confronting the hostile crowd of Northern Indians in the famous flagpole incident, covered later.[148]

Sitting Bull of the South was again photographed at least twice by Frank Currier in Omaha, Nebraska, in May 1875, with Red Cloud and the already photo-savvy Brule chiefs Swift Bear and Spotted Tail. In one image, the members of this joint Oglala-Brule delegation, on their way to Washington, are flanked by Julius Meyer, a young enterprising Prussian-born Jew who operated the "Indian Wigwam," a popular curio store.[149] Julius and his brothers were well-known figures in Omaha. In his "Indian Wigwam" advertisement, Meyer, who spoke some Pawnee and Lakota, identified himself as "Indian Interpreter, Indian Trader and Dealer in Indian, Chinese and Japanese Curiosities. Tomahawks, Bows & Arrows, Tipi Covers, Pipes," and even "Scalps"![150]

In another photograph, the same four Lakota chiefs are seated, with Meyer standing behind them with mixed-blood interpreters Louis Bordeaux and Billy Hunter Garnett.[151] As Frank Goodyear wrote, "Meyer acted as their host in Omaha and was the person responsible for taking them to [Frank F.] Currier's studio. [... Of course,] the delegation demanded to be paid for participating in this photographic session. Meyer ended up covering all their expenses in Omaha and giving these four leaders two ponies each." Significant of the first image, aside from being a relatively early portrait of noted Lakota chiefs, are again the white and darker cotton shirts, and dark silk neckerchiefs worn by the Indians. Behind the group, partially visible, is what Goodyear describes as an "elaborately painted backdrop." An

l-r.: Sitting Bull the Oglala, Swift Bear, and Spotted Tail;
standing: Julius Meyer and Red Cloud.
Studio photograph by Frank F. Currier, Omaha, Nebraska, May 1875.

indication that already by the 1870s such decorated backdrops were in use among Midwestern photographers.[152]

The name "Sitting Bull," being that of the Oglala, is also listed as No. 152 in James H. Hamilton's *Catalogue*, and as No. 30 "Old Sitting Bull of the South" in *Western Stereoscopic Gems* by Mitchell, McGowan & Co. During the early troubles at the newly established Red Cloud Agency, Sitting Bull of the South flexed his muscle against the more belligerent Northern faction in an incident that, in October 1874, saw the Agency flagpole chopped down by angry Northern Indians. "A group of Akichita or Indian camp police arrived on the scene led by Sitting Bull of the South who carried a distinctive three-blade club [symbolic of his status as a head akicita]. These Indians rushed between the troops and the angry warriors and with their clubs beat the hostiles back."[153]

For his courage, as a member of the 1875 Sioux delegation to Washington, the Oglala Sitting Bull received an engraved "presentation" gun (valued at $500) from President Ulysses S. Grant as a token of appreciation and friendship. The golden side-plate of the Model 1866 Henry repeating rifle was inscribed: "Sitting Bull from The President For Bravery & True Friendship." The following year the Oglala headman loaned his gun to a friend, one of the many Lakota who in the spring of 1876, left the agencies to join the hunting bands under Crazy Horse and the Hunkpapa Sitting Bull. In a strange but telling anecdotal detail of the larger drama that unfolded on the banks of the Little Bighorn and thereafter, the very rifle donated by the President of the United States to the "friendly" Sitting Bull would find its way to the allied village of the more famous "hostile" Sitting Bull, and it would be used in defeating the 7th U.S. Cavalry, almost to the day of the 100th anniversary of the birth of the Nation.

In late fall of that year, the Oglala Sitting Bull, whom the Americans regarded as one of their best friends among the Lakota, left Red Cloud Agency and proceeded to Crazy Horse's village on the Yellowstone between the mouths of the Tongue and Powder rivers. There he recovered his gun, and a number of cavalry horses. The friendly Sitting Bull urged the Northern Indians to negotiate peace with the Bluecoats and eventually left Crazy Horse's camp with a group of "hostiles" to meet with Col. Nelson A. Miles, commanding officer at Tongue River cantonment.

In mid-December, as these Sioux approached the post they were met by Crow scouts who, after faking friendship, killed five of them including Sitting Bull, capturing his gun. Sitting Bull must have been carrying also his famous bladed club, as both rifle and war club were given to Col. Miles. After Gen. Miles's death, the family donated the weapons to the Museum of the American Indian-Heye Foundation in New York, now NMAI. Also chief Red Cloud, on that famous 1875 trip to Washington, received a silver mounted rifle from Commissioner of Indian Affairs John Q. Smith. And this gun too (valued at $250) was carried into battle against the Americans, not by the famous owner, but by his son Jack in the Rosebud fight of June 17, 1876. On that occasion, young Jack Red Cloud did not live up to his father's reputation as a warrior, and he managed to have his gun captured, again by the Crow.

A war club similar to that of the Oglala Sitting Bull, the three blades mounted on a long effigy-style handle decorated with brass tacks, is held by He Dog in a classic photograph of this close comrade of Crazy Horse's taken at Red Cloud Agency by D.S. Mitchell in 1877.[154] The effigy may actually represent the head of a raptor, eagle or hawk. He Dog carried his impressive club to Washington, as seen in the Sioux delegation photo taken in the Capital City that October, 1877, and in his portrait. Most important, as it relates to what Sandoz incorrectly labeled the "white-man's clothing" of the Indian in the tintype, in the studio photograph by Charles M. Bell, He Dog is dressed as in the Mitchell image: long-sleeve white shirt, dark vest, same large German silver cross, same long beaded ear-pendant with large abalone shell. He, or possibly the photographer, only substituted a full war bonnet for the single eagle feather in the Mitchell photo. The leader of the Sorebacks Oglala clung to his bladed club, reflecting his status as head solider.[155]

Iron Crow, Red Bear, Running Antelope

Another member of the 1877 Oglala delegation, the one Crazy Horse was supposed to have joined, was Iron Crow (Kangi Maza, ca. 1849-1925). A few years younger than Crazy Horse, Iron Crow had fought at the Little Bighorn and followed Tašunke Witko to Camp Robinson. Like He Dog, he too had no objection to being photographed by D.S. Mitchell at Red Cloud Agency. His stereo-portrait was listed as No. 21 in Mitchell and McGowan's *Stereoscopic Gems*. Iron Crow was one of the Crazy Horse loyalists. After the chief's death, Iron Crow traveled with the Sioux delegation hoping to secure the old promise of a separate agency for the Northern Indians.

Nothing was accomplished in Washington, and actually both Red Cloud and Spotted Tail were ordered to move their agencies to the Missouri. Angry and disillusioned, Iron Crow took advantage of the confusion with the removal and "slipped away to join Sitting Bull in Canada."[156]

After Tašunke Witko's death, fear of intra-tribal revenge, punishment by the U.S. military, disenchantment with agency life, and the illusion of lasting freedom across the 49th parallel, together triggered the stampede to Canada of several Northern thiyóšpaye. The thiyóšpaye, "they live together," was the basic unit of Sioux sociopolitical organization, the term designating an extended family, or group of families. "They" being male blood relatives, or "brothers" – in the Dakota-type kinship system this included siblings and parallel cousins[157] – plus their wives and offspring, and occasionally other consanguine and affine relatives. Hassrick wrote that at the core of Lakota societal fabric, "the bilateral nature of Sioux kinship system involved [...] a strong sense of consanguine unity on the part of the lineal and collateral family members. The lineal family of grandfather, father, and son, with their male blood brothers as collaterals, was the basis of the thiyóšpaye and band organization."[158] As Bray put it, a number of Lakota headmen "were early committed to a break for Canada. Significant among these was the Sans Arc Decider Red Bear [whose] personal ties to the exiles in Grandmother's Land matched his political disillusionment. [...] His kola, or pledged comrade, was Spotted Eagle, the Sans Arc war chief who had led part of their Bull Dung tiyospaye [...] into Canada with Sitting Bull."[159] Noteworthy in terms of Lakota photographic history: shortly before fleeing to Canada, Red Bear (Mato Luta), a veteran of the Custer fight, was photographed with his family in front of his tipi by Private Charles Howard at Camp Sheridan-Spotted Tail Agency in the fall of 1877.[160] It is telling that the Sans Arc chief and Crazy Horse sympathizer would allow not just a civilian but an actual soldier with a camera to photograph him and his family at such a critical moment. A further indication that the Lakota had by then established an articulate and mostly tolerant and often friendly relationship with photography.

This had already been the case of another famous Lakota contemporary of Crazy Horse, Hunkpapa chief Running Antelope (Tatoka Inyanke ca. 1821-1896) who had touched the pen in 1868 at Fort Laramie. He was photographed by Gardner in Washington in 1872, and a few years later by James H. Hamilton who listed him together with Two Bears (No. 86) in his *Catalogue of Stereoscopic Views*. The face of Running Antelope was reproduced posthumously in the popular etching on the $5 Silver Certificate issued by the U.S. Mint in 1899.[161] Running Antelope's dignified features are fairly loyal to the original, but the three eagle feathers and the barely visible short arrow (representing a battle wound) decorating his hair in the Gardner photo, were substituted on the silver certificate with a striking, highly symbolic, Plains Indian eagle feather wapha'ha.[162]

Crazy Horse the Man

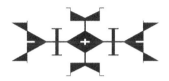

"[…he] would go about the village without noticing people or saying anything. In his own teepee he would joke, and when he was on the warpath with a small party, he would joke to make his warriors feel good. But around the village he hardly noticed anybody, except little children. All the Lakotas like to dance and sing; but he never joined a dance, and they say nobody ever heard him sing."

John Neihardt, based on Black Elk's testimony, 1930 [163]

"A little before we got to the Agency, Lieutenant Clark, acting as General Crook's staff, came out to meet Crazy Horse, about four miles north of the Agency. He shook hands with Crazy Horse and other Northern chiefs out there on the prairie, and the Northern Indians dressed up Lieutenant Clark, an army officer, with the Indian dress, a war shirt, war bonnet and pipe. They shook hands with the left hand because the heart is on the left side. Some old [Indian] fellow said 'Shake hands with him with your left for that is the side your heart lays.' […] So we got along with Crazy Horse pretty good, just the same as any friendly Indian, for some time, and in the month of August we got news that the Nez Perce had broken out and were working toward Wyoming."

Billy Hunter Garnett, interviewed by Gen. H.L. Scott and
Maj. James McLaughlin, Pine Ridge, 1920 [164]

"1877-'78 – Crazy Horse came to make peace and was killed with his hands stretched out winter."

Baptiste Good's Winter Count, translated by Rev. Wm. J. Cleveland, Rosebud Agency, collected by Dr. W.H. Corbusier, Camp Sheridan, 1879-1880 [165]

Those who have written about Crazy Horse consistently stressed first and foremost the Lakota chief's warrior spirit and military prowess. Horn Chips testified that "Crazy Horse was not accounted good for anything among the Indians but to make war; he was expected to do that; he was set apart in their minds to make war, and that was his business."[166] In the pragmatic mind of the Lakota, what Tašunke Witko was meant to be synonymous of, and be best at, was "war." Dakota Sioux author Allen C. Ross-Ehanamani even drew a comparison between Crazy Horse and German Field Marshal Erwin Rommel (1891-1944), the "Desert Fox," one of Hitler's most capable generals (who later committed suicide having been accused of treason).[167]

Crazy Horse was a leading member of the Kangi Yuhn military sodality, the Crow Owners Society, of which he and He Dog were made lance bearers in 1870. As such, they "were expected to be at the head [...] when attacking the enemy and not to turn back [...] to thrust their lance into the ground [...] pinning themselves in position to fight to the death or until freed by another society member. [...] Bonds of kinship, not exclusively based on genealogical relationship, united fellow society members and contributed to a sense of tribal unity."[168]

Three years later, with the widening chasm between hunting bands and agency Indians, Crazy Horse withdrew from the Crow Owners and created a new society, the Hokši Hakata, or "Last-Born Child." Bray pointed out that, unlike other Lakota warrior societies, Crazy Horse's own, true to his free spirit and disdain of exhibitionism, had no regalia, nor hierarchy of officers, except perhaps for the role of eyapaha, "announcer," played by Shell Boy. About forty in number, they included Crazy Horse's own cousins Kicking Bear (Mato Wanahtake) and Eagle Elk (Wamble Hehaka), Good/Pretty Weasel (Itunkasan Wašte), Low Dog (Šunka Kucigala), Flying By/Come Flying (Kinyan Hiyaye), the already mentioned Short Bull, and others. Eager to follow the charismatic Crazy Horse, these famous Lakota warriors became in essence Tašunke Witko's personal, albeit ultimately ineffective, bodyguard.

Crazy Horse's martial predisposition was combined with his modesty and deep spirituality, leading Charles Eastman, interviewed by Eli Ricker in August 1907, to again portray the late Oglala warrior as "brave noble, chivalrous man, always a gentleman, quiet in demeanor, not boastful, silent, never self-seeking, a high-minded man, a pure patriot who loved his people – imbued with the spirit of the highest patriotism, [who] fought for his country as long as there was any hope of success. He disdained politics, all scheming and intriguing."[169] In his *Tasunke Witko Woihamble*, Francis White Lance listed the seven sacred laws of the Lakota which Crazy Horse sought to adhere to: wačante ognake, generosity; wausila, empathy; yuonihan, honor; wačin tanka, open mindedness; wowahala, humility; ohitika, bravery; woksape, wisdom.[170]

Even in faraway Japan, the mystique of the legendary warrior turned Crazy Horse into a sort of Lakota samurai. The exotic interpretation was rendered by Prof. Juri Abe, well versed in Lakota history and culture.[171] Drawing from her own family history with samurai roots, Prof. Abe saw in the Lakota war chief the embodiment of the true spirit of bushido. For Abe, it was the same indomitable, generous, and honorable spirit exhibited throughout his life by Michitsura Nozu, a high ranking imperial officer who was Crazy Horse's contemporary. Col. Nozu was also the first Japanese ever to visit Fort Laramie and thence Camp Robinson, less than a year before a fatal soldier's bayonet – and his own knife – were thrust into Crazy Horse's body. Juri Abe wrote that Nozu was an "intrepid man, resolute, with presence of mind and above all unselfish, the true expression of shin no bujin [true warrior], which befits him best." Abe speculated that "if we see it this way, then we can think that the spirit of Crazy Horse, killed several months later at Camp Robinson, might have called to that far away land the spirit of a kindred man, a warrior who came from a distant country." Perhaps, then, the samurai sword that Colonel Nozu allegedly presented to

Red Cloud on the occasion of their brief encounter at Red Cloud Agency in October 1876, was actually intended for Crazy Horse.

Crazy Horse's war exploits are no doubt defining of his historical persona. But in our attempt to unlock the "mystery" of the tintype, we needed to look beyond the "mystic warrior" image to better understand Crazy Horse's "the man" off the battlefield. An insight into this side of Crazy Horse's character and personality was gained by his looking at his relationship with the women in his life, his interaction with the mixed-bloods, the composition of his thiyóšpaye at Red Cloud Agency, and, equally important, his search for peace and the goodwill he exhibited during the last months of his life.

Black Buffalo Woman

Competition for women was strong among the Lakota. Marriages were for the most part happy and long-lasting, but when adultery occurred it was often the cause of violent confrontation between Sioux men. Although, ideally husbands were to control their jealous and possessive impulses. If they so wished, they had the right to reclaim their wife back. Relatives of the involved parties generally mediated a non-violent resolution and arranged for compensation. At times, a "crime of passion" occurred, uxoricide being more prevalent. These episodes were extreme and outside the prescribed cultural norm, thus were recorded on winter counts. The Cloud Shield winter count, for example, has it that in 1784-85, "an Omaha woman living with the Oglala, attempted to run away and they killed her." In the same Cloud Shield, the winter 1799-1800 is remembered because "a woman who had been given to a white man was killed because she ran away from him." Another dramatic example is the American Horse winter count, where the winter 1804-05 bears the pictograph of a Lakota woman pierced by an arrow or lance: "An Indian woman, married to a white man, was unfaithful, she was killed by a man named Ponka." And again, from the Long Soldier winter count for 1852-53, we know that a "woman was killed by intent by husband who was mad."[172] Stanley Vestal recalled that in the early 1850s when the Hunkpapa headmen decided to test the character of their four prospective paramount chiefs, they "agreed that a sure way to test [them] would be to steal their wives and see how they took it. [...] As had been expected [...] all lost their tempers when they found men meddling with their wives, and one of them went gunning for the disturber of the domestic peace."[173]

Crazy Horse, too, became involved with another man's woman. The affair nearly costing him his life and resulted in the famous facial scar that, like the tintype, has been the topic of much debate. We discuss the scar in great detail later. There are several versions of the entire imbroglio involving Crazy Horse, Black Buffalo Woman, and the latter's husband No Water. A Lakota supporter of the tintype who identified himself as "Chief Piercer at the Woptura [Horn Chips] Sundance in Wanblee" wrote that: "[in 1862] Crazy Horse was 20 years old. It was the same year that Black Buffalo Woman was married to No Water. The marriage had taken place at about the same time the photo [tintype] was made. They made sure Crazy Horse wasn't around because they were afraid that he would have interfered. What people never knew was that Crazy Horse, and Black Buffalo Woman had been married in a private ceremony a few years before, the same day that No Water's [older] brother 'one of the twins' [Black Twin] had died going down inside a cave with Crazy Horse, behind a water fall on the west side of the Big Horn Mountains. He had been sucked down a worlpool [sic] that emptied out into a river on the east side of the mountains. Crazy Horse was blamed for the death, and even though he was not to blame, he still felt guilt all the same. The marriage between him and Black Buffalo Woman was never spoken of after that, and she was given to No Water."[174]

Although other sources indicate a later date and different circumstances for Black Twin's death, the fact remains that he was a conservative leader of the Northern Oglala who, like the younger Crazy Horse, opposed White encroachment on Lakota lands.[175] If indeed Crazy Horse was somehow linked to, though not responsible for, Black Twin's death – a death He Dog placed around 1875 – it is understandable that his relatives, particularly after the Black Buffalo Woman trouble, would place blame on Crazy Horse and that, conversely, he felt the guilt.

Crazy Horse's reserved and modest demeanor combined with his proverbial generosity and distinguished war record, contrasted with No Water's boisterous behavior and occasional drinking. Tašunke Wiko's idiosyncratic and withdrawn personality made him even more attractive to Black Buffalo Woman. For his part, Crazy Horse probably saw not only the beauty of her Lakota femininity and the romance of her embrace (soon to be abruptly interrupted), but also the lost attention and warmth of his long gone mother. All would have been fine, except that Black Buffalo was already tied to a band leader who, in turn, was compelled by his status if not necessarily by his love for his unfaithful wife, to save face. That she and No Water had children further complicated things. As for Crazy Horse, recently appointed one of the four Oglala shirt-wearers, accepting Black Buffalo Woman in his lodge meant violating the precepts of unselfishness and self-denial required of his office.[176]

Though his facial features were deceptively pleasant, Tašunke Witko was the bravest of the brave, a manly Lakota. He embodied the individualism of the warrior ethic, living dangerously, each moment to the fullest. But he also felt a profound sense of duty and concern for the welfare of his thiyóšpaye and the wider tribal camp. These traits defined the basic, complementary, and at times contradictory ideal of Lakota manhood. In the end, in Crazy Horse's unique personality and psychological make-up, the recent incident, and subsequent demotion mattered little. He knew where he stood in his commitment to defending the freedom and independence of the Lakota, shirt or no shirt. As for the disruption of tribal unity, following Lakota norm, relatives on both sides mediated and succeeded in diffusing, at least temporarily, a potentially explosive situation. Assured that Black Buffalo Woman would not be punished upon her return to No Water's, Crazy Horse agreed to give her up. No Water remedied to the bloody injury inflicted to a fellow tribesman by sending him horses that were accepted. The incident was officially closed, but resentment continued on.

His close ties to Red Cloud and own position of leadership within the Badger Eaters band kept No Water involved in tribal politics. Later in 1877, he too joined the ranks of Lieut. Clark's Indian scouts at the Agency. And it was "White Hat" Clark who, in the final hours of Crazy Horse's life, offered No Water $200 for the apprehension of the Oglala war chief. No Water never pocketed the money, but he managed to run two ponies to death in his hot pursuit of Crazy Horse on his way to Spotted Tail. His eagerness to sell the old rival to the Bluecoats and his declared intention to shoot Crazy Horse put an even deeper wedge in the already existing fracture between their respective kinfolks for years to come, just like an old Southern Italian *faida* between families.

The fall-out from the adulterous affair was summarized to Eleanor Hinman in the summer of 1930 by He Dog, thru interpreter John Colhoff: "The trouble [between Crazy Horse and No Water] flared up once more after it was supposed to have been quieted. There were several bands encamped near the mouth of the Big Horn river. They had been hunting buffalo along the Missouri. Some were through dressing their meat and others were not. Iron Horse [Crazy Horse's brother in law] and Crazy Horse had finished and were coming back with their ponies loaded with packs of meat. A man named Moccasin Top was still dressing his kill. [He] owned a fast buckskin horse, and had it tethered near him while he worked. No Water came along that way and saw Crazy Horse coming. He untied the buckskin horse of Moccasin Top and jumped on it and started off across the prairie pretty fast. Then Crazy Horse came along and saw Moccasin Top. He said, 'Are you here? Then who was the man who just rode off on your buckskin horse?' Moccasin Top said, 'That was No Water.' Crazy Horse said, 'I wish I had known it! I would certainly have given him a bullet in return for that one he gave me.' Crazy Horse, continued He Dog, chased after his rival, but No Water was able to get away crossing the Yellowstone River." Many people, including Bad Heart Bull and He Dog himself, whose father was related to No Water's father, "came to be drawn into the quarrel" sparked by the affair with Black Buffalo Woman.

Even Chips was caught up in it. "No Water's friends," explained He Dog, "accused Chips, the medicine man who gave Crazy Horse his war medicine, of giving him a love-charm to make this woman run away with him. They were going to kill Chips. The Black Twin (Holy Black Eagle) [one of No Water's brothers] tried to get Chips to acknowledge that he had given Crazy Horse a love-charm, but Chips stoutly denied it. He said he knew nothing whatever about the affair. So after a while they let him go. After that Chips stayed away from the Badger band."

No Water, for his part, quit the Northern Oglala and, again according to He Dog, "went south among the Loafer Indians at Red Cloud Agency and never went back. He stayed at the agency all through the war with the white people and had nothing to do with the hostiles [...] My father and No Water's father were related; that's how Bad Heart Bull and I came drawn into the quarrel." He Dog then added that, when months after the incident Black Buffalo Woman gave birth to a light haired girl, village gossip had it that "this child was Crazy Horse's daughter, but it was never known for certain. This daughter," concluded He Dog, "is living now [1930]."[177]

It may also be true, if we are to believe stories gathered among old-timers at Pine Ridge by David H. Miller, that Crazy Horse followed his Black Buffalo Woman affair with a similar, equally brief, escapade. Bray commented that "the gossip may be just that, but one alleged affair has some support. According to modern Lakota informants, Crazy Horse had an adulterous affair with Shell Blanket Woman, wife of Sans Arc warrior Stands Straddle. Legal testimony from the 1920s establishes that Stands Straddle divorced his wife about 1873, possibly following the affair with Crazy Horse."[178] Be that as it may, the more notorious and potentially tragic liaison was with Black Buffalo Woman and the resulting trouble with No Water. When Vittorio Zucconi visited Pine Ridge in the mid-1990s, he met a descendant of No Water who, as noted, upon learning the Italian journalist was researching the life of Crazy Horse, gave him a cold shoulder and referred him to someone else.

Black Shawl

While still recovering from No Water's gunshot wound, in the summer of 1870 or 1871 Crazy Horse married Black Shawl, Tašina Sapa Win (ca. 1843-1927). Crazy Horse was about thirty years old (maybe younger?) and a recognized war leader, yet lagged behind in establishing his own nuclear family. The marriage to Black Shawl was to begin a new season in Crazy Horse's life. But also in this, Tašunke Witko was not destined to fulfill that human aspiration, deeply felt by the Lakota, of seeing one's own children and grandchildren grow up and prosper. To her credit, Black Shawl gave Crazy Horse the warmth of domestic life he had experienced only briefly in his childhood. Black Shawl was about the same age as her husband. She was the daughter of Old Red Feather and Red Elk Woman, and the sister of Iron Horse and Young Red Feather.

Of the other known women with whom Crazy Horse had, or was said to have had, a relationship, romantic or otherwise, Black Shawl was apparently the only one to give him a child. Tragically consistent with Crazy Horse's adverse destiny, the parenting of their beloved daughter Kokipapi, They Fear Her, was short-lived. The little girl passed away in the fall 1873 when only two-and-a-half years old. Unclear what actually happened, her young life was truncated by a sudden, infective illness, perhaps whopping-cough or influenza. Whatever the cause, the loss touched Crazy Horse to his very core, nearly killing him of an unbearable heart break that affected him for the remaining four years of his life. He had lost his own mother as a child, and recently also both his step-brother and his best friend.

All through these family tragedies and difficulties, Black Shawl was the reserved, soft spoken, and supporting wife who embodied the ideal of Lakota womanhood. She will remain loyal to Crazy Horse for the entire duration of their marriage and long after her husband's premature death. Tašina Sapa Win honored Tašunke Witko's memory by never becoming another man's woman. Black Shawl was photographed at Pine Ridge Reservation in 1888,[179] where she lived with her seventy-year-old mother, as Bray put it, "in the Spleen, or Melt, band camp (site of modern Holy Rosary Mission), [...] next to the family of Black Shawl's brother Red Feather. As two widows, the women would have lived in their natal tiyospaye, which the Spleen likely represents."[180] She died around 1927 of influenza; like her little daughter, the victim of a White man's disease. Strangely enough, in his own diary Jesse Lee wrote that Black Shawl had died shortly after Crazy Horse and that her body had been placed next to that of her late husband on the scaffold overlooking Camp Sheridan.[181]

The Larrabee Woman

In 1877, Tašunke Witko was an attractive Lakota in his prime, with the charisma of an undefeated war chief, though he was beginning to lose his grip on some of his old supporters and was regarded as a troublesome rival by agency chiefs. Not far from Red Cloud Agency and Crazy Horse's lodge lived Joseph Larrabee (Larabee, Laravie, etc.), known as Joe Hunška, Long/Tall Joe, a thin and tall fellow with a long beard, and his large family, two wives and nine children. Years later, Tom Laravie, one of Long Joe's sons, related the following to William J. Bordeaux, the French-Sičangu interpreter and author of *Custer's Conqueror*: "My father [...] was married twice. His first wife was a full-blood Cheyenne and she was called Chi-chi by her tribesmen but the Sioux referred to her as Shahunwinla meaning Cheyenne woman. From this union four daughters were born [...]. They were my half-sisters."[182] One of the four Larrabee girls was Helen, nick-named Nellie, known among the Lakota as Ištaglewin, Brown Eye Woman. She was about eighteen years old, perhaps younger, and considered one of the most attractive and sought after mixed-blood unmarried women at the Agency and reportedly "very pretty."[183] Rumors had it that Lieut. William "White Hat" Philo Clark was among her suitors, perhaps even her secret lover. She had been betrothed to a Loafer Band Oglala named Little Bear (Matočiga), also known as Sioux Bob. But then in the very spring of that eventful year of 1877, the legendary war chief, who was about twice Nellie's age, arrived at the Agency with his large band and Little Bear was pushed aside. Nellie Brown Eyes eventually caught the Oglala war chief's attention. Her youth and beauty impressed Crazy Horse's senses and possibly his heart and he wasted no time. After presenting Long Joe with horses as customary, Crazy Horse took Nellie into his lodge as his second wife.

As with other aspects of Tašunke's life, there are conflicting stories regarding the true nature of Nellie's involvement with Crazy Horse. Some suggest that she was pushed into his lodge by Lieut. Clark to mellow the chief down. And, possibly, to serve as an informant for the astute Lieutenant. Despite her relatively young age, Nellie was an intelligent and crafty woman who rose to the occasion. We do not know whether she truly loved her famous husband or simply played the part, and was paid for it. It has also been said that Nellie compounded Crazy Horse's final troubles by influencing his refusal to travel to Washington. Perhaps, her true intent was to protect Crazy Horse, confiding to him what she might have heard Clark say, that the plan was to arrest Crazy Horse and take him to a far distant island. Speculations aside, her female presence was needed in Crazy Horse's lodge, particularly in light of Tašunke Witko's own Lakota wife Black Shawl's frail condition. By the time he took Nellie in, Crazy Horse had left Tall Bull's lodge and moved into a tipi of his own. Nellie would help with the lodge daily chores and give the isolated and disillusioned Tašunke needed emotional support.

According to Victoria Standing Bear Conroy, a maternal second cousin of Crazy Horse,[184] the increasingly ostracized war chief "only had Miss Laravere [sic] a month or so when he was killed."[185] Mrs. Conroy and Nellie's own step-brother confirmed later that it is odd that no child was born of their relationship – if it was ever consummated, and there is no reason to believe it wasn't – adding yet another puzzle to the many enigmas of Crazy Horse's private life. That Crazy Horse would choose a young Cheyenne "breed" as his second wife instead of an eligible full-blood wiyan waštewin from a prominent Lakota thiyóšpaye, in line with the principle of marriage alliances, may also reflect the void that was created around him by agency Indians. And conversely, Tašunke's own lack of interest for political networking through marriage. As for Crazy Horse's second wife, unlike Black Shawl who remained loyal to her husband's memory, Nellie Larabee later married a Brule named Greasy Hand (ca. 1851-1933), aka Albert Crazy Horse. They lived in Wamblee and had two children, Richard Crazy Horse (1893-1941) and Julia Crazy Horse (1910 - ca.1940).

Speaking of women and conflict, an old grudge over a woman was apparently also at the root of the rancor Little Big Man harbored against the war chief. The circumstances are unclear surrounding an old confrontation between the two close friends, which apparently left a bad mark in Little Big Man's heart. In his interview with Walter Mason Camp held at Pine Ridge in 1910, Horn Chips did not give a specific date or place for the incident, but mentioned it right after, perhaps in conjunction, with the Little Bighorn: "Crazy Horse, in camp, one time had forbidden Little Big Man to sleep with one of the squaws. They got into a fight over it and were never friends after that."[186] Assuming the translation was correct, what could have led Crazy Horse to dictate whether Little Big Man, himself a leading akičita, could or could not sleep with a woman remains unclear. If the Horn Chips story is true, then Little Big Man's behavior after surrender and his own version of what really happened in front of the Camp Robinson's guardhouse now make more sense.

Mixed-Bloods – "Iyeška"

Increased interaction with Whites placed new pressures on the traditional composition of Lakota bands, with the emergence of a previously unknown social (and later political) entity, the mixed-bloods. They were for the most part, French or French-Canadians whose incorporation in Lakota societal fabric initially proved beneficial. Referred to as iyeška, "translators," they played a crucial role as both economic middlemen, cultural brokers, and relatives in the transitional years of treaty making and the establishment of the agencies. Crazy Horse's personal relationship with the mixed-bloods was generally positive, and it was one of them, Baptiste "Little Bat" who in 1877 mediated Crazy Horse's acceptance of photography. Before that, another mixed-blood by the same first name, Baptiste "Big Bat" Pourier

(1843-1932), the famed French trapper, scout, and interpreter who had no love lost to the Indians, had his own personal exchange with Crazy Horse. Big Bat had married a part Oglala and part French-Canadian woman of the Oyuhpe Band, one of Fast Thunder's sisters and a cousin of Crazy Horse himself. He was present when Crazy Horse was mortally wounded, and held the war chief in high esteem. Interviewed by Eli S. Ricker in 1906, Pourier declared that "Crazy Horse was as fine an Indian as he ever knew."[187] Big Bat acknowledged the straightforwardness of the war chief with whom, early on, he had established a rapport of mutual respect: "Bat says […that] when Crazy Horse stole two blooded mares from him at Fort Laramie […] Bat went to him and asked for them, and Crazy Horse told his wife to get them, but she did not want to […] give them up – but he ordered her again to get them, saying they belonged to Bat, and she delivered them. Bat says he was the only Indian who would give them up." Perhaps, Big Bat captured the true essence of Tašunke Witko the man and patriot when he stated that "Crazy Horse fought only for his country, and was not a bad Indian at all."[188] Considering the paramount importance of horses in Lakota culture, the behavior exhibited by Crazy Horse is consistent with his direct, unassuming but determined personality, which the equally determined Pourier understood and appreciated.

Stealing horses was a brave deed and Crazy Horse was particularly good at it, as Billy Garnett recalled in his 1907 interview with Eli S. Ricker.[189] Now, for Crazy Horse to give them back to their owner was a gesture of generosity and goodwill. It was precisely his seemingly distant but generous nature, more than his undisputed courage and war record, to win him the respect, even the liking of the mixed-bloods; hardy fellows who understood the Lakota way and language. As historian Robert A. Clark wrote, in the beginning at Camp Robinson "Crazy Horse's ability to command respect extended beyond the Sioux. He also gained prestige among the army officers. And as his stature grew at Red Cloud Agency, jealousy among the chiefs began to work its way into agency [and tribal] affairs."[190]

Crazy Horse was not much of a talker, rather, a doer. When he did speak, he went straight to the issue, without engaging in oratorical performances.

Even in that, Tašunke Witko departed from Lakota norm that emphasized good oratorical abilities. Interviewed in the early 1930s by Stanley Vestal (Walter S. Campbell), Mnicojou chief White Bull (1849-1947), Sitting Bull's eldest nephew who shared many battles alongside the Oglala war chief, stated through interpreter Sam Eagle Chasing, "Crazy Horse spoke seldom: when he did speak, he hit the nail on the head."[191]

Even the dubious Frank Grouard could not subtract himself from Crazy Horse's captivating personality, whatever his true feelings towards him might have been. According to his biographer Joe DeBarthe, "Grouard says that the Ogallala chief was a fine looking savage in 1873, when he first met him. A trifle less than six feet tall, he was straight as an arrow. He was naturally spare, and could stand any amount of hardship. He was proud of his people and their history and, like Sitting Bull, was opposed to any and all intercourse with the whites. Grouard says Crazy Horse was the bravest man he ever met. Reserved at all times, his counsel was greatly sought." Crazy Horse could also be very passionate, generous, and especially caring with those in need. It was in Crazy Horse's tipi that Grouard "found shelter and protection when Sitting Bull sought to destroy him, and the regard the two men had for each other transcended the affection of brothers."[192] We will discuss Little Bat later.

Thiyóšpaye

The composition and strength of Crazy Horse's thiyóšpaye at Red Cloud Agency progressively shrank, reflecting the unsettled climate that ultimately (shortly before and after the war chief's death) saw the defection of some of his closest friends and the breakouts of many Northern lodges to Canada. Keeping in mind the relatively fluid nature of the Northern Indian camp organization in the spring of 1877, the Surrender Ledger compiled by Lieut. Charles A. Johnson and Red Cloud Agency chief clerk Charles P. Jordan on Sunday, May 6th of the same year provides a fairly accurate picture of the composition of Crazy Horse's camp circle at the time of his arrival at the Agency. The head count listed a Northern Indian contingent of 217 adult males, 312 adult females (of which some 16 were widows, head of household), plus 370 children about equally divided between boys and girls, for a total of 899 people. The Northern Camp, erected at some distance from the larger Oglala tribal village a few miles from the Agency, comprised 145 lodges, divided into eight sub-circles identified with their respective leaders: White Twin with 39 lodges, Charging Hawk with two, Black Elk with 37, Knife Chief with eight, Horned Horse (Little Bull) with 13, Crazy Horse himself with seven, Little Big Man with 30, and He Dog with nine.[193] The sensationalist media in the East reported an inflated "500 warriors" still at the command of Crazy Horse.[194]

The Ledger shows that Crazy Horse had no surviving consanguine siblings, nor any children. In the eyes of the Lakota, therefore, he was considered a "poor" man. On the other hand, Crazy Horse's affine kindred was complex, as shown in records later made public by the Clown family. According to the latter, after the death of his first wife, Crazy Horse's father married the two eldest Corn daughters, and later also Red Leggings. The Corn brothers Ashes (ca. 1830-ca. 1890), Bull Head (ca. 1831-1923), and Spotted Crow (ca. 1833-??), thus became Crazy Horse's [step-]lekši. The large number of Corn siblings implies that, reflecting his status and Lakota marriage practices, Chief Corn had more than one wife. From Worm's union with Red Leggings a daughter named Iron Cedar (later Julia Iron Cedar Clown) was born ca. 1865. She was a younger [step-]sister (tanka) to Crazy Horse. She stayed at Spotted Tail. Worm went to Red Cloud in May 1877, and returned to Spotted Tail after his son's death.

While it does not change the overall issue pertaining to the diminished strength of Crazy Horse's thiyóšpaye at Red Cloud, Kingsley Bray provides a different reading of the birth of Iron Cedar. Bray suggests that Red Leggings married a Mnicojou man named Woman (or Woman's) Breast and from that union Iron Cedar was born. Possibly by yet a different wife, Woman Breast, also fathered Leo Combing, James Bear Pipe, Peter Wolf, and Coming Home Last. The Clown family disagrees. Worm, Woman Breast (Breast of Woman), also known as Kills at Night, was one and the same person, that is, the elder Crazy Horse. Still according to them, feeling threatened after the killing of his son Waglula wanted nothing to do with the Oglala, whom he blamed for Crazy Horse's death, and spent his final years, about 1881 to 1900, moving between Rosebud, Cheyenne River, and Standing Rock reservations. He assumed the name of Woman's Breast to elude the U.S. government.

Ephriam Dickson sees Worm and Woman's Breast as two different people. Woman's Breast and Red Leggings (and other wives?) were parents to Shell Blanket (ca.1848-1894), Leo Combing (ca. 1851-1932), James Bear Pipe (ca. 1854-1892), Peter Wolf (ca. 1858-assassinated in 1918), Comes Home Last (ca. 1864-??), and Sacred Girl (ca. 1868-??), and of course Iron Cedar. In 1884, Iron Cedar Woman married a Sans Arc man named Heyoka, Clown, born ca. 1865. As a boy he had been at the Little Bighorn and was later known as Amos Clown. Julia and Amos Clown appear in their old age in an undated photograph published by Donovin Sprague of Crazy Horse Memorial.[195] The *Authorized Biography* notes that Julia and Amos's son Moses Clown (1891-1917) most resembled "Crazy Horse in appearance of any of his nephews." Indeed, the small photographic portrait published on the back cover of the first DVD actually shows a resemblance to the Indian in the tintype, as does the sketch of Crazy Horse drawn posthumously on description provided by Julia Clown/Iron Cedar Woman.

With combined genealogical information given by Sprague, and by Victor Douville of Lakota Studies Department at Sinte Gleska University, Bray further suggests that Crazy Horse's often cited kinship to Spotted Tail through Worm's remarriages to the Brule chief's sisters Gathers the Grapes and Corn Woman, can be explained as follows: "These women were not biological or full-sisters to Spotted Tail. A woman that Spotted Tail called 'mother,' perhaps a sister of his biological mother Walks With the Pipe [of the Wazhazha band, usually associated with the Sičangu], married Mnicojou chief Corn. Their children would have been 'brothers' and 'sisters' to Spotted Tail. I therefore suggest," concluded Bray, "that Gathers the Grapes and Corn [Woman] are the same women as Iron Between Horns and Kills Enemy (although I am not sure which one corresponds to which!)."[196] The comprehensive Crazy Horse genealogy compiled by Francis White Lance offers additional comparative information not found elsewhere.[197]

Luther Standing Bear, who was then a child, recalled that after the surrender of the Northern Indians, his father's lodge at Spotted Tail Agency received the visit of Crazy Horse himself: "He did not carry anything with him, and he was dressed very poorly. There was nothing fancy about him in any way."[198] A simple and modest man, but by no means a meek personality. While through his deceased mother, his remarried father, and his half-sister's kindred he had many relatives there, Crazy Horse lacked a strong network of close blood relations. He was practically alone, hence poor. The previously mentioned Victoria Conroy, half-sister of Luther, was the daughter of Brule headman Standing Bear (Sr.), first cousin of Crazy Horse through Worm's sister Rattle Stone Woman and her husband One Horse. In a 1934 letter to Gordon McGregor, [199] Conroy commented specifically on the composition of her second cousin's immediate family: "I am writing to you today about my relationship to Crazy Horse. There are no living blood relations nearer to him than my sister and I. There are many who claim relationship, but they were related to him by marriage [only]."

The Peace Road

Crazy Horse's opening to peace complicated, rather than facilitated, his position at Red Cloud. As a "de facto" new agency chief and Army scout, he became an involuntary challenge to the already established Oglala hierarchy. Hence the growing ostracism and isolation, and the urgency for Crazy Horse to secure an agency of his own for those Northern Indians who still wished to follow him. In his July 1930 interviews with Eleanor Hinman, He Dog underscored that Crazy Horse's willingness to travel to Washington was tied to the key issue of a separate agency back in the North Country. "Crazy Horse," explained He Dog through interpreter Thomas White Cow Killer, "said to me that if they would have the [Northern Indians] agency moved over to Beaver Creek [in eastern Wyoming], then he would go to Washington as they asked him. The reason he gave for this condition was that Beaver Creek was in the middle of the Sioux territory, while the location of Fort Robinson was on the edge of it." A week later, again through interpreter John Colhoff, He Dog reiterated the same point: "When we first came down to the [Red Cloud] agency, Crazy Horse was willing to go to Washington. He said to me, 'First, I want them to place my agency on Beaver Creek west of the Black Hills. Then I will go to Washington – for your benefit, for my benefit, and for the benefit of all of us. And that is the only reason why I will go there.'"[200]

His disposition was made clear by his trusted friend He Dog who, with the aid of pictographs, recounted the life-story of Crazy Horse. In one of the captions comprising the so-called *Eagle Hawk Narrative* accompanying the sketches, we read, "He Dog and Crazy Horse were protecting the Black Hills, and they had a battle [along the Little Big Horn River on June 25, 1876]. American Horse and Afraid of His Horses were then friendly chiefs, and they were on the side of the whites. After the battle, American Horse and Young Man Afraid of His Horses went out to meet the two warring chiefs, Crazy Horse and He Dog, [...] and they took some presents – two blankets and horses – and each made a special talk to Crazy Horse and He Dog. [They told them] to surrender and live in peace with the whites; that they wanted their children learn the white man's way and go to school; that they wanted peace between the Indians and the whites, and for that reason brought presents and these horses. So Crazy Horse said he would [make peace], and the others who were sitting down on the ground were all in favor of it also. He said he would take the pipe of peace and smoke, and he said the reason he was at war was that he [had been] protecting the Black Hills, because there was a lot of riches in the Black Hills..., but he said 'Now I will smoke, and everything will be in peace henceforth.'"[201]

Tašunke Witko led his people to Camp Robinson on May 6, 1877. His demeanor on the day of his surrender speaks volumes of the truthfulness of his peaceful disposition: "Lieutenant Clark had gone out early in the morning to a point seven or eight miles from the post to meet the incoming party. Crazy Horse, upon learning who he was, remained silent, but was not at all ungracious or surly. He dismounted from his pony, sat down upon the ground, and said that then was the best time for smoking the pipe of peace. He then held out his left hand to Clark telling him 'Cola (friend), I shake with this hand because my heart is on this side; I want this peace to last forever,'"[202] As several of his contemporaries later reported, Tašunke Witko was a man of few words but of clear and determined actions. He wanted to show both the Americans and the Agency Indians his sincere desire to getting along with the Whites, despite the undeniably profound distrust he must have nurtured towards them. He Dog put it best when he stated, "If I heard Crazy Horse say it once I heard him say it many times: I came here for peace. No matter if my own relatives pointed a gun at my head and ordered me to change that word I would not change it." Hunts the Enemy (1847-1910), son of Brave Bear and nephew of Red Cloud, had brought tobacco to Crazy Horse in early January 1877, preceding Spotted Tail and Red Cloud. In his 1907 interview with Judge Ricker, George Sword (as Hunts the Enemy was now known as a Captain of the Pine Ridge Indian Police) underscored that Crazy Horse "Came in good faith, to have permanent peace with the whites – to stop bloodshed on both sides."[203]

An opinion also held by Billy Garnett, who stated that "There cannot be the slightest question, for the evidence of circumstances points unmistakably that way, that Crazy Horse had come into the [Red Cloud] Agency with nothing but honorable intentions to accept the terms of the government and the inevitable situation of affairs."[204] Billy Garnett echoed He Dog recalling that a couple of weeks after the historic hand-shake, "[I] went out to the Crazy Horse village and told Crazy Horse that Lieutenant Clark would make him a scout and nineteen of his Indians, so when I told him that, they jumped at the chance. They came and got arms and pistols. So Crazy Horse was a scout. He started in in about the same month, about May. So we got along with Crazy Horse pretty good, just the same as any friendly Indian for some time. [...] In the month of August we got the news that the Nez Percé had broken out and were working for Wyoming."[205]

Even the following mundane episode also related by Garnett to Judge Ricker is indicative of Crazy Horse's good disposition, before rumors, innuendos, and plain lies began poisoning the air around him: "On his arrival at Red Cloud, Crazy Horse was not surprised with any new proposition; [.... he] was arranging in his mind for the Washington mission, and [...] his frame of mind was tranquil and pacific." Garnett invited Crazy Horse, Little Big Man, and a few others to dinner, and "It was on this occasion that [Tašunke Witko] remarked that he would begin to learn the use of the fork at the table. He said he had to do it." Ever straightforward and a practical man, Crazy Horse went on to ask Garnett "Questions about traveling to Washington; how the Indians were provided for; all of which were answered to his satisfaction."[206] As Thomas Powers wrote, "Use of the fork was soon followed by use of the chair. Crazy Horse seemed to pick up quickly the fact that in crowded meetings the man who sat in the chair was in charge of the room. The chief clerk at the agency than summer, Charles P. Jordan, remarked that when Crazy Horse came to see the agent, James Irwin, 'he was always accompanied by a body-guard of men,' as many as six or eight in all. Crazy Horse did little talking but sat in a chair. The men with him sat on the floor."[207]

The testimony rendered by Louis Mato (Bear) Bordeaux (1849-1917), who also knew Crazy Horse, to Eli S. Ricker in 1907, echoed the Oglala hero's true feelings. While in the Adjutant's Office at Camp Robinson, the very day he was going to die, Crazy Horse reiterated that peace with the Whites had been his aspiration since the early spring of that fateful year: "[Tašunke Witko] said that when he came in from the north and met the officers and others on Hat Creek, he presented the pipe of peace to the Great Spirit there and said he wanted peace, he wanted no more war, and promised he would not fight against any nation anymore, and that he wants to be at peace now."[208] That Bordeaux reported fairly accurately the chief's words is assured by the fact that he spoke Lakota (his mother's tongue) and that when Crazy Horse finally came in, he was the official interpreter at Spotted Tail Agency and nearby Camp Sheridan. Bordeaux went on to emphasize contextually the profound meaning of what Crazy Horse had said. "Mr. Bordeaux," Ricker continued, "explains that when an Indian presents the pipe to the Great Spirit it is the holy pipe; to the wild Indian this act and vow was in the nature of an oath, as such obligations are among civilized peoples; to the Indian it is a holy, sacred act, solemn and to be kept with honor."[209] Shortly after coming in, the Northern Indians were ordered by Col. Ranald S. Mackenzie (1840-1889) to surrender all their weapons – those still in their possession, tucked away after the original confiscation. Crazy Horse himself, though "sick as he was" with indigestion, "went from tipi to tipi, consuming nearly the entire night, coaxing and commanding by turns, that if any guns could be found they must be turned in by daylight."[210]

Good feelings prevailed, and on May 24th Crazy Horse again showed his congeniality, nurtured undoubtedly by the anticipation of good news regarding the new agency and the buffalo hunt, soon to be delivered in person at Red Cloud Agency by Gen. George Crook himself. Less than a year after stopping Crook's advance at the Rosebud, and shortly thereafter defeating Custer at the Little Bighorn, Crazy Horse agreed to a lengthy interview with *Chicago Times* newspaper correspondent Charles Diehl. In the presence of Crazy Horse, who listened carefully, often nodding in approval and interjecting only once, were headmen Horned Horse (Little Bull) and Red Dog. The translation provided by Billy Garnett with the assistance of "Little Bat" Garnier gave telling details of the Custer Battle, the Rosebud fight, and the Sibley scout.[211] The positive mood continued the following day, May 25th, with a great council held with Gen. Crook and his staff. Judging from eyewitness accounts, the grand parade of several hundred Indian scouts, the friendly shaking of hands between "Three Stars," Crazy Horse, and the other chiefs, the speeches, and the colorful backdrop of a multitude of curious Indian women and children assembled on the nearby sloping bluff must have been a sight to behold. We do not know whether photographs were taken, or are now lost.

The event was recorded in writing by Robert Strahorn who, as noted, in 1876 had accompanied Gen. Crook against Crazy Horse.[212] Strahorn, a correspondent for the *Denver Rocky Mountain News* under the pen name "Alter Ego," also sold his dispatches to the *Chicago Tribune*, the *New York Times*, and other papers: "Camp Robinson, May 25. At noon to-day the principal warriors at the agency to the number of 600 were passed in review by Gen. Crook. Lieut. Clark formed them in line on the plain at the east of the agency buildings, Gen. Crook taking his station in front of the centre. The Indians were broken into a column of 18 platoons, and executed the march past in good style. Having been again wheeled into line, the chiefs rode to within a few paces of Gen. Crook where they dismounted and shook hands with him. Crazy Horse, who now saw the General for the first time, knelt on the ground as he shook his hand. His example was followed by the others. Little Big Man was conspicuous by his almost complete nudity. Gen. Crook now led the way to the agency. [..] All the principal men having assembled inside the agency stockade, an interval of silence ensued while the Indians arranged the order of precedence in speeches, and the council was opened by Crazy Horse, who is notably a man of few words, seating himself on the ground in front of the General. He spoke in a low voice as follows: 'You sent us tobacco and provisions when we were hungry, to our camp. From the time I received it, I kept coming in and toward the post. All the time since I came in, I have been happy. While coming this way [prior to May 7], I picked out a place and put a stick in the ground for a place to live hereafter, where there is plenty of game (He meant where he wants the agency). All of these relations of mine who are here, were with me when I picked out this place. I would like to have them to back with me and stay there with me. This is all I have to say.'"[213]

Speaking from the heart, with simple words Tašunke Witko expressed a most profound aspiration: to return as soon as possible with his followers to the North Country. He wanted his agency there to live in peace, nothing more. The other chiefs who spoke were, in order, Young Man Afraid, Red Cloud, No Water, again Red Cloud, Iron Hawk, High Bear, Little Wound, and finally Spotted Tail. The latter gave a longer and more elaborate harangue which, in substance, could not have been farther from Crazy Horse's. Sinte Gleška closed his talk by praising himself for succeeding in "getting Crazy Horse in," expressed his desire to have his children "brought-up like white men," and urged Gen. Crook "to ask the great father to send a Catholic priest to us – one that wears a black dress." He also insisted upon Bouchey [F.C. Bouncher] and Bissnett [Joe Bissonette] "for traders. We were raised with these people, and when we get hungry they will give us something to eat." Gen. Crook's reply to Crazy Horse and the other chiefs was polite, condescending, and inconclusive, particularly with regard to the thorny request of a separate agency "in the upper country." "I cannot decide these things myself. They must be decided in Washington." If Crazy Horse really understood Gen. Crook's words as they were translated by interpreters Joe [Jose/Joseph] Merrivale and Tom Dorion, it must have been quite a sobering disappointment. As William Bordeaux later wrote, "According to the statements [by] those who knew him Crazy Horse entertained no exceptional ill will toward the Government, but he believed that man had been created by the Great Spirit to enjoy what nature offered and that he was meant to be free." [214]

Writing in the 1950s, Robert T. Grange, Jr., curator of the Fort Robinson Museum, commented that "Great excitement developed among the Indians around Camp Robinson as a result of the killing of Crazy Horse and serious trouble was threatened, but the efforts of Indian leaders prevented a violent outbreak. In his report of the incident, Lieut. Clark listed the Arapaho, Black Coal and Sharp Nose, and the Sioux leaders Red Cloud, Young Man Afraid of His Horses, American Horse, Yellow Bear, Little Big Man, Big Road, No Water, Three Bears, and No Flesh as the men who prevented an outbreak by controlling their people. That so important a man as Crazy Horse could be killed in such a way without any more serious consequences than a few day's uproar was an indication that the war with the Sioux was about over."[215] The only expression of dissent was a number of Northern Indians breaking away and heading north in the midst of the confusion created by the removal of the Red Cloud and Spotted Tail agencies.

A year later, in September 1878, what remained south of the Northern village also split. Those under Crazy Horse's father Worm, who blamed Red Cloud for his son's death, had had enough of running away and opted to remain among the Brule under the protection of Spotted Tail. Others, mostly Oglala, including Crazy Horse's widow Black Shawl and her mother Red Elk Woman, returned to their kinfolk, now settled at Pine Ridge. Then there were those, among whom, as Bray wrote, "A sentiment existed to break away for sanctuary with Sitting Bull's people in Canada. Just as Worm had foreseen, the lure of the last buffalo herds, and the collapse of hopes of a northern reserve, had caused mass breakouts during the previous winter. His brother Little Hawk had joined the flights, along with old war comrades of his son like He Dog and Big Road, Low Dog and Iron Crow."[216] The dream was short-lived. Within the next three years, most if not all had re-crossed the medicine line to resettle at various agencies within the Great Sioux Reservation.

A year after the death, with a large giveaway honoring Crazy Horse's name, Worm ended the Ghost Owing mourning period, finally releasing his son's nagila to the Happy Hunting Grounds. Free at last. Only the Lakota present at the tearing down of Crazy Horse's Ghost Lodge understood the profound significance of the moment. With very few exceptions, to the Whites on the frontier, the military, and enemy tribes, the passing of Crazy Horse was welcome news about an obstinate war chief, soon to be forgotten. Years later Jesse M. Lee, who had since risen through the ranks and retired as major general, wrote to Brininstool what, at the time seemed a fair assessment of the destiny that expected the fading memory of Crazy Horse. This, of course, before Eleanor Hinman gave voice to the Indian testimonies, before Mari Sandoz romanticized the "mystic warrior," and before William Bordeaux, too, recalled the Indian version of what had happened to Crazy Horse. Lee wrote, "There is no Indian journalist, author or reporter to present the chief's side of the story of his tragic fate. With the lapse of time, his name and fame may linger for awhile in the traditions of his tribe, and then fade away forever. History will make but little record of him, save to note a point perhaps in the onward march of our Christian civilization."[217] The sympathetic general was to be proven wrong.

Photography and "Good Behavior"

"Soon the soldier chiefs were speaking well of the hostile Crazy Horse, calling him a fine, quiet, and modest man, one much concerned with the welfare of his people. Even his anger at the picture men, those with the black box who would catch his shadow [...] seemed good to them."

Mari Sandoz, 1942

Three weeks after Crazy Horse and Lieut. Clark shook hands, a patronizing editorial in the *New York Herald* of May 28, 1877, applauded the government's new direction in dealing with the Sioux and was particularly prophetic regarding the fate expecting Crazy Horse and, later, Sitting Bull. "It remains to be seen," read the paper, "whether the new management of Indian affairs at the Red Cloud and Spotted Tail agencies shall be better or worse. It has much to be urged in its favor. It deals with the red men on the basis of justice [!], giving proper encouragement to the well-disposed, and assuring the evil minded they cannot escape punishment if they persist in wrong doing. With its well organized establishment of Indian soldiers [scouts] under the guidance of officers of the regular army, the ingress or egress of Indian truants is next to impossible; the savages being divided among themselves they can offer but a weak and short-lived resistance, hence submit readily to the rules of discipline. It is the old adage of 'Divide and conquer' over again."[218] Seven months earlier, writing soon after the Custer debacle, a Cheyenne, Wyoming Territory, newspaper had also emphasized on the Indians' internal split and welcomed the government strong hand: "The Indians are utterly divided and have given up their old insolent and arrogant bearing. They see now that nothing but good behavior can save them from sure and swift punishment."[219]

"Good behavior" was also alluded to in the annual reports agents in the field submitted to the Commissioner of Indian Affairs to reassure Washington that progress, though slow, was being made, particularly among the Sioux. For their part the Sioux, like other Indians, were adjusting by necessity if not reluctantly to the new situation. Famous Lakota leaders like Red Cloud, Spotted Tail, and later Sitting Bull, in time established a tolerant, complex, symbiotic rapport with photography.[220] Frank Goodyear pointed out that the photo-savvy Red Cloud "Used photography as a means of simultaneously paying deference to and resisting those who sought to subjugate the Lakotas [...]. The process of 'mimicry' allowed him to remain engaged in deliberations with government officials while at the same time offering him the opportunity to sabotage their authority."[221] Group delegation and individual portrait photography "served as a stage on which Native Americans and non-Natives continued to engage in a larger trans-cultural [and more peaceful] conversation." Individual differences in temperament and personality-type notwithstanding ("while Spotted Tail had a lively vein of humor in his character, and loved to indulge in a little joke, Red Cloud was all dignity and seriousness"),[222] photography became an important new interpreter for American Indian chiefs.

It had not always been like that. In the beginning, some Lakota leaders expressed uneasiness with what they perceived as a suspicious tool and the intrusive behavior of photographers. During his first trip to Washington in the spring of 1870, Red Cloud resisted being photographed. There are two versions to the story, one claiming that Mathew Brady actually convinced the wily chief to visit his popular studio on Pennsylvania Avenue, but that the impatient Red Cloud, who had greater worries on his mind, would not sit still and the *exposure* turned out blurred and unusable. Another story, reported that same year in *Frank Leslie's Illustrated Newspaper*, maintained that the chief refused on the grounds that "he was not a white man, but a Sioux, and that he was not dressed for the occasion." The *Leslie's* journalist added his own "ignorant Indian" stereotype, stating that, purportedly, the refusal to be photographed was motivated by "fear." Red Cloud and the other chiefs were worried "the Great Spirit would be angry with them, and they would die."[223] Never mind that if Red Cloud and fellow Lakota, articulate and intelligent as they had demonstrated to be time and again in their negotiations, ever expressed such feelings through an interpreter, they were most likely playing the White man's game simply to be left alone. And perhaps, eventually require later good payment for their pictures to be taken. In true Lakota fashion, Red Cloud and the others probably laughed wholeheartedly amongst themselves of the gullibility of the White man.

Red Cloud proved this two years later in 1872, back at Fort Laramie. The camera was there, and again photography lost the match with the shrewd, middle-aged Lakota. The unyielding leader of the Bad Face Oglala, "brushed aside" U.S. Commissioners F.R. Brunot and Robert Campbell's suggestion that the council be held in a large tent, and demanded instead that they meet on the fort commandant's veranda. There, Mahpiya Luta became enraged by the presence of a "shadow catcher" and "he stopped his speech to order that [the] photographer be chased away!"[224] Fear of the Great Spirit, or of losing his soul, had nothing to do with the refusal to pose for Gardner. As earlier in the City of Washington, the chief simply had no time for such ancillary performances, nor was he in the right state of mind for picture taking. Serious issues were at stake: intrusions of settlers on Lakota lands, location of his agency, right to trade at Fort Laramie, annuities, internal dissention. Not a good disposition towards photographers and their trappings. In fact, both Red Cloud and Crazy Horse had been absent from the photographic portraits taken earlier at the Laramie Treaty in 1868. On that historic occasion, Gardner photographed without problems the Peace Commission meeting with the Cheyenne and the Arapaho on May 10th, and with the Hunkpatila Oglala of Old Man Afraid on May 24-25th.

Red Cloud's unwelcoming reaction to the camera was harmless, and while photography was a relatively safe endeavor at the forts and vicinities, it could be a very dangerous craft on the open range. Poor Ridgway Glover experienced that, paying with his own life. Apparently, for some Indians even the showing of a photograph portraying a close relative could cause problems, as the murder of young acting agent Frank Appleton, discussed below, proved in 1874 at newly established Red Cloud Agency. Generally speaking, however, these were exceptions to a less bloody rapport between photography and Indians, as the welcome accorded to Lieut. Thomas

Wilhelm and his camera at both Red Cloud and Spotted Tail agencies that same tense year 1874 showed.

After opening to peace, Crazy Horse, too, did his best to accommodate. From learning the strange table manners of the White man, helped in the task by Billy Garnett, to accepting an invitation from another friendly mixed-blood, Little Bat, to visit the "pictures" log-house at the Agency and have his photograph taken might not have been too big of a deal for Crazy Horse. The evidence points that way, challenging the Sandoz stereotype of an intransigent Crazy Horse "frozen in war time" to his very death. That portrayal still pervades both the scholarly literature and the popular perception of the great Oglala. Martha Sandweiss, perpetuating the Crazy Horse myth of stubborn refusal to the camera, stated that, "In retrospect, one can only admire the prescience of Crazy Horse, the Lakota leader who, unlike his contemporary Sitting Bull, steadfastly refused to be photographed."[225]

Sandweiss confused the issues and compared two different situations. Neither the Oglala war chief nor the Hunkpapa spiritual leader of the Northern coalition had ever dealt with a photographer before their victory at the Greasy Grass in '76. The same historical confusion and negative theme underscored the writing of Red Cloud's photo-biographer Frank Goodyear who subscribed to the "hatred" view concluding that, in contrast to the openness towards the camera adopted by Mahpiya Luta, "The famed warrior Crazy Horse [...] never posed for a photographer, a decision indicative of his unyielding commitment to a campaign of warfare against the United States."[226] The latter part of Goodyear's statement is incorrect. Like Sandweiss, Goodyear does no justice to the complex persona of Tašunke Witko. Nor does he address the equally complex and rapidly evolving events and circumstances that followed the Little Bighorn, Crazy Horse's yielding to the peace faction in the Northern Circle, his decision to report to Red Cloud Agency, not to mention signing up as an Army scout!

Crazy Horse saw a camera for the first time after his arrival at Camp Robinson. Sitting Bull, too, was first photographed after he crossed into Canada and submitted to the status of non-belligerent guest-refugee enforced by the RCMP, the feared Red-Coat Mounties. True to his unselfish nature and love of his People, Crazy Horse put aside distrust, reluctance, and well-founded suspicion, even hate, leading his followers to what only less than a year earlier had seemed the unthinkable. Horn Chips confirmed that Crazy Horse had spoken warm-heartedly to Lieut. Clark, employing conciliatory words, explaining the defensive nature of his previously "hostile" stand, and now his desire for peace. "I have been a man of war and have always protected my country against invaders," Crazy Horse reportedly said. "Now I am for peace. I will look at the ground and fight no more. I will settle down and attend to my own business."[227] That is why he shook hands with Clark with his left hand, the side of the heart. Posing for a photograph, like other Lakota chiefs and headmen had done and were still doing, could represent an additional concession to goodwill. Even Sandoz implicitly recognized that.[228]

Touch the Clouds, as we noted, was himself first photographed by James H. Hamilton at Spotted Tail, and again in full regalia by Julius Ulke and Mathew Brady in Washington, only shortly after Crazy Horse's death. Would such a close kin, still in mourning, accept to be photographed had such an act been considered offensive to the memory of his deceased relative and inconsistent with Lakota ways and beliefs? Obviously not.

Cochise, Inkpaduta, and Crazy Horse

Despite the thousands of photographic portraits of American Indians that were taken from the mid-1850s to the late 1900s, obviously many Native persons, including famous ones, eluded the camera. Whenever we do not seem to have a documented photograph of a certain historical Indian figure, the gap is more likely due to a series of fortuitous circumstances such as advanced age, premature death, remote settlement, ongoing war, or no photographer at hand, rather than the subject's avoidance of, objection to, much less "fear" of, photography itself. A classic example is that of Cochise (Gochi/Chees/KaChis, ca. 1815-1874), the legendary war chief of the Chiricahua who, together with his father-in-law Mangas Coloradas

(Dasoda-he, ca. 1795-1863)[229] tried to defend the Apache Homeland from White encroachment. Gen. Oliver O. Howard (1830-1909) met Cochise in 1872 and described him as "A man fully six feet in height, well proportioned, large, dark eyes, face slightly painted with vermillion, unmistakably an Indian. […] He gave me a warm grasp of the hand […] his face was really pleasant to look upon, making me say to myself, 'How strange it is that such a man can be the robber and murderer so much complained of.'" No documented photographic portrait of Cochise is known to exist, but it has been speculated that "possibly a photograph from life was made sometime in 1872 […] while visiting Fort Bowie [Arizona Terr.]." This alleged and long-lost photo might have been the basis of a painting entitled "Cochise by W.S. Sutter 1872" showing an Indian whose face "Definitely has Cochise's high cheek bones, Roman nose, and dark eyes – as well as a pleasant but somewhat melancholy mouth."[230]

We can also infer Cochise's features from those of his two sons. Naiche (Nachez, ca. 1856-1919), the youngest son who was said to resemble his father the most.[231] Naiche joined Geronimo's fight, and he was photographed by Camillus S. Fly (1849-1901) in 1886 in northeastern Sonora, Mexico, in a classic view of the two chiefs on horseback, flanked by Geronimo's second cousins Perico (holding a child), and Fun, both standing.[232] Naiche, who later became a U.S. Indian scout, was also photographed the same year by Frank A. Randall in 1884 at San Carlos Reservation, Arizona (1854-1916).[233]

In keeping within the Sioux, two other notable examples of "missing photos" stand out, again pertaining to war leaders who, like Cochise, strongly opposed the Americans: Inkpaduta, Red Tip/Scarlet Point, the "renegade" Dakota chief,[234] and for those who do not believe in the tintype, our own Crazy Horse. The consensus among historians and tribal members alike has been that both Inkpaduta and Crazy Horse wanted nothing to do whatsoever with photographers. Interestingly, the "faceless" aura affected in diametrically opposite ways the mystique of their historical persona. The older Inkpaduta (ca. 1810-1879) is an enigmatic figure that, according to both White and Indian historians, left behind a trail of bloody deeds.

"His name," wrote Mark Diedrich, "was linked to the murder of the principal chief of the Wahpekute tribe (his own relative), and in 1857 he was the leader in the infamous massacre of about forty white settlers on the Minnesota-Iowa border. [...] Inkpaduta's raid [...] helped prompt the larger Sioux uprising of 1862 in Minnesota."[235] Ostracized by his own people, with a small band of "renegades" Inkpaduta fled west. He joined Sitting Bull and Crazy Horse and fought alongside them in the Battle of Lodge Grass Creek, 1874, and two years later at the Little Bighorn. Inkpaduta and his warriors, who at the Greasy Grass were camped near the Hunkpapa on the southern end of the great village, were among the first to respond to Reno's attack. The defense mounted by Inkpaduta's forty or so warriors, that was quickly joined by the much stronger Hunkpapa contingent and soon reinforced by the Oglala akičita led by Crazy Horse not only stopped the Reno, but rendered his re-positioning in the timber precarious and untenable.

We know little about the specific role the fiery Inkpaduta himself played in the Custer fight, but we do know that the Santee chief never came to terms with the Americans. He was the only major Sioux leader never to make peace with, never to surrender to, and never to be captured by the United States of America. Adding to Inkpaduta's aura of "sanguine renegade" (alternatively, "unsung hero" for his admirers like Charles Eastman)[236] was the fact that he too, apparently, was never photographed. The reason given by his biographers sounds familiar and understandable, given the bounty that had been put on his head. According to Van Nuys, "If, which is highly unlikely, he ever had the opportunity, it would not have been characteristic of him to permit one to be taken."[237] In the end, keeping with his elusive character, the wily old Wahpekute died in obscurity and forgotten in voluntary exile in Canada.[238] Inkpaduta is still today an Indian leader without a face.

Conversely, other prominent Santee chiefs who were Inkpaduta's own contemporaries, posed for the camera. Including the famed Little Crow (Taoyateduta, ca. 1810-1863), Mdewakanton leader of the tragic 1862 Dakota Sioux Uprising, who was photographed without any problems by Zeno Shindler as early as 1858 when a Santee delegation visited Washington and New York.[239] But even the absolute stance against any photographs of Scarlet Point has been challenged. There is a slim possibility that Inkpaduta may have actually been "captured" by the camera, if only once. An image was published for the first time by Diedrich, who wrote, "This photo [...] was only recently discovered, and is purportedly of Inkpaduta [...]. No known photograph of him was thought to exist. Yet, this slightly out of focus portrait portrays an Indian who fits Inkpaduta's general facial description – long, slim face, with high cheek bones, sunken black eyes, and a large mouth with unusually big canine teeth. If it indeed is Inkpaduta, it probably was taken before the 1857 Spirit Lake massacre."[240] Maxwell Van Nuys strongly doubts the photo and actually notes that the Wahpekute chief "had a broad face [with] smallpox scars." The same author thinks that a lithograph of Inkpaduta's brother Sintomniduta ("All Over Red") is the closest likeness to him.[241]

Pictures aside, what strikes here is the parallel to the search for a Crazy Horse photograph, but with a major difference. Unlike the Santee "renegade" chief, the younger Oglala warrior eventually emerged as a charismatic hero with a powerful, quasi-religious aura that has spread all over the world to a degree perhaps unparalleled by any other of the equally popular Indian leaders. For many White and Indian Minnesotans and Iowans alike, Inkpaduta came to epitomize a "devilish" figure tarnished by the "bloody crimes" he committed. The opposite is true of Crazy Horse, despite his war record that is not at all inferior to that of the sanguine Wahpekute. It was Inkpaduta who, after joining the Northern Village in April 1876, "acclaimed Crazy Horse as a worthy heir – a 'swift hawk' against his people's enemies." Scouting alone in the Black Hills, Crazy Horse had recently "spied a small party leaving the French Creek diggings. Prospector Charles Metz, with his wife, their maid Rachel Briggs, and three other men, was returning to Cheyenne. As they passed through Red Canyon, Crazy Horse picked off the party one by one. The maid fled up the canyon, but her body was found with a single arrow through the back. In the lone warfare style of a Thunder Dreamer." Crazy Horse did not claim the Metz killings coups, but to Inkpaduta what mattered was that the Oglala war chief had struck the enemy, like a "swift hawk."[242] Inkpaduta's admiration would not tarnish by association, Crazy Horse's image. As the pages of history turned, Crazy Horse was recognized as a hero whose actions were nobly motivated and even, possibly, spiritually inspired, hence the label "mystic warrior" later coined by Sandoz and borrowed freely by those who followed. The "sanctification" of the legendary Oglala was also a reflection of his elusive nature and ultimate martyrdom.

Crazy Horse, Jesus, and John Doe

The religious overtones associated with the figure of Crazy Horse were reiterated three decades ago by Richard Moves Camp (b. 1956), a descendant of Horn Chips and a respected Oglala yuwipi wičaša, who drew a symbolic parallel between Tašunke Witko and no less than Jesus Christ. "Crazy Horse is like another famous leader who lived a few thousand years ago," stated Moves Camp in an interview. "His name was Jesus. At one time even his own disciples disowned him. But today, everyone seems to want to get on the bandwagon."[243] Crazy Horse's ultimate betrayal, violent death, and being a man without a "recorded" face is indeed reminiscent of similar aspects in the life of Jesus. The comparison should not, by any means, be offensive to either Christians or traditional Indians alike. Crazy Horse himself is said to have alluded to such similarity of destiny. While living among his Mnicojou relatives in his youth he might have seen Jesuit father Jean De Smet (1801-1873) during a visit at Fort Pierre. Or later in 1868 on the Powder River, when the Belgian missionary visited Sitting Bull on his peace commission trip. Crazy Horse listened to Sitting Bull speak well of the Belgian black robe seeking peace between the Indians and the Americans. Shortly after the killing of Crazy Horse, Mrs. Lucy W. Lee, wife of Lieut. Jesse M. Lee, sent a letter from Camp Sheridan to the Editor of the *Greencastle Star*, which read in part, "Crazy Horse was a very religious man [...] he was sincere and faithful in his belief [...]. Through Father De Smet and other missionaries who visited the Missouri River country, he had gained a very clear knowledge of Christ and His life upon this earth, and he had taken Him as an example and pattern for him to imitate. In his troubles with the whites, he likened them to Christ's persecutors."[244] Kinsley Bray gives such an assertion the benefit of the doubt: "Although uncredited to any primary source, and to be assessed critically given Mrs. Lee's role as Spotted Tail Agency schoolteacher, the statement squares nicely with the evidence for regular visits to Fort Pierre. De Smet's 1848 trip is the only one that fits the chronology. During the days after Crazy Horse's death Lucy's husband, Lt. Jesse M. Lee, extended much kindness to the mourning family – so this may be evidence of the highest caliber."[245]

Whether or not Crazy Horse was influenced by Father De Smet, the fact remains that some significant parallels have been drawn between the figure of Crazy Horse and that of Jesus. Like the Nazarene, the "mystic" Oglala was in his thirties, "barely thirty-three years" according to Eastman,[246] when he voluntarily walked into a trap. In both cases, locations were symbolic, with friends and foes coexisting somehow, under the authority of a foreign conqueror. Like Jesus, Crazy Horse, too, was first honored, then betrayed by some of his closest friends and handed over to his enemies by treachery, jealousy, and false witness. A shameful act still affecting the conscience of many Sioux tribesmen. "A disgrace, and a dirty shame; we killed our own man," later declared an elderly Lakota.[247] The mortal wound inflicted to Crazy Horse in northwestern Nebraska, though less inhumane than the cruel flogging and agonizing crucifixion of an equally innocent man on Jerusalem's Golgotha nearly two thousand years earlier, was perpetrated by a soldier of an invading army. Similarly, the death of these two men who had inspired a large following, was mourned only by their closest relatives and friends, fearful of reprisal. No one had dared step in to defend their leader, none rose against the executioners and their accomplices to avenge them.

Even the exact location of the two innocent victims' graves was long left to speculation. Perhaps, a secret guarded jealously by a chosen few. As for Crazy Horse, it is generally believed that his remains were hidden in a small cave in the Badlands, or buried near Wounded Knee Creek.

In early November 1877, as the Oglala, Brule, and the Northern Village under Low Dog crossed the Nebraska line and moved onto the Great Sioux Reservation, Crazy Horse's family secretly selected what they thought would be the final resting place for the body of their slain relative, tightly wrapped in its burial bundle. "Although the exact location of this second burial is obscured by enigma and misdirection," Bray wrote, "Horn Chips [who accompanied the small burial party] indicated it was in Pine Ridge north of the head of Wounded Knee Creek. [...] Worm and Horn Chips buried Crazy Horse in a rude coffin they had fashioned. Wood was scarce, and Crazy Horse's legs had to be unjointed at the knees." The body was eventually exhumed by Horn Chips in fall of 1878 and again secretly reinterred one final time in a cliff along White Horse Creek, a few miles from the Oglala community of Manderson.[248]

There is also another significant parallel between Jesus and Crazy Horse, as they seemingly left no positively recorded likeness. Was Jesus, though born a Jew, truly light-haired as Christian iconography generally portrays him? Probably not. Conversely, why was Crazy Horse light-haired, even curly-haired when young, if he was a full-blood Lakota? Hair color aside, in both cases history had in store a surprise. A funerary linen cloth allegedly impressed with the facial features and full-length battered body of Jesus surfaced in Europe during the Middle Ages and is today preserved in a church in Turin, Italy. The Sindone [Shroud] is accepted as authentic by Roman Catholic faithful, although the Church of Rome has not yet officially declared it so. Many scientists and skeptics regard it a hoax, but recent new findings have given renewed scholarly credence to its authenticity.[249]

More secular in nature is yet another ideal comparison that has been suggested between the persona of Crazy Horse as portrayed in Mari Sandoz's novel and the fictional character of John Doe. In his edited version of the autobiography of Red Cloud – Crazy Horse's nemesis at the Agency – R. Eli Paul suggested that "literary scholars may want to compare Sandoz's Crazy Horse to another popular hero of her day. Filmmaker Frank Capra's quiet, reserved, heroic character of John Doe shared a similar destiny to Crazy

Horse […]; each was felled by darker forces and treacherous, conspiratorial colleagues. Gary Cooper [who interpreted the character of John Doe] had Edward Arnold; Crazy Horse had Red Cloud."[250]

"Wolf" for the Bluecoats

Another major discrepancy between myth and reality is the fact alluded to earlier. Ten days after coming to the Agency, not even a year after defeating Gen. Crook at the Rosebud, and then Lieut. Col. Custer at the Little Horn, the "wily," fiercely anti-American, intransigent, determined, uncompromising Oglala war-chief Crazy Horse and fifteen of his headmen enlisted as U.S. Army scouts at Camp Robinson. Until recently, very few people, either Indian or White, knew or would have admitted that the very Crazy Horse, the mystic warrior of the Lakota, the unyielding "hostile," together with his best akičita had actually become "wolves for the Blue Soldiers", to borrow from Thomas Dunley's pioneering work.[251] As far as Crazy Horse and his men were concerned, their main reason for signing up as Indian scouts was to demonstrate right from the start their good intentions as they awaited the assignment of their own northern agency. And, at the same time, ensure that their families be safe, clothed, and fed, now regularly drawing their Army pay and government rations. Since hunting (and possibly raiding) as a way of life was to be given up, soldiering their own camps for the Bluecoats was the only thing left for them to do. True, they had fought long and hard for their land, the Sacred Hills, the buffalo, and they still had the illusory wish they could live off the chase once they were allowed to return north, but they had given their word for peace. Now they also subjected themselves to the authority of a White soldier chief.

Lakota men had practical needs and immediate concerns, with little time left for philosophical considerations on the incongruity of scouting for the Army. Formerly "hostile" Cheyenne and Arapaho had already done that. Other Lakota too were also wearing the buttoned blue coats and insignia of Indian scouts. Now Crazy Horse and his loyal warriors, having been forced under the terms of peace to give up their guns and, temporarily, also their horses, were able through enlistment to have their mounts and weapons back. Imperative above all, for a Lakota, was his horse-mobility. The breaks and stampedes of Crazy Horse's followers and sympathizers away from Red Cloud and Spotted Tail to Canada in the wake of Tašunke's death will prove that. But for now, enlistment with the rank of sergeant reasserted the camp chiefs' leadership and authority in a midst of a volatile situation. Given the circumstances, it was the necessary, right thing to do.

Red Cloud himself a few months earlier had accepted Lieut. Clark's offer that officially reinstated him to his Agency leadership position. Billy Garnett recalled that Lieut. Clark had directed him, as interpreter, to summon Red Cloud to the lieutenant's quarters where the White officer addressed the Oglala with these words: "You have been dismissed as chief by Gen. Crook who placed both agencies under Spotted Tail. […] Now, I want you to go out and bring Crazy Horse and all the people he claims in. […] We want to have some of these northern Indians with Crazy Horse go to Washington with the delegation to let them know that we are at peace; and Gen. Crook is a friend of mine, and if you do as I tell you I'll have him to reinstate you to your place; and I will make you First Sergeant; that is as high as I can place you, for it is the highest office in the Indian scout service; I have all the other chiefs on the agency enlisted; but I will recognize you as the highest officer among the chiefs; so that you can have control of your people. I will assist you with all the rations you think you will need." Needless to say, Red Cloud's reply was "How!"[252]

The younger Hunkpatila war chief was no exception. Tašunke Witko, too, was sworn in to serve "honestly and faithfully as a Scout for three months." Reflecting the status and respect the Military accorded him, Crazy Horse was given the rank of First Sergeant, a recognition Red Cloud, American Horse, Spotted Tail and other agency chiefs did not like. Crazy Horse was placed in charge of Company C, one of the five Indian scout companies under the command of Lieut. Clark at Red Cloud, and Capt. George M. Randall at Spotted Tail. Crazy Horse was joined by Northern Oglala wakičunze Little Big Man, Big Road, Iron Crow, and his [step-]uncle Little Hawk, who were enlisted as Sergeants. Others who raised the right

THE UNITED STATES OF AMERICA.

OATH OF ENLISTMENT AND ALLEGIANCE.

STATE OF *Wyoming* } *ss:*

TOWN OF _____

I, *Crazy Horse*, born in _____, in the State of *Wyoming*, and by occupation a *Scout*, Do HEREBY ACKNOWLEDGE to have voluntarily enlisted this *12* day of *May* ~~three months~~ 187*7*, as a ~~Soldier~~ *Scout* in the Army of the United States of America, for the period of ~~FIVE YEARS~~, unless sooner discharged by proper authority: And do also agree to accept from the United States such bounty, pay, rations, and clothing as are, or may be established by law. And I do solemnly swear, that I am _____ years and *Scout Three* months of age, and know of no impediment to my serving honestly and faithfully as a ~~Soldier~~ for ~~five years~~ *months* under this enlistment contract with the United States. And I, *Crazy Horse* do also solemnly swear, that I will bear true faith and allegiance to the **United States of America**, and that I will serve them honestly and faithfully against all their enemies or opposers whomsoever; and that I will observe and obey the orders of the President of the United States, and the orders of the officers appointed over me, according to the Rules and Articles of War.

Crazy × Horse (L.S.)

Subscribed and duly sworn to before me, this *12* day of *May* A.D. 187*7*.

W. Clark
1st Lieut 2nd Cavalry
Recruiting Officer.

I CERTIFY, ON HONOR, That I have carefully examined the above-named recruit, agreeably to the General Regulations of the Army, and that, in my opinion, he is free from all bodily defects and mental infirmity, which would in any way, disqualify him from performing the duties of a soldier.

W. Clark
1st Lieut 3rd Cavalry
Examining Officer.

I CERTIFY, ON HONOR, That I have minutely inspected the above-named recruit, _____, previously to his enlistment, and that he was entirely sober when enlisted; that, to the best of my judgment and belief, he is of lawful age; and that I have accepted and enlisted him into the service of the United States under this contract of enlistment as duly qualified to perform the duties of an able-bodied soldier, and, in doing so, have strictly observed the Regulations which govern the Recruiting Service. This soldier has *Black* eyes, *Black* hair, *Copper* complexion, is _____ inches high.

W. Clark (L.S.)
1st Lieut 2nd Cavalry
Recruiting Officer, United States Army.

[A. G. O. No. 73.]

Crazy Horse's Oath of Enlistment and Allegiance as
a U.S. Army Scout, May 12, 1877.

hand were Hunkpatila elder Iron Crow along with other nine Northern Oglala. Also Tašunke's own kola He Dog, the elder Iron Hawk, Horned Horse who had stopped grieving for the death of his son the previous summer at Greasy Grass, and several others signed up. The historic episode was reported in *The Cheyenne Daily Leader* on May 16, 1877, and read in part: "Red Cloud [Agency], May 15. Lieut. Clark, of Gen. Crook's staff, has enlisted Crazy Horse and fifteen of his head men. This was done to better control the Indians at the Agency. A remarkable scene occurred when the red soldiers were sworn into Uncle Sam's service. They swore with uplifted hands [...] Three of the leading chiefs have been advanced to the grade of [First] Sergeants: Spotted Tail, Red Cloud and Crazy Horse. The latter said at the last council before his enlistment, that he wanted to "get along straight and well" at the Agency, and "that he would like a hundred of his best men enlisted."[253]

Within the perpetuation of distorted myths, such an important step taken by Crazy Horse was barely touched upon by his early biographers. Western historian Steven Ambrose, whose *Crazy Horse and Custer* was long regarded a classic, actually hinted with an ambiguous language that the Oglala chief did not enlist: "Lieutenant Clark tried to get Crazy Horse to join up as an Indian scout, but Crazy Horse refused."[254]

Ambrose must have been the source of Russell Freedman's assertion that "Crazy Horse was under great pressure to lead the scouts, but he objected [and] when Clark persisted, Crazy Horse threatened to take his people and head north."[255] Here, admittedly, we are dealing with two different issues: signing up as scouts at Camp Robinson, and going on the war-path for the Americans in pursuit of the Nez Perce. Sandoz accepted the first as fact, without dating it, but inserting a misleading "finally" in her sentence as if the episode had occurred well after the surrender and after considerable pressure from the military: "As scouts they would get a horse and a Sharps carbine each, [...]. So Crazy Horse and twenty-five of his followers finally joined."[256] Billy Garnett told Eli S. Ricker that he "kicked to Clark against making any of C. Horse's band scouts, and against making C. Horse a scout and giving him and them arms so soon after they had submitted.

The scouts were armed with Sharp's carbines (for horseback use) and the six-shooting revolvers such as used in the army."[257] Crazy Horse re-enlisted on July 1, 1877, as First Sergeant of Company C Indian Scouts. Sergeants included: Big Road, also known as Wide Trail; Little Hawk, known earlier as Long Face; Jumping Shield; and Little Big Man. Corporals were Iron Hawk, He Dog, Four Crows, and No Water.

Confusion and Betrayal

It was Lieut. William "Philo" Clark (1845-1884) who eventually betrayed his solemn hand shake with Crazy Horse. A coetaneous of the war chief, Clark was a clever officer, a reliable subordinate in the military hierarchy, and a firm intermediary with the Indians. To his credit, Lieut. Clark had a reputation "of feeling and thinking like the Indians themselves." His practical need and intellectual interest later led him to author a pioneering study, *Indian Sign Language,* published posthumously in 1885.[258] From his "intelligence office" at Camp Robinson, Clark ran a network of Indian informers and spies, commanded the Indian scouts, and shrewdly exploited the tension that soon brewed at Red Cloud Agency. He, too, was ultimately partly responsible for the death of Crazy Horse.

Friswold drew a concise but insightful biographical and psychological sketch of the New York-born Second Lieutenant who served as aide-de camp to Gen. Philip Sheridan and George Crook. "Clark," wrote Friswold, "proved to be one of the ablest of the young officers coming along after the Civil War, commanded troops in the field, had an excellent record as a staff-officer and more than fulfilled the expectations of his superiors." This included his handling of the Northern Indians and their charismatic war chief. "When Crazy Horse did come in on May 7th," Friswold concluded, "there was even more friction and backbiting, and you may be sure that Clark did his share to keep it going and building up. A rumor here, an innuendo there, one chief apparently being favored over another, all these things kept the Indians divided just at a time when even a united front would not have been too effective in dealing with the whites. The old principle of 'Divide and Conquer' was again proved effective."[259]

In what Bray called a life characterized by enigma about the future and misunderstanding due to cultural and language barriers, plus a good dose of intra-tribal jealousy, the request that Crazy Horse, Touch the Clouds, and the other Northern chiefs should again "put blood on their faces" and go after the Nez Perce, showed that the Americans double-talked. In a dramatic meeting, held the end of August, present on one side Lieut. Clark flanked by interpreter Frank Grouard, and Three Bears representing the agency Oglala, on the other Crazy Horse, Touch the Clouds, High Bear, and other head warriors, the tall Mnicojou spoke on behalf of the Northern Indians and of Crazy Horse, denouncing the soldiers' hypocrisy. "We washed the blood from our faces," Touch the Clouds began, "and came in and surrendered and wanted peace." He, Crazy Horse, and the other Northern chiefs had done what they had been asked; honoring their side of the agreement. They had been ordered to give up their guns, and they did. They had been asked to enlist as scouts to keep order and peace in the camps, and they did. They had been told they could not hunt the buffalo, and they didn't. Using metaphors to emphasize the point, Touch the Clouds remarked that, as the Soldiers would do with a horse, they had turned the heads of the Northern Indians towards Washington. Now, the Great father, the "Gray Fox" (General Crook), and "White Hat" had changed their mind. "You ask us to put blood on our faces, but I do not want this," he continued, "neither does Crazy Horse."

After Touch the Clouds sat down, Crazy Horse stood up, and using the same "blood" metaphor reiterated what his Mnicojou relative had just said: "The big chief, Gen. Crook, sent out word to us that if we would come to the Agency we would be well treated, and should live in peace and quiet. We believed him, and we came in with our hearts good to every one; and now we are asked to put blood upon our faces and go on the warpath, almost in the same breath with the request to go on a mission of peace to Washington."[260] Crazy Horse had now sad proof that the White chiefs, those who held his destiny in their hands, spoke with a forked tongue. All the assurances, especially those of a separate agency in the north, were lies. Innuendos, rumors, wrong assumptions, flat-out lies, made-up stories, bad translations, envy, jealousy, women and revenge, tribal politics and power struggles, even strictly personal dislikes, together created very "bad winds" at Red Cloud Agency.

Crazy Horse sought refuge and support at Spotted Tail, but there, too, he was persona non grata, and was taken back to Red Cloud. At Camp Robinson, his many enemies prevailed over his few loyal friends and on September 5, 1877, *Tašunke Witko Ktepi*, they killed Crazy Horse, as reported in some winter counts. Bayoneted by a soldier guard who had the tip of his blade on the chief's back to prod him along. Bayoneted "on purpose," according to a testimony rendered to Mrs. Richard Stirk by the sister of Tašunke Witko's wife.[261] Even on his very death bed, the sincerity and goodness of Crazy Horse's heart, his desire for peace, showed. The agonizing Lakota addressed Lieut. Jesse Lee, with the following words rendered in translation, again, by Louis Bordeaux: "I don't blame any white man; but I blame the Indians."[262]

For years, Lakota old timers spoke softly about those tragic days, as much of the blame fell upon some of their most popular leaders. He Dog declared the whole affair was "due to the resentment and jealousy on the part of the chiefs and headmen of the other tribes."[263] Tassels in the tragic mosaic of betrayal and death were also the false rumors spread by agency scout Woman Dress (ca. 1846-1921) who accused Crazy Horse of plotting to kill Gen. Crook. "The origin of the Crook murder story," wrote Bray, "remains a tantalizing clue in the intrigue against Crazy Horse. [...] Woman Dress belonged to Red Cloud's Bad Face band, was the chief's first cousin, and 'always stayed with Red Cloud,' according to Red Feather."[264] Only a few years younger than Crazy Horse, he and his siblings Charging Bear, Bear Foot, and No Neck, all sons of the late Chief Smoke, were part, to varying degree, of an elaborate network of spies set up by Lieut. Clark, to whom they all reported. The anti-Crazy Horse intelligence apparently included also brothers Little Wolf and Lone Bear, cousins of Woman Dress. The two had been with Crazy Horse at the Little Bighorn and surrendered with him. And like him had enlisted as scouts. Although they and others later denied circulating rumors against Crazy Horse, finger pointing went full circle, falling back on Woman Dress. "This is probably simplistic scape-goating," according to Bray, as all those mentioned above, plus the ever present and ambiguous Frank Grouard (De Barthe notwithstanding) were Clark's informers, all reporting on Crazy Horse.[265]

What happened on the Camp Robinson grounds represents one of the great tragedies in Lakota history, precisely because of the complicity of many fellow tribesmen. Turning Bear, a Brule warrior who signed up as scout but was still sympathetic to Crazy Horse, had escorted the Oglala war chief from Spotted Tail Agency back to Camp Robinson that fateful September day and was present when Crazy Horse attempted to avoid arrest and was bayoneted. Interviewed by William Bordeaux, Turning Bear stated that the mortally wounded chief whispered to him these rather tell-ing words: "I hold no ill will against any of them although some whom I believed to be my friends have betrayed me."[266] Crazy Horse may or may not have been aware of Woman Dress and the others, but he sure felt betrayed by Little Big Man. "This Indian," wrote later Maj. (then Lieut.) Henry R. Lemly, eyewitness to the killing, "was known to the officers as a paid spy in the employ of the Agency."[267]

Less than a month later, on September 29, 1877, Little Big Man was awarded an unusual silver medal for so-called "gallant services rendered to the Whites at the death of Crazy Horse."[268] Baptiste Pourier, who was in Lieut. Clark's quarters when Crazy Horse was wounded, heard the commo-tion in front of the guardhouse, especially the cries of Little Big Man. Thirty years after the tragic event, Pourier recalled that, for always portray-ing himself as the tough guy, Little Big Man surely made a very big deal of the small cuts the received in the scuffle: "Little Big Man seized him, but Crazy Horse cut him across the base of the forefinger – a slight wound only – but Little Big Man howled and cried and acted the baby as though he was half killed."[269]

Luther P. Bradley, who had replaced Ranald Mackenzie as Commanding Officer of the Black Hills District at Camp Robinson with the rank of Lieut.

Col., 9th Infantry, objectively reported Little Big Man's own defense: "Crazy Horse suddenly drew two knives, and with one in each hand started to run amuck among the officers and soldiers. Little Big Man [...] jumped upon Crazy Horse's back and seized his arms and elbows, receiving two slight cuts in the wrists [...]. Here, there is a discrepancy. Some say that the death wound of Crazy Horse was given by the sentinel at the door of the guardhouse, who prodded him in the abdomen with his bayonet in return for the trust with a knife made by Crazy Horse. Others affirm that Little Big Man, while holding down Crazy Horse's hands deflected the latter's own poniard and inflicted the gash which resulted in [the chief's] death. Billy Hunter, whose statement was written out for me by Lieutenant George A. Dodd, Third Cavalry, is one of the strongest witnesses on the first side, but Little Big Man himself assured me at the Sun Dance in 1881 that he had unintentionally killed Crazy Horse with the latter's own weapon, which was shaped at the end like a bayonet (stiletto), and made the very same kind of a wound. [...] Little Big Man further assured me that at first it was thought best to let the idea prevail that a soldier had done the killing, and thus reduce the probability of any one of the dead man's relatives revenging his taking off after the manner of the aborigines. [...] I give both stories, although I incline strongly to believe Little Big Man."[270]

Even in death, Crazy Horse remained enigmatic. Bray concluded that "although early controversy existed over whether Crazy Horse was killed by one of the guards or by his own knives, deflected in the struggle with Little Big Man, the weight of evidence has always favored the former. [...] Although not definitive, the balance of evidence suggests that Crazy Horse's killer was Private William Gentles, Company F, Fourteenth Infantry."[271] Not so, according to Ephriam Dickson, who found inconsistencies in Gentles's military record specifically pertaining to his service at Camp Robinson that tragic day in September.[272]

Mrs. Lucy W. Lee was the wife of Lieut. Jesse M. Lee, who will later serve as Recorder for the Reno Court of Inquiry convened in Chicago in January, 1879. Despite the prejudices of the time, both husband and wife shared good sentiments towards the Indians. In a long letter from Camp

Sheridan to the editor of the Greencastle, Indiana, *Star*, on September 18, 1877, Mrs. Lee wrote, "My next letter to your newsy newspaper was to have been a description of the Indian mode of burial; but I will defer that, and give you an account of the week of excitement we have just passed through, and which I hope will be the last of the kind while I remain here." After recounting, with patronizing but caring tones the last events that lead to the killing of Crazy Horse, and the concerned role played by her husband, she spoke sympathetically of the late chief: "Thus ended the career of Crazy Horse, one of the bravest of Indians. No doubt he was a very bad man, and had done some wicked things, but there is something to say in his defense: He felt that he and his people had been most cruelly dealt with by the whites, who were taking all their country from them without giving them any equivalent, and he was trying to help his people out of this bondage. Finally, he, a 'wild Indian of the north,' was induced, by offers of complete pardon and safety for himself and his followers, to come in to an agency and live a life that was new and strange to him, and many promises of good treatment and privileges were made to him. After his many years of wild roaming life, it seemed almost as though he was deprived of his liberty. Then, instead of leaving him in peace and quiet, to get used to his new mode of life, he was talked to, morning, noon and night, until his mind was in a whirl of confusion, which prevented his sleeping, as he sent word to Spotted Tail 'for twenty seven nights he had neither rest nor sleep.'"[273]

"Fear" as Savagism

The violent passing of Crazy Horse and the apparent lack of a photograph of him reinforced many myths and legends, including the "fear" story originally reported by McGillycuddy. Actually, in 1926 Billy Garnett had written to the doctor that, "Crazy Horse never had a picture taken that I know of, and if there was one taken, some one sneaked up and took it, for he never would consent to be photographed." As Garnett explained, the reason why Crazy Horse refused to pose publicly in front of a camera had nothing to do with "fear," nor the lack of a photographer nearby, but simply because in those days Indian chiefs and headmen had their photo taken as a sign of prestige and status, something Crazy Horse shied away from as "[he] was a very modest man, considering his fighting ability, and bravery."[274] Which suggests that an indoor setting, the faster process of the tintype, and the request coming from a relative or friend, may have won his reluctance.

Trimble himself, while accepting as valid the unproven supposition – on the authority of Tom Buecker – that "Crazy Horse was never in the vicinity of a photographer," admitted that this latter reason seemed to him more logical than the "myth" created by McGillycuddy. "Although I am not an expert on Lakota religion and culture," Trimble continued, "I have never read or heard from a credible source of any Lakota taboo against having one's image captured by photography; certainly not fear of death. Great Sioux leaders like Sitting Bull, and even several holy men of the time, willingly posed for photographs. Red Cloud," he under-scored, "is second only to Lincoln in having his portrait done by photog-raphy." Trimble's reasoning was right on target, questioning the validity and motives of McGillycuddy's categorical assertion so often quoted as "proof." Although he did not exclude a priori the possibility of a photo-graph, he too fell in the a-temporal "mortal enemy" stereotype of the war chief, without considering the events that followed Crazy Horse's coming to Camp Robinson. Trimble attributed the refusal not to supernatural fears but rather simply, in his view, to the chief's dislike of the White man: "If Crazy Horse did refuse to have his picture taken, it would be more likely that he wanted to do nothing to satisfy the curiosity of whites, whom he considered his mortal enemies, or that he might indicate participation in an alien culture he despised."

While it is certainly true that Tašunke Witko despised the Americans for their intrusion and devastating impact on the Lakota world, some-what naively he believed Gen. Crook's vague assurances of long-lasting peace. Little did he know that by 1877, a separate northern agency ran contrary to the government plan to move the Red Cloud and Spotted Tail agencies from Nebraska to the Missouri River "where supplies could be more economically delivered by river boat."[275] Still, while Crazy Horse waited in vain for the fulfillment of a broken promise, he did his best to get along with military officers and White civilians, including the local photographer(s). This is a rebuke to both hostility theorists and the advocates of a lack of interaction with "shadow catchers." In the end, the very Billy Garnett, having heard of, perhaps having seen too, the Crazy Horse tintype for the first time after the death of Little Bat, or of his wife, conceded, according to Eleanor Hinman, that both he and McGillycuddy were wrong that there was no picture of Crazy Horse.

Bruce Brown, a retired investigative reporter, inspired by a dream worked on a digital pastel portrait of the great chief. "Trying to portray Crazy Horse," he wrote in his fictionalized "conversations" with Tašunke Witko, "is a difficult proposition since he is the only great figure in American history who never allowed his soul to be captured, as the Sioux conceived it, meaning he never allowed his visage to be captured in life, either by photograph or artist's portrait."[276] While the popular notion of Indian "fear" of the camera is likely based on occasional episodes and tribal differences, the overall stereotype attributed to all Indians, and Crazy Horse in particular, is greatly exaggerated. Tom Buecker correctly recognized that although [in the beginning] some Indians resisted being photographed, many others had no qualms."[277] Attributing "fear" of a technological innovation such as the camera, was part of the colonizing and patronizing discourse that deprived the American Indian of his own intelligence, humanity, and sensitivity. It was part of the broader characterization of Indian inferiority.

Historian Robert F. Berkhofer referred to that persistent White assumption that defined Indian character by presumed "deficiency" associated with "savagery." This included also lack of "civilized" emotions that rendered Indians persistently serious, stern, inexpressive, and "morose." When "fear" of the camera was overcome, that lack of expression was reflected in the photographs. Obviously, the imperturbability of official Indian portraits simply mirrored the formality of the occasion, the novelty of the camera, and the interaction with a stranger and his machine. The same applied to period photographic portraits of White and Black Americans. The technology of the time required longer times, it was necessary to remain still, and a serious facial expression was then the norm; a behavioral rule that cut across cultural, socioeconomic, and racial boundaries. There were, of course, exceptions. In her book on Gertrude Käsebier's portraits of Sioux performers in Cody's *Wild West* show, Michelle Delaney expressed surprise at two photographs of Joe Black Fox as he "seems quite at ease with Käsebier and being in front of a camera." Delaney continued, "Black Fox almost smiles, grinning for the portraits." Reflecting the entrenched and erroneous stereotype of the "stolen soul" theme, Delaney expected otherwise: "This is generally uncharacteristic for Native Americans – in 1898 many still believed in the potential for the lens to steal their soul." To Delaney's surprise, "Black Fox poses dutifully in his feather headdress and then playfully with cigarette in hand, relaxed, wrapped in a blanket [etc.]."[278] And why shouldn't he, we may ask?

Alleged Painted Portraits

The "fear factor" and "bribery" tales were just that. What about Crazy Horse sitting for an artistic sketch or painted portrait? Here, too, "stories" claimed to be "history" did not pass our scrutiny. This was the case of Henry H. Cross (1837-1918), a New York-born artist and contemporary of Crazy Horse.

Adventurous and free-spirited, Cross studied art in Paris at a young age, and upon his return to the States traveled west. Following the 1862 Uprising in Minnesota, he took portraits of the Dakota Sioux who were sentenced to death by hanging at Mankato (the lowest point in Abraham Lincoln's otherwise meritorious presidency).[279] Cross later joined P.T. Barnum's circus, and visited frontier military posts, painting local scenery and portraits of soldiers, Indians, and settlers. Including a painting titled *Camp of Sitting Bull in the Big Horn Mountains 1873*, purportedly from life, even though the tipis in the background are disproportionally big.[280] Cross also painted an alleged, utterly unrealistic "portrait" of Crazy Horse. The colorful artwork, now in the Chicago History Museum, shows a stocky, muscular, broad-chested warrior wearing a big eagle-feather war bonnet (!), a single large shell (abalone?) necklace, a buffalo-skin skirt (!), and holding a lance and a shield. That the painting was intended to portray Crazy Horse is shown by the prominent scar visible on the Indian's face. Cross's *Crazy Horse* is nothing but an unhappy idealized caricature attempt at recreating the likeness of the famous war chief. Even more puzzling is the handwritten presentation note on the right hand corner of the painting itself that reads, "Tosunke [sic] Witko (Crazy Horse) Ogalala Sioux Painted from Life at Wood Mountain N.W. Territory, 1876. HH Cross. Presented to My Friend R.R. Ricketts."[281]

This fantasized portrait might have later inspired a sketch of Crazy Horse by Eugene H. Bischoff for a popular, early 1950s, American Indian "read and color" booklet. Wearing a magnificent war bonnet, Bischoff's *Crazy Horse* has a scarf tied around his neck and holds a pipe in his right hand. No scar is seen on the face otherwise defined by handsome features, piercing eyes, and high cheekbones.[282]

Another Crazy Horse portrait-related saga appeared some decades ago from the incautious pen of the late Evan S. Connell. In his award winning *Son of the Morning Star* (a likely spurious name),[283] the famous author made reference to an alleged encounter between a young Western artist and the Lakota war chief. Inspired by Edgar Paxson's world famous six-by-ten-foot oil panorama titled *Custer's Last Stand*, Connell wrote that "Paxson was adept at sign language, as well as being able to speak several Indian dialects, and a number of surviving warriors led him around the famous field. Gall, Two Moon, Hump, Crow King, White Bull, and Crazy Horse, all posed for him, according to his grandson." Recognizing the uniqueness of Paxson's accomplishment as a painter, Connell resurrected the old saga of Crazy Horse's stubborn opposition to photography. "That Crazy Horse should pose for a picture is surprising," he argued, "considering his obstinate refusal to be photographed, though there is a difference."[284]

Our reading of the historical and biographical documentation pertaining to Paxson revealed otherwise. In fairness to E.S. Paxson's grandson, William Edgar Paxson, it was Connell himself who stretched his imagination. This is what William Paxson wrote in the lavishly illustrated biography of his grandfather: "Edgar set out overland in early 1877. He soon viewed the rolling hills and prairies surrounding the Little Bighorn for the first time. In the years to come he would return several times, going over the battlefield with Indian participants and soldiers who were close to the tragedy. [...] He noted, in his journals and letters, his trips in 1877, '82, '84 and '96. The Sioux chief Gall and the Cheyenne Two Moon [...] held Edgar in high regard and gave him many details of the actual fighting [...] Edgar interviewed other Indian participants [...] and made sketches of them at the same time."[285]

Edgar Samuel Paxson (1852-1919) learned the trade of painting carriages and signs in New York State. Driven by the lure of the West, "He arrived in Montana in 1877 where he worked for a stagecoach company, as a guide, and other frontier jobs; the following year he moved to Deer Lodge where he painted signs and scenery for theatrical backdrops."[286] There is no mention of Crazy Horse "sitting" for E.S. Paxson, nor Paxson visiting Camp Robinson and Red Cloud Agency in 1877. Obviously, Crazy Horse could not have sat for a portrait in '82, or thereafter. The incongruity of Connell's allegation stands out. Paxson was never in the presence of Crazy Horse, knew very little of him and certainly had no available visual representation of the Oglala chief. Paxson's lack of knowledge, influenced by Indian stereotypes and popular perceptions of what the late formidable warrior Crazy Horse "should" have looked like, was reflected in that same famous scene that Connell praised as the artist's "most thoroughly researched" giant *Last Stand*.

The large oil painting, finished in 1899, purportedly reproduces chief Crazy Horse (on the right side of the painting) charging on horseback, wearing a long sleeve red shirt, breastplate, long-tail war bonnet, holding a Winchester in one hand and a three-blade war club in the other.[287] We said earlier that the club was cherished by Sioux head warriors as a symbol of their status and prowess in battle. Perhaps Paxson saw the famous D.S. Mitchell (1877) photograph of Crazy Horse's kola He Dog holding a similar weapon. Or perhaps Paxson saw a photograph by L.A. Huffman (1880) of Spotted Eagle, who had fought alongside Crazy Horse at the Little Bighorn. The Sans Arc head warrior is shown holding a gunstock-style war club with its three prominent knife blades and long handle decorated with brass tacks.

Compared with eyewitness accounts of Crazy Horse's much simpler, Spartan-like, nearly naked, body-painted, single-feathered (albeit here wrongly tied) battle attire, (rendered by Oglala artist Eagle Lance, better known as Amos Bad Heart (Buffalo) Bull (1869-1913)[288] Paxson's *Crazy Horse* looks highly romanticized and conjectural, largely the fruit of his own artistic imagination, with the exception that Paxson wanted to identify his subject as Crazy Horse by tracing a big visible scar on the Indian's left cheek. As for later idealized representations of the great Lakota patriot, Mari Sandoz's first edition of *Crazy Horse* has on the front cover the embossed drawing of a Plains Indian on horseback wearing a war bonnet, very unlike the protagonist of her book.

We do not know whether a contemporary drawing depicting Crazy Horse from life exists somewhere, perhaps the work of an artistically gifted Camp Robinson soldier or officer, or a Red Cloud Agency employee. Or even sketched by one of the visiting newspaper correspondents who made it to that corner of Nebraska during the summer of 1877. Such a portrait has yet to be located. In a 1950s letter to Will G. Robinson, Col. W.A. Graham, author of the classic *The Custer Myth*, had it that, "In a conversation with Mrs. R.S. McLaughlin (daughter-in-law of the Major [James McLaughlin, Indian Agent at Standing Rock]), she told of loaning a portrait of Crazy Horse to Congressman [Usher L.] Burdick, and was unable to get it back." Painted portrait or photo we do not know, but Robinson was "inclined to mistrust her judgment."[289] Still, with regard to a possible, painted or sketched portrait of Crazy Horse from life, Michael Samuel once again contradicted popular belief when he wrote, "There was a portrait 'not a photo' made of him on a stump just outside his lodge on Beaver Creek, just east of Camp Robinson in 1877 not long before his death. His hair was down on one side, and tied up on the other. It was done so in order to hide the medicine stone tied in his hair just behind his left ear. He was also wearing a coat made from a pendelton [sic] blanket made by his newest wife, Nellie Larabie."[290]

Michael Samuel does not identify the author and whereabouts of this alleged portrait, but the reference to the Pendleton blanket-capote suggests he may be referring to the same alleged sketch of Crazy Horse already mentioned by Tom Buecker[291] and Donovin Sprague.[292] Both scholars clarified the misidentification. The sketch is based, again, on the noted stereoscopic photograph of Brule warrior Crazy in the Lodge, taken by Stanley J. Morrow in 1876.

Crazy in the Lodge, by Stanley J. Morrow, 1876.

Although, as noted, Morrow correctly identified his subject as "Crazy-in-the-Lodge, head warrior under Spotted Tail", the same image was later reproduced and incorrectly labeled "Crazy Horse."[293] Expanding on what Buecker had written, Sprague explained that "in 1996 a sketch of this photograph was published in [...] *Indian Country Today* as the only sketch of Crazy Horse. Below the sketch contained the information that the French artist Frank Taurillo sketched it in 1872. The sketch was donated to Tim Giago, then editor of *Indian Country Today*, by Ed Putnam of Gilroy,

California. Giago claimed to have the only sketch of Crazy Horse. Clearly, the artist had made a sketch of the Crazy in the Lodge photo, adding the name of Crazy Horse to it."[294] Likely inspired by the 1876 Morrow photograph was also a sketch of Crazy Horse made in 1934 by a Mormon missionary and authenticated by Julia Clown. [295] The features in the sketch (in the possession of The Clown Family) are softer and more pleasant than those in the Morrow photo, showing a vague resemblance to the Indian in the tintype. [296]

Morrow's photo of Crazy in the Lodge was later rendered as artwork by Hodges Soileau who contributed to the confusion by labeling it *Crazy Horse* in the 12-stamp series *Great American Indian Chiefs*, issued by the Marshall Islands, 1999.[297]

Crazy Horse, sketch by a Mormon missionary, 1934, with vague resemblance to the tintype Indian.

"Crazy Horse", by H. Soileau, is actually Crazy in the Lodge; 60c stamp, Marshall Islands, 1999.

Names

So much has been written, alleged, flatly denied, purportedly authenticated, attributed to, and even stated on behalf of Crazy Horse that it is difficult to separate fact from fiction, and all that falls in between. As we said in the beginning, we can only give voice to, and evaluate, all sides with an open mind and an open heart, in the hope that truth will eventually prevail, as it usually does. An open mind, however, implies also a critical eye, cognizant that too much unwelcome "dust" has been stirred up around the heroic figure of Crazy Horse. There is even approximation when it comes to well-established and undisputed historical facts.

Relating the circumstances of Crazy Horse's surrender, Vine Deloria, Jr., renown Sioux scholar and acclaimed American Indian intellectual, wrote in his Introduction to the new reprint edition of Sandoz's classic biography that, "So finally in May [...] Crazy Horse led his people to the Pine Ridge Agency."[298] It is well known that Crazy Horse surrendered and was killed at Camp Robinson, today a national historic landmark, in northwestern Nebraska, and not at Pine Ridge, South Dakota, where the Red Cloud and his Oglala relocated in 1878. Those interested in the life of Crazy Horse also know that a small pyramid-like stone monument, similar to the one erected at Fort Sill, Oklahoma, in memory of Geronimo, was dedicated at Fort Robinson on September 5, 1934, with a large Indian participation that included descendants of the Lakota hero.[299] In fairness to Deloria, perhaps he confused the Pine Ridge crest overlooking Camp Robinson and nearby Red Cloud Agency with the one later to be officially named Pine Ridge Agency across the territorial/state line.

Speaking of pines, we may reconsider what Wikipedia says of Crazy Horse's alleged Lakota birth name Čaóha, (Čháŋ Óhaŋ), "Among Wood/ Trees," also rendered "In the Wilderness." There seems to be something curiously odd in this "wilderness" attribute. When did the Lakota make theirs the Euro-American dichotomy, rooted in ancient Greek philosophy, juxtaposing the "civilized," advanced world to the "natural," primitive wilderness? Did the Lakota living in the buffalo days really refer to the trees that darken the HeSapa, as "wilderness"? Luther Standing Bear (1863-1936), son of the homonymous mixed-blood Brule maternal cousin of Crazy Horse, provided an answer: "For the Lakota there was no wilderness … nature was not dangerous but hospitable, not forbidding but friendly."[300] Early Lakota testimonies do not mention Čaóha / Čháŋ Óhaŋ, or other relating to "trees" and "wilderness" among the childhood, youth or early adulthood names of Crazy Horse. They do list what translates into English as Curly Hair, Light or Yellow Fuzzy Hair, Buys a Bad Woman, Crushes Man, Horse Partly Showing, Horse Stands in Sight, and other renditions of these and similar names in Lakota.[301] In his personal story narrated to Stanley Vestal, for example, chief White Bull (One Bull's elder brother) recalled the name "Breaks-the-Head" by which Crazy Horse was also known among the Mnicojou.[302] Calling again into account the issue of translation, and given that the Lakota equivalent was apparently not recorded, the name mentioned by White Bull could well be another rendering of "Crushes Man." Or, yet an altogether different name. Both evidently referring to some memorable war deed by Crazy Horse. As for Čháŋ Óhaŋ, the Crazy Horse family tradition pointed to the general location of his birth, the wooded Black Hills, hence the toponym recorded as one of his early names.

Regarding to more famous patronymic in Lakota, Feraca rendered it Tashunke Witko and commented that, like other details of the chief's life, "The origin of the name Crazy Horse […] is shrouded in legend. Many authorities maintain that the name was bestowed at birth when a wild horse came charging through the encampment. However," continued Feraca, "I have met Sioux Indians who present other versions. One of the most common is that the name is connected with the chief's practice of rubbing his horse with sacred stones before setting out to do battle, thus giving the mount extraordinary courage and making it impervious to bullets and arrows."[303] Feraca added that he was told by yet another aged, full-blood Sioux that the family name "Crazy Horse" had a very ancient origin, dating back to when the Lakota first acquired horses. According to oral tradition, one such šunkawakan, the mysterious large dog-like animal, had been captured by the great-grandfather of the war chief's own father. The latter too, had carried that ancient family name before passing it on to his son. The eccentric animal, a fired mustang, was roped shortly before the Lakota conquered the Black Hills from the Kiowa and the Cheyenne. It was a very fine-looking horse but, unlike other horses in the still small family herd who responded well to voice and lariat, the beautiful mustang remained independent, exhibiting a bizarre, witko, that is "crazy" behavior. The People named that strange-behaving animal's first owner with the attribute of his horse, Tašunke Witko, His Horse Is Crazy.

Other Indians who carried that same name, like Horn Chips' lesser known brother, and Greasing Hand who married Nellie Larabee after the Oglala war chief 's death, were not blood kin, did not belong to the direct line of descent of the true Crazy Horses. Horn Chips, interviewed by Judge Ricker in 1907, gave his own explanation for the name Crazy Horse: "He was born with light hair and was called by the Indians the light-haired boy. [...] His grandfather Makes the Song, had dream that Crazy Horse would be called Crazy Horse. When Crazy Horse was just 21 years old the Oglala had a fight with the Crows and Rees, and others whose language they could not understand and in this fight he counted his coup in this manner: A Shoshone lay dead on the field in a position that none could approach to strike the body. Crazy Horse's horse became unmanageable and carried his rider wildly about and up within reach of the Shoshone body and Crazy Horse struck and counted coo [sic], and from the crazy conduct of the horse the rider was dubbed Crazy Horse."[304] So, even on the matter of Crazy Horse's name, testimonies are either contradictory or, as in the case of Chips, somewhat deficient. Horn Chips explained the circumstances of the name change, but not the origin itself of the famed name, except referring to Makes the Song's dream.

Nothing of what we have discussed so far is by any means intended as a patronizing criticism of the opinions of deserving, long-gone photographers, artists, and historians. Much less a disrespectful slight to the memory of the late Vine Deloria, Jr., who contributed so much to the American Indian intellectual renaissance, and much more. We all make mistakes, in good faith. We only wanted to underscore how much doubt, confusion, uncertainty, approximation, and outright invented "history" surrounds the deserving name and memory of Tašunke Witko. It is indeed difficult to keep Crazy Horse in focus, to use a photographic analogy. And while some basic facts can be objectively revisited and re-evaluated, other issues including the long-standing debate over the existence of a photographic portrait, are more complex to unravel and have often been obscured by misconceptions, myths, tales, even lies.

Marshall has it right, only with an open mind and a sincere heart we may search for the true nature of Crazy Horse's remarkable persona and the possibility that, in the end, he too might have agreed to have his picture taken, provided a "shadow catcher" was in the area. Again, here too, the long-standing tale of Crazy Horse "never" being in the vicinity of a photographer has been disproved by historical evidence.

"Shadow Catchers" in the Midst

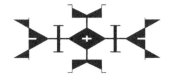

Like the pieces of a tragic puzzle, the antecedents to Crazy Horse's surrender and killing at Camp Robinson were set less than a decade earlier, in the provisions of the Fort Laramie Treaty of 1868. A treaty, we have seen, documented in Gardner's photographs. According to the provisions of this historic document – later invoked by the late Russell Means in his peripatetic and illusory crusade for an independent "Lakotah Republic" [305] – all Sioux bands were to relocate within the boundaries of the newly established Great Sioux Reservation, settle on arable lands, if they so wished, "to commence farming," and refer for all sorts of services, including schooling for their children and the routine distribution of annuities to "some place on the Missouri River, near the center of said reservation" where "the agent for said Indians shall in the future make his home." This was agreed upon on paper by the contracting parties. To be noted, however, that as far as the Sioux were concerned, the chiefs and headmen who signed in 1868 did not represent, nor did they speak, for the entirety of the Lakota Nation. They certainly did not speak for Sitting Bull or Crazy Horse. Furthermore, the specific provisions of the treaty, expressed in the usual awkward legalese of such documents (compounded by implicit or hidden meanings) were only ambiguously explained to the Indians through faulty translations. Laramie 1868 did not find an easy, speedy and peaceful application. As far as the Oglala and the Brule in particular, were concerned, it would take a decade before the two large Lakota tribes crossed the Dakota border to settle at their current agencies, again, within the boundaries of what was then the unified Great Sioux Reservation.[306]

Red Cloud Agency, Nebraska, from an illustration in
Harper's Weekly, May 18, 1876.

While officially pacified, Red Cloud Agency in northwestern Nebraska was a harbor of discontent. In 1873-1874 it counted some 9,300 Sioux, plus 1,200 Cheyenne, and 1,000 Arapaho. The traditional ingredients of Lakota intestine factionalism still in place, they were aggravated by dependence on poor quality annuity goods and reduced mobility. Still at large were the hunting bands under Crazy Horse and Sitting Bull who refused to abide by treaties they had not signed, and would not accept being told what to do or not to do in their own country. The new arrangement was particularly hard on young agency Sioux men, torn between the magnet of the still free Northern Indians and the authority of the agency chiefs. It was hard because while the older generations had already gained status the traditional Lakota way, by counting coups and cutting horses to paraphrase Anthony McGinnis,[307] younger ones could not freely follow the warrior tradition. Thus, they could not make a name for themselves doing what a true Lakota man was supposed to do which was win war honors and steal horses, in addition, of course, to providing for his family and protecting the women and children. Since food and protection were no longer a major issue after most of the Lakota had settled near their respective agencies, and the distribution of annuities took poor-quality but generally sufficient care of the People's bellies, only the former was left. Younger men had to find a way to release aggression and gain prestige to be respected members of their own thiyóšpaye, let alone acquire standing within the tribe. Among the Oglala, notorious for their aggressive and insubordinate temper, this created a potentially explosive situation.

In the very winter of 1873-1874, Dr. John J. Saville,[308] newly appointed agent at Red Cloud Agency, experienced firsthand the dangerous volatility of a seemingly pacified yet overtly hostile situation, especially when family groups from the Northern bands temporarily reunited with agency relatives for the winter months and expected to be fed and clothed by the agent. To keep discontent and threats of violence under control, and to provide a deterrent to aggression against civilian agency officials, military intervention from Fort Laramie was sought, leading to the establishment of army posts at Spotted Tail and Red Cloud agencies despite strong Indian opposition. The former post was named after Gen. Philip H. Sheridan. The latter, where Crazy Horse was to meet his tragic destiny, was named after Lieut. Levi H. Robinson who, together with Corp. John Coleman, in February 1874 had been killed near Fort Laramie by a Sioux war party, apparently from Lone Horn's camp. At the very Red Cloud Agency, young clerk Frank Appleton,[309] Agent Saville's own nephew, had also recently been killed by an Indian.[310] Billy Garnett identified the killer as Kicking Bear (1846-1904), later a Ghost Dance leader, son of Oglala chief Old Black Fox, a signer of the 1868 Treaty, and Iron Cedar Woman, one of Sitting Bull's sisters. By marrying a niece of Mnicojou chief Big Foot, Kicking Bear became a cousin of Crazy Horse, to whom he was very loyal, as were his brothers Flying Hawk (1852-1931) and half-brother Young Black Fox (1844-1881). Others say Kicking Bear's father Black Fox was Worm's brother, thus also making him a cousin of Crazy Horse."

According to Garnett, Kicking Bear murdered Appleton to avenge the killing of a relative slain by Whites in the Platte country.[311] Yet, only a few months after the killing, while visiting the agency in May 1874, Lieut. Thomas Wilhelm gathered the following cryptic testimony of the incident, subsequently published in his official *Memorandum*: "One day an Indian came to the quarters of Mr. Appleton, and picked up a photograph, taken of a party of Indians while on an eastern trip in which the Indian's father appeared. The buck ran with the picture at full speed to his tepe [sic], showing it to his friends; then brought it back to the owner, evidently with some friendly impression, and said 'someone may be killed here to-night; if you are called for do not come out.' Appleton paid no attention to the admonition. He was called for by an Indian in the middle of the night, and obeyed the call. As he turned to enter his door, the Indian shoot him in the back, climbed over the stockade and disappeared."[312]

George Hyde does not mention a possible connection with photography and provides yet a different account of the incident, brewed as it were in the climate of heightened factionalism, unrest, and dissatisfaction that marked the establishment of Red Cloud Agency in Nebraska.[313] According to Garnett, Red Cloud, Young Man Afraid, and Little Wound rushed to the agency to the dying man's bedside. Red Cloud, who had just lost his own son and had fresh the signs of self-inflicted mourning wounds, shed tears and expressed his condemnation and anger towards the "bad Indian" up north, referring to Crazy Horse's Hunkpatila Oglala to whom also Kicking Bear belonged. The incident created great excitement in the Indian camps. As Harry Young recalled, "They came from all directions, the chiefs all sitting in council, trying to decide what was best to do. They held the agent as a hostage until a decision was made. The younger Indians wanted to burn the Agency, kill us white men, and go north. American Horse [...] made the Indians a final talk, telling them if they were brave and wanted to fight the white man, that they could go down to Fort Laramie on the Platte River and find plenty of them, including the soldiers, but they must not harm us white men on the Agency; that some of us were married to their people, and were building them an Agency and treating them kindly. This seemed to quiet them."[314]

Less threatening turned out to be the pioneering photographic experience of Lieut. Wilhelm himself, who, in the above mentioned *Memorandum*, while reporting on formal military matters, went also into lengthy details about his ad-hoc camera work among the same turbulent Sioux at Red Cloud and the quieter bunch at Spotted Tail. Accompanied by Lieut. William H. Carter, Wilhelm visited Red Cloud camp where he met agency trader John W. Dear (misspelled Deer in the report),[315] and Joseph Larabee (referred to as "Joe, the half breed interpreter"), the latter to become Crazy Horse's father in-law three years later. Lieut. Wilhelm was invited inside the lodge of chief Blue Horse who in 1869 had assumed the leadership of the Loafer Band after his brother Big Mouth had been killed by Spotted Tail.[316] Šunketo (or Šunkehinto) had already been photographed by Glover in 1866 at Laramie and was also a signer of the 1868 Treaty. In 1872 Blue Horse had traveled to Washington with Red Cloud's delegation and was photographed by Alexander Gardner.[317]

Blue Horse was about the same age as Red Cloud and would later participate in the famous meeting of agency chiefs held with Gen. George Crook at Col. Luther Bradley's residence during the crisis that led to the attempted arrest and subsequent killing of Crazy Horse. Back to Lieut. Wilhelm. That same day the officer with a camera visited Blue Horse, his party also witnessed a "thunder and lightning dance or ceremony" which included a dog feast and a game of shinny. At this point, recalled the lieutenant "we next located our instrument and obtained a number of photographic views. While we were preparing for one of these, we saw an old Indian by the name of Linenfoot, walking diagonally into the field of view. As we had some apprehension of getting him to stand by himself, we intercepted him at a favorable point, and before the 'how' was fairly exchanged, the impression was made. He is what we would call the town crier [...]." Wilhelm then met another Lakota headman who is often featured in early photographic portraits, one actually produced by the crafty lieutenant himself at the Indian's own request: "We also met Red-dog [Šunke Luta], who is a jolly old Indian, and famous among his people for his bloody work in the Fetterman massacre. He asked us for a photograph of himself, which we had made for him. At this he was apparently very much delighted."[318]

Ephriam Dickson pointed out that Red Dog was a Hunkpapa by birth who had "married an Oglala [a sister of Red Cloud] and eventually became a primary spokesman for the Oyuhpe Band who had settled at Red Cloud Agency."[319] He was the father of noted Oglala warriors Fills the Pipe and Kills a Hundred. Red Dog's name is also found among the Indian portraits comprising the *Western Stereoscopic Gems* advertised by Mitchell and McGowan of Omaha, Nebraska, and in J.H. Hamilton's *Catalogue of Stereoscopic Views* where he is listed alone and with his daughter. Whether the Mitchell and McGowan, and the Hamilton images are new portraits, different from the one, or the ones, taken by Wilhelm has not yet been ascertained. Clearly, Red Dog belonged to the category of prominent Sioux who had established an early, positive rapport with photography.

Not so ready and agreeable, instead, was the older and craftier Red Cloud, whom Wilhelm met the following day, May 22, 1874. "In a conversation with Red Cloud to-day," he wrote, "we asked among other things, that he permit us to take a photograph of himself. He stated that he would afford us the opportunity, but not now, or not until we should return from the White Clay, as in the first place he was not in the proper dress for such a thing, nor was it the proper day. For the latter we could not account, unless he referred to the fact that it was Friday, as it had been represented through the half breeds to some of the Indians, we are told, that Friday is our unlucky day."[320] Previously, while waiting to witness a "squaw dance," Wilhelm "obtained a photograph of a group of tepees [sic], in which the one belonging to Red Cloud is the most prominent."[321] Red Cloud's refusal was a shrewd tactic to enhance his prestige and worth, particularly at a time when his authority was being challenged on both sides, by the militant element of the tribe for not being sufficiently tough with the Whites, and by the U.S. military for not doing enough to control his "bucks." Lieut. Wilhelm's comments, collected in the field from the mixed-bloods, are particularly revealing of the complex state of affairs at Red Cloud Agency: "We were informed by a half breed that the old man is abused on all sides; that his identification with the whites has brought against him the more radical of his tribe, and his weakness in controlling his people has brought the white element also against him. His refusal to declare war against the Government, when the troops entered his country, brought down on him also several of his war chiefs, who have taken great pride in the fact that, through their encouragement, the Platte River which is the southern boundary of their hunting grounds, has lately been known as the dead line."[322]

On May 23, Wilhelm returned to Red Cloud, "and upon entering the village we were met by Grey-eye who is remarkable for nothing but begging and indolence. The object in our early movement was to get a small group of Indians to stand for a negative. We did our best to include Grey-eye and certain others; but on account of superstitions we were about to fail. Mr. Deer [sic] at this time came to our assistance. He finally succeeded in making up a group consisting of Red Cloud's chief warriors, namely Blue Horse, Sioux Bob, and Collar Bones. They insisted upon Mr. Deer and the writer standing immediately in their rear, evidently to give confidence to their position."

In his excellent survey of early photographers at Red Cloud and Spotted Tail agencies and nearby army posts, Dickson recognized that in Crazy Horse's times, the Lakota reaction to the camera was not always negative. Still, quoting the above episode, Dickson reiterated the old argument that "on account of superstitions" Grey Eye probably escaped the lieutenant's camera. Assuming he was the same individual, the charge of "superstition" may not be as sound as it seems. As we noted earlier, Grey Eye and his family had already been photographed without any apparent problem by Gardner at Fort Laramie in 1868. Furthermore, Grey Eye also had a rudimentary command of the English language and he understood very well the non-threatening nature of photography. In any case, back to Wilhelm and his camera.

News of the officer-photographer's presence sparked the lucrative interest of other Indians who saw an opportunity to make an easy buck, offering themselves for a portrait. Immediately after the picture-taking inside Mr. Dear's stockade, Wilhelm relates that, "An Indian by the name of Spider, notorious for his thefts and falsehoods, rode up, rigged in an old shirt, with two large glass studs in its front, and red leggings. He demanded five dollars from us for the privilege of photographing him. His horse was milk white, with the mane and tail painted bright yellow. As we were slow to accept this proposition he became somewhat insolent. Long John who has been very friendly to us during the several days here, took up the matter in Spider's own language, and no doubt saved us some embarrassment. The

Indian finally rode off."[323] Born about 1840, Spider, Iktomila, also known as High Hollow Horn, was Old Man Afraid of His Horse's son-in-law and at times acted as a spokesman for Red Cloud. The early 1877 "Register of Indians at Red Cloud" lists Spider as head of family in Young Man Afraid of Horse's camp.[324]

In retrospect, and in light of other practical matters including mazaska requests as the one just reported, we should be cautious using "superstition" as a blanket reason for Indian rejections to the camera. We may be closer to the truth if we place occasional negative reactions in historical and socio-cultural perspective. In the behavior exhibited, and the apparent reasons given by some Indians, "superstition" was but a stratagem to prolong the negotiation, make oneself more desirable as a subject, and eventually justify the price asked for consenting to be photographed. An episode that occurred years later among the Canadian Blackfoot is revealing of the American Indian traditional predisposition for pranks and "leg pulling" with disingenuous White men.

When the camera showed up in Indian Country, north and south of the medicine line, it became fair game for Indian humor. English-born Anglican missionary Canon H.W. Gibbon Stocken recalled that his life-long Blackfoot friend Silas Wolf Collar, whom he had instructed in syllabics, was also very intrigued by the camera: "Seeing me taking a photograph one day, Silas asked me all about the process and then asked me to teach him. This I did and he turned out some very fair prints, doing everything himself." Silas, who was highly respected within the tribe, obviously used his home advantage and, continued Stocken, "he took one or two pictures that Indians would not have allowed me to take." Sometime later, the notorious impersonator Sylvester Long, better known under his spurious Indian name of Long Lance (Buffalo Child),[325] wrote a book "in which Silas Wolf Collar is reported to have attributed his ability and knowledge of syllabics and photography to supernatural power." As Stocken explained, when Long Lance visited Wolf Collar, "after Indian custom, Silas began to 'pull his leg,' in which he was adept. He surrounded his life with remarkable supernatural powers, including his knowledge of Blackfoot syllabics, and of photography, and ended by referring the budding journalist to [...] myself for confirmation."[326]

The episode speaks volumes. While it is understandable that nineteenth century and even early twentieth century photographers and writers believed what Indians told them about the camera (and other matters as well), to insist nowadays on the ethnographic tale of Indian "supernatural fear" of photography only perpetuates the old "primitive savage" stereotype. Of course, it does not mean that occasional instances of genuine fear, concern, or prohibition based on religious belief, did not occur. But with the wealth of new documentary evidence available, we should see through the old ethno-blanket tales of Indian "fear and superstition" and focus instead on the historical truth.

Returning to Lieut. Wilhelm, he arrived at Spotted Tail Agency on May 28, where he met several Brule signatories of the 1868 Treaty, some of whom had already been photographed by Gardner at Laramie or later in Washington, namely Swift Bear, Roman Nose, and Big Partizan. The latter, listed in the Laramie Treaty also under his Lakota name Bella-tonka-tonka[327] was described by the lieutenant as "the great Medicine Man. He is very old, and acknowledged by his people as careful, honest and upright, and is charged with such papers as may relate to their relations with the Government."[328] Spotted Tail himself received the young officer kindly. The Brule chief wished to impress his American guest with symbols of his status and friendship with the White man. Sinte Gleška also wanted to convey the progressive image of a chief who was familiar with the black box the lieutenant carried with him. He made a point of showing Wilhelm his most prized possessions, photographs included. "He seemed very glad to see us, and at once led the way to his lodge," recalled the officer. "He waived his hand for us to be seated upon a piece of canvas, on one side facing the entrance. After some little delay, the interpreter made his appearance, when the usual exchange of greetings took place. Spotted Tail then drew forth numerous articles of value given him by the government, and individuals, whilst on his trips East at various times. Among them was a massive silver medal, with an impression of Andrew Johnson on one side, and the words 'Spotted Tail's Friendly Indian' on the other. He displayed a fine white linen banner [...] marked 'Spotted Tail's Friendly Band.' He also handed us photographs of himself and favorite wife." The fact that the Brule chief kept those photos among his prized possessions is indicative of the value he attributed to his own printed image.

Catching the moment, Lieut. Wilhelm sought to expand the nature of his official visit to the friendly chief and his band with his own active interest in photography. He noted that meanwhile other chiefs had joined them in Spotted Tail's large lodge, namely "Crow Dog, Black Crow, Crazy-in-the-Lodge, and Windy Man, the four head soldiers, together with Rising Sun, Blue Teeth, Eagle Man, White Hat, Tall Man, Crooked Foot, Present[s]-the-Pipe, Hunts-the-Bear, High Bear, Whirl Wind, Scratching Head, Belt, and Picket Pin. [...] We," continued the lieutenant, "had a great desire to obtain some photographs while here, and took advantage of the display of Spotted Tail's photograph to open the subject through the interpreter. [...] Eventually, [Spotted Tail] turned to the Indians present, and made known to them our desire, saying that he hoped our effort would be encouraged, and this nonsensical superstition laid aside; that his picture had been made very often, and even now was floating beyond the great water. He stated no harm had ever befallen him on that account; that his people had attracted so much attention in the East, that [...] the people of which must certainly have but a limited idea of their location and manner of living, and that it would be highly beneficial to spread true pictures of their people [...] &c. The pipe was freely passed around, and considerable said on various subjects."[329]

No further details are given on the picture taking effort, but we can reasonably assume that Lieut. Wilhelm succeeded in his picture taking. His reference to Crazy-in-the-Lodge is particularly interesting. As we saw earlier, a photo portrait with that name is attributed to Stanley J. Morrow, and has often been mistakenly identified as that of Crazy Horse. Partly on the dubious similarity of their names. In Wilhelm's case, both he and his interpreter clearly knew who was who in the Brule camp, and if a photo of Crazy-in-the-Lodge was indeed taken by Lieut. Wilhelm, it certainly came with proper identification. So, the Morrow image could actually be a "lost" Wilhelm's photograph. Conversely, Morrow may have taken his own photo of Crazy in the Lodge, the one generally attributed to him.

Of interest was also Wilhelm's encounter with another famous Lakota chief often featured in early photographs, and his daughters: "As we departed for our own camp we fell in with Two Strike and his two daughters; all were mounted, the daughters riding side by side (astride, as all squaws ride) in rear of the father. They are apparently about 18 or 20 years of age, and were profusely decorated with bead work. One had a saddle cloth almost a solid mass of beads; each had her hair in two braids down the back, their faces very bright with vermillion."[330] Unfortunately, the technology of the time was still far from color photography, but the lieutenant's narration gives a clear sense of the impressive, colorful nature of Sioux formal attire in those early agency days; especially the members of a chief's household. Proudly, Spotted Tail returned the visit to the American officer's camp. The chief and his followers "about 250 or 300 in number, all well mounted on ponies [...] presented an appearance certainly beyond all description [...] we could distinguish the great variety of brilliant colors in dress and plumage [...] the spectacle was one of the grandest we have ever witnessed."[331]

The *Memorandum* authored by Lieut. Wilhelm and his surviving images are precious. The tintype reproduced by Dickson shows the interior of the defensive stockade around trader John W. Dear's store with a number of individuals identified: Lieut. W.H. Carter of the 6th U.S. Cavalry, Soreback Band chief Red Leaf, interpreter Billy Hunter Garnett, artist Jules Tavernier, trader J.W. Dear, and Lieut. James Buchanan.[332] Tavernier (1844-1889), a French painter who accompanied Lieut. Wilhelm's expedition, drew sketches for *Harper's Weekly* depicting the Western landscape, life at the Agency and in Red Cloud's village, and even of the dramatic yearly sun dance, reproduced with artistic license in the January 2, 1875, issue of *Harper's*.[333] During the ceremony, lightning struck the sacred pole, an ominous sign that forced Tavernier and Clark to quickly leave the sun dance grounds least they be clubbed to death by enraged akičita. After their withdrawal, however, they remained in the vicinity without additional problems.

Lieut. Wilhelm's visit was eventually forgotten, and while photography could be used as a tool for establishing a dialog outside the realm of politics, internal tribal affairs and the thorny issues of agency location, trading, government rations distribution, stealing of Indian horses by White rustlers, and so on, were more serious matters that deeply preoccupied Indians and Whites alike at both agencies. Worrisome, too, for Red Cloud, Spotted Tail, and the other agency chiefs was the permanent military presence on their lands. They had voiced strong opposition to the establishment of army posts near the agencies, fearing troubles. In fact, the Army's resolve was seriously tested by young Sioux warriors who fired upon the soldiers who had originally set up a tent encampment close to the agency stockade and blockhouse. There is an interesting drawing of this very first camp, titled "Pencil sketch of Camp Robinson Red Cloud Agency 1874" by Lieut. W.H. Carter who, perhaps inspired by Wilhelm and Tavernier, also made a sketch of a Sioux tipi village, still near Red Cloud Agency, with Crow Butte in background.[334] Although crude, the sketches are historically valuable, the latter actually similar to a stereo view of a "Sioux Village on White River" taken only a few years later by Private Charles Howard. The sparsely wooded foothills of the butte in the Carter sketch were the subject of an 1877 panoramic photo captioned "Crow Butte, Nebraska" by Private Howard.

Despite the young akičita's show of force, the soldiers were there to stay. The permanent garrison quarters were built in earnest and the site was officially called Camp Robinson. Of particular relevance to the Crazy Horse picture question is an important detail reported by Robert Grange in his history of the post, but long overlooked or purposely ignored by the "no picture" supporters. Grange specified that the description that followed had been written when the old post was under construction in the fall of 1874: "The camp is 160 yards square. Officers' quarters are on the north, infantry barracks on the east and west and cavalry barracks, guard house and storehouse on the south sides. The barracks are built of logs [...] have shingle roofs, log walls, window sashes and are floored. [...] other buildings of the early post were constructed of logs, slabs, or boards. [...] In addition to the military buildings there was a post trader's residence and store-saloon, and next to it a small log building housing a photographer's studio."[335]

The log cabin studio was actually located at the nearby Agency. The opening of a photographic studio at such a remote post, in the midst of the unsettled Oglala, was remarkable, and an indication of the profitable nature of Western and Indian photography. The studio's successful activity with both White and Indian patrons was corroborated later by eyewitness accounts and reports, including that of Robert Strahorn. Visiting Camp Robinson and nearby Red Cloud Agency in early 1877, just a few months before Crazy Horse's surrender, Strahorn wrote that the photographic studio was housed in a permanent structure, a log cabin conveniently positioned near Mr. Dear's trading store at Red Cloud Agency. It did a good business producing views of the busy agency and photographic portraits of the Indians.[336]

That a photographic studio was already operating at Camp Robinson - Red Cloud Agency and that it was patronized by local Indians is an important reminder that by 1877 the agency Sioux, along with the Cheyenne and the Arapaho there, were well accustomed to "shadow catchers" in their midst, and to having their picture taken. In hindsight, we may critically wonder why, if a photographer was present at Red Cloud in the spring 1877, he did not document Crazy Horse's surrender. The answers could be many, including that he may have been temporarily absent. More likely, given the volatile situation and the potentially dangerous nature of the event, most Northern Indians still being unfamiliar with the camera, picture taking was purposely avoided. Camera technology required prolonged exposure time, and the intrusive presence of a photographer with his "looking box" on a tripod could have been perceived with suspicion or hostility by the Northern Indians. Shortly thereafter, however, under different circumstances, James H. Hamilton did photograph several Northern Indians. And, that fall, he actually photographed the surrender at Spotted Tail Agency of the defeated remnants of Mnicojou chief Lame Deer's band. The stereoview is listed as "No. 107. Surrender of Lame Deer's Band" in Hamilton's *Catalogue*. A tragic coincidence, Lame Deer (?-1877) himself was killed on May 7 at Muddy Creek, Montana, during a clash with Col. Nelson A. Miles, perhaps a premonition of the destiny that would soon befall Crazy Horse.

Who the original photographer that set up business at the agency was, we still do not know. We also do not know how long the photographic gallery remained in continuous operation, whether it changed hands, between whom, and when. Ephriam Dickson discovered a small carte-de-visit print in the photographic collection of the Nebraska State Historical Society with the imprint "Hamilton & Smith's Gallery of Art, Red Cloud Agency, Nebraska,"[337] but it is not known whether this is the unknown photographer(s), a subsequent partnership, or what. Most likely the imprint refers to Charles Lewis Hamilton (1837-18??), a Kentucky-born photographer who had previously operated a studio at Fort Randall on the Missouri, Dakota Territory. Charles L. Hamilton was at Red Cloud Agency in early 1876, but it is not clear how long he remained there. Dickson also noted that in this specific photograph the background does not match that in the "alleged" Crazy Horse tintype. We suggest that this fact alone does not mean much. A different backdrop could have been temporarily substituted for a one-of-a-kind sitting with Crazy Horse.

Some time ago, Terry Clark (Little Fox), identifying himself as North Dakota Pembina and Red River Métis, suggested that José Maria Mora (ca. 1846/49-1926) made this kind of ornate backdrops, similar to the one in the tintype. Cuban-born Mora was a famous New York photographer who took studio portraits of Lieut. Col. George Armstrong Custer in both civilian dress and military uniform during the latter's visit to New York in March 1876. Actually, Custer's last photographs were taken a month later in the same city by William R. Howell (1846-1890),[338] right on the eve of the historic campaign that put him, dramatically, face to face with Crazy Horse. Returning to Mora, Clark wrote that the New York photographer "made this type of backdrops of the 1870s. [...] Now, let's say that the photographer of Crazy Horse did not have these backdrops. It is o.k. [...] Maybe the U.S. military officers [at Camp Robinson] had this back-drop in their possession in their mess at barracks. This was the old west [...] and they had some comfort with them. I spent over 20 years in the U.S. military (U.S. Navy) [...] I have been to isolated regions around the world [...]. You bring things with you to ease your mind. This backdrop looks to me like some backdrop of an opera setting."[339]

Terry Clark did not provide additional information on the subject, but it is significant that the Hamilton & Smith's imprint on the carte-de-visite cited by Dickson is artistically elaborate. Also significant, their photographic establishment at Red Cloud Agency is referred to in that same imprint as a "gallery of art," not simply a "studio." Leaving us wondering about the interior decor of the photographic business and the different backdrops, even opera-style ones as suggested by Terry Clark, that might have been used there. Only a few years later, the same David F. Barry had a similar ornate backdrop with painted column – almost identical to the one in the tintype – in his temporary studio at Fort Buford. There, in May 1881, Barry photographed the Northern Indians who returned from Canada to surrender. One group photo in particular shows Crow King, Major David Brotherton, and Low Dog (more on him, later), seated, and behind them, standing, George Fleury, the resident mixed-blood interpreter.[340]

If we do not know what the picture gallery at Red Cloud looked like inside, unless we accept the tintype was taken in that very studio, we do know what it looked like outside. Again, this is historically remarkable, and proof of the photographic surprises contextually supportive of the case for a Crazy Horse photograph that have surfaced in recent years. The photograph in question was originally posted on the online thread on Pvt. Charles Howard and, as we mentioned earlier, it was so historically significant that Tom Buecker chose it as the cover illustration of his photography book on Red Cloud Agency.[341] "[Peter T.] Buckley," wrote Buecker, "added this unique image of a photographer taking a picture of an Indian group to his collection of stereo views. The 'Gallery' seen here was a log structure near the post trader's store at Camp Robinson. An *Omaha Daily*

Bee article about Indian scouts at Camp Robinson provided details: 'Many of them are having their picture taken at the little log cabin gallery near the sutler's (post trader's) store.'" Oddly, however, Buecker seems to downplay the importance of the presence of a photographic studio and gives only a matter-of-fact comment about the skylight: "Permanent photography studios were not regular fixtures at frontier posts, including at Camp Robinson or at Red Cloud Agency. Evidently visiting photographers set up shop in the log structure shown here. Between the two log structures a crude sign was hung reading 'Pictures,' which remained as long as a photographer was present. A portion of the studio skylight can be seen on the roof of the larger cabin."

In fact, the outdoor scene on a bright-sunny day says much more. A photographer is standing next to his camera on a tripod in the process of taking a picture of a group of Indians, one man and eight women, standing in a row outside the log cabin picture gallery. The Indians all diligently face the photographer, apparently lined-up according to their approximate age; the older woman, likely the wife, standing next to the sole Indian man in the group. Except for the absence of a long breastplate, the Indian man in the photograph is dressed just like the Indian in the tintype: long white shirt over dark leggings, beaded moccasins, and trade blanket draped over his shoulders. He also wears a dentalium choker, and what appears to be brass bracelets. The Indian women, too, have a combination of typical 1870s Agency Sioux dresses. Some wear long one-piece calico dresses, others their fine, fringed, long buckskin dresses. They also wear the typical large woman leather belts. Some also have plaid trade blankets and long beautiful dentalium earrings.

Additionally, there are two male figures standing inside the log cabin, on the door threshold. The one in the back is barely visible, the other in the front, wearing not leggings but trousers – an indication he may be a mixed-blood interpreter helping the photographer – is holding what seems to be a cat in his arms. Outside, near the left-hand corner of the log house, partially hidden from the view of the Indian group being photographed, an Indian figure wearing a hat stands, fully wrapped in a blanket.

"165. Photographing Indians at Red Cloud", in J.H. Hamilton's
Catalogue. The canvas skylight cover is visible on the roof of the
log-cabin photographic gallery; large PICTURES sign in the background.
The tall Indian with long white shirt, stroud leggings, and blanket
near the door is dressed like the Indian in the tintype.

The photographer in the foreground next to the camera has a noticeably
large military-style holster at his waist. He looks like a robust man, just like
James H. Hamilton was. He is holding his hat in the air, possibly indicating
to the Indian group where to look, at the same time signaling the exposure time to whomever, behind him, is in turn taking this rare image of
a photographer in the act of photographing Indians. Two photographers
were working their camera simultaneously at Red Cloud Agency.

The photograph is also extremely important from a documentary
perspective because it shows two additional key elements that support,
contextually, our case for the Crazy Horse tintype. On the far right, in
the background behind the younger Indian women, on the side of the
log house is a large sign carved on a rectangular wooden board that reads
"PICTURES." Most interestingly, again in favor of the tintype portrait of
Crazy Horse taken indoor, on the plank roof of the photographer's log
cabin is a very noticeable, large, rectangular light-color cover. It was most
likely made of thick off-white canvas, known as "duck cloth," like that

of 1870s U.S. army tents, at the time also increasingly used by Indians for their tipis as a substitute for now scarce buffalo hides.[342] This functional feature, and the relatively large size of the roof opening, allowed natural light to illuminate the studio directly from the ceiling for indoor photographs. The rectangular cut-out skylight ceiling area, in correspondence of the canvas cover, might have had a removable wooden section of planks or boards inside, sized to match the opening, to be easily taken down and reinstalled as needed. The skylight section of the wooden roof was a clever practical solution to the all canvas tent-like roof used in some log house field studios out West. A famous example of the full tent roof over log-walled structure was the photographic studio, "Our Gallery at Deadwood," D.S. Mitchell set up in the Black Hills in 1876.[343]

Neither Tom Buecker nor Ephriam Dickson connected this "new" vintage photograph of the Red Cloud gallery to the Crazy Horse tintype debate. Dickson, however, did express his great surprise at this and other Peter T. Buckley Collection images originally posted on-line: "I am speechless! […] They are absolutely astounding! They include a mixture of D.S. Mitchell, Private Charles Howard, Stanley J. Morrow, and James [H.] Hamilton. There are views I have never seen before of Red Cloud Agency and Camp Robinson […] I think that the wonderful photograph of the photographer taking the group shot at his studio is by James H. Hamilton. It is possibly his image # 165 labeled 'Photographing Indians at Red Cloud.'" On the same Charles Howard thread, Dickson added an interesting comment on another image. The comment implicitly supports what we said earlier about the biased "fear factor" long attributed to the "ignorant [!] Indians" vis-à-vis the more objective, natural curiosity the same Indians actually showed for photography. "There is also one [photograph] in the Heritage Auctions series," Dickson wrote, "showing two native individuals looking at a viewer and stereo cards. I suspect that this is Hamilton's '# 170, 'Learning the Use of the Stereoscope.'" If Dickson and later Buecker accepted that the Hamilton image "Catalogue No. 170" (and others in the Buckley Collection) correctly corresponded to the stereoview showing the two Indians with stereoscope and stereo pictures (likewise other Hamilton stereoscopic views), why should not also No. 104 correctly identify its subject, whatever the identification maybe. We accept the Hamilton identification as "Crazy Horse."

Regarding accuracy and matching clothing, the two Red Cloud Agency Indians in the Hamilton photo wear white cotton shirts, stroud leggings, trade blankets; one also seems to be wearing a neckerchief, while the other has a metal armband.

"170. Learning the Use of the Stereoscope", in J.H. Hamilton's *Catalogue*. The photograph, taken in the summer 1877, shows "Indian man's dress" common at Red Cloud Agency during Crazy Horse's time.

Not only was there a professional photographic "gallery of art" with a large "Pictures" sign outside and a skylight opening on the roof at Red Cloud Agency in 1877, but also amateur camera workers as well, both civilian and military, who were at one point or another operating their "nosed boxes" at Camp Robinson - Red Cloud Agency before, during, and after Crazy Horse's stay. A few decades ago, no one would have thought how pervasive the presence of photography in the Sioux Country was during Crazy Horse's time. As Buecker wrote, "Photographers on their way to or returning from the Black Hills regularly paused for several days [and even longer] at Camp Robinson, where they set up temporary studios to provide soldiers, civilians, and native customers with tintypes and other forms of indoor photography. [...] After a local photographer returned from a trip to Red Cloud Agency and Camp Robinson, a North Platte newspaper reported that he had cleared two hundred dollars in one week, adding, 'the 'soger' [sic] boys and Indians are profitable patrons of picture makers.' [...] Between 1874 and 1877 no less than nine photographers visited Camp Robinson and Red Cloud Agency."

Irish-born Albert E. Guerin (1848-1889), who had a studio in St. Louis, stopped at Red Cloud Agency in the fall of 1875 while working as official photographer on Lieut. Col. Richard I. Dodge and Prof. Walter P. Jenney's follow-up expedition to the Black Hills.[344] Their mission was to confirm the presence of gold reported the previous year by the large Custer expedition of July-August 1874 which, in addition to scientists and embedded journalists, also included a talented photographer, William H. Illingworth (1844-1893).[345] Illingworth did not make it to Red Cloud, but Guerin did in early October. As Dickson wrote, "Besides a series of view of the Black Hills, Guerin also made at least one photograph of Red Cloud Agency [...] 'It was ration day for the Indians,' Colonel Dodge wrote in his official report of the expedition, 'and hundreds [of Indians] were collected, in their holiday costume, making a picturesque sight.'" The image Guerin took is a distant panoramic stereoview of the agency buildings "showing considerable activity outside the warehouse and issue room. A second photograph of the agency from 1875 may also be Guerin's."[346]

To be noted, with respect to the state of affairs at Red Cloud and Spotted Tail agencies, that as with the Custer intrusion the previous summer, also Lieut. Col. Dodge's walk in the Black Hills, the Sioux sacred HeSapa, went, for all practical purposes, mostly unchallenged by the Lakota. Col. Dodge actually called it "a delightful picnic" despite the absence of the fair sex. While in the Hills, Guerin also took group portraits of "Indian chiefs & interpreters," including Red Dog and other Sioux from Red Cloud Agency who were traveling with Sen. William Allison's Black Hills Commission.[347] Paradoxically, instead, shortly after the flagpole incident, the Sioux, believing the bearded White man with his long wagon train and military escort were after gold, tried to prevent Yale College professor Othniel C. Marsh (1831-1899) from entering the Black Hills - Bad Lands region on a paleontological expedition. The scientist's true intentions eventually prevailed and the suspicious Indians relented. Red Cloud befriended the professor and asked him to take back East, along with his precious bones, proof of the Sioux being cheated by Agent John J. Saville. Professor Marsh took the matter to heart, an investigation followed, and Dr. Saville was removed from office.

Years later, in January 1883, accompanied by mixed-blood interpreter Ed Laramie, Red Cloud visited Prof. Marsh in New Haven, where the two old friends were photographed together shaking hands by Frank A. Bowman. Bowman also took a number of individual portraits of the popular Sioux chief, who donned an elegant black suit and short hair. Replying to a local reporter, the photographer said, "I feared that Red Cloud would be a difficult subject to handle, but he was not. On the contrary, he was much more patient and civilized than the ordinary customer. [...] Through the whole ordeal he showed a spirit of outmost patience."[348] What a change. A little over ten years had passed since the Oglala leader had stood somewhat reluctantly for the first time in front of the camera. It was during the 1872 delegation trip to Washington, when he sat alone for Mathew Brady, and shaking hands with his wašiču friend William Blackmore for Alexander Gardner.

The first solo photographic portrait of Red Cloud back at his agency was actually taken in December 1876 by Stanley J. Morrow.[349] A few years earlier, in 1869, Morrow had established a Photograph and Ambrotype Gallery in Yankton, Dakota Territory, gaining a reputation for excellence, especially his early American Indian portraits. In late summer 1876, at the height of the Black Hills gold rush, he set up a tent studio in Deadwood where thousands of miners were flocking. Morrow documented Gen. Crook's return from his nearly disastrous summer campaign against Crazy Horse, Sitting Bull, and the Northern Indians, which Morrow dramatized by staging scenes of soldiers butchering their own horses to avoid starvation.[350]

In late October 1876, Morrow reached Red Cloud Agency where Col. Ranald S. Mackenzie had just surrounded the camps of Red Cloud and Red

Leaf. A small number of guns and over seven hundred ponies were confiscated; some forty-eight horses were from Red Cloud himself, who was placed under military arrest. A detachment of one hundred Pawnee scouts led by Frank and Luther North aided Col. Mackenzie's 4th U.S. Cavalry in the operation. Adding insult to injury, the hated Pawnee were rewarded with a horse each from the captured Sioux herd. Then, on October 24, before a large assembly Gen. Crook thought of publicly punishing Red Cloud for his recalcitrance and stonewalling in the government takeover of the Black Hills, which was actually a blatant violation of the 1868 treaty. Gen. Crook proceeded to name Spotted Tail paramount chief of all the White River Sioux.[351] Morrow took an outdoor, panoramic, restaged view of the event. Standing in front of the two-story agency building, at the center of a large gathering are Gen. Crook, Spotted Tail, and Red Cloud.[352] Emboldened by the White soldier chief's recognition, Spotted Tail also stood with his family before Morrow's camera; a proud-looking, statuary Sinte Gleška flanked by his wife and daughter (all three wrapped in blankets), a classic image that has been reproduced many times.[353]

The official dethroning of Red Cloud and the investiture of Spotted Tail was a formality that meant little to the agency Oglala, and equally to the Brule. Both continued to handle their internal affairs according to traditional Lakota custom. Despite his anger and frustration, when Morrow returned to Camp Robinson in early December, Red Cloud was persuaded by Mr. Dear, able in such negotiations, to be photographed: "Through the kindness of the Indian trader, Mr. Dear, I was enabled to procure some good negatives of Red Cloud, today, it being the first time he ever gave a sitting to a photographer."[354] The only known Morrow photograph from that sitting portrays a stern, mature Red Cloud in dark civilian clothing, seated outdoors with hat in hand, the trader store's palisade as backdrop. Unaware of the Brady, Gardner, and Currier portraits, Morrow erroneously assumed his were the first photos of the Oglala chief. Dickson writes that "Stanley Morrow retuned to Yankton in mid-December 1876 and continued his photographic trips on the Missouri River for several years. He also expanded his operations establishing galleries at Fort Keogh and

Fort Custer, Montana, and he accompanied the reburial party to the Little Bighorn Battlefield in 1879."[355] Apparently, Morrow was not at Red Cloud Agency when Crazy Horse was there.

The photographer who was present in the late spring to early-fall 1877 at Camp Robinson-Red Cloud Agency was James H. Hamilton (c. 1839-1897).[356] A Kentuckian, James was the younger brother of previously mentioned Charles L. Hamilton. Charles owned a "Photograph and Ambrotype Gallery" in Sioux City, Iowa, "practiced photography in Fort Randall, Dakota Territory [...] during the Civil War era," and later, as we already said, was also briefly at Red Cloud Agency.[357] It was in his brother Charles Hamilton's Sioux City shop that James became seriously interested in photography. In early 1864 James crossed the wide Missouri and opened his own gallery in Omaha, Nebraska, where he produced "some very fine card pictures." Dickson adds that "there, in addition to portraiture, [James H.] also made his first Indian portraits."[358] In a reversal of roles, after the Civil War young William Henry Jackson himself worked as an apprentice in James H. Hamilton's studio. Hamilton eventually sold his business to brothers William H. and Edward Jackson and returned to Sioux City, a boomtown for frontier photographers, where in 1868 he opened a new gallery.

A couple of years later, his interest in American Indian and landscape photography took him south, again crossing the Missouri to the Omaha and Winnebago Agencies, where he produced Indian portraits and outdoor views. These and most other Hamilton images were later advertised as Hamilton & Kodylek, from the name of his new partner, Austrian-born John Kodylek. [359] Dickson pointed out that the early 1870s were a time of intense competition in Sioux City. Not only selected images but also entire stocks and even studios were sold and purchased between local photographers, at times making the paternity of early images difficult if not impossible. In 1873 Hamilton took his camera north to Dakota Territory. Dickson noted that "part of the driving force to expand his offerings was the growing competition in Sioux City. His primary rival for Indian photographs was Byron H. Gurnsey [1833-1880 or 1890], who had opened a studio in the city in the spring of 1870 with William Illingworth [1842-1893]." Samples of Gurnsey's stereographic series *North Western Views*, published in Sioux City, Iowa, and *Rocky Mountain Views*, from his studio in Colorado Springs, are in the National Anthropological Archives. Hamilton purchased a number of Gurnsey and other frontier photographers' negatives and marketed them under his own imprint.[360]

This brings us back to the *Wi'iyohi* article and photos that in 1947 had raised the hopes of Will Robinson and others that a photographic portrait of Crazy Horse had finally been found. As Tom Buecker wrote, "The case on this one was nearly closed, but Robinson [...] wanted more conclusive proof. [...] An answer for Robinson's nagging question was found at the Smithsonian's National Museum of Natural History [where the National Anthropological Archives were then located]. In its [NAA] extensive Native American photo collection existed the same image, attributed to a photographer named B.H. Gurnsey of Sioux City. The photo Robinson thought to be Oglala Crazy Horse was 'Chak-ur-T-kee' a Pawnee chief."[361] Furthermore, Buecker concluded, "Other Gurnsey-attributed photos cast some doubt on the authenticity of the Nellie Laravie photo." Later, Jack Heriard echoed the "Pawnee chief by Gurnsey" identification, and posed the question whether the same image may have actually been purchased and intentionally misidentified by James Hamilton as the portrait of Crazy Horse listed as No.104 in his *Catalogue*. As we noted earlier, that was not the case.

Still, Heriard's view was shared by Ephriam Dickson who, referring to the old stereoscopic image originally investigated by W.G. Robinson, wrote: "One image in the Hamilton series is known with the name Crazy Horse handwritten on the <u>reverse</u>; it has been shown to actually be of a Pawnee named 'Chak-ur-t-kee,' an image actually made by Byron Gurnsey and later reprinted by Hamilton." Dickson went on to notice that "there still may be a Hamilton image out there waiting to be discovered. However, of the number of Hamilton Indian portraits from the agencies from 1877 that are known, none of them have the backdrop visible in the Crazy Horse tintype. Hamilton instead used a blanket, tree branches and other props in his temporary studio."[362]

Leaving aside, for the moment, the argument about the backdrop, we know from the W.G. Robinson correspondence that the "Crazy Horse" identification penciled on the Gurnsey stereo was done by the brother of Blanche M. Lewis, not by Hamilton. It is true that this portrait of Chak-ur-T-kee with the Hamilton imprint is in Hamilton's own *Catalogue*, but it is listed as "No. 168. Pawnee Chief," not as Crazy Horse. With all likelihood, Hamilton did not report the Indian's personal name because it was a picture by someone else, of an Indian he did not know. Conversely, as we said, Hamilton knew exactly who Crazy Horse was. He had seen the Oglala war chief alive at Camp Robinson and at nearby Red Cloud Agency. The Gurnsey paternity of the original image is pretty much settled. Likewise, the name of the subject, who appears as "Chak-ok-ta-kee, or The Man That Strikes His Enemies, Pawnee chief," in an original stereograph in the Princeton University Library.[363] Not fully agreed upon, instead, is the Pawnee tribal identification. Unlike the Sioux, there are considerably fewer Pawnee images of the same period to compare the Gurnsey photo with. Thomas Kavanagh looked at the Pawnee photos in the NAA and did not include the Gurnsey image in his survey. Kavanagh did offer interesting clues on the wide range of dress, hair style, and accessories Pawnee men wore in the late-1860s and early-1870s; some did have buckskin dresses with fairly long fringes.[364]

An alternative tribal identification was given in 2008 by Cowan's Auctions in the advertisement of a "cdv of Chak-uk-t-kee, Arikara Chief." The long caption read: "No imprint, but known in stereo format as the work of Byron H. Gurnsey, [...], ca. 1870. Erroneous pencil inscription, verso: Standing Rock Indian. [... In 1871, Gurnsey] sold his studio and many of his glass negatives to J.H. Hamilton [...]. As a merchandizing ploy, after the death of the Oglala Sioux chief Crazy Horse in 1877, Hamilton & Hoyt re-issued this image in stereo format as 'Crazy Horse.' The Arikara were an expatriate group of the Skidi Pawnee. Gurnsey photographed the Arikara Head Chief, Son of The Star [aka Rushing Bear] in the same setting, but never made any Pawnee portrait."[365] We have not seen the stereo portrait of "Chak-uk-t-kee" with the Hamilton & Hoyt imprint and

Chak-ur-t-kee (Chak-ok-ta-kee), by Byron H. Gurnsey, no date;
published by J.H. Hamilton, "168. Pawnee Chief"
in *Catalogue of Stereoscopic Views* (1878).

their identification as "Crazy Horse," and we assume we are probably dealing with the same photo referred to earlier by Dickson. Still, the suggestion
that Hamilton (& Hoyt) purposely misidentified a Crazy Horse portrait
seems unlikely. Several U.S. Army officers and soldiers, agency personnel, post-traders, mixed-blood scouts, and interpreters, even journalists
and occasional visitors, not to mention many Lakota, Cheyenne, and
Arapaho, had known or seen Crazy Horse at Camp Robinson, Red Cloud,
and Spotted Tail agencies, and would have clearly been able to tell that
the Indian photograph advertised as "Crazy Horse" by Hamilton and Hoyt
was not the late Oglala war chief. While anything is possible, the overt
falsification of an Indian portrait as that of Crazy Horse, whose notoriety

had just begun to spread after his surrender and death, would have back-fired, causing a negative reaction and a bad name for the photographer (or photographers) business. Surprisingly, still today the photographic portrait of Chak-uk-t-kee is identified as "Crazy Horse" in a website on the Little Bighorn.[366]

It was the discovery of gold in the Black Hills in the early 1870s, and the coming to an end of the Sioux and Cheyenne war of 1876-1877, that had given new impetus to photographic activities in the region.[367] Charles C. Hamilton, who was then sixteen years old, some fifty years later recalled his experiences as he joined his father James on the photographic trip to the Hills of the spring-summer 1877, with the usual stops at Red Cloud and Spotted Tail Agencies. His testimony provides key evidence that as a professional photographer his father was very much interested in American Indian portraits at a time when Crazy Horse was also at Red Cloud. Charles C. Hamilton, who had become a respected Judge in Iowa recalled that by early July his father was already at the agency: "About this time I received word from my father that he had arrived at Red Cloud Agency, having come from Sioux City on the Union Pacific train to Cheyenne, and from there to Red Cloud [...] by [wagon] train. He asked me to join him there as soon as it was safe to travel. [...] Finally, a train was organized [in Crook City, where the youth was at the time] with sufficient number of people. [...] After a trip devoid of excitement, I arrived and joined my father. This was a Government post [Camp Robinson] with barracks sufficient to accommodate about 1,500 soldiers of cavalrymen, and a couple of companies of artillery. The intention of my father in going to Red Cloud Agency," son Charles explained, "was to obtain photographs of the fort, the agency, the noted officers of the Army, the leading scouts, and the leading chiefs of the different tribes." At this point in the narration, Judge Hamilton interjected the old tale of Indian superstition. "My father," he continued, "succeeded in securing negatives of the leading government officers, and of the leading white men scouts, but had difficulty in securing pictures of the Indian Chiefs. The Indians," he explained to his audience, "had a superstition about having their pictures taken, and would not consent unless some white man was beside them and had his picture taken at the same time. But my father very readily secured their pictures without their knowledge or consent."

James H. Hamilton made extensive use of tintypes. "In those days," Charles recalled, "photographers were making what is known as tin type pictures. In taking a tin type, four pictures are made with one exposure. When my father was ready to take a picture, we would have the Indian seated upon a bench about two or three feet from a white man, and would then make an exposure and secure the tin type pictures. This was supposed to be but one exposure, but in fact produced four tin types. It was then necessary to take another picture, so that each of the persons could have one. A negative was then substituted and a new lens put in the camera. A focus was made on the Indian alone, and a good negative was thus procured. A tin type was given to the Indian and to the white man and all was lovely."[368]

We already commented on Charles Hamilton's impressionistic account of Indian dress at the agency. What is interesting, notwithstanding the Indian superstition story, is that after the initial resistance, his father James was granted permission to witness and photograph the most sacred of Lakota ceremonies: "While at Red Cloud, we had the privilege of witness-ing and taking pictures of a Sun Dance. This was a dance and ceremony wherein the young men of the tribe were initiated into manhood and became members of the warrior body.[369] [...] My father had difficulty in securing the pictures of this ceremony, but the Indians finally agreed to permit the pictures to be taken [...] and a number of fine negatives were secured."[370] The reference to the Sun Dance picture taking is significant in many respects: not only for the concession granted to an intruding stranger and photographer, but also because it proves that James H. Hamilton was already at Red Cloud Agency by June when he photographed the large Crazy Horse sun dance on June 29. It was hosted by the Northern Indians and included the sham battle previously referred to.

This could be the sun dance generally alluded to in their eyewitness accounts by Camp Robinson Commander Col. Luther Bradley, by Lieut.

William P. Clark, by Lieut. Frederick G. Schwatka (who later published a popular article on it),[371] by interpreter Billy Garnett, and others. Hamilton lists a "No. 128. Sun Dancer" in his *Catalogue*. The image has yet to be positively identified but six hand-colored photographs of a sun dance by an unknown photographer were recently sold by Cowan's. Undated and apparently old, they were tentatively dated by the auctioneers at ca. 1880-90s, though they could be earlier.[372] One photograph in particular, with handwritten caption "The Brave at the Pole of Torture," seemingly shows a lone sun dancer (with evident re-touching by the photographer) reminiscent of the old painting of a Sioux sun dancer by George Catlin, and later photographs.

Whether those images could actually be Hamilton's, we do not know. What is certain is that James H. Hamilton was one of the earliest known "shadow catchers" to produce a photographic portrait of a Lakota sun dancer. Hamilton's presence at the sun dance indicates that he spent more than a couple of months at Red Cloud Agency. Enough time to become acquainted with officers, mixed-bloods, and especially with the names and faces of prominent Indians, the ones he photographed and later listed in his *Catalogue*, Crazy Horse included. It has also been suggested that the Indian portrayed by Hamilton and listed as Crazy Horse could actually be his father Waglula, but this is utterly unlikely. Hamilton knew who the Oglala war chief was and there does not seem to be any valid reason to doubt his listing of "No. 104" as the real Crazy Horse. Hamilton's own son Charles recalled that at Red Cloud and Spotted Tail agencies his father secured portraits of "all the leading Indians," and Crazy Horse was certainly one of them. Had Crazy Horse been an exception, Hamilton's father would have undoubtedly expressed his disappointment for such notable omission – as D.F. Barry later did, though based on false pretense – and his son would have remembered it.

James H. Hamilton was not only a traveling photographer, but also an enterprising businessman who took advantage of what was an important aspect of Indian life at the agencies: trade. Indians loved to trade, both for economic and social reasons, and the opportunity to do so at a place other than the agency trader's store was appreciated. This gave Hamilton yet another chance to interact with his potential subjects. We know Crazy Horse visited the trader stores at both Red Cloud and Spotted Tail agencies. Nothing precluded him from also visiting Hamilton's big trade wagon, perhaps accompanied by Nellie, Little Bat, even Grouard as interpreters. This was a good opportunity for the photographer-trader to also discuss picture taking in the private setting of the local photo gallery with a skylight. As Hamilton's son recalled, "My father had a side line in this business. The soldiers and Indians were all anxious to secure pictures, and he traded tin types for buffalo robes, moccasins, beaded leggings, and other wearing apparel of the Indians. When we started back to the Black Hills from Red Cloud, we had a large wagon of furs and trinkets." Trading photographic portraits for goods proved advantageous to all parties involved. Hamilton's imposing physique and kind manners probably also helped with the Indians. "My father," reiterated Charles Hamilton, "pursued the same tactics at Spotted Tail Agency as he had at Red Cloud, and secured negatives of the leading officers of the Army, of the Indian Chiefs, and leading Scouts."[373]

Precisely how many negative plates, stereoviews, or tintypes of Indians James H. Hamilton took that summer, we may never know, but given his photo-for-trade offers, certainly a considerable number. Some were posted by Heritage Auctions and more recently published by Tom Buecker. The fact that, until now, no surviving tintype with the same backdrop from Camp Robinson-Red Cloud Agency has positively been identified as a James H. Hamilton cannot be argued against the eyewitness testimony of his son. By their own nature, tintypes generally did not bear the maker's imprint, and their small size lent them to be easily damaged or lost. From his son's narration, we know that James H. Hamilton also had a "little portable studio [...] located along the banks of a little stream west of the barracks" that he utilized for indoor portraits.

Two sample photographs taken by Hamilton at Spotted Tail, "No. 108. Sioux Belles" and the previously mentioned "No. 129. Touch-the-Cloud" (both in his *Catalogue*) show two different, simple backdrops. For the Crazy

6

133. Gray Wolf, Winnebago Chief.
134. Sioux Squaw.
135. Arrapahoe Village and Sand Buttes,
136. Pappoose in Cradle, Strapped to Pony.
137. Indian Graveyard at Red Cloud.
138. Red Cloud Village and Sand Buttes.
139. Red Dog and Daughter.
140. Group of Sioux Chiefs.
141. Four Bears, Sioux Chief.
142. Sioux Brave.
143. Yankton Sioux Chief.
144. Santee Sioux Chief.
145. Cooking Scene at Arrapahoe Village.
146. Indian Guarding Prisoners.
147. Arrapahoe Squaws & Ponies at Red Cl'd
148. Red Clrud's Lodge.
149. Crow's Breast, Sioux Chief.
150. Making Love to the Squaws.
151. Warrior, with War Bonnet.
152. Sitting Bull.
153. Big Little Man.
154. Family Group at Red Cloud.
155. Arrapahoe Chiefs and Village.
156. Arrapahoe Chief.
157. American Horse's Village at Red Cloud
158. Arrapahoe Squaw.
159. Group at Red Cloud.
160. Two-Strike and Family.
161. Children in the Wigwam.
162. Sioux Squaw, and Pappoose in Cradle.
163. Travay.
164. Group at Spotted Tail Agency.
165. Photographing Indians at Red Cloud.
166. Village at Spotted Tail Agency.
167. Spotted Tail's Daughter.
168. Pawnee Chief.

7

169. Sioux Traveling.
170. Learning the Use of the Stereoscope
171. Roman Nose, Sioux Chief,
172. American Horse's Lodge.
173. Ponca Chiefs.
174. Group of Chiefs at Bismarck.
175. Black Eagle.
176. War Dance.
177. Sioux Hunter.
178. Sioux Squaw in buckskin suit.
179. Son of a Star, Sioux Chief.
180. Group of Chiefs.
181. Interpreter and Sioux Chiefs.
182. Warrior and Squaw.
183. Dressing Beef.
184. Squaw in Fancy Dress.
185. Sioux Warrior.
186. Courting.
187. Upper Missouri River Sioux Warrio
188. Arrapahoe Brave.

LANDSCAPES.

189. Lone Rock, and view of Sioux Falls
190. Lovers Retreat, Sioux Falls.
191. Rapids and Island at Sioux Falls.
192. Main Falls, looking southwest.
193. Main Falls, looking southeast.
194. Middle Falls in winter.
195. Lower Falls.
196. Lower Falls in winter.
197. Town of Sioux Falls.
198. Split Rock and Palisades.
199. Palisades, looking east.
200. Palisades, looking northeast.
201. Palisades, looking northwest.
202. Palisades, looking south.

J.H. Hamilton's *Catalogue of Stereoscopic Views of the Northwest,*
Sioux City, Iowa (1878).
Continued through page 179.

8°

203. Spirit Canyon.
204. Natural Bridge Piers at Dell Rapids.
205. Group at Dell Rapids.
206. Pipestone Falls.
207. Pipestone Quarries.
208. Pipestone Falls and Quarry.
209. Pipestone Towers.
210. Minnehaha Falls in winter.
211. Minnehaha Falls in summer.
212. Bridal Veil.
213. Dells of St. Croix.
214. Taylor's Falls on St. Croix.
215. Crow Butte, Neb., looking east.
216. Crow Butte, Neb., looking northeast.
217. Sand Buttes at Red Cloud Agency.
218. Bear Buttes, Black Hills.
219. Crook City, Black Hills.
220. Whitewood, near Crook City.
221. Mining on the Whitewood.
222. Eagle's Nest, near Deadwood.
223. Montana City, Black Hills.
224. Elizabethtown, Black Hills.
225. Main Street, Deadwood.
226. Deadwood.
227. Deadwood Gulch.
228. Deadwood Towers.
229. Central City.
230. Mining near Deadwood.

CATALOGUE

OF

STEREOSCOPIC

VIEWS of the NORTHWEST

INCLUDING VIEWS OF

Sioux Falls Pipestone Quarries, Dakota, Minnesota, and Black Hills Scenery.

Also a large and Complete Assortment of

INDIAN SCENES,

Representing Distinguished Chiefs and Promi-
nent Characters, Villages, Wigwams, Fam-
ily Groups, Dances, Burial Scenes,

And other peculiarities of the uncivilized tribes of the Northwest

Published and for Sale by

J. H. HAMILTON, Sioux City, Iowa.

Special Wholesale Rates to Dealers.

Catalogue.

1. Spotted Tail, Sioux Chief.
2. Council of Omaha and Winnebago Chfs.
3. Eba-hom-ba, Omaha Chief and Warriors
4. Omaha Indians starting on a hunt.
5. Social Smoke—Omahas.
6. Omahas, with lodge in the woods.
7. Omaha Council.
8. Omaha Brick Yard.
9. Group of Omaha Chiefs.
10. Omaha Pipe Dance.
11. Winnebago Council.
12. Pa-de-gi-he, Omaha Chief.
13. Omaha Village Scene.
14. Prairie Scene at the Omaha Agency.
15. Omaha Warrior.
16. Omaha Squaws and Pappoose.
17. Gi-he-ga, Omaha Chief.
18. Torrega, Iowa Chief.
19. Omaha Family.
20. Chief's Son.
21. Scene at Omaha Pipe Dance.
22. Group of Dancers.
23. Mud Wigwam.
24. Omaha Pappoose.
25. Num-ba-douba, Omaha.
26. Iowa Chief.
27. Omaha Hunter.
28. Omaha Village.
29. Iowa Chief and Wigwam.
30. Omaha Agency.
31. Omaha Brave.

3

32. E-ba-hom-ba, Omaha chief with pipe.
33. Omaha Lodge.
34. Prairie Scene, with Indians.
35. Group of Omahas.
36. Yellow Smoke and Wash-co-mo-ni, chfs
37. Omaha Squaw and Sick Pappoose.
38. Iowa Chief and Interpreter.
39. Scene at Omaha Agency.
40. Shauga-skah, Omaha chief.
41. Big Bear, Omaha chief.
42. Omahas, with Packed Ponies.

WINNEBAGO INDIANS.

43. Standing Buffalo, chief.
44. Winnebago Children.
45. Winnebago Squaws and Pappoose.
46. Indians on the Prairie.
47. After receiving Annuity Goods.
48. Pet Elk.
49. Group of Winnebagoes, with ponies.
50. Squaw, with pappoose on a board.
51. Waiting for Annuity Goods.
52. Group of Winnebagoes.
53. Waiting for Soup.
54. Group of Winnebago Squaws in woods.
55. Group of Winnebagoes on prairie.
56. Winnebago Pappoose.
57. Walk-in-the-Evening and Bear's Skin.
58. Squaw, with pappoose on her back.
59. Winnebago Wigwam.
60. Interior of Wigwam.
61. Group on Issue Day.
62. White Swan and Son.
63. Receiving Annuity Goods.
64. Bark Wigwam.

4

Cooking Scene.
Chief's Daughter.
Squaws.
Issuing Goods to Winnebagoes.
Green Cloud.
Winnebago Squaw.
Hunting for Travelers.
Becoming Civilized.
Squaw Carrying Wood.
Squaws Standing for a Picture.
Squaws on Horseback.
Squaw Chopping Wood.
Indians Wrestling.
Squaws dressed low-neck & short sleeves
Squaws and Dogs in front of a wigwam
Boy Shooting with Bow.
Tree Climber.
Winnebagoes Playing Moccasin.
Winnebagoes on Prairie.
Squaw and Pappoose.

SIOUX INDIANS.

Rushing Bear, Sioux Chief.
Two Bears and Running Antelope.
Sioux Medicine Man.
Sioux Squaw.
Sioux Warrior.
Chief and Daughters.
Red Dog's Daughter.
Sioux Chiefs at Standing Rock Agency.
Bear's Rib and Long Fox.
Starving Warrior.
Brule Sioux Chief.
Iron Horse, Sioux Chief.
Group of Sioux Chiefs.

5

98. Medicine Bear, Sioux Chief.
99. The Grass, Sioux.
100. Mrs. Galpin and Sioux Chiefs.
101. Black Hawk, Sioux Chief.
102. Sioux War Dance.
103. Spotted Tail's Squaw, No. 4.
104. Crazy Horse.
105. Arrapahoe Warrior.
106. White Thunder, Sioux Chief.
107. Surrender of Lame Deer's Band.
108. Sioux Belles.
109. Dancing Party.
110. Scalping Scene.
111. Group of War Dancers at Spotted Tail.
112. Black Elk, Sioux Chief.
113. Red Dog, Sioux Chief.
114. Red Dog's Daughter.
115. Muggins, Sioux Warrior.
116. Roman Nose and War Pony.
117. Arrapahoe Village.
118. Medicine Man at Red Cloud.
119. Red Cloud's Village.
120. White Goose, Sioux Chief.
121. Burial Tree at Red Cloud.
122. Pretty Bear, Sioux Chief.
123. Emigrants Surprised.
124. U. S. Indian Soldier under Spotted Tail.
125. Spotted Tail's Son.
126. Black Crow, Sioux Chief.
127. Spotten Tail's Son and Family.
128. Sun Dancer.
129. Touch-the-Cloud.
    Led principal charge, under Crazy Horse, in Custer Massacre.
130. Two-Strike, Sioux Chief.
131. Sioux War Dancers.
132. Gray Wolf and Family.

Horse tintype, Hamilton must have utilized the permanent gallery of art near the trader's store. Whether the more elaborate backdrop was his, or belonged to the log cabin studio we do not know. We already noted the rafters in the ceiling visible in the tintype, indicating it was taken in the log cabin gallery with skylight for indoor photography. The same gallery with canvas skylight is seen in another "Peter T. Buckley" image, also published by Buecker: "Horse racing was a popular pastime at the agency and Camp Robinson, especially when many mounted troops were stationed there, and that was the case in the summer 1877. Large numbers of soldiers, civilians and agency Indians viewed the races. [...] In this view riders and mounts pose near the photographer's gallery at the completion of a race: two other men stand on the gallery's roof (the white skylight is visible)."[374]

Jack Heriard, for one, pointed out that photo-historians who possess Hamilton photographs – not necessarily from his 1877 stay at Red Cloud – "have not been able to match [the tintype's] backdrop with other Hamilton photos. There are no known photos by Hamilton or the other photographers visiting Camp Robinson with their subjects posed in the studio setting pictured in [the tintype]."[375] Actually there seems to be evidence to the contrary. According to the late Tom Buecker, this backdrop was the same as the one used in some sittings in Hamilton's well-known Sioux City, Iowa, studio. Specifically, based on information he had originally received from Thomas Wright, Buecker stated that the same backdrop appeared in a studio portrait of either Red Cloud or Red Feather.[376] However, Buecker took this fact to prove that the Indian in the tintype could not be Crazy Horse because Crazy Horse never traveled to Sioux City.[377] It does not seem to be a valid argument. J.H. Hamilton's published *Catalogue* bears on the front the Sioux City, Iowa, imprint, but the stereoviews taken at Red Cloud and Spotted Tail listed in that very *Catalogue*, too, have the same Sioux City imprint of his permanent studio, even though technically the photographs were not taken in Sioux City.

At a closer look, the backdrop in the tintype appears to be a composite of two different style backdrops, the ferns to the right, and the column to the left of the Indian, separated by a vertical line, visible behind the

Indian's left arm (again, the tintype is a positive/mirror image). Nothing prevented Hamilton from using the artistic, composite backdrop available in the large log cabin "gallery of art," the permanent studio with a skylight and a large "Pictures" sign posted outside at Red Cloud Agency.

Less than a month after Crazy Horse's death, while the large Sioux delegation was in Washington to meet with Pres. Rutherford B. Hayes and preparations were underway for the transfer of Red Cloud Agency to the Missouri, Private Charles Howard (1842-??), 4th U.S. Infantry, arrived at Camp Robinson with the mapping expedition of Capt. William N. Stanton.[378] Born in 1842 in Virginia, Howard was a musician who enlisted in 1875 and was assigned to the 4th Infantry Band. The following year he was at Fort Bridger, Wyoming Territory, producing photographs and tintypes. He must have been fairly well known, as Capt. Stanton requested to the commanding officer at Ft. Bridger that the "soldier with a camera" be assigned to his expedition. As noted, Howard arrived too late to see and even possibly photograph Crazy Horse, but he sensed the historicity of the moment and his privileged position to document, if not the face, at least the temporary grave where the mortal remains of Crazy Horse were laid to rest on a hill near Camp Sheridan. Dickson pointed out that Howard was "at Camp Robinson Sept. 30 to October 4 and from Oct. 25 to Oct. 28, 1877. Crazy Horse had already died by this time [...]." Specifically, with regard to the backdrop of our tintype, Dickson noted that "only one image showing a backdrop is known by Private Howard. It dates to the 1878-80 period and is different than the Crazy Horse tintype."[379]

Sometime in September or October 1877, Maine-born photographer Daniel S. Mitchell (1838-1929) was at Red Cloud Agency, and later at Spotted Tail, where he took local views and portraits of Sioux and Arapaho Indians. He had been running a successful studio in Cheyenne, Wyoming Territory, but like other camera workers he was drawn to the Black Hills by the large influx of prospectors and the bustling new towns. Mitchell actually partnered with another photographer, Joseph H. McGowan, as his assistant, and together they traveled the region with their tent studio taking excellent scenic stereoviews and portraits, later advertised as "Class D. - Indian Chiefs Portraits" of their *Western Stereoscopic Gems*, by the Great Western Photograph Publishing Co., based in Omaha.[380] We do not know exactly when Mitchell arrived at Red Cloud Agency, but circumstantial evidence suggests it must have been shortly after the death of Crazy Horse, so he cannot be a candidate for either a photograph or our debated tintype of Crazy Horse. D.S. Mitchell's large number of portraits of Lakota (mostly Oglala), and Arapaho men and women, do attest that, as Dickson put it, their "concerns about the camera robbing them of their personal power had largely disappeared."[381] And also that despite the recent crisis and volatile climate aggravated by the government plan to relocate the agencies to the Missouri, "shadow catchers" were still welcome at the troublesome Red Cloud Agency and at the friendlier Spotted Tail Agency. Dickson also pointed out that Mitchell had a painted backdrop, but it was different from the one in the Crazy Horse tintype. Furthermore, Dickson continued, Mitchell "does not list a portrait of Crazy Horse in his catalog of views; seems he would have had he had taken one. The fact that the Oglala headmen are wearing their Ulysses S. Grant Indian Peace Medals suggests that the portraits were made after the delegation had returned from Washington D.C. in October 1877, after Crazy Horse died."[382]

Before the end of that tragic year, but again shortly after the death of Crazy Horse, another photographer stopped at Red Cloud Agency. Traveling from the Hills back to Sidney, Nebraska, a connecting point between the Black Hills Stage Route and the Union Pacific Transcontinental Railroad, David Rodocker (1840-1919) visited the Agency. There, wrote Dickson, "he made at least five images. His view of the agency buildings shows them completely deserted, suggesting that he might have passed through in late October after the Oglala had already departed for their new reservation in Dakota Territory. Views of Indian camps in the area, however, suggest that a few families had not yet joined their relatives at the new Red Cloud Agency."[383]

While recognizing that at least five known photographers passed through Red Cloud Agency and Camp Robinson in 1877, Ephriam Dickson felt that "only one – James Hamilton – can be shown to have been there during the period that Crazy Horse was also there. None of the backdrops used by four of the photographers (the fifth one is not known) match the Crazy Horse tintype." Therefore, interpreting the general view on this matter, he concluded that "based on the information we have about the photographers, the timing of their visits and their known backdrops, I find it highly unlikely that the tintype discussed was taken at Camp Robinson in 1877."[384] Conversely, and indicative of a more open mind, another objective and rational critic like Thomas W. Wright had given the Crazy Horse tintype the benefit of the doubt. "The tintype which Fred Hackett turned up has THE BEST CLAIM TO BEING an authentic picture of the noted chief," he wrote.[385]

The tintype had a great advantage. No lengthy exposure time was needed; no negative was produced. Instead, a positive photographic image was impressed directly on a small plate of iron ("ferro," in Italian) varnished with a sensitized film. The resulting impression was one of a kind, to be kept by the subject of the image itself. With a special four-lens camera, four positive identical tintypes were produced with a single exposure, but again, no negative. The four small images were then cut into four separate originals of the same subject. Unless they were mounted on a piece of cardboard, and even then not always, tintypes did not carry the photographer/studio imprint logo impressed on the back. By 1877, the Sioux were very familiar with tintypes. They had been for a good decade, since Glover and Gardner at Fort Laramie, and later Lieut. Wilhelm at Camp Robinson, blazed the photographic trail into Lakota Country.

In a recent article on the "controversial" Crazy Horse tintype, Angela Aleiss quoted the professional opinion of Mark Osterman, Photographic Process Historian at George Eastman House International Museum of Photography and Film in Rochester, New York. Osterman explained that the tintype in question "is a ferrotype [tintype] made with a <u>four-lens Bon Ton camera</u> [...]. The original plate was size 5" x 7" and the four individual images were cut from the plate and generally inserted into or pasted from behind to a paper mat. The black edge on the right and top shows that this image was on the top right of the set of four." What happened to the other three identical copies is unknown, although Carroll Friswold, Jr. stated his father and Fred Hackett had seen another tintype identical to the one published by Vaughn and Friswold himself. It is logical to assume that, if indeed James H. Hamilton was the photographer, "104. Crazy Horse" in his *Catalogue* could be an altogether different photo as the same catalogue lists the images as "stereoscopic views." Returning to Aleiss's article and what she called "the photo's Victorian-florid backdrop," again Osterman acknowledged that "fancy backdrops were common for studio portraiture in the U.S."

The same authority, evidently unaware of the existence of the permanent photographic studio at Red Cloud Agency, a fully furnished self-identified "Gallery of Art", and that the log-cabin housing it was actually equipped with a large skylight, argued against the Crazy Horse identification of the tintype precisely based on the key elements we instead maintain in its favor. "It is a skylight studio portrait and not taken in a tent," Osterman stated. He pointed out the gradient of light coming from behind the background to the right "as a sign. The elaborate set seems to indicate that the studio was located in a large city like Chicago or New York rather than a military camp in western Nebraska." We never suggested the tintype was taken in a tent, having verified since the beginning that there was a photographic gallery at Camp Robinson-Red Cloud Agency by the time of Crazy Horse's surrender. Furthermore, there seems to be no logical reason why an elaborate backdrop like the one in the tintype could not be have been used in that same permanent "gallery of art," or photographic studio.

By 1877, the Agency had grown to a bustling small border town. In addition to the "pictures" studio, there was also a "restaurant" and a post office at Red Cloud Agency. Osterman does provide an interesting analysis of the interior details of the alleged "large city" studio setting seen in the tintype. As Aleiss wrote, "Osterman describes the object on the left as a typical studio photographer's 'posing chair' facing backward. 'The box with the knob is that part of the chair that allows the arm/back rest to move up and down' he says. A cast iron 'head immobilizer' would have been placed behind the subject to prevent him from moving during the six- to 20-second exposure required for the photo." Osterman determined that "this is another potential clue that the image was taken in a city. An itinerant photographer working in a studio/darkroom tent would generally use a much lighter chair." Still, he admitted that "the floor, chair, and background smack of the 1870s," adding that photographers would reuse the same equipment for years later." Drawing a presumptuous conclusion, he stated, "So this could be as late as the 1880s or even the 1890s. Very difficult to say."

Aleiss closed the article with the intriguing rhetorical question: "So who really is that stoic-looking man in the Crazy Horse tintype?"[386] The answer is, "Crazy Horse."

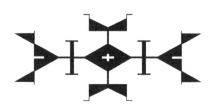

PART II

The Face of Crazy Horse

"A good man and good to look at."
Victoria Standing Bear Conroy, in Jean Hammond 1986

"I showed the picture to Dewey Beard just before he died.
He looked at a long time. And said it looks like Crazy Horse."
Jake Herman, letter to J.W. Vaughn, 1956

The Age Question

No one really knows exactly what year Curly Hair was born and conversely, how old Crazy Horse was when his blood was spilled irreversibly on the Camp Robinson ground. The age question is intriguing in its own right, and there are estimates that can help us postulate, if nothing else, whether the individual in the tintype could possibly match the age attributed to the Lakota chief at the time of death. Together with other evidence, age has been crucial in discarding photographs of older-looking Indians purportedly identified as Crazy Horse.[387] Still, the age discrepancies pertaining to the famous Oglala are noticeable. Assuming there were no problems with translation, or purposely misleading answers, first and foremost there are the testimonies of Crazy Horse's own father Worm and his spiritual mentor Horn Chips; both made Crazy Horse about thirty-seven years old when he was mortally wounded. He Dog thought his kola was even older, about thirty-nine, while Charles Eastman, as we said, was quite certain

Crazy Horse was thirty-three when he died. In a 1927 reply letter to Dr. McGillycuddy, Billy Garnett gave a similar age assessment of the Oglala war chief. "As you know," he wrote, "Crazy Horse was an Indian just a little past 30 years old when he was killed."[388]

First Lieut. Walter S. Schuyler, Gen. Crook's Aide-de-Camp, in an interview to the *Chicago Tribune* dated only a few days before the "hostile" Crazy Horse and his Oglala were to surrender at Camp Robinson, underscored the Northern Indian's impressive war record with respect to his relatively young age, having not yet reached his thirtieth birthday: "The chief fighting man is Crazy Horse, as a chief, and he had the best fighting element with him. He is no doubt the bravest man. […] He is only 29 years of age."[389] The completely revised Crazy Horse biography on Wikipedia takes a middle of the road approach and proclaims that the great Lakota was thirty-five when he was killed. The on-line thread "Crazy Horse and Relatives" gives him born in 1840, hence 37 years when he died. A word of caution was spoken by William J. Bordeaux (1884-1965?), the mixed-blood Brule son of Louis Bordeaux (1849-1917), the noted French-Brule interpreter and rancher who had known Crazy Horse personally. W.J. Bordeaux acknowledged that "the task was no easy matter for he lived in a time when scant attention was given to the recording of noteworthy events. As a result," he continued, "even the place and exact date of his birth, hence his accurate age, have been a matter of controversy among his own tribe."[390] Bordeaux's cautionary approach is noteworthy and admirable. Today, most sources place the date of Crazy Horse's birth around the year 1840-1841, the "Stole-One-Hundred-Horses Winter" (alternatively, "One Hundred Horses Were Returned Home Winter") according to some Oglala winter counts, and the location of his birth being "at the foot of Bear Butte, near the present Fort Mead, South Dakota."[391] Foremost among the non-Indian biographers of the great chief, Bray, too, gives the Black Hills, actually a Kapozha ("Travel light") camp along one of the creeks that flow into the forks of the Cheyenne River, as Pehin Yuhaha's place of birth in the fall 1840. In Bray's map of the Lakota world in Crazy Horse's youth, the birthplace is marked Bear Butte.[392]

The certainty of many writers clashes with W.J. Bordeaux's words who, as just noted, insisted that "the exact location of the birthplace of Crazy Horse has never been absolutely established and opinions differ. While some have declared that he was born near Laramie, Wyoming, others have believed that it was in the Dakota Region."[393] Bordeaux did not reach his conclusions based solely on speculation. He had interviewed "several near relatives of the noted warrior, including a full [sic] sister, Mrs. [Julia] Clown [...] at her home, about seven miles East of the Thunder Butte Sub Station on the Cheyenne River Indian Reservation, [and] she told me [...] that Crazy Horse was born somewhere near the mouth of the Laramie River in the southeastern part of Wyoming. As to the date of his birth, Mrs. Clown and her husband agreed that it was in the spring of the year that Left Hand Big Nose was killed by the Shoshones [1839]." So, according to Julia Clown, Crazy Horse would have been about 38 years old when he was killed. Still, not all Indians who had known Crazy Horse intimately would speculate on his age. Crazy Horse's brother-in-law Red Feather, one of those who "knew him well, knew everything about him," candidly admitted that he did not know Crazy Horse's age, "or where he was born, or where he was buried."[394] The "I-know-nothing" attitude Feraca compared to the omertà of old generation Southern Italians, reflected a combination of truth and desire to shroud the memory of the Lakota hero in a blanket of silence. With regard to Crazy Horse's wife Black Shawl (ca. 1843-1927), despite her health condition she lived into her early eighties before succumbing to the influenza epidemic that hit Pine Ridge in the late 1920s. Her photograph, dated 1888, was published by a number of authors.[395] To keep with the controversy of the Crazy Horse tintype, also in the case of his wife Black Shawl, not everyone agrees with the identity of the woman in the picture.[396]

Uncertainties also pertain to the circumstances that led to the death of Crazy Horse's mother by suicide, and, again as already discussed, to the complex and controversial identification of Crazy Horse's closest relatives and their descendants. Case in point, Julia Iron Cedar Woman (Mrs. Amos Clown), cited earlier. According to Lakota custom and kinship terminology

Julia Clown was considered "sister" to Crazy Horse, while biologically she probably was a "half-sister," or a cousin. Her own date of birth is unclear, as is her true relationship to Crazy Horse. Hardorff identified her as "Mrs. Joe Clown" born in 1832,[397] while according to Raymond Clown, one of her descendants, she was born in 1864 or 1865, after the death of Crazy Horse's biological mother. The *Authorized Biography* adds new information but does not resolve the issue. As we have repeatedly seen, the fact remains that among the Lakota themselves there are today conflicting (and confusing) claims regarding who is truly related, more or less directly or indirectly, to Crazy Horse and who is not, yet claims to be. Not to mention the Canadian element, still poorly known. In this regard, Tony Whirlwind Horse, former BIA superintendent at Pine Ridge, commented two decades ago that "after Crazy Horse was killed, many of his band went to Canada. They've never come back. We may never know the truth."[398]

The resulting in-feuding, the charges and counter-charges, the accusations and recriminations within and between those who claim to be Crazy Horse descendants are also due to the uncertainty that to this day embraces some of the most basic facts regarding not just Crazy Horse himself, but also his father Worm, his mother Rattling Blanket Woman, and his wife Black Shawl. The difficult scenario is rooted in a combination of factors, including the disintegration of Crazy Horse's own thiyóšpaye, the Canadian diaspora of many Northern Indians after his death, coupled with the curtain of silence that soon followed for fear of revenge and retaliation, in time leading to faulty or incomplete family oral histories. All of the above were compounded by the difference between English and Lakota kinship terminologies, and the confusion created by agency officials on reservation records when applying the Euro-American kinship system to Lakota names and relationships.[399]

General Appearance

In his previously cited critique of the elusive Crazy Horse photo question, Tom Buecker quoted Richard G. Hardorff in support of his skepticism of the tintype as a possible likeness of Crazy Horse: "The subject's broad [?] facial features and lack of a prominent scar and clothing 'contradict all statements made about the likeness of Crazy Horse by those who associated with him.'"[400] A similar view on the alleged consistent character of the testimonies regarding Crazy Horse's general likenesses was later expressed by Charles Trimble who stated that "descriptions of Crazy Horse's facial and physical features are abundant, both from Lakotas and a few whites who knew him well. These are included in letters, transcripts of interviews and in books based on those primary sources, and all are consistent in their descriptions."[401] Such alleged consensus about Crazy Horse's features and appearance, particularly in the months following his surrender does not, at closer scrutiny, always stand when dealing with specific details. On almost every aspect of his persona we find different or conflicting statements and testimonies. The differences and discrepancies are at times minor, other times too significant not to raise questions about the objectivity and validity of the alleged consistency of opinion ascribed to Crazy Horse's contemporaries by modern scholars.

Discrepancies do exist and, to some extent, they may be the result of poor or faulty translations rendered by interpreters. The old Italian proverb *traduttori, traditori,* "translators, traitors" fits the case, as exemplified by the incident involving Grouard's vile rendering of Crazy Horse's words on the Nez Perce campaign, whatever the Oglala war chief's true feelings might have been. In the summer of 1881 a reporter for the *Leavenworth Weekly Times* traveled to Fort Yates to see the "hostiles" who had recently returned from their Canadian exile. Through an interpreter, he recorded the words of Low Dog, Crow King, Hump, and Iron Thunder, but he was soon made aware of the limits of translations: "There has been a great desire to hear the Indian account of the Custer fight. All these hostiles were in it. Captain Howe, who is highly regarded by the Indians, told me that Low Dog, chief of the Ogalallas, and recognized by the Indians as a great warrior, had promised to give him an account of the fight, and invited me to hear it. I took pencil and paper and with Low Dog's consent noted it down. I have it almost word for word as translated by the interpreter but I regret exceedingly that the interpreter did not give me a literal translation. All Indians use a great many gestures and signs, and the interpreters tell me that it is very difficult to do more than give the substance of what they say."[402]

Translations were, by their very nature, approximate at best, especially in a turbulent context of pivotal events such as the Custer fight, the confiscation of Indian ponies, the illegal taking of the Black Hills, the killing of Crazy Horse, the transfer of the Oglala and Brule agencies from Nebraska to South Dakota, and the stampedes of Northern Indians to Canada. In the dynamics of the verbal exchanges they were asked to translate, these cultural brokers and linguistic mediators often had vested interests of their own, either as a group on at a strictly personal level, besides their own likes and dislikes, blood relations, official duties and obligations, and even fears, as seems to have been the case of Frank Grouard. It is difficult to evaluate objectively the validity of this or that oral testimony, not so much as far as the general picture is concerned, but the specific details.

With regard to Crazy Horse's adult life, especially the last few months before his death, we do not think that this important point has been taken sufficiently into account. In addition to approximate, misinterpreted or misunderstood, and even altogether fallacious translations, the discrepancies we encounter on many specific aspects of Crazy Horse's persona may also reflect the subsequent mythologizing and hero-making, whereas the image became, as it often happened in many other instances in history, the substance. There is the additional complication, faced early on by Eleanor Hinman, and referred to also elsewhere, pertaining to the wall of silence that not a few traditional Sioux raised when it came to discussing issues, events, and peoples directly relating to Crazy Horse, particularly because of the circumstances that had led to his murderous death, the very Lakota involved, to varying degrees, in the entire affair.

Hinman, though well intentioned and sincerely motivated, was not so lucky nor welcome by Crazy Horse's surviving relatives at Pine Ridge. When she drove up to Manderson, in the heart of the reservation, she was met by silence: "Luke Little Hawk, approached by John Colhoff on behalf of the interviewer, replied in effect that no questions had been asked about Crazy Horse at the time of his death, and he did not care to answer any now." Nicholas Black Elk, the world-renown Oglala wičaša wakan related to Crazy Horse through the latter's paternal grandfather Makes the Song,[403] asked Hinman for excessive compensation "as another form of refusal" to cooperate. Other Crazy Horse relatives were equally tight lipped. Jealousy and betrayal had undermined the warrior's commitment to peace. If successful, it would have made him a double winner, in war and peace, overshadowing the agency chiefs. Instead, he met betrayal and death. "The interpreter Emil Afraid-of-Hawk," explained Hinman, "told us that Crazy Horse's relatives had repeatedly refused to make any statement about him to white people or indeed to Indians of the opposite faction."[404]

The discrepancies specifically regarding Crazy Horse's features cannot be attributed exclusively to inaccurate translations. Nor can we logically blame solely the factionalism that pervaded Lakota tribal affairs during and following Crazy Horse's last days. True, they may have reflected the different way each player looked at this controversial, idiosyncratic, aloof, and troublesome man called Crazy Horse. Then again, something does not make sense in the contrasting and contradicting eyewitness impressions, accounts, and descriptions, by both Indian, mixed-blood, and White contemporaries. With regard to the latter, for example, how can we reconcile attributes like "fine looking and intelligent," "good looking," even "girlish looking boy" employed by Lieut. John G. Bourke, Lieut. Jesse Lee, and Agent James Irwin respectively, in defining Crazy Horse's features, with diametrically opposite reports of a "disfigured face," "dogged and morose," "ugly scar," "brutal expression," and the like given by other White eyewitnesses? Were the former descriptions closer to the "physical" truth, and the latter biased by personal dislike? Probably so.

Selective testimonies about Crazy Horse's features, when read taking into account the necessary approximation of what may have been said, lost, or added in translation, and other cultural and personal factors, do present a challenge. But if we can see through the contradictions, with an open mind, then a clearer and more objective portrait of the great Indian patriot emerges. A portrait, we believe, that closely coincides with the image impressed on the tintype. To begin with, the overall physical appearance ascribed to the Oglala war chief does not contradict, but rather strongly corroborates the identity of the Indian in the tintype as a likeness of Crazy Horse. Lieut. Jesse Lee, a military officer accustomed to "sizing" Army recruits, was very surprised when he first met Crazy Horse, whom he expected to be much taller and more physically imposing, like many other Lakota. Lee estimated Crazy Horse to be "not over five feet six inches in height."[405] Frank White Buffalo Man, Hunkpapa from Little Eagle, later testified that his own aunt had known Crazy Horse: "She said Crazy Horse was about five feet, seven inches tall."[406]

The tintype Indian matches these and similar estimates and description of Crazy Horse being a small man among the Lakota, of average built again tending to small, with a relatively small and "strait" nose, meaning, lacking the broadness, prominence, even the "hump" typical of many of his Lakota contemporaries. We have the faces (and noses) of Red Cloud, Spotted Tail, Roman Nose, Whistling Elk, Slow Bull, Little Hawk, Little Big Man, Woman Dress, Young Man Afraid, American Horse, No Neck, Hunts the Enemy (George Sword), Iron Tail, even his kola He Dog, Short Bull, and others whose photographs are positively identified, to compare with the tintype Indian. Similarly, the lips and mouth, in the latter are not excessively pronounced, actually well proportioned, almost delicate like those of a youth, even bordering the feminine. Hence the Sioux testimonies that, while being an adult Lakota male, Crazy Horse did not quite look like the rest of them. A close-up of the face and expression of the Indian in the tintype, fits the "girlish looking boy" characterization previously cited. We address this again later, but for now we can say that possibly a "mark," or indentation, is detectable on the left side of his chin near the mouth.

The Indian in the tintype also fits the approximate age attributed to Crazy Horse at the time of his surrender and death – early to mid-thirties. Most Indian contemporaries also spoke of Crazy Horse's overall pleasant features, his complexion being rather "light" for a Lakota. The subject in the tintype matches such general attributes. The fact that his hands appear otherwise dark, is not atypical in vintage photographs. It also reflected the season, late-spring or summer, when the image was taken. Those familiar with historic photographs of Plains Indians know that most subjects seen in photographs, presented very dark, tanned faces, hands, and forearms, due to constant exposure to sun and prairie winds, whereas the rest of the body, legs especially but also the chest, when shown occasionally in vintage photographs, appear lighter, sometimes much lighter.[407]

When Sioux and non-Indian contemporaries spoke of Crazy Horse's skin color, they obviously referred to his "natural" tone which tended to be lighter than the average Lakota. Even though Donovin Sprague disagrees with the identification of the tintype as Crazy Horse, suggesting instead the name of No Neck, one of the sons of late chief Smoke and himself an Oglala band chief loyal to Red Cloud, his reproduction of the tintype, along with the photos of Iron Tail (same page), and American Horse and Sword (both opposite page) is positioned in such a way to give support to the lighter complexion comparison. And, compare also the darker complexion of Crazy Horse's Oglala contemporaries Stabber (Wačapa) and Stands First (Toka Najin) in 1870s photographs.[408] The Indian in the tintype and No Neck are clearly not the same person, even though Donovin Sprague, contacted by phone, insisted they are, primarily on the (not so valid) reason that they had the same hair partition line.

Still regarding the tintype Indian's general appearance, his overall dress is simple and typical of the time. It includes the long white cotton shirt commonly sold at agency trader's stores in the 1870s, distributed as government gifts or annuities, and dark, most likely blue stroud leggings with period fringe decorations. Brass arm bands, beaded moccasins, and a (red) wool trade blanket decorated with large beaded strip, also typical of the period, complete the attire. The overall demeanor is composed

Composite comparison of the tintype Indian (l) and No Neck (r).
Note the different complexion colors. No Neck had a complexion much darker than
Crazy Horse who was known as the "Light Skinned Warrior."

and dignified, as if aware of the uniqueness of the moment. The facial expression is firm and determined but not tense, as compared, for example, with similar period photos (in Feraca's article) of Woman Dress, standing and wearing an almost identical outfit, or of Little Big Man, seated, also with a white shirt under the vest, wearing a large medal, perhaps the one he received for his role in the Crazy Horse affair. The lack of a war bonnet or weapon (notwithstanding what Michael Samuel wrote, also to be discussed later), and the subject holding in his left hand – the side of the heart – his wotawe (again, below in detail) compares nicely with the generalized description of Crazy Horse's low-key, simple, dignified appearance. In the words of William Bordeaux, "Throughout his colorful career he never became unduly conceited and he was never seen in gorgeous costumes such as the feathered war-bonnet or in the buckskin war shirt trimmed with weasel tails or in a decorated robe. He showed no signs of personal pompousness."[409]

Luther Standing Bear was fourteen years old when he first saw Tašunke Witko at Spotted Tail Agency in the summer 1877. He confirmed the impression of Crazy Horse being modest in dress and countenance, a telling statement about his personal nature. Luther saw Crazy Horse in his father's lodge: "He was a little man of slight built. He did not carry anything with him, and he dressed poorly. There was nothing fancy about him."[410] Aside from what Hardorff called "broad facial features" and "the lack of a prominent scar," which can be debated, it is surprising that the same Hardorff expressed "skepticism" on the identification of the tintype as Crazy Horse based on what he described as "the overall gaudy regalia worn by the subject of this picture." Which, he argued "seems to contradict all statements made about the likeness of Crazy Horse by those who associated with him."[411] How can the absence of a war bonnet or other elaborate eagle feather arrangement, absence of traditional pipe and beaded pipe bag, absence of a weapon (war club, pipe tomahawk, gun, even sword), combined with the presence of a simple cotton shirt rather than the traditional painted, quilled/beaded, fringed buckskin scalp/war shirt, and how plain stroud leggings without beaded border strip, and a breastplate, albeit a long one, be considered "gaudy regalia"? As we detail in our assessment of the breastplate and armbands, the elegant attribute better fits, for example, American Horse (next page), Young Man Afraid, Touch the Cloud, Little Wound, or Little Big Man, (even Billy Garnett) who, that fall in Washington, were photographed both in group and alone wearing "gaudy regalia."

Crazy Horse's lack of ostentation and quiet demeanor matches the overall appearance of the Indian in the tintype. Again according to Hardorff, "From composite statements of Indian contemporaries, Crazy Horse emerges as a man of medium stature and light frame and weight; [...] He] lacked the prominence of cheekbones so typical of his race."[412] Horn Chips, through interpreter, stated that "Crazy Horse was a man small in stature, rather light in frame and weight, [and] light complexion."[413] He was corroborated by Little Killer, who had been close to Crazy Horse before and after the surrender. In his interview with Hinman he described the war chief as "a short little man."[414] Newspaper correspondents expressed judgments at times differing from, at times converging with, those of the Indians. One writer reported that Crazy Horse "was a very young-appearing man, although 37 years of age."[415] Another made him "slender, and about 35 years old."[416] Still another saw him "thirty-eight years of age" adding that "he is not unlike other fine-looking and intelligent Sioux, though bearing himself with greater dignity than any of them."[417]

American Horse in full regalia, studio portrait by Charles M. Bell, Washington, Oct. 1877. The long white cotton shirt is visible under the traditional fringed and beaded buckskin war/scalp shirt.

Lieut. John G. Bourke, 3rd U.S. Cavalry, author of the frontier classic *On the Border with Crook*, visited Crazy Horse's lodge near the agency soon after the surrender. He was accompanied by the ambivalent Frank Grouard – a spy for the military by his own admission – who had previously lived in semi-captivity among the Northern Indians and knew both Sitting Bull and Crazy Horse intimately. Consonant with traditional Lakota hospitality and his new good disposition, Crazy Horse welcomed Grouard and Lieut. Bourke, who later remembered his first encounter with the war chief: "I saw before me a man who looked quite young, not over thirty years old, five feet eight inches high, lithe and sinewy, with a scar in his face." Like Lee, Bourke too was accustomed to judging physical types and heights, estimating Crazy Horse to be "about 5'8'," just like the Indian in the tintype. Bourke added that "the expression of his countenance was of quiet dignity, but morose, dogged, tenacious, and melancholy." This was not surprising, as the Oglala war chief was aware he had placed himself in an unknown situation and among potential enemies, Indian and White alike, no matter how sincere his peaceful intentions were. According to Bourke, Crazy Horse, was "at least in the first days of his coming upon the reservation, gloomy and reserved."[418]

After his first enlistment in Lieut. Clark's Indian scouts, and the return of weapons and horses to him and his chiefs, Crazy Horse began to relax, interacting with both agency Indians and local Whites, also gaining some weight. The days of physical hardship and fighting now over, he partook of the temporary peace and the fattening (if not necessarily nutritious) government rations, pure lead for a traditional Lakota stomach. Crazy Horse attended dog feasts and ceremonial gatherings, not least the big council sponsored by Little Wound. If he kept eating voraciously, it was a typically Lakota and indeed generalized Indian trait. Sioux men were brought up to endure hunger and occasional famine, and when food was plenty, it was customary to overeat, to show appreciation to the host and, of course, just to make sure. It was impolite not to fully partake of feast whenever food was offered. In the end, Crazy Horse actually suffered from severe indigestion and other intestinal problems, as reported by a correspondent, George P. Wallihan, who signed himself "Rapherty" in *The Cheyenne Daily Leader*, May 16, 1877: "His illness was caused by over-eating and the sudden change from buffalo straight, and but little of that, to wheat bread, coffee, sugar and strawberries and cream, which are furnished at this place of plenty, and it nearly killed him."[419]

When the young reporter, just arrived at Red Cloud a few days after the surrender, arranged with the help of post trader Dear and Frank Grouard a visit to Crazy Horse's lodge, the war chief, he wrote, received him and his two lady companions with some distance. If true to a degree, it was probably due to the White paper-man being a total stranger, and perhaps Crazy Horse still recovering from his severe indigestion. Details of the visit later reported between the lines by the same narrator, describing the traditional reception with the pipe being passed around the circle of Northern chiefs and guests, including the two ladies, speak to the contrary. Young Wallihan, like his father Samuel, was no Indian lover, and his writings reflected a racist attitude and a profound dislike of the Red Man, especially those responsible for Custer's death. Wallihan described Crazy Horse, dubbing him with offensive sarcasm "Maniacal Equine," as "quite ungracious" and "sullen." Thomas Powers pointed out that the young journalist "failed to mention two gifts presented by the chief to his guests. To Ella, whom Wallihan married soon afterward, [Crazy Horse] gave the pipe which had passed around the circle, and to the young reporter he presented a ledger book containing eighteen drawings."[420]

Crazy Horse's actions prove once again the fallacy of the "irreconcilable enemy and hater of the White man" portrayal, and actually denotes the kindness, sensitivity, and generosity of his character, even when confronted by a rude wašiču. Donating his čannupa to a stranger, an unmarried young White woman who apparently showed a kinder attitude than her arrogant fiancé, would have been enough. But, as always, Crazy Horse did more. He gave the journalist precisely what he thought his guest might appreciate, a sample of the Indians' own way of recording important events, through picture-writing. The Oglala war chief (again, despite his temporary illness) even took the time to explain the content of his gift to Wallihan, who later wrote the ledger-book, in the words of Crazy Horse translated by Grouard, "pictured the life of a famous warrior," but that the chief did not identify himself as the protagonist. If indeed some of the pictographs represented his own war deeds, consistent with his modest and reserved nature, Crazy Horse did not wish to acknowledge. Conversely, and indicative of Wallihan's presumptuous attitude, the young White man refused to express appreciation for such a personal gift with the added bonus. Let alone the pipe the Oglala leader gave to his soon-to-be bride. Outrageously, years later Wallihan even commented on the unpleasant "Indian odor" retained by the pages of the ledger book. A smell that, in his words, "does not yield to fumigation" and remained "the smell of Indian" even after forty years.[421]

The portrayal of a stoic, perpetually "gloomy," "morose," "melancholy" Indian does not do justice to the real Crazy Horse. The Wallihan episode proves it clearly, as it also disproves the "profound hatred towards Whites" attribute often bestowed upon Crazy Horse. If prior to surrendering Crazy Horse had expressed such feelings and fought heart and soul against the Americans, there were valid reasons. Now it was time to give peace a chance. Interacting with his former enemies, Crazy Horse tried to discern between those he could be kind to, and those he should better keep away from. He could also be agreeable to a degree, and generous to White perfect strangers. He was finally able of smiling, and even laughing at seemingly serious issues when he felt at ease among relatives and friends.

When He Dog asked his kola whether he would consider him an enemy if he relocated his own lodge at some distance, Crazy Horse laughed wholeheartedly like a man who held no grudge, remarking his friend was free to do as he pleased. When a dubious character like Frank Grouard visited him, Crazy Horse was found pensive in his lodge, but changed his mood and expressed joy in seeing his old "friend." Lieut. Bourke, who was there, wrote that "[Crazy Horse] behaved with stolidity, like a man who realized he had to give in to Fate, but would do so as sullenly as possible. [Yet] while talking to Frank, his countenance lit up with genuine pleasure."[422] Grouard himself confessed that he often dressed in Indian clothing, white cotton shirt, leggings, moccasins when visiting the Northern camp, to better fit in their midst. Crazy Horse, a pure heart, took it at face value, as a sign of respect and friendship, either not realizing Grouard was actually spying on him, or just not worrying himself about that. Crazy Horse apparently trusted "the Grabber," hence the positive expressions reported by Bourke. Still, with the entire world weighing on his shoulders, compounded by a sensitive and introverted nature, a family history rid with deep sorrows, a de facto prisoner status, and an uncertain future, no wonder Crazy Horse could at times appear "sullen and morose."

As a Lakota warrior who had never before interacted directly at length with the Whites, actually regarding them as mortal enemies, it is remarkable and indicative of his intelligence, open-mindedness, and sincere desire for peace that Crazy Horse showed kindness to an ungrateful visiting stranger like Wallihan. Obviously, in his ordinary daily interaction within his own camp and with fellow tribesmen, Crazy Horse remained himself: a war chief, leader of a faction that intended to return to the open plains, albeit within the yet to be defined boundaries of their elusive new agency in the North Country, as "promised" by Gen. Crook. In a situation that soon began to deteriorate, Tašunke Witko asserted his authority and therefore appeared, in Agent James Irwin's own words, "lordly and dictatorial [...] with his own people and other bands of Sioux." Still, Irwin also admitted in the same letter to the Commissioner of Indian Affairs in Washington that much of what was going on with Crazy Horse, the Nez Perce crisis, the promise of the new agency, the conflicting talks about the buffalo hunt, and the delegation trip to Washington, all contributed to creating confusion and misconceptions. "I think," stated Irwin, "that most if not all the difficulty arose from a misconception of Crazy Horse's character."[423]

After the killing of his son, Waglula was quoted as saying that "his boy [...] would never have fought the whites but they (the military) hunted him and his village in their own country, and they had to defend themselves, or all would have perished. He had enough buffalo in that country to last several years, and (he) wanted to stay. He fought only the Crows and the Snakes and stole their ponies. But he was not let alone. Every courier that came north to him said, 'Come in! Come in! Or the Gray Fox (Crook) will drive you after Sitting Bull.' At last he came. Spotted Tail and Red Cloud, the greatest chiefs of the Brules and the Oglalas, had to stand aside and give him the principal place in council, and on this account they and their young men became jealous. They were the cause of their poor boy lying there. He was killed by too much talk."[424]

Undoubtedly, during the few months that preceded his assassination, Crazy Horse must have reflected upon the incongruity of what was happening to him, his followers, the Lakota Nation as a whole. He must have asked himself who were these milahanska and what right they had to come to his Country and tell him what to do or not to do, where to go or not to go. Precisely what Sitting Bull had been saying. A Virginia-born, ex-confederate soldier turned "squaw-man," Frank H. Huston showed insight into the Northern Indians perspective, referring specifically to Sitting Bull, but the same applied also to Crazy Horse's frame of mind. Huston understood that the problem was not Sitting Bull and the other hostile chiefs, but the unwillingness of the Whites (prospectors, settlers, missionaries, Government, and Army) to simply leave them alone. "I find almost no one," commented Huston few years after Crazy Horse's death, "with a proper understanding of the attitude of [Sitting] Bull et al. As Tatanka (i.e. Sitting Bull) said, 'We ask only to be let alone.' Kettle (i.e, Black Kettle) said the same. 'All we wish is that you yellow-faces keep out of our country. We don't want to fight you. This is our country. The Great Spirit gave it to us. Keep out and we will be friends.'"[425]

In his May 1930 letter to Eleanor Hinman, Dr. McGillycuddy eulogized Crazy Horse as follows: "He was but thirty-six. In him everything was made secondary to patriotism and love of his people. Modest, fearless, a mystic, a believer in destiny, and much of a recluse, he was held in veneration and admiration by the younger warriors, who would follow him anywhere. These qualities made him a danger to the government, and he became persona non grata to evolution and to the progress of the white

man's civilization. Hence his early death was preordained."[426] It is difficult to comment objectively on Crazy Horse's already complex psychological profile, particularly during those difficult months leading up to
his murder. Still, in retrospect, and always keeping in mind the deleteri-
ous impact of intertribal warfare on the American Indians' own destiny,
it is hard not to empathize with Crazy Horse and Sitting Bull, and for
that matter with Indian patriot chiefs of the likes of Chief Joseph, Dull
Knife, and Little Wolf, but also Geronimo, Pontiac, Tecumseh, Black Hawk,
Osceola, or lesser known leaders of faraway Indian resistance as Kamiakin
and Captain Jack, all with their own shortcomings and unique histories,
but acting in the best interest of their people as they understood it. Some
were eventually portrayed in photographs, others not, as was the case,
many maintain, of Crazy Horse.

One of the most categorical pronouncements in this regard was that
of Henry Standing Bear, the son of mixed-blood Brule headman Standing
Bear and a maternal cousin of Crazy Horse. In a 1910 interview conducted
by Walter Mason Camp, the younger Standing Bear unequivocally stated:
"His likeness was never photographed or sketched, although false photos
have been published. The true features of the great warrior chief of the
Oglala will never appear in history."[427] Henry Standing Bear spoke specifically of "published photos," so we can assume he was not aware of the
tintype. It would have been revealing to know his opinion on the tintype,
and whether this portrait could have been used as the model in the carving
of the Crazy Horse Monument. The granite features that are already clearly
defined will inevitably, in time, become "the face" of the Oglala war chief
even though the monumental sculpture, as we said earlier, since its inception was intended to be more symbolic and evocative than "realistic."

Certainly not as challenging as the gigantic carving, but conceptually equally difficult, have been attempts over the years to reconstruct on
paper a reliable and consistent portrayal of Crazy Horse's physical appearance, his facial features in particular. William J. Bordeaux, too, searched
for a photograph, but to no vale. "The question has been raised by some
scribes and historians," he wrote, "as to the existence of a photo taken of

the noted warrior. A thorough search by the author for a picture of him brought no results, for none was ever taken of him." He added that "a near image described by the author's father, Louis Bordeaux, Mrs. Clown, the warrior's '[step-]sister, and other close associates, gave a fair legible facial and figured idea of [Crazy Horse's] appearance, as to his height, weight, and poise. Height about, 5' 11", weight 175 lbs., complexion rather light for an Indian [....]."[428] The description inspired a black and white sketch drawing published as frontispiece in *Custer's Conqueror*, the profile is that of an "odd" looking Indian purportedly said to be "very close" to what the real Crazy Horse looked like.

"Crazy Horse", sketch in W.J. Bordeaux, *Custer's Conqueror* (1952). Aside from the overall oddity of the sketch, the vertical scar on the left cheek is not supported by eyewitness accounts.

Bordeaux's quantified data differ from those later summarized by Hardorff: "From composite statements by Indian contemporaries, Crazy Horse emerges as a man of medium stature (5ft., 8 inches), and light in frame and weight (140 lbs). His hair was of a sandy color, fine in texture, and reaching well below his waist. Of light complexion, his face was narrow, lacking the prominence of cheekbones, with a sharp straight nose."[429] Hardorff echoed "Big Bat" Pourier who recalled that "Crazy Horse was a slim, light man; weight about 140 pounds."[430] Given a logical degree of approximation, these descriptions do fit the tintype.

While this and other reconstructed drawings of Crazy Horse's face differ considerably from each other, as noted there was consensus among Indians of the overall pleasantness of his features, and his well-proportioned body type. Indian testimonies, but also some non-Indian ones, tend to concur on the overall "good-look" of Tašunke Witko. This, combined with a seemingly aloof, silent, and intriguing personality, must have been a powerful magnet for

Lakota women who crossed his path and, conversely, a reason for envy, jealousy, and resentment for many Lakota men. The Black Buffalo Woman precedent and possibly others testify to Crazy Horse's attractiveness and his ascendant on women. A fact also implied by Lieut. Henry R. Lemly, 3rd U.S. Cavalry, who had orders to escort the would-to-be-imprisoned Oglala chief to Fort Laramie, thence to Omaha and beyond. In a letter he sent to Brininstool in 1925 regarding the murderous affair, Lemly stated that "Crazy Horse was a lithe, slender Indian of medium or more height, weighing perhaps 155 to 165 pounds [...] Louis Richard's daughter, who fled to Crazy Horse, was said to be very pretty. Crazy Horse must have been good-looking to have attracted her."[431]

Victoria Conroy, who was related to Crazy Horse through Worm's sister Rattle Stone Woman, reiterated the positive impression of a good-look-ing, well-proportioned man. She was about eleven years old when the war chief was killed, and since her father Standing Bear's thiyóšpaye was close to that of Crazy Horse's, she saw him often up close: "A good man and good to look at. He wasn't short, he wasn't fat, he wasn't skinny. His nose wasn't big, it wasn't crooked. His face was small, like his waistline."[432]

Aside from the issue of the face wound, discussed below, and keep-ing in mind Victoria Conroy's and similar testimonies we should also ask to what extent did Crazy Horse present "typical Sioux" features. Perhaps, like those of the Indian in the tintype seen by Feraca. We have noted that Crazy Horse's relatively small nose and well-proportioned mouth gave him a look that was indeed a bit unusual when compared to the average Lakota adult male of the 1870s. But here, too, "typical" is a potentially misleading and ambiguous term. Social scientists and philosophers have long argued over the validity of characterizing ethnic groups according to certain shared somatic traits. There is no question that the Sioux, like other tribes, had distinctive tribal features that were uniquely theirs and distinguished them from other Indians. Such features reflected a combina-tion of strictly morphological and phenotypical traits deriving from hered-itary/genetic, dietary, and environmental factors, but also a set of band or tribally specific, distinctive cultural elements, such as hair style, dress, ornaments, body alterations, tattoos, and the like.

Many nineteenth-century photographs show that there was also heterogeneity within the Lakota, as shown for example in the facial features and body types of Little Big Man and Touch the Clouds, or the same Red Cloud and Spotted Tail. On the other hand, as in any other human population, similar traits being genetically determined and preserved – with obvious individualization – were passed on to the next generation. Jack Red Cloud was said to be a "spitting image" of his father. More directly related to Crazy Horse, a group photograph of brothers Joe (Joseph) Horn Cloud (standing, wearing civilian clothing), Daniel White Lance (seated, left,

(l-r) Daniel White Lance, Joseph "Joe" Horn Cloud (standing), and
Dewey Beard (aka Iron Hail), survivors of the Wounded Knee massacre:
"White Lance and Beard were wounded [...] their father & mother,
two brothers, and Beard's wife and child were killed there. Dec. 29, 1890."

wearing beaded scalp-shirt, holding a revolver and a pipe bag), and Dewey Beard who authenticated the tintype (seated, right, also wearing a scalp-shirt, holding a pipe and a pipe bag) show a remarkable resemblance to the Indian in the tintype. Francis White Lance recalled that several members of the Horn Cloud (Mahpiya He) family were killed at Wounded Knee, while others survived, including the three brothers and their seventeen-year-old sister Alice.

On genealogical information provided by Francis White Lance, Donovin Sprague reiterated that "the family came from the northern Lakota and settled at Pine Ridge Reservation following the killing of chief Sitting Bull [...] The Horn Cloud family belonged to the tiospaye (extended family) of Spotted Elk who became known as Chief Big Foot (Si Tanka)."[433] Daniel White Lance's eyes, the uniquely puffed eyelid folds and eyebrows, but also nose and cheeks, even the philtrum (the vertical groove between nose and upper lip), and chin, are remarkably similar if not almost identical to those of the Indian in the tintype.[434]

Composite comparison of Daniel White Lance (l) and Crazy Horse (r).
Note Crazy Horse's unique light brown hair in comparison to
Daniel White Lance's darker hair

Anthropological studies have underscored the presence of regional variations among prehistoric and historic American Indians, but also heterogeneity within each tribal group. Writing on the skeletal biology of the Plains, Laura Scheiber concluded that "a more generalized connection between prehistoric and known historic groups has been suggested for the Northwestern Plains. [...] Native people living on the Northwestern Plains, such as the Arapaho, Blackfoot, Cheyenne, Crow, Gros Ventre, Kiowa, and Teton Sioux differ from their neighbors in the Great Basin to the west because of long-term geographic and linguistic barriers. So-called Siouan traits include larger statures, higher orbits, and longer and larger crania when compared to individuals from the southwest part of the region. [...] The most striking change through time is a decrease in cranial vault height [...] This change could be a selective response to environmental change or a result of gene flow from Eastern Siouan speakers, or [...] other unknown factor. Changes in craniofacial morphology could also be a result of cultural changes, [...] with survivors of disease effectively creating a bottleneck or founders' effect that restricted the gene flow into future generations. [...] Heterogeneity is common within populations and suggests unique combinations of formerly distinct and autonomous band origins for some historic sociopolitical entities."[435]

Anyone familiar with historic American Indian photographs knows how distinctive somatic differences between tribes can be, and also within the same tribe. What to make, then, of the search for your "typical Sioux features"? Here, again, the coin has two sides. After viewing hundreds of nineteenth century Lakota photographs, the impression one gets is that while the individual Indians portrayed undoubtedly share common Siouan denominators, as alluded to by Feraca, ethnographic images also show considerable internal variation in body type and facial features. Crazy Horse's Oglala contemporary Short Bull testified thru interpreter that Tašunke Witko did not look like your "typical Sioux." But he then associated Crazy Horse to the "general Sioux type" exemplified, for example, by Bad Heart Bull. In Short Bull's own words, "Crazy Horse was a man not very tall and not very short, neither broad nor thin. [...] He was a trifle under six feet tall. Bad Heart Bull was the same general type. But Crazy Horse had a very light complexion, much lighter than the other Indians. [...] His features were not like those of the rest of us. His face was not broad, and he had a sharp, high nose".[436]

Once again, such discordant views are, to say the least, intriguing and perplexing. Here, too, we could invoke the critical element of translation that, like a distorting filter, might have at times misconstrued what had originally been said in Lakota. Equally troubling is the description made in late May, 1877, by Robert Strahorn of the *Chicago Tribune* who reported that Crazy Horse was "a very small man who has been so cut up by wounds that he is very ugly."[437] Such negative attributes clash with the words of U.S. Indian Agent Dr. James Irwin, also already cited, whose comparative models were indeed the "hard" faces of other prominent Lakota (and Cheyenne and Arapaho) warriors and headmen at Red Cloud Agency. As noted, Irwin described the facial features of an adult Crazy Horse in an altogether different light, as those of a "bashful girlish looking boy." "Girlish"?! "Boy"?! The possible rationale here is that Agent Irwin used such ambiguous terms to avoid appreciative ones like "pleasant" or even "good looking" for an Indian whom he otherwise regarded "a man of small capacity, brought to notoriety by his stubborn will and brute courage,"[438] and later "very impudent and defiant."[439] A contradiction of attributes coming from the same source. Still, Irwin's description of Crazy Horse's features is a total opposite to the "ugliness" presumably impressed on the chief's face by his famous scar.

Face Wound and Scar

Much of what has been said and written about Crazy Horse's facial features is closely tied to the purportedly very visible and presumably very ugly scar that some asserted disfigured his face. Would not Crazy Horse's cousin Eagle Elk (1851-1945?), interviewed by John Neihardt in 1944, have stressed or at least mentioned the scar's negative impact on his famous relative's face, had the same scar been so visible, repulsive, and truly "ugly"? Instead, according to Wamble Hehaka, "Crazy Horse was not a tall man – not too small a man, but just above a small man. [...] His complexion was not so dark [either]. He was a very good looking man; his face was fine."[440] If the scar had been indeed prominent, but not "repulsive," would not Eagle Elk add at least something to the effect that the bullet fired by No Water, and the resulting wound, while visible, did not alter Crazy Horse's good looks?

Doubts about the true "ugly" extent of the face wound are cast by another remarkable eyewitness account rendered to Josephine Waggoner in 1936 by Susan Bordeaux Bettelyoun (1857-1945). Susan was the daughter of interpreter James Bordeaux (1814-1870), the burly Missouri River French trader called Mato (The Bear) by the Lakota, and Red Cormorant Woman (Huntkalutawin, ca. 1820-ca. 1880), a sister of Brule chief Swift Bear. Upon getting married, Red Cormorant took the name of Marie Bordeaux. Her daughter Susan was about twenty years old when Crazy Horse surrendered, so as a young adult her memory was sharp. She was at Camp Sheridan in July 1877, specifically at the local postmaster and trader store when Crazy Horse visited there. Susan Bettelyoun's testimony is precious: "My husband, Chas. Tackett [she had married him in 1874] was a scout but when he was not on duty he clerked in [George H.] Jewett's store, and had waited on Crazy Horse. My mother-in-law and I drove up [in our horse wagon] to the store one day when Crazy Horse was there; she pointed him out to me. He was a very handsome young man of about thirty six years or so. He was not so dark; he had hazel eyes, nice long light brown hair. His scalp lock was ornamented with beads and hung clear to his waist; his braids were wrapped in fur. He was partly wrapped in a broad cloth blanket, his leggings were also navy blue broad cloth, his moccasins were beaded. He was above the medium height and was slender."[441]

Comparing Susan Bordeaux Bettelyoun's description with the tintype, it is likely that Crazy Horse had his picture taken between June and July, 1877: the tintype matches very closely many of the details she gave. Then again, the main elements of white shirt with metal arm and wrist bands, dark stroud leggings, and beaded moccasins were typical Indian attire at the Lakota agencies, as documented in many photographs. The inseparable red blanket is another positive indicator, along with the braids wrapped in otterskin, distinctive of a war chief. Still regarding Crazy Horse's handsome features, Charles Eastman later gathered a positive consensus among the old timers who had known the Oglala war chief. "He was an uncommonly handsome man," concluded the famous Santee doctor and author, "[…] physically perfect, an Apollo in symmetry. Furthermore, he was a true type of Indian refinement and grace. He was modest and courteous as Chief Joseph."[442] It is interesting that Dr. Eastman used the same "Apollo" analogy with Crazy Horse as Catlin had done with Lone Horn.

This takes us back to the unsettled issue of the scar. Like many other aspects of Tašunke Witko's life, conflicting opinions, testimonies – both contemporary and posthumous – abound about the famous wound inflicted by No Water. The violent confrontation could have ended the life of Crazy Horse, who probably would have been forgotten by history. It was on that occasion that Little Big Man, at the sight of the enraged husband bursting into the tipi gun in hand, held Crazy Horse's arm brandishing a knife to defend himself from his attacker. Why did Little Big Man do that, we do not know. He will do the same thing seven years later at Camp Robinson, with more tragic consequences. No Water was son of the late (Old) No Water from whom he had inherited the leadership of the Hoka Yuta, the Badger Eaters band. The disputed PteSapa Wiyan, Black Buffalo Woman, was an attractive nice of Red Cloud, who apparently had arranged her marriage with No Water. True, at the time of the affair with Crazy Horse, Black Buffalo Woman and No Water were already parents of three children; in the Lakota way, an indication of a good marriage, blessed with a full lodge. Their eldest son was named (Young) No Water. Ten years after his father's attack on Crazy Horse, Young No Water, too, was himself involved in a brawl, of a different nature. In 1880 at Pine Ridge, he attempted to kill Indian Agent Dr. Valentine McGillycuddy, in a mix of personal grudge and political enmity. Regarding Crazy Horse and Black Buffalo Woman, much gossip surrounded their troubled affair.[443]

Everyone agrees that about ten years or less before his death, Crazy Horse was shot in the face by No Water with a small caliber bullet. The angry husband of Black Buffalo Woman had apparently borrowed a small handgun from his kinsman Bad Heart Bull. There is disagreement as to the exact location and date of the episode. Some say it happened in the Big Horn Country while others, including Hardorff concluded that the "shooting took place on Powder River during the summer of 1870."[444] William J. Bordeaux suggests an earlier date, perhaps the fall of 1866.[445] There are also doubts about the exact dynamics and outcome of the incident. According to some accounts the small projectile actually penetrated Crazy Horse's face, according to others, it simply grazed it. As for the type and make of the handgun fired by No Water, according to Lone Eagle, it was a .41 caliber Derringer palm-pistol. Even though the .41 rimfire bullet traveled at low velocity for a gun (circa 425 feet per second), at close range it could kill. This issue is important with regard to the extent of the damage a small bullet could produce on the victim's face, depending also on the angle of impact, relative distance, and other ballistic factors. What is certain is that as a result of the close-range firing and the bullet impact, some kind of marking was left on Crazy Horse's face. Anything beyond that is more a matter of opinion, conjecture, conflicting testimonies, and discordant recollections than factual truth, and it remains, therefore, open to question.

The divergence of opinion is striking. George Washington Oakes, a teamster who saw Crazy Horse at Camp Robinson, recalled that the Oglala war chief "had quite a scar on his left cheek."[446] Other eyewitnesses, especially women, did not refer to the scar as a defining element of Crazy Horse's facial features, while giving other details of Crazy Horse's face, hair, and dress. This is odd, as women tend to be particularly attentive to facial features and possible alterations. More so, if we consider another account, that of a *New York Sun* reporter who met Crazy Horse shortly after his surrender and spoke of a "bullet wound through his left cheek [...that] disfigured his face and gives the mouth a drawn and somewhat fierce or brutal expression."[447] As we saw earlier, Victoria Conroy said nothing of the "ugly scar" on Crazy Horse's face. Neither did Red Feather, Tašunke Witko's brother-in-law, who simply stated that "Crazy Horse was a nice-looking man."[448] Their silence casts a shadow of doubt on the description so often reported – echoing the *Sun* editorial – that "his left cheek was disfigured by a stained scar of a bullet wound, giving his mouth a drawn and somewhat fierce expression."[449]

It is a fact that some kind of a stained scar or "mark" altering the natural skin-color tissue was present on Crazy Horse's face; left side of the mouth and cheek, as visible in the tintype. The distinctiveness of the feature seems to be up to the judgment of each viewer, some emphasizing it, others downplaying and even ignoring it. When in 1954 Feraca viewed the tintype said by Jake Herman to be Crazy Horse, he disagreed with the identification precisely because, Feraca argued, the subject in the small picture apparently lacked a visible scar on his face. Feraca also stressed that the Indian in that very tintype had pleasant features, contrary to what most non-Indian sources he was familiar with maintained. "A small number of Pine Ridge Sioux," wrote Feraca, "sincerely believe that they possess tintypes or other pictures of Crazy Horse. None of these pictures look alike. Jake Herman, a mixed blood and former publicity man for the tribe will show any interested party a tintype of a good-looking young warrior with typical Sioux features. Crazy Horse is said to have had a scar on one cheek as a result of a bullet wound. Just which cheek was scarred is a matter of much disagreement, but Jake's warrior has no scar at all." Actually, the scar is there, but barely visible in the original small-size tintype. Feraca rejected Jake Herman's identification. Years later Steve reiterated that same point to Randy and me, while enjoying foamy water in the park behind the BIA.

Like everyone else, Steve expected the bullet wound scar to be very pronounced, hence his negative verdict on the tintype. Jake Herman thought otherwise and, as Feraca reported in his Crazy Horse article, the Oglala spokesperson had a very plausible explanation: "Jake said the scar was slight and probably wouldn't show."[450] Especially in a front view; simple as that. When Luther Standing Bear saw Crazy Horse at Spotted Tail Agency in September 1877, he would have certainly noticed the scar on the chief's face had it been "big" and "ugly" enough to "disfigure" his left (or even his right) cheek. To an agency Sioux teenager, as Luther was at the time, a war chief of the Northern Indians with a prominent scar on his face would have no doubt remained impressed in his mind for the rest of his life. The "ugly" scar would have reinforced the heroic image of the free and fearless warrior-chief that defined Crazy Horse, especially after his victories at the Rosebud and the Little Bighorn. In later years, Standing Bear did not even mention a scar, let alone a big and prominent one, whereas he did recall Crazy Horse's light brown hair.

Lakota naming tradition calls for an additional consideration. If the incident was so significant in Tašunke's life that it cost him his Shirt Wearer status, and if the resulting scar was so noticeable that, according to some, it altered his facial expression, wouldn't the Oglala give Crazy Horse, without replacing the established patronymic, also a second name, say, the Lakota equivalent of "[His] Wounded Face," or "Shot in the Face," even "Scar Face"? This is a common practice among the Sioux and other American Indians. There is a "Shot in the Face" cited in the Little Bighorn literature.[451] In fact, similar renaming cut across ethnic boundaries. A popular example from the history of organized crime during the prohibition era illustrates the point. In an altogether different time and place, but conceptually similar situation involving a woman. It had as the main protagonist noted Neapolitan-born mobster Alfonso (Al) Capone. Capone became known as "Scarface" because of a facial wound he received from the brother of the woman whom he had made unwelcome appreciations to. Being protective, even violently possessive of one's own female relatives was one of the traits Feraca maintained Southern Italian men shared with their Sioux counterparts. Crazy Horse's affair with Black Buffalo Woman, No Water's rage, and the resulting wound were defining moments in the Oglala warrior's life. If it resulted in a very visible and prominent badge of "shame" impressed by a jealous husband on a fellow tribesman responsible for disrupting his conjugal life, it makes little sense that not even a nickname was bestowed on Crazy Horse.

American Indian history offers many examples of prominent individuals whose face was somewhat disfigured by a scar, regardless of how it was procured, and renamed accordingly. Scarface Charley was one of the leaders of the 1872-1873 Modoc war in the Lava Beds of Northern California who, after the execution of Captain Jack, was removed with the remnants of his people to Indian Territory. The prominent scar on his right cheek is clearly seen in a close-up photograph reproduced by Brown and Schmitt.[452] His scarred face is also visible in a group portrait taken by McCarty of Baxter Springs, Kansas, of Modoc men, including Scarface Charley, with wives and children after removal.[453]

Closer to Crazy Horse, two Lakota warriors were wounded in the face, but survived, at the Little Bighorn. One was White Mountain, HeSká, also known simply as Mountain. Born around 1836, this Oglala was already a mature warrior when he was hit by a trooper's musket ball in his left eye, while withdrawing from the battlefield. Enraged at the Bluecoats, after a brief stop in camp to be medicated, the brave, bandaged-up Mountain quickly rejoined the fighting and counted coup.[454] Alongside the wounded warrior were his sons Rock, Lone Hill, and High Wolf, and his wife Red Bird, Zitkalalutawin, one of the warrior women in the Custer fight.[455] When the big village separated, Mountain, still with his left eye bandaged, stayed with Crazy Horse as part of He Dog's thiyóśpaye, and surrendered with them the following May at Camp Robinson. After nearly a year, his wound had probably healed completely. Perhaps, for protection, he still wore a bandage. In the Crazy Horse Surrender Ledger, compiled on May 6th, 1877, by Lieut. Charles A. Johnson and Charles P. Jordan, chief clerk for Red Cloud Agency, the veteran warrior was still listed as Mountain, member of the He Dog tipi circle. Mountain was head of household, his lodge comprising three adult males, two adult females, two boys and one girl.[456] Eventually, the very noticeable scar in his left eye led him to change his name to Išta Ogna Opi, "Wounded Eye," better known to Whites and mixed-bloods as Shot in the Eye. His wife too became known as Susie Shot in the Eye. Twenty years later, the elderly couple, like many other Indians, were photographed by Frank A. Rinehart (1861-1928), at the 1898 Indian Congress Pan-American Exposition held in Omaha, Nebraska. The old wounded veteran of the Little Bighorn also posed for De Lancey Gill in Washington in 1907. He died after 1910.

The other Oglala warrior to assume a name from a shooting that occurred at the Greasy Grass was Red Horn / Horned Bull (born ca. 1847, or ca. 1851), wounded in the face while pressing Reno's hasty retreat across the Little Bighorn. Red Horn was part of the Big Road (Wide Road, ca. 1834-1897) band of Bad Face Northern Oglala who later in 1877 fled to Canada. They surrendered in 1881. In his commentary to the Big Road pictographic roster originally published by Garrick Mallery in 1886, Ephriam Dickson captioned the Red Horn Bull glyph as follows: "An Oglala by this name could not be identified in either the Sitting Bull Surrender Census or in [Maj.] McLaughlin's annuity list for 1881, but he does appear in the transfer list to Pine Ridge (May 1882). In the Big Road Roster, he is shown as a head akičita. This individual is probably Red Horn Bull, Tatanka Heluta [...] who by 1890 was a member of the Hokayuta band living in the White Clay District at Pine Ridge."[457]

After the Wounded Knee tragedy, Red Horn Bull together with Iron Tail, Black Fox, High Heron, and other former "hostiles" joined *Buffalo Bill's Wild West* show and they were photographed in American and European cities. Red Horn Bull's badly wounded, partially disfigured left side of the face is seen in a photographic portrait taken by Gertrude Käsebier in her New York studio.[458] Interviewed by Eli S. Ricker in 1906, Red Horn / Horned Bull was referred to as "Shot in the Face" by interpreter Nicholas Ruleau.[459] He was erroneously identified by Pugh Young Man Afraid of His Horses, paternal nephew of Young Man Afraid, as the Indian in the *Wi'iyohi* purported photograph of Crazy Horse that Will Robinson had sent him for identification: "I don't agree [sic] with you [...] also that picture you have which you said it was Crazy Horse. I will tell you who that picture is. His name is Red Horn Bull who was shot through the mouth at Custer Battle as you notice he is dark complexion Mr Crazy Horse is a light complexion man medium height light hair handsome pleasant face medium built."[460]

Also pertinent to our issue, the census of Crazy Horse's band contains several male names specifically descriptive of facial features: White Face, Black Eye Lid, Scabby Face, Wrinkled Face, Hole in Face, Thick Face, and that of a woman, Crooked Mouth. Speaking of names, a brief digression to acknowledge that the Ledger also features a number of scatological or foul names, such as Shits on His Hand, Pisses in the Horn, Soft Prick, and Bull Proof, the latter a woman. "These names," commented Bruce Brown who posted a transcription of the Ledger originally published by Buecker and Paul, "may reflect the Sioux habit of enlisting a winkte (a male transvestite, whom the Sioux believed had the power of prophesy) to give children 'joke names.' On the other hand," Brown continued, "it has also been suggested that members of Crazy Horse's band may have used these names at time of surrender as a passive form of disrespect for the surrender process."[461] Comparing the Crazy Horse's *Surrender Ledger* with the Sitting Bull's *Surrender Census* edited by Ephriam Dickson[462] where both descriptive and foul names are also present (for example, "Makes Dirt/ Dung with Dirt" in He Dog's Oglala band and "Urinate in the Horn" and "Rotten Puss" both in Hump's Minicoju band), the latter explanation seems most plausible. We should not forget that Crazy Horse's own spiritual mentor and close friend Horn Chips, yuwipi and rock dreamer, was also known as Long Turd.[463]

Back to the scar, given all of the above, it surprises us that Crazy Horse did not acquire yet another appellative related to his injury. Unless, as said, the scar was neither that pronounced nor that ugly. A possible reason why Short Bull, while giving a detailed portrait of the chief's features, did not mention the gunshot wound on his face. Neither did Little Killer. It would seem that, at least for some of his Indian contemporaries, the 'famous' wound was not actually a defining element of Crazy Horse's facial features. Accounts also differ regarding the details of the damage inflicted by the vengeful No Water. He Dog, interviewed by Hinman in 1930, stated that "No Water shot him just below the left nostril. The bullet followed the line of the teeth and fractured the upper jaw,"[464] along with the version reported by Mari Sandoz: "The flash strung the eyes of Crazy Horse, the bullet crashed through his upper jaw, and he fell forward."[465] We cannot double-guess what He Dog actually said in Lakota, and the interpreter's choice of words in translation, that is, what the latter understood, changed, added, or subtracted. There is no reason to doubt He Dog's words. Let us assume he used the verb pawe, "to bleed at the nose" to indicate what happened after the bullet hit Crazy Horse's face. Pawega means "to break" or "to intersect." Words that to an interpreter's ears might have sounded similar, could have meant two slightly different things. William J. Bordeaux said that "when [No Water] fired the bullet only grazed the cheek of Crazy Horse," likely producing a heavy nose bleed.[466] In a letter to Will G. Robinson dated October 25, 1951, the same Bordeaux specified that "according to the information given me by his sister Mrs. Clown and other near associates the scar which was more or less faint, was a flesh wound [...] right across his left cheek. The wound was caused by a gun shot at close range."[467] Eagle Elk stated simply that No Water shot his rival "through the head below the eye."[468] Opta in Lakota can mean both "through" and "across." Generally speaking, in English the former indicates "in" one side and "out" the other, while still in English the latter refers to a movement from one side to the other. Interpreters could have attributed alternative meanings to what had been said in Lakota, perhaps inserting either unconsciously or purposely, their own thoughts on the issue.

The question remains of the true extent of the visible damage caused by the small bullet fired by No Water. If what was generally reported about the incident is correct – the bullet entering and exiting somewhere on Crazy Horse's face – from a strictly ballistic and forensic perspective the projectile seemingly traveled subcutaneously on soft tissue. The resulting scar therefore occurred mostly inside the left cheek. Big Bat Pourier said that the chief was slurring when talking, a likely consequence of the impact of the bullet on the soft tissue inside his mouth, and reason why perhaps Crazy Horse, already a withdrawn character scarred by personal tragedies, had become even less talkative after the No Water incident. Regarding the visual impact of the wound, probably only the points of entry and exit of the small bullet were visible on the surface of the skin; with pulling of the skin due primarily to the already mentioned subcutaneous scar.

Frank Grouard (1850-1905), the Tahiti-born French-mulatto "renegade" who had lived with the Northern Indians and then, in 1875, moved back to the military camp close to Red Cloud Agency, gave a recollection that would strengthen the argument in favor of limited visible surface scarification. A scar that might have become less noticeable as Tašunke gained weight at Camp Robinson. Considering that "The Grabber" knew Crazy Horse well (whether he actually betrayed him with his faulty translation of the Nez Perce affair, or by spreading rumors against Crazy Horse, is open to debate), it follows that his recollections of Tašunke Witko's face should be fairly accurate. Yet, Yugata did not speak of "ugly" scars, "fierce and brutal expression" and the like, but simply of "powder marks on one side of his face". This is exactly what is seen in the tintype. A similar testimony, though worded differently by interpreter Peter Schweigerman, came from no less than Horn Chips himself who reiterated that "the wound [inflicted] by No Water for Crazy Horse taking his wife did not change the color of his complexion," this cryptic translation possibly meaning that the wound/scar did not alter the skin surface, hence, his look. If it did not impress Grouard and Horn Chips, two independent observers accustomed to seeing facial wounds (and mutilations) all of types, then the scar-alteration could not have been that "ugly". On their testimonies, Hardorff concluded that the visual result of Crazy Horse being shot in the face was "a powder-stained scar on his left cheek which he carried the rest of his life."[469] How big of a scar it was, Hardorff could not say, but we can now see it in the enlarged detail from the original tintype.

William J. Bordeaux, who gathered testimonies in the Lakota language, also wrote that when No Water fired, "the bullet only grazed the cheek of Crazy Horse." While most authors claim the chief fell unconscious from the shot, Bordeaux went on to say that Tašunke Witko "immediately came running towards [No Water] in order to grapple with him. As the two men struggled, Touch the Clouds came between them and took the gun away from No Water."[470] As for the exact location of the scar, Chips identified the lower right side of Tašunke's face. "This wound was on his face," said Chips, "the ball entering at the side of his nose, low down on the right side, and coming out at the base of the on the back side."[471] Left or right side could be a problem with translation, or the visual memory of the

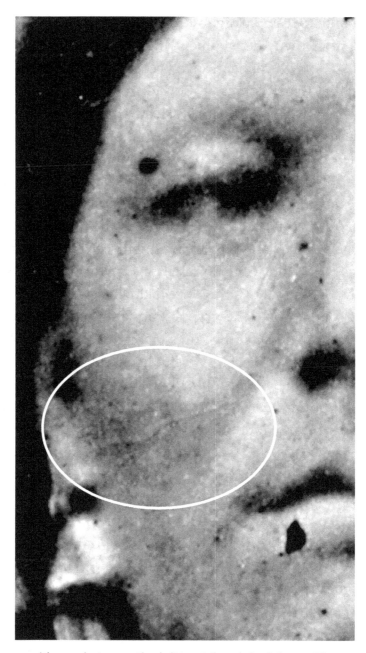

Crazy Horse, with scar between the left nostril and the left ear. The scar matches what William J. Bordeaux wrote, that according to information provided by Mrs. Clown, Crazy Horse's sister, and others who had known Crazy Horse, the scar "was a flesh wound [...] right across his left cheek". He Dog, too, confirmed that the bullet entered below the left nostril and the scar followed the line of the upper jaw. Exactly what is shown in the tintype The enlarged detail also shows the black powder marks reported by Frank Grouard.

speaker who used his own perspective, or both. Most testimonies speak of left cheek/side, consistent with the scar visible in the tintype. [472]

Returning once again to the size, shape, and visible impact of the wound mark on Crazy Horse's face, Mari Sandoz identified the wounded area just below the left nostril, and reported that official government records spoke of a small hole on Crazy Horse's face. "I found the scar described in the AGO records a small hole under the left nostril with a slight ridge outside it," Mari Sandoz wrote to Will Robinson in 1937.[473] She also added that, were it not for that "slightly haughty cast" – in the words of an Army officer who had known Crazy Horse – the chief's face showed "mildness and gentleness [...] more the face of a holy man as his father was, than the fierce, relentless warrior the Army knew he could be." Like the Indian in the tintype. As noted, contrary to newspaper articles and other accounts, other eyewitnesses indicated that Tašunke Witko's facial features were indeed pleasant and good looking.

It is unfortunate that the twenty-one pictographs drawn by He Dog to illustrate the main episodes in Crazy Horse's life, from his initiation as a wičaša yatanpi (a man spoken well of / a shirt wearer, in 1868 – according to other accounts, earlier in 1865), to his killing in 1877, have been lost.[474] It would have been revealing to see whether He Dog regarded the scar so prominent and defining a feature of his kola's face to reproduce it as a distinctive mark, even in a small pictographic portrait of his friend. We just do not know for sure to what extent Crazy Horse exhibited an "ugly scar" on his face as several newspapers, copying each other, reported in 1877. [475] True, some non-Indian sources described the negative visual impact of a scar on Crazy Horse's face: "A bullet wound through his left cheek, obtained, it is said, in a personal feud which first gave him notoriety, disfigures his face and gives to the mouth a drawn and somewhat fierce or brutal expression."[476] But if we compare such a strong description with the testimonies to the contrary previously cited, it is to be wondered how a "few powder marks" or even a "minor scar" could result in the "disfigured face" of some editorials. Similarly, how the "mildness and gentleness" of a "girlish looking boy,"(!!) or even better, "a very handsome young man" could turn into a "somewhat fierce or brutal expression." These incon-sistencies are also reflected in the reconstructed portraits of Crazy Horse drawn over the years by both Indian and White artists.

On the lasting impact of the small bullet fired by No Water on Crazy Horse's facial-maxillary bones, we have Horn Chips' testimony. In the same interview given in 1907, Chips maintained he was the only one left who knew where Crazy Horse's body was buried: "Crazy Horse was [originally] buried on the Beaver [Creek] by the cliffs […] in a frame house [pine coffin] lined with scarlet cloth." This, footnoted Hardorff, was "the cliff burial near Camp Sheridan where on September 6 relatives sepulchered the remains of Crazy Horse in a coffin draped with red blankets, on a three-feet-high scaffold."[477] Horn Chips continued, through Schweigerman: "When the Indians went down to the Missouri River the body was removed to White Clay Creek and buried; and when they returned, Chips and his brother went and took up the body to see if it had been disturbed, and finding that it had not been, they re-interred it." Reassuming once again the various locations, after the scaffold on the bluffs overlooking Camp Sheridan, and the interment on White Horse Creek, right above Manderson, the chief's mortal remains finally found permanent rest near Wounded Knee, "where it is now."

Chips had put Crazy Horse's bones "into a black blanket and laid them in a butte rock cave. There is no petrifaction, no flesh," the old medicine man explained, "nothing but bones. The shot through the head by No Water shows in the skull."[478] Again we are left to wonder where exactly "in the skull" the small bullet showed. Most sources agree that, Crazy Horse also had a bullet wound scar on his arm, from the Pawnee, and one in his left calf from the Ute. As for the burial site, its general location was apparently known to Jesse Lee, who sympathetically wrote: "Crazy Horse is forever at peace! He sleeps in an obscure and lonely grave on the cliffs of Wounded Knee Creek where it may be that his hovering spirit, in the closing days of 1890 […] caught once more the sound of the white man's guns that sent to bloody graves in indiscriminate slaughter, men women and children of a kindred band."[479]

In a sketch drawn sometime prior to 1940 based purportedly "on descriptions of old men and women who knew Crazy Horse personally," Oglala Lakota artist Andrew Standing Soldier (1917-1967) drew a long, visible scar on the subject's right cheek.[480] The scar runs under the right eye fully across the right cheek bone. According to Trimble, who published a copy of the portrait in the previously cited article, "Relatives and close friends of the war leader reportedly pronounced it an excellent likeness." The location and visible size of the scar seems however inconsistent with, and actually contradicts most testimonies regarding the point of entry of the small bullet and the path it followed. Such a frontal "cut" across the cheek could have most likely been produced by a knife or, but difficult to conceive, by a brushing bullet that hit the face as the intended victim instinctively jerked his head quickly to avoid the frontal impact. The prominent frontal view of the scar is not the only problem with the Standing Soldier sketch of Crazy Horse.

Crazy Horse, by Andrew Standing Soldier, sketched before 1940.

Although admittedly inconclusive, the results of an informal survey conducted by the present writer among a cross-section of American Indian, White, Asian, and African American visitors outside the National Museum of the American Indian in Washington are worth mentioning. Without identifying the portrait by Standing Soldier as that of "Crazy Horse," the question was asked, "How old do you think the Indian in this drawing is?" The overwhelming response was that the sketch likely identified "an Indian in his forties," for some even older. With regard to the facial wound, when asked what kind of weapon they thought could have produced that visible scar on his cheek, again the overwhelming response was "a knife." Finally, most of the respondents did not think the Indian in the drawing could be considered particularly "good looking." This puts the Standing Soldier's artistic likeness at odds with the general perception among the Lakota that, again in the words of Victoria Conroy, Crazy Horse "was a good man and good to look at."[481] Susan Bordeaux Bettelyoun went even further and used the adjective "very handsome" in her recollection of Crazy Horse, features the handsome Lakota warrior had inherited, along with his unusually brown hair, from his mother Rattling Blanket. Like Grouard and Horn Chips, Susan Bettelyoun too made no mention of any disfiguring "ugly scar" on the chief's face.

This does not mean a scar was not there. Simply that, as Jake Herman maintained, the scar did not show that much, especially seen from afar. In a postscript in a long letter to J.W. Vaughn verifying the tintype as a portrait of Crazy Horse, Herman cited a Lakota elder who had known the war chief: "As for the scar on the Chief Crazy Horse cheeks, Patrick Apple told me once that [Crazy Horse] had a scar on the cheek but it was small. Patrick rode and fought with the Chief. He knew him well."[482] There is also the ancillary evidence of the pictographic sketch of the killing of Crazy Horse, drawn by eyewitness American Horse as the glyph for the year 1877-78 in his own winter count. While American Horse drew the victim's braided hair (an alternative interpretation could be that one of the two lines represents the single feather resting upside down on the back of Crazy Horse's head) no mark appears on the profile showing the left side of the Oglala war chief's face.[483] Given the crude nature of the drawing, just a small line across the left cheek would have rendered the idea, again, provided the scar was indeed a defining feature on Crazy Horse's face. Apparently, for American Horse it was not.

There is yet another iconographic representation of the face of Crazy Horse in a notebook of drawings by Arnold Short Bull, dated ca. 1885-1890. The notebook was acquired directly from Short Bull around 1909 by ethnomusicologist Natalie Curtis Burlin. She had collected songs and stories from Short Bull and other Lakota elders, and published them along with photographs she obtained a couple of years earlier in her classic anthology of American Indian lore, *The Indians' Book*.[484] Short Bull's notebook is now part of the vast collection of Native American ledger art at the Hood Museum, Dartmouth College in Hanover, New Hampshire. In typical ledger-book style, with the action generally moving right to left, the drawing in question shows Crazy Horse on horseback, facing back and firing his pistol revolver at five Crow or Shoshone warriors chasing him while shooting bullets and arrows. Even though Short Bull clearly shows Crazy Horse's right side of the face, there is no mark visible to represent a wound. Again, while this cannot be argued as "proof," both the American Horse and the Short Bull drawings invite caution when speaking of the facial wound as a "defining" element of Crazy Horse's otherwise pleasant features. If the wound was so noticeable, applying artistic license Short Bull could have drawn the "defining feature" on the visible side, the important message being the presence of the wound itself, not specifically on which cheek. Equally important and characteristic of Crazy Horse was his long, light brown hair. In Short Bull's color drawing the hair is indeed long, reaching below the waist, but the color is typical "Indian" graphite-dark, like that of his pursuers, even though the artist had available a yellow-brown tone that he used, for example, for some of the enemy horses.[485]

There is a significant historic parallel to Crazy Horse's facial wound. It relates to the coetaneous wašiču nemesis of the Lakota chief himself, the very Thomas Custer (1845-1876), younger brother of the Glory Hunter. Crazy Horse and Tom Custer got a glimpse of each other, perhaps even more, "wounded face" to "wounded face" at the Little Bighorn. In his biography of Tom Custer, Carl F. Day went into details regarding the young officer's facial wound. In 1876, it was such a defining feature of Capt. Tom Custer that the Arikara scouts recruited at Fort Lincoln for the Sioux Campaign dubbed him accordingly, "Wounded Face." As with Crazy Horse's, Tom Custer's wound, too, was not very recent, being over ten years old. It was inflicted by a Confederate Rebel Colors bearer at the end of the Civil War and, like in Crazy Horse's case, had it been only slightly more to the center of the face, it probably would have cost him his life. The incident took place in early April 1865, as Col. Charles E. Capehart recalled in a letter to Libby Custer: "I saw [Tom Custer] capture his second flag. It was in a charge made by my brigade at Sailor's [Sayler's] Creek, Virginia, against Gen. [Richard S.] Ewell's Corps. [...] We were confronted by a supporting line. It was from the second line that he wrestled the colors, single-handed, and only a few paces to my right. As he approached the colors he received a shot in the face which knocked him back on his horse, but in a moment he was upright in his saddle."[486]

Day dwelled on the Confederate soldier shooting Tom Custer in the face, but after consulting the primary sources, he pointed out that "there has been confusion over the extent of the wound. Tom and Armstrong [his famous older brother]," explained Day, "both state in their letters that Tom was shot through the right cheek, with the bullet exiting under the right ear. In his application for reinstatement in the army, Tom wrote he, 'received a severe wound through my right cheek....' Tom's medical records," Day noted, "continue the confusion. His medical report of 9 April [1865, just days after the fact] listed his injury as a gunshot wound to the face and neck. Two days later Tom reported to the medical officer at City Point, Virginia, where his wound was listed as being restricted to the face. A photograph that appears to have been taken shortly after the event clearly shows what appears to be a scar or some minor tissue damage to his right lower jaw extending to a point just below the right ear. It seems clear from the photographic evidence that Tom's wound was not as severe as he and Armstrong stated." Day's observations inspire caution in all those who have tried to extrapolate, even exaggerate, on the true extent of Crazy Horse's facial wound. "Had the bullet entered the mouth," Day concluded, "or the soft tissue of the throat, it would have probably struck one of the major vessels and Tom would have bled to death."[487] The cicatrix is visible in Tom Custer's right profile view, but is not detectable in a front view of his face.

As a footnote to the Crazy Horse face wound, there are also two dissenting testimonies on the alleged Crazy Horse skull accidentally found by a trapper over two decades after the chief's parents had interred it with the rest of his remains. In a long letter to Will G. Robinson, Dean O'Bannon of Dallas, Texas, explained why he thought the Indian in the *Wi'iyohi* cropped photo was indeed Crazy Horse, and he referred also to a recent issue of *Frontier Times* magazine: "The base theme for this article was an interview with two Indians who were present at the time Crazy Horse was killed. The interview was conducted in the year 1909 by a man named Lone Eagle. A portion of this story deals with the mystery concerning the remains of Crazy Horse. It seems that a trapper named White found a skull in the badlands between Wounded Knee Creek and Porcupine Creek. This was in the year 1883 or 84. The skull had two marks on it, one on the upper jaw just below the corner of the nose, and one higher up between the cheekbone and the eye. White said that he found this skull with some bones and a set of travois poles. After showing the skull to several old Indian women who had known Crazy Horse well, they stated that it was definitively the skull of the same man. This skull was given to a relative and at the request of Black Shawl [Crazy Horse's widow] was crushed and buried near the present Rockyford [sic], South Dakota. The Indian in the photo that you have has these marks on his face and unless I am mistaken, he also has what appears to be a scar on his left cheek [...] also unless I am mistaken the clothing of the man in your picture is Oglala."[488]

This latter reference is interesting as it echoes what Pugh Young Man Afraid of His Horses had written nearly a decade earlier, that the man in the photo was actually Oglala, specifically Red Horn Bull, a veteran of the Custer Battle. Regarding Crazy Horse's remains, Pugh Young Man Afraid of

His Horses had written that "when Crazy Horse was killed [...] his parents and few relatives did took [sic] the body on travois to Spotted Tail Agency [...] which they stayed over night there then the group moved the next day headed east three days. One day his father said to the group we will stop here as the body is spoiling and smell so they camp on Porcupine Creek at the big elm tree which is east of Porcupine Store now. Next morning before any-body was up his father and mother took the body and gone from the camp and they came back near noon without the body. [...] Also I heard about that skull found on Wounded Knee, but you know there was silver in the teeth of that skull which I don't think Crazy Horse had any silver teeth."[489] The "search for the lost trail" of Crazy Horse's remains led Cleve Walstrom, a Kansas mortician, to identify over twenty possible burial sites described in his book by that title also endorsed by Richard Moves Camp.[490]

Hair Color and Style

One area of almost unanimous consensus deals with Tašunke Witko's hair color, texture, and style, both in his childhood and adult life. "Crazy Horse was born with light hair," stated Horn Chips, "and was called by the Indians the Light Haired Boy. His hair was always light [meaning, did not change much over time]. It did not reach to the ground as stated by Garnett, but did reach below his hips."[491] Like the Indian in the tintype. Red Feather, Black Shawl's brother, stated that Crazy Horse had "brown – not black – hair."[492] Luther Standing Bear later recalled that the Oglala war chief had "light brown hair, which was of a fine texture, and not like the black, coarse hair that Indians usually have."[493] Little Killer said that Crazy Horse "did not have black hair; he had brown hair like a white man."[494] Similarly, Susan Bordeaux Bettelyoun stated that Crazy Horse had "nice long light brown hair. His scalp lock was ornamented with beads and hung clear to his waist; his braids were wrapped in fur."[495] Susan's nephew William J. Bordeaux "darkened" the color of Crazy Horse's hair to "long dark brown." Later, he specified that on the night of his death, as Crazy

Horse was laying in pain on an improvised bed made with blankets placed on the floor of the dimly lighted room, "he was nude except for his breech cloth and his face was ghastly. His long brown hair was unplaited and came down to his waistline conforming with his athletic features and fair complexion [sic]."[496]

In the previously cited interview with John Neihardt, Eagle Elk remarked that "Crazy Horse was not a tall man – not too small a man [either], but just above a small man. His hair was not so dark as the other Indians; it was rather brown [...] His hair was braided down on both sides. That is how he wore his hair all the time."[497] Here, too, "all the time" must be understood as "customarily." Most sources confirm that in battle Crazy Horse wore his hair loose, like a rainstorm from which came the hail symbolized by painted dots on his face and body. The previously cited Mnicojou chief White Bull recalled that in battle Crazy Horse wore his hair "loose and flying."[498] The Indian in the tintype wears his hair in "posed" fashion, only one long braid partially wrapped in otter-fur on his left side, reaching below the waist, like Susan Bettelyoun, Jessie Eagle Heart, and others said. The other braid is behind his right shoulder. As noted, the lighter shade on the top of his head near the partition line, showing the lighter color of Crazy Horse's hair, was due to the illumination produced by the skylight in the Red Cloud Agency photographer's studio. Our subject wears earrings adorning his ears. They appear to be small shells with tin cones attached, again, typically consistent with Crazy Horse's period.

Eyes

The impression one gets by looking at the eyes of the Indian in the tintype is that he may be affected by mild strabismus, as seen in the composite close-up of Daniel White Lance and Crazy Horse, previously discussed. This is also consistent with Short Bull's statement that Crazy Horse's eyes never looked straight. Given the small size of the original image, and the unusual circumstances of this single sitting, it could also be that the subject temporarily focused his eyes at an angle that gives the above impression. Hardorff

As a war chief, Crazy Horse wrapped his long light brown hair in otterskin that
reached below his waist. All other personal details in the tintype match
Susan Bordeaux Bettelyoun's description of Crazy Horse.

summarized the sketchy references to Crazy Horse's eyes with a somewhat revealing statement that supports the "unfocused" impression one gets by looking at the tintype Indian's eyes. He cited a *New York Sun* article of May 23, 1877, describing the surrender of Crazy Horse. The newspaper referred to the Northern Indian leader as "the ablest of their chiefs, not excepting Spotted Tail. [...] not unlike other fine-looking and intelligent Sioux, though bearing himself with greater dignity than any of them. His eyes are exceedingly restless and impress the beholder fully as much as does his general demeanor."[499] And again, wrote Hardorff, Crazy Horse's eyes had "a wandering gaze that rarely focused straight at another person."[500]

As with the facial wound and hair color, not all accounts agree on the color of Crazy Horse's eyes. Little Killer, younger brother of Club Man who surrendered with Crazy Horse in 1877, years later commented on the war chief's eyes, saying that "his eyes were black like a Lakota's."[501] For Susan Bordeaux Bettelyoun, instead Crazy Horse had "hazel eyes."[502] William J. Bordeaux concurred with his paternal aunt that the famed Oglala's eyes were "light brown."[503] Black Elk (Hehaka Sapa, ca. 1863-1950), the Oglala visionary and later Catholic convert recalled instead that his cousin, a small slender man among the Lakota, had eyes that "looked through things." The tintype clearly shown that the Indian has light-colored eyes and a penetrating stare.

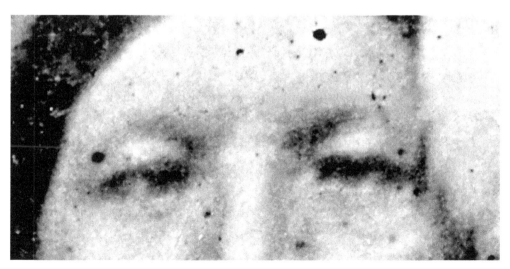

Crazy Horse's light-brown eyes as per Crazy Horse's own sister Mrs. Clown and "penetrating stare." Enlarged detail from the tintype.

White Shirt and Stroud Leggings

With game becoming scarce and trade goods increasingly available, especially after the 1850s-1860s treaties, the Lakota, Cheyenne, and Arapaho
traded regularly at Fort Laramie and later at Red Cloud and Spotted Tail's
agencies. At treaty negotiations, the government shipped vast quantities of presents as a sign of largess, goodwill, but also power, to appease
and reward loyal chiefs, and smooth the ground with the more recalci-
trant ones. Indians, for their part, expected largess and generosity of the
White Father, and eagerly looked forward to these donations. During the
1860s, large quantities of bulk commodities and government surplus items
destined to such distributions converged at Fort Laramie. The abundance
inevitably led also to bribery, corruption, and conflict among and between
the independent mixed-bloods and the local White post traders licensed to
do business with the Indians. Presenting the case of John Loree, appointed
agent for the Upper Platte Agency who speculated on the annuity goods
that, based on the Treaty of 1851, were to be distributed for free to the
Indians, Tom Buecker wrote that "by the early 1860s, the Indian trade on
the northern Plains was still open-ended for enterprising individuals." At
this same juncture, the United States government appointed Indian agents
who had the authority to license traders near their respective agencies. The
Museum of the Fur Trade recently obtained a document that illustrates
the struggle between old-time traders and a greedy agent for control of
the trade with the Indians: "The deposition signed in 1864 by trader and
freighter John R. Colombeo denouncing agent Loree's irregularities, listed
among the typical goods, referred to as annual presents of said Govt. to the
Indians of his Agency [...] twelve bales of (12) shirts; each bale containing
about one dozen (12)."[504] Loree eventually fled the agency with his pock-
ets full of "Indian" money.

A few years later, Seth E. Ward, the post trader at Fort Laramie with
whom Loree had both dealings and frictions, reported in his ledger the
prices and quantities of gifts intended for the historic treaty of 1868.
They included, first and foremost, weapons and ammunitions (rifles, bulk

powder, bar lead, percussion cups), and then hardware (kettles, pots and tin pans, butcher knives, awls, and needles), blankets (typically three-point), red and blue cloth (stroud/flannel), clothing (both surplus military uniforms and civilian shirts, handkerchiefs/neckerchiefs), miscellaneous items of adornment (packaged vermillion and glass beads, combs, umbrellas, eye-goggles), staple items and groceries (sugar, coffee, tobacco, hard tack), and riding equipment (lariats, bridles, saddles). Specifically regarding shirts, the Ward's ledger lists them of different types: unspecified shirts, woolen shirts, flannel shirts, and white shirts.[505]

A vast amount of White-man's goods, from early trade items to treaty presents, government annuities, and "stolen" goods, flooded the once exclusively "drawn from Nature" market of the Great Plains. Besides what they received at negotiations, and what they purchased or exchanged directly with traders, the Sioux periodically drew government rations as provided by the 1851 and 1868 treaties. In a relatively short time, they and other Plains tribes had become accustomed to, and increasingly dependent upon, Euro-American textiles, like those just mentioned. Indian men in particular began wearing white and brightly colored/patterned cotton, muslin, mixed-linen, flannel or woolen shirts, in addition to other articles of clothing such as military jackets, civilian vests, hats of all kinds, scarves, silk handkerchiefs, and so on. These were initially integrated with, and eventually completely substituted for, traditional clothes; similarly for Indian women and children.

Of course, Indians were not just passive recipients of the "new fashion" wave, and expressed their aesthetic taste introducing distinctive design patterns and preferred colors, thanks also to the widespread adoption of vitreous pony and seed-beads, and color-cloth. As Robert Murray wrote, "Indian women were skilled seamstresses, as evidenced by the many surviving museum examples of their workmanship. Naturally then they asked for specialized cloth items" especially "striped bed ticking," "blue drilling," "scarlet cloth," and "blue cloth."[506] They expressed their creative and decorative skills in what can be regarded as the artistic equivalent of the equestrian revolution. Thanks to new metal sewing kits of penknives, awls, scissors, needles, thimbles, and cotton thread, they integrated cloth and the ubiquitous trade beads with the traditional porcupine quills, horse hair, and vegetable fibers. Moccasins survived the longest in the rapidly changing Lakota wardrobe, but they too benefited from cloth and beads for decoration. The National Museum of the American Indian and other museums in the U.S., Canada, and Europe, have beautiful samples of Lakota and Plains Indian beaded footwear from Crazy Horse's time. The Indian in the tintype wears beaded moccasins with typical Lakota geometric design. This combination of "mixed" dress, whereas Lakota and other Plains Indian men wore white shirts together with stroud leggings and traditional beaded moccasins, is seen in many period photographs and ledger-art drawings.

White cotton/muslin shirts are especially noticeable in the black and white photographs of 1870s Indians taken in the field at Red Cloud and Spotted Tail agencies and other localities, and of the members of the Indian delegations to Washington taken in the studios of Zeno Shindler, James McClees, Alexander Gardner, Charles Bell, Mathew Brady, and others. The historic portraits consistently show Lakota, Cheyenne, and Arapaho (and other Plains tribes) chiefs and headmen wearing candid white shirts, dark vests, and neckerchiefs, or Ascot ties, plus occasional metal (nickel/German silver, or brass) armbands, attesting to the widespread use of this type of clothing and accessories in Crazy Horse's time. Shirts are generally worn over stroud leggings and beaded moccasins. Leaving aside for the moment the breastplate issue, individual and group photographs of Red Cloud, Spotted Tail, He Dog, Young Man Afraid of His Horse, Hunts the Enemy, Little Hawk, Sitting Bull the Oglala, Three Bears, Red Dog, even Little Big Man and many more match in the main the clothing of the Indian in the tintype. But also the striking Gardner portraits from the waist up of Brule chief Yellow Hair (PehiZi), and Hunkpapa headman Black Horn (HeSapa), the latter holding a long, 1840 model Army sword cradled in his left arm, and a small paper fan in his right hand.[507] Byron H. Gurnsey, too, whose "Chak-ok-ta-kee/Chak-uk-t-kee" photograph was central to the early Crazy Horse picture debates, took photographic portraits of Sioux delegations passing through Sioux City, Iowa. One portrays the leading members of the 1870 Brule delegation to Washington, namely Fast Bear, Spotted Tail, Swift Bear, and Yellow Hair, the first three wearing white shirts and neckerchiefs, the latter a striped color shirt and a short, German-silver neck-pendant.

By the late 1860s-early 1870s, cotton/muslin shirts, either plain white, or brightly colored with stripes, floral, or geometric pattern designs were very common among the Sioux. In his recollections of a pitched battle fought in the spring 1873 with the Canadian Red River Métis who were hunting buffalo south of the Canadian border on the Rosebud, White Bull had joined his maternal uncle Sitting Bull in fighting the Slota. As Vestal wrote, "White Bull was wearing his war-clothes; he was all dressed up. He wore beaded moccasins and leggings, a red shirt and a bone breastplate." Later White Bull will mention also wearing "dark blue woolen legging [sic]" as part of his own war attire.[508] When White Bull and his younger brother One Bull, along with Crazy Horse, Sitting Bull, Gall, Four Horns, Low Dog, Big Road, Spotted Eagle, Makes Room, Two Moon, Ice, and the other chiefs and headmen of the Northern hunting bands of a likewise brave heart gathered on the banks of the Little Bighorn, the thousands of Indians there must have offered an impressive sight. Not only from the sheer extent of the village, the number of lodges, the huge pony-herd, but also the variety of clothing. The men, as we gather from the Indians' own iconographic accounts, wore leggings, breechcloths, and war shirts made of buckskin, integrated with similar articles cut and sewn from trade cloth, stroud, or flannel.

There were also many white cotton/muslin shirts and old surplus military uniform jackets. Indian women wore both traditional, fringed, long buckskin dress, or a similar long dress cut and sewn to fit from stroud, other trade cloth, or blankets. Both buckskin and stroud dresses were usually decorated with elk teeth, porcupine quill, and beadwork, and tied around the waist with a large leather belt to which a knife-sheath with a sharp butchering knife and awl in its beaded case were usually secured. Inkpaduta's Santee, camped near Sitting Bull's Hunkpapa at the southern end of the village. Being refugees from the east, poorer, and having been exposed earlier to trade and acculturation, these Dakota wore almost exclusively textile clothing they made and were known as "Waist and Skirt People," their women wearing settler-type or wraparound skirts made of trade cloth, or full calico dresses.

White muslin/cotton shirts, similar to the one worn by the Indian in the tintype, were also worn by at least two Arapaho and certainly by some if not many of the Lakota and Northern Cheyenne who fought at the Little Bighorn. We have the testimony given in 1920 to Col. Tim McCoy by Waterman and Left Hand, two of the five young Northern Arapaho who somewhat accidentally were themselves protagonists of the epic battle, and they specifically made reference to white shirts. The five young warriors had recently left Red Cloud Agency, where the Arapaho also camped, intentioned on a war party against the Shoshone when they ran into a small band of Northern Indians. Forced to follow them to the big village, the Arapaho were suspected by the Sioux of being Army scouts and might have been killed had not been for the intervention of Cheyenne chief Two Moon who spoke on their behalf, saving their lives. The next day, the Arapaho fought bravely against Custer and his men. In typical war-narrative fashion, Waterman took great care in describing his attire for that historic event: "During the battle I was dressed in beaded leggings, breech-clout [sic], a white shirt, and a large war-bonnet. My face was painted yellow and red, and around my neck, tied in a deer-skin medicine bag, was a certain root, which was my medicine."

The other warrior, Left Hand was actually part Blackfoot and Cheyenne, but had always lived among the Arapaho, possibly having been captured as a youth and adopted by his Arapaho father named Cherry. Left Hand also related his war exploits at the Little Bighorn: "During the fight I counted thirteen coups. I was dressed in a shirt and breech-clout. My medicine was a piece of buffalo hide made into a cross with two feathers in it, which I wore in my hair." In the melee, Left Hand killed a Lakota warrior with his lance that he had mistaken for a Crow or Arikara scout, himself risking to be killed in retaliation by the angry Sioux.[509] We do not know what color Left Hand's shirt was, but given Waterman's testimony, and the fact that the Arapaho were coming from the agency, we may assume it was also white. There are two earlier photographs of an Arapaho identified as Left Hand, taken by Gardner in Washington in 1872, in which the subject wears a white shirt under the usual dark vest, and a large white neckerchief, similar to that of the Indian in the tintype. He may or may not be the same person; John Koster implies he is.

In his *Catalogue*, W.H. Jackson listed a Left Hand as a Southern Arapaho.[510] An enigmatic Hunkapapa Lakota also known as Left Hand, Čatka, originally enlisted as a U.S. Army Scout in December 1875, one of the five Dakota who had joined Gen. Custer. He mustered out six months later in early June while serving under Gen. Alfred Terry column. Left Hand went on to join his people in the hostile camp where his body was found in an abandoned tipi after the battle, the circumstances of his death unknown. His unusual story was related by John Koster who noted that Left Hand's "role in the battle and manner of his death remain a mystery."[511] We know, however, what he wore, thanks to the testimony of Arikara scout Young Hawk who recalled that when Left Hand's body was found, "he had on a white shirt. The shoulders were painted green, and on his forehead, painted in red, was a sign of a secret society."

These and other testimonies show the widespread use of cloth-shirts, white in particular, by the Indians at the Little Bighorn and at the Sioux agencies. Photographs taken at Camp Robinson, Red Cloud, and Spotted Tail, 1874 to 1877, prove that this article of wašiču wardrobe was largely in use. Especially popular was the three-quarter "long-John" coarse all-cotton or mixed-linen long white shirt. Comfortable and practical, as we just heard it complemented breechcloth and leggings, both made of soft buckskin at that time. With regard to the old-style leggings in particular, chiefs and head warriors favored the soft, white buckskin, called hunská ("clear white leg"). By 1877, even earlier, buckskin had been mostly replaced by blue, red, or other dark color trade cotton stroud. The long shirt reached below the loin area, in the old days covered by a buckskin čehgnáke ("penis cover") and now by a long rectangular stroud/flannel breechcloth held around the waist by a leather belt.

Some of these recently adopted breechcloths could be quite long and nicely decorated with appliqué and beadwork. An example is a late 1870s-early 1880s photograph marketed by Lucien Stilwell of Deadwood, showing a full length studio portrait of Lone Dog (Šunke Išnala/Wanjila), the Lower Yanktonai chief signer of the 1877 Agreement at Standing Rock. Besides the long breechcloth, and the long (coyote or wolf?) tail hanging from one of his arms, what is interesting in this photograph is the backdrop with ferns similar to those in the tintype. White cotton/muslin shirts, undershirts, and longjohns were of course also used by White civilians and Army personnel – they were common merchandise on the trader's store shelves at the forts and nearby agencies.

When Crazy Horse and his long caravan of tired and hungry followers finally approached Camp Robinson, on April 30, 1877, supplies of clothing and food were sent out by the military authorities as goodwill presents to alleviate the destitute condition of the Northern Indians. The two groups met on the banks of Hat Creek, some forty miles from the post. The rescue train, under the command of 2nd Lieut. J. Wesley Rosenquest of the 4th U.S. Cavalry included ten supply wagons loaded with rations and a one hundred beef cattle herd, escorted by some fifty Oglala enlisted as Indian scouts. The scouts were led by American Horse who, as reported in the *Denver Daily Tribune*, "Desired to make a great spread and ado of their mission, and [...] to create a stunning sensation in the Crazy Horse camp by exhibiting to the suffering hostiles a first class toilet. Accordingly, they bought up all the white shirts at the trader's store, and carefully stowed them away in their gaudy saddle pouches. They rode out to within five miles of the Crazy Horse camp, halted by the side of a stream, bathed and donned their reception attire. Other garments were thrown aside and the clean, white linen put on with its full length exposed. [...] These white-robed reds soon made a triumphant entry into the dilapidated Crazy Horse village. [...] the thoroughly wild Indians, who had never seen such a fluttering of white flags, were greatly rejoiced there were so many peace ensigns to welcome them in."[512]

Billy Garnett who was present, may have also had a white shirt on, and Red Cloud too, who with his own party of nearly one hundred strong, had rendezvoused earlier with American Horse and Rosenquest's convoy on the Laramie and Black Hills Road, some three miles below the Hat Creek stage station. Garnett recalled that, "Chief American Horse, true to his instinct as ever to help himself, posted his scouts in line in front of all the others and had them sitting down facing the Indians coming from the north. [...] and when Crazy Horse men came up they presented each Indian scout including American Horse and the Lieutenant who was surprised to get one, a pony. This Lieutenant Rosecrans [sic] shook hands with Crazy Horse and all the chiefs. It has been said that Lieut. Clark was the first army offi-cer ever known to shake hands with Crazy Horse, but this is a mistake." Only the next day did Lieut. Clark leave Camp Robinson to meet Crazy Horse some two miles north of Red Cloud Agency: "The chiefs sat down in a row and they told Clark to advance and shake hands with them, using the left hand, they using the same; for, they say, the left hand is next [to] the heart, but the right hand does all matter of wickedness. Crazy Horse presented the Lieutenant a war bonnet, war shirt, pipe and beaded sack for tobacco and kinni kinnick and pipe."[513] Gifts were also presented by He Dog.

American Horse and Red Cloud wore their dark blue Indian scout jack-ets showing their rank. The two chiefs later wore the popular and prac-tical agency white shirt in Washington. American Horse wore his under his war shirt in the famous Lakota delegation photograph taken that fall in the Capital City after Crazy Horse's death. Two years prior, the Oglala Sitting Bull was photographed by Frank Currier at Omaha in 1875 with Little Wound, Spotted Tail, Red Cloud, and Julius Meyer, again shown wearing a white cotton shirt. Red Cloud, too, had one under his tailored double-breasted dark-color jacket. White cotton shirts had been intro-duced and adopted earlier among other Sioux divisions as seen, for exam-ple, in the 1858 McClees Studio photo of Yankton chief Struck by the Ree. Shown seated in his white shirt and waist-high blanket, next to inter-preter Charles Picotte and chief Smutty Bear, the three were part of a large Yankton delegation to Washington.[514] Several of the Dakota Indians photographed later in Washington by Shindler in 1867 also wore white cotton shirts. But even at the famous 1868 Fort Laramie gathering the two historic Gardner photos the "Interior of Council Chamber" show, seated to the right of a shirtless Old Man Afraid, an aged Lakota chief (unidentified) wearing a long sleeve white shirt, his head wrapped in a large neckerchief.[515] The same applied to the 1872 Sioux delegation photographs taken by Alexander Gardner in Washington. One example for all is the photograph of Brule chief Swift Bear, shown seated, holding an eagle feathers fan with a blanket wrapped around his waist. He wears a white cotton shirt, dark vest, and a long neckerchief over which shines a large peace medal.

Swift Bear (Mato Luzahan, 1827-1909), by A. Gardner, Washington, 1872.

As we said earlier, many of the Indians photographed at Red Cloud and Spotted Tail agencies, 1874 to 1877, are wearing white cotton/linen shirts. At the great council with Gen. Crook on May 25, 1877, held inside the Red Cloud Agency stockade, Iron Hawk, also known as Sweater, spoke after Red Cloud's second harangue. The respected, elderly Northern Oglala who was related to orphaned brothers Woman's Dress and Keeps the Battle, reportedly wore a "modern white shirt, buttoned in front, the bosom on his back."[516]

The above contradicts what Judge Charles C. Hamilton recalled in his previously cited Address before the Academy of Science and Letters in Sioux City, Iowa, regarding the dress of the Indians at Red Cloud and Spotted Tail agencies in 1877: "The Indians we saw out there were real Indians. They were dressed as frontier Indians are supposed to be dressed. All wore beaded moccasins. The rest of their clothing was made of deer-hide or buck-skin, profusely beaded. Their head dress was made up of feathers, and all of the men wore their scalp lock neatly braided, surrounded by a big ring of bright red paint."[517] Many of them did, but not all. It is true that some of the surviving James H. Hamilton photographs show, for example, two "Sioux Belles" (No. 108 of his *Catalogue of Stereoscopic Views*) wearing traditional, fringed, long buckskin dresses, and beautiful, long dentalium earrings. Other images, as that of "Two-Strike, Sioux Chief" (No. 130) and "Two-Strike and Family" (No. 160) clearly reflect otherwise. Two Strike (Numpkahapa, 1831-1915), famous Sičangu headman (photographed in his scalp shirt a couple of years earlier by Gardner), is wearing a clear cotton shirt. In the family stereoview portrait, his two wives wear long trade cloth/stroud dresses. They were customarily embellished with elk teeth, as in this case. The women also wear again long dentalium earrings, dentalium shells being symbols of wealth and status. Like his father, son Little Hawk too, seated, wears a long sleeve white cotton shirt with brass armbands, stroud leggings, and beaded moccasins. Two-Strikes' younger daughter sitting next to Little Hawk wears instead a white buckskin dress, also a sign of her family wealth and love; well-dressed children brought honor to their parents and grandparents.[518] Private Charles Howard lists

"Two Strikes [sic] and family" (No. 64) among his stereoviews again raising the question whether we are dealing with the same image or two different ones.

Yet another notable example of common "agency dress" are the white shirt, stroud leggings, and trade blanket Red Dog wears in an undated stereoview portrait by James H. Hamilton. We have also seen the remarkable J.H. Hamilton stereoview (No. 165) of the large Indian group photographed outside the log cabin studio in 1877. Similarly telling is the family portrait of American Horse with wife, son, and daughter, also taken by Hamilton in front of the same log cabin photographic studio. American Horse is wearing a white long sleeve shirt with brass armbands, short two-row hair-pipe breastplate, dentalium chocker, braids wrapped in otterskin, and beaded blanket, just like the Indian in the tintype. His son seats between his legs, also wearing a boy-size white shirt and a short five-row dentalium breastplate. His wife Spotted Elk Woman, donning long detalium earrings, wears a fine trade shawl over a calico dress. The little girl on her lap poses in her stroud dress finely decorated with elk teeth again, indicative of a much loved and well taken care of daughter of a chief. The old Heritage Auctions – mistakenly regarding both American Horse and his son as "females" – labeled the group portrait as "Sioux Squaws." J.H. Hamilton had listed it in his *Catalogue* as "154. Family Group at Red Cloud." Tom Buecker reproduced the same stereoview in *The Last Days*, but titled it "Photograph of an agency family" without recognizing it as American Horse's.

Did James H. Hamilton's son, later the honorable Judge Charles Hamilton, purposely "lie" about the Indians' dress at Red Cloud? Obviously not. He simply recalled the strong visual impact, the emotional experience of a sixteen-year old White boy in the midst of the most formidable and belligerent Indians of the Plains. Many were the very Sioux who had defeated Gen. Custer only a year earlier and were just now beginning to adjust to agency life. Young Hamilton certainly saw warriors on horseback, in buckskins and war bonnets, and women with long, beaded fringed buckskin dresses. All of which must have made not a small impression on him. Lakota still wore clothing made of buckskin, but mostly during cere-monies, or special occasions, such as posing for a photograph, especially women. When on delegation trips, Indians too, traveled with a suitcase carrying their traditional buckskin shirts and leggings, and richly beaded moccasins. It was a matter of pride, of course, a statement of tribal identity, to impress their White hosts, and to pose for the photographer.

Lakota chiefs, with the notable exception of Crazy Horse and Sitting Bull, loved pageantry and making a good show of themselves, especially when other leaders, Indian and White, were present. Chiefs and headmen took along beaded trade blankets, war bonnets and other eagle feather ornamentations, ceremonial pipes and pipe bags, large German silver crosses, impressive bear-claw necklaces, and dentalium or bone hair-pipe breastplates. Some, like He Dog, had their war clubs, others, even swords and sabers.[519] With pride they donned fringed and painted war shirts beaded and decorated with human and horse hair, feathers and bonnets, peace medals, and held their long-stem catlinite pipes and fringed and beaded pipe bags, and more. Posing for the camera was part of diplo-macy and the Washington show. Depending on the circumstances, dele-gation Indians switched clothing back and forth. By now, however, cloth was preferred in everyday life, being more practical, easily available, and less odorous. Back at the agency, particularly among the recently surren-dered Northern Indians, long-sleeve, coarse white, natural or ivory tone, or colorfully patterned cotton/muslin shirts were substituting for the once predominant buckskin.

Women, likewise, rapidly replaced, at least for everyday camp and agency life, their long buckskin dress with long red, blue stroud, flan-nel, or calico dresses tied at the waist with a large leather belt. Attached to the belt they usually carried a large butcher knife in scabbard and an awl also in a beaded scabbard. As early as 1868, Gardner's photographs attested to that at Fort Laramie, as did those of the "shadow catchers" who came through Red Cloud Agency in 1877. Oral testimonies specifically pertaining to this mundane aspect of tribal life corroborated the same. Interviewed by Eleanor Hinman at Pine Ridge in the summer of 1930, with

Mrs. Annie Roland interpreting, Red Feather recalled that "Crazy Horse had never been to an agency since he was a young man. Neither had I. [...] When [the Northern Indians] were only about one day's journey from the fort, the people from the agency brought out rations to them. When they got to the fort, the agent gave them rations, clothing, and blankets. Everyone was very jolly. All the women made new clothes. Before they all wore buckskin, but now their clothes were of bright-colored cloth."[520]

As for the men, again the cloth-shirt, either soft or coarse white, or brightly colored cotton/muslin, was unquestionably common clothing at Red Cloud Agency in 1877, even earlier. A period photograph portrays a stern looking Red Cloud, 1872, wearing a white long-sleeve undershirt and his usual dark vest. Another image is that of an equally stern Spotted Tail, 1870, wearing a light-color patterned long sleeve shirt. In 1877, Young Man Afraid and He Dog, are both also wearing almost identical tops of white shirt, dark cloth vest, and big German-silver cross on their chest, symbolic of the four sacred directions.[521] There is a group photograph, possibly by Gardner, of three members of the famous 1872 Sioux delegation to Washington, flanked by Julius Meyer standing and donning an otter turban with tail, fringed buckskin jacket, belt with beaded knife sheath, and beaded leggings. The Indians next to Meyer are, left to right, Brule headmen The-One-Who-Runs-the-Tiger and Bald Eagle, both seated, and Gassy, standing, wrapped to his chest in the ever present trade blanket. All three wear white cotton shirts, the two seated Indians also have white neckerchiefs, stroud leggings, beaded moccasins, and their personal blanket resting on their lap.[522] Photographs taken in 1875 near the Black Hills and at Red Cloud by Albert E. Guerin show that white cloth shirts and dark vests, blankets, and hats had replaced buckskin among Indian males as standard dress. The only exception, of course, traditional moccasins. Guerin's photographs captioned "Indian Chiefs & Interpreters" are indicative of the dress already worn at the agencies.[523]

The Indian in the tintype wears precisely the kind of clothing in use among Lakota, Northern Cheyenne, and Northern Arapaho men at Red Cloud Agency in 1877. There is an abundance of contemporary individual

Indian and group photos taken by different "shadow catchers" in the months immediately preceding and following the surrender and death of Crazy Horse. They all show that the long white cotton/muslin shirt and indigo-blue or red trade stroud or flannel leggings were ordinary among agency Indians. In addition to visual evidence, there are also eyewitness accounts of what not just Indians in general, but Crazy Horse specifically usually wore when visiting the agency trader's store and nearby Camp Robinson. Similarly, there are also testimonies describing what he actually wore the day he was killed. There appears to be some disagreement about his leggings, not the shirt he wore and the red blanket he customarily carried. Specifically regarding the leggings: because of the abrasive contact with the horse's flanks (often sweaty), with prairie dust, and the habit of sitting cross legged directly on the ground, leggings needed to be changed or replaced altogether more often.

There are other testimonies supporting Crazy Horse's use of a white cotton/muslin shirt, together with white buckskin or white or blue stroud leggings. According to a White Bull's testimony mailed by Walter S. Campbell to Eleanor Hinman in 1932, even before his surrender Crazy Horse used a white muslin shirt as part of his normal attire. Sometime between the victory over Custer (June 25-26) and the battle at Slim Buttes (Sept. 8, 1876) White Bull was a visiting guest in Crazy Horse's lodge. As he recalled, "That evening Crazy Horse wore white cloth leggings, and a white muslin shirt for a robe. His face was not painted. […] He was] about his own height (5 ft 10 [inch]) now – perhaps taller once, but slimmer, with a light complexion."[524]

So, as far as Crazy Horse's leggings are concerned, what may be reported by one eyewitness, may not coincide with another's. Michael Samuel, who supports the tintype as a true likeness of Crazy Horse, gave new details about the white shirt. According to him, Crazy Horse had purchased it in 1862, at the trader's store near Fort Laramie, along with "a shawl as a gift for Black Buffalo Woman, a long ribbon for his mother 'Gathers Her Berries' that he wore in the photo in his hair on the right side, and a shirt for himself. The shirt," Samuel explains, "was not what he wanted, but it was all that was left. It was a longjohn shirt with buttons part way down the front, and it had no collor [sic], so he took the shawl and used it as a scarf to cover up these things. Crazy Horse borrowed the Moccasins you see in the photo because his were ragged. He also took off his Breech cloth because it was not very fluttering. Then he took out the Longjohn shirt tail from his leggings to cover himself with. You will notice how it was wrinkled from being tucked in."[525]

White Calf, a twenty-three-year-old Oglala scout at Red Cloud Agency saw the stabbing of the war chief and was interviewed by Hinman at Pine Ridge in 1930: "I was in Red Cloud's band at the old agency near the fort [Camp Robinson]. I was a scout [...] I was right there at the time Crazy Horse was killed. [...] Do you want to know how Crazy Horse was dressed, at the time he was killed? He wore beaded moccasins, buckskin leggings, and a white cotton shirt. He had a red blanket." [526]

The killing of Crazy Horse (1877), by Bad Heart Bull (ca. 1890), shows how Crazy Horse was dressed when he was mortally wounded. Like the Indian in the tintype, Crazy Horse is wearing a white cotton shirt, beaded moccasins, blue stroud leggings, stylized blanket wrapped around his waist, and enhanced Ascot tie just like the tintype. Different details apply to Little Big Man who is holding Crazy Horse's arm while a soldier lunges forward with his bayonet.

Woman's Dress (ca. 1877) dressed like the Indian in the tintype, enlisted as scout by Lieutenant Clark at Camp Robinson, was the cause of a report that Crazy Horse was planning to murder General Crook in council.

Lieut. William Philo Clark and Oglala chief Little Hawk, by D.S. Mitchell, Red Cloud Agency, 1877. Little Hawk, Crazy Horse's uncle, is dressed like the Indian in the tintype, white shirt, trade blanket with large beaded strip, stroud leggings, and Ascot tie.

Red Blanket

We just heard from White Calf, and a number of other eyewitness testimonies confirm, that Crazy Horse generally carried a red blanket, which he regarded one of his most cherished possessions that he also had the day of his death. It would make sense that such a prized item should also be part, if one was taken, of his photographic portrait. The Indian in the tintype clearly holds over his left forearm a blanket, most likely red with light-color border trim, decorated with a large beaded strip. Michael Samuel, again, links the identity of the Indian in the tintype as Crazy Horse to his famous blanket: "Over his right (i.e., left) arm he draped the red blanket."[527] As we saw earlier, other sources indicate that Crazy Horse had raided that *šinaša*, scarlet blanket, in 1867 from a wagon train on the Tongue River and, in the words of William Bordeaux, he "wore [it] thereafter until the time of his death."[528] Michael Samuel however maintains that, as with the white shirt and other items previously described, Crazy Horse had purchased the red blanket at the Laramie trader's store in 1862: "Just before this Photo was taken He had stopped at the trading post that was just a little North and East from the Fort itself. He had purchased the Blanket you see. It was Red with White trim. He had wanted a solid red blanket to use as his burial blanket, but that was all they had left."[529]

Whatever the circumstances, Crazy Horse was in the habit of carrying a red blanket. We do not know whether the one he had the day he died was his old one, another old one, or one more recently acquired, either as a gift, or at the Red Cloud Agency trader store. We know that, the day of his surrender, as a gesture of goodwill and tribal reconciliation, he presented chief Red Cloud with a horse and a red blanket trimmed with fine porcupine quillwork. Indian scout White Calf, who with his friend Red Feather was standing near the Adjutant's office and saw Crazy Horse being escorted, still unknowingly, to the guardhouse, recalled that when the Oglala war chief was killed he "had a red blanket."[530] He Dog, who was also present, confirmed it. "I was present at the killing of Crazy Horse," he stated in his 1930 interview. "The next day when I went to the [Camp] Robinson I was told that Crazy Horse had escaped [...]. The Indian police were given orders to bring him back. Next day [Sept. 5th] they brought him back. I was still encamped at the White Butte, and they brought him past my camp on their way to the fort. I saw them coming and sent orders for them to bring Crazy Horse into my tipi. I meant to give him a good talking-to. But police didn't stop, they took him straight on to the fort. When I saw this, I could only put on my war bonnet and get my horse bareback and follow. When I came to the fort I found Crazy Horse in the lead on his horse, wearing a red blanket. A military ambulance followed – a couple of army officers were in it, but no Indians. I rode up on the left side of Crazy Horse and shook hands with him. I saw that he did not look right. I said, 'look out – watch your step – you are going into a dangerous place,'"[531]

Based on He Dog's and other eyewitness testimonies, Bray drafted a detailed reconstruction of the chief's last moments, and the red blanket is again mentioned. After Crazy Horse was bayoneted outside the guard-house, "for a moment he crouched, then the upper part of his body sagged, and he lay in the dust."[532] Touch the Clouds and He Dog rushed to his side. Shortly thereafter, a Brule named Closed Cloud stepped outside the guard-house carrying the chief's red blanket, with the intention of spreading it over him, at which the wounded man reacted furiously. At that He Dog grabbed the blanket, folded into a pillow, and placed under Crazy Horse's head. He Dog himself also recalled that at that point he tore in two the large agency blanket he was himself wearing "and used half of it to cover him. He was gasping hard for breath. 'See where I am hurt,' he gasped. 'I can feel the blood flowing.' I," continued He Dog, "pulled back his shirt and looked at the wound. He was thrust nearly through twice. The first stroke went from between the ribs in the back, on the right side, and very nearly came through in front under the heart. A lump was rising under the skin where the thrust entered. The second wound was through the small of the back, through the kidneys."[533]

Other warriors spread their own blankets on the ground, repositioned the mortally wounded chief there, and used them to carry him to the Adjutant's Office. There Crazy Horse was gently placed on a pile of blankets laid on the floor, as his death bed. Shortly before midnight, with his weeping father Worm and one of his step-mothers, besides Dr. McGillycuddy, Bat Pourier, Capt. Kerrington, Lieut. Lemly, and Touch the Clouds present, Crazy Horse finally ended his earthly suffering and journeyed on to the spirit world. The tall Mnicojou symbolically closed the curtain on his cousin's troubled life by pulling the chief's red blanket over his face while uttering these tragic words, "It is good, he has looked for death, and it has come." Mahpiya Ičantagya, himself will pass away at Cheyenne River Reservation on September 5, 1905, the 28th anniversary of Crazy Horse's death, and he too was wrapped in a red blanket. Photographs of the large Sioux delegation to Washington in the wake of Crazy Horse's death, show several Indians with blankets like the one of the Indian in the tintype: dark in color, usually red with a large beaded band and light-color border trim. A similarly large, agency-issue red blanket with light-color border trim is shown covering the wooden box containing Crazy Horse's body in the scaffold burial erected near Camp Sheridan. It is visible in the two photographs of the scaffold grave, surrounded by a tall fence of large pine boards, taken by Private Charles Howard in October 1877.

Crazy Horse's grave, by Pvt. Charles Howard, near Camp Sheridan, Oct. 1877. In this photo, taken from a different angle than the one discussed earlier, the red blanket draping the scaffold is also clearly visible. E.A. Brininstool obtained a few pages of Lieut. Jesse Lee's diary, now lost, where Lee had written: "Whenever I get out my quarters I see the the red blanket in which his body is wrapped, and thus is recalled to my mind and heart Crazy Horse's pathetic and tragic end." As seen in the tintype, when Crazy Horse posed for his photograph, he folded his cherished blanket around his left arm, as a war chief of his ranking would do. In the tintype, the width and light color of the border trim of the blanket touching the log-cabin studio floor is the same as that of the blanket on the scaffold.

Wotawe

Like all other Lakota, Crazy Horse had also his own wotawe, a protective charm or charms. His was given to him by his mentor Ptehe Woptuha, Horn Chips, himself a "stone dreamer." Since Crazy Horse's life was centered on his identity as a warrior, his wotawe was especially meant to shield and protect him in battle.[534] In his 1930 interview with Eleanor Hinman, Red Feather stated that "during war expeditions he wore a little white stone with a hole through it, on a buckskin string slung over his shoulder. He wore it under his left arm. [...] A man name Chips, a great friend [and spiritual mentor] of his, gave it to him."[535] This tunken medicine was extremely powerful, imbued with wakan power, hence "heavy," a reason why, according to Lakota oral tradition, Crazy Horse's war ponies could not last long. He Dog related the same: "Crazy Horse always led his men himself when they went into battle [...]. He headed many charges and was many times wounded in battle, but never seriously. He never wore a war bonnet. A medicine man named Chips had given him power if he would wear in battle an eagle-bone whistle and one feather and a certain round stone with a hole in it. He wore the stone under his left arm, suspended by a leather thong that went over his shoulder."[536]

Interviewed a year later by Mari Sandoz, with John Colhoff translating, He Dog provided additional details: "Chips made medicine for Crazy Horse [and gave him] a sort of black stone – like a good-sized marble – covered with buckskin and with one of the two center feathers of an eagle. (Each eagle has two exactly-matched feathers in his tail, bilaterally placed). The other feather he wore in his hair in battle. His eagle wing-bone flute (from the same eagle) was made to wear over his neck on a rawhide string. All the medicine, head feather and flute were from the spotted eagle."[537] The stone with the hole in the middle, and the lanyard with the eagle feather decoration attached to it, is clearly visible in the tintype, hanging from the Indian's left arm, along his left thigh, just near the left knee. The rawhide string running through it, is also noticeable. After Chips gave Crazy Horse his second medicine bundle, the Oglala war chief owned two sacred stones: one in the small buckskin pouch near his heart – as shown also in the tintype (resting on the otter fur); the other, as previously noted, with a hole and a string through it. As Francis White Lance put it, "The lanyard with his stone medicine and eagle feather are right below his left hand."[538] White Lance further suggests that Crazy Horse had, altogether, seven sacred stones, although two in particular were his favorite. One was for his horse when going into battle, the other, the heart stone medicine, he carried all the time on the same side of his heart next to his eagle-bone war whistle.

The revised "Crazy Horse" entry on Wikipedia, mostly based on the second DVD, states that Chips gave Crazy Horse a black stone (inyan sapa) "to protect his horse, a black and white paint he had named 'Inyan' meaning rock or stone. He placed the stone behind the horse's ear, so that the medicine he received from his vision quest [a medicine bundle, the white owl and the red-tail hawk as animal protectors, his face paint consisting of a yellow lightning bolt down the left side of his face and white powder marks to symbolize hailstones, and a sacred song] and the medicine that Horn Chips had given him would combine to make his horse and himself as one in battle." Adding to what was already stated by He Dog, most sources agree that Crazy Horse's wotawe included also a small medicine bag given to him by Chips sometimes after the No Water incident. It was made of tanned buckskin and it contained the dried heart and claws of a spotted eagle.[539] This is probably the medicine bag referred to by He Dog and Eagle Elk who recalled that Crazy Horse "wore a strand of braided buckskin; at the lower end was something like medicine, tied up in the buckskin. He had an eagle-wing whistle tied on. He had it with him all the time."[540] "Like medicine" must be understood as the small tanned buckskin sack container, hence itself wotawe.

This description matches exactly the tintype. Hardorff, rephrasing the Chips, Eagle Elk, He Dog, and other testimonies suggests that, closely connected with his single spotted eagle feather, Crazy Horse's "medicine pouch contained the heart of the same spotted eagle, one of his wing bones supplying the whistle which he wore around his neck." Furthermore,

Crazy Horse's wotawe is clearly visible in the tintype. Top arrow shows the eagle-bone war whistle Crazy Horse always had leaning on his heart. Middle arrow shows the spotted eagle feather attached to the lanyard.Bottom arrow shows the sacred stone with a drilled whole to attach it to the lanyard as per Red Feather, Crazy Horse's brother-in-law.

Hardorff continued, "To evoke the spirit blessings of the eternal beings, he carried a little round stone under his left arm. Wrapped in a rawhide, the stone was adorned by the second bilateral tail feather off the spotted eagle, the whole being suspended by a leather thong that passed over his right shoulder." Crazy Horse's cherished his medicine pouch, and he had it with him at all times as Eagle Elk stated.

The Indian in the tintype appears to be holding in his left hand a leather pouch to which is attached a thin leather thong that, draping his knuckles, hangs down with what seems to be two small round (leather) knots from which hangs a large eagle tail feather. It is safe to assume this is the wotawe described earlier. Hardorff elaborated on the issue of the stone pouch and feather attached stating that "the stone spoken of by He Dog was a wasicun tunken, a sacred stone, perhaps one of the small, translucent, hemispherical stones found near anthills. Invested with a protective spirit helper, such stones were placed in a small buckskin bag. In the case of Crazy Horse, this bag was laced with a rawhide string which was worn over the right shoulder, suspending the stone under his left arm. [...] Although He Dog spoke of a black stone, Red Feather recalled it as being white, which may suggest translucency."[541] Thomas Powers emphasized Crazy Horse's wotawe: "Horn Chips made for him a whistle to blow as he rode into battle. About the year 1862 or 1863, according to Red Feather, Horn Chips prepared for Crazy Horse the most powerful of all his protections. It was made from a rock, drilled through the center, which Crazy Horse was to wear on a thong under his left arm."[542] This stone is clearly visible with the thong going through in the tintype, by his left knee. The matching evidence of the wotawe alone should be enough to authenticate the tintype as Crazy Horse.

Crazy Horse's protection in battle also included facial decoration, consisting of "white dots and a vertical 'zig-zag' streak of red lightning," which he drew with his finger.[543] Testimonies relate that, before going into battle, the Oglala war chief painted his face with a zigzag line, representing lightning, his loosened long hair symbolizing rain, and random white dots on his face and body representing hail. The whole attire evoked the powerful, striking, thunderous forces of Wakinyan. Whether the zigzag line was red or yellow is a matter of debate. Again, the Mnicojou descendants specify that the latter was the color used by Crazy Horse himself, the former by his father Worm, hence the confusion. Regardless, as Hardorff put it, "It must have been an imposing sight to see him in mounted action, long hair of both horse and rider trailing in the wind, because in combat he never braided his hair or knotted his horse's tail. [...] It was said of him that he always led the charge, well in advance of his line of warriors, not allowing anyone to get ahead of him."[544]

With regard to Eagle Elk's statement that Crazy Horse "did not paint [himself]," Hardorff falls into a semantic trap when he footnotes, presumptuously correcting, the old warrior's recollection. "Eagle Elk is mistaken. In preparation for combat," insisted Hardorff. "Crazy Horse painted his face with the powerful symbols of the Thunder Beings – a red zigzag line to represent lightning, and random white dots representing hail. Ritually applied, these painted images were part of the wotawe which made Crazy Horse bulletproof." Once again, the problem here was not Eagle Elk's assertion, but what he really meant to convey with it. It was customary for warriors to fully paint their faces, and often their bodies, with their sacred color, or combination of colors, according to personalized "dreamed" patterns and designs.

What Crazy Horse did instead was minimal in comparison to the norm, but still powerful and beautiful in its simplicity. Eagle Elk was conceptually right. Crazy Horse did not fully cover his face with paint. He dotted it and put a strike of paint to symbolize lightning. That was enough to evoke the tremendous power of the Thunder Beings; minimal decoration, similarly on what is believed to have been Crazy Horse's scalp shirt, already mentioned. There is agreement that Tašunke Witko did not wear the typical eagle feather war bonnet of a chief, but a single feather of wamble gleška, the spotted eagle. Some suggest the feather was of a red-tail hawk, but the eagle feather appears in many accounts. He Dog, through interpreter Thomas White Cow Killer, testified that Crazy Horse "never wore a war bonnet. [...] The one central feather that is in the middle of the war-eagle's tail,that was the feather he wore in his hair."[545] If we again read Eagle Elk correctly, Crazy Horse actually wore that single eagle feather only as part of his war attire, placing it his hair "just before the start of a battle," and evidently removing it once back to camp. Parading with his eagle feather tied to his hair, either up or down was not part of his customary behavior or attire.

This too would be in line with his love for simplicity, reflected when going into battle, in minimal facial and body paint decoration, complemented as it were by the ritualized renewal of his close connection with the powers of his wotawe. Thus, before the fight, Crazy Horse prepared himself and his horse with ritual acts: "He got off his pony and got a little dirt from a molehill and put it between the ears of his horse, and then he took some [more] and got it in front of the horse and threw it over toward the tail, and then he got around behind the horse and threw some toward his head. Then he went up to the horse and brushed it off and rubbed it in. Then he rubbed a little on his hand and [brushed it] over his [own] head. Then he took a spotted eagle feather and," Eagle Feather explained, "put it upside down on the back of his head instead of standing up, as most [warriors] did."[546] One wonders why, if that was the case, Amos Bad Heart Bull drew his otherwise faithful sketches of Crazy Horse in his nearly naked battle attire, with a single eagle feather standing up on the back of the war chef's head. Also the reconstructed sketches of Crazy Horse published in Bordeaux's *Custer's Conqueror*, in Carroll's *Eleanor H. Hinman Interviews*, and in Trimble's "What did Crazy Horse look like?" (the Standing Soldier's drawing) are clearly different from one another in the facial features, they all claim to represent a close likeness of the chief, all showing the subject wearing a single feather standing up, rather than upside-down on the back of the head as related by most eyewitness testimonies.

In the 13 cent U.S. stamp dedicated to Crazy Horse a partly visible eagle feather is drawn standing up. More puzzling, even the large marble Crazy Horse 1/34th scale model on the veranda overlooking, about one mile distant, the gigantic Crazy Horse Monument features, off and on, a removable single (marble) feather standing up. According to the original design, a huge "hand-built, 44-foot feather" is supposed to be placed on the granitic head of Crazy Horse, also standing up. Perhaps, what we are currently discussing here may convince the Crazy Horse Memorial Foundation to rethink the feather issue and reposition the planned stone feather somehow upside down, or as if it were flowing in the wind together with the loose hair. The feather standing up in the marble model appears esthetically unpleasing to the eye, let alone it being historically incorrect. Braids aside, the two upside down feathers in the good old Indian Head Nickel may give the Crazy Horse Foundation a better idea for a possible alternative. An upside down spotted eagle feather is correctly shown in yet another reconstructed but still conjectural portrait of Crazy Horse published in Hardorff's *The Oglala Lakota Crazy Horse*. The sketch is consistent with the text that expands on the previously cited Eagle Elk and similar testimonies. Crazy Horse, writes Hardorff, "never wore a war bonnet or any of the gaudy trappings so cherished by the peoples of the plains. [...] His spirit powers were evoked by the winged beings – a spotted eagle – who dictated that he wear a single feather on the back of his head. The bilateral tail feather was worn pointed down, which is the position of the eagle's tail just prior to the kill."[547]

The Indian in the tintype does not wear a war bonnet, nor an eagle feather standing up. We cannot see, hence we cannot tell whether he does wear a single tail feather of the spotted eagle, or red-tail hawk, hanging upside down in the back of his head. We do not think so. Again, we regard its absence consistent with what was implicitly stated by He Dog and explicitly by Eagle Elk, as the eagle or hawk feather specifically was to be worn only in battle. The subject in our tintype does wear, hanging upside down on the right side of his head, the white eagle plume distinctive of the Mnicojou, and indicative of his kola status, as Crazy Horse was. Still in reference to the tintype Indian, Francis White Lance pointed out that "the eagle plume on his head is worn Northern style where [Crazy Horse's] mother is from (Miniconjou)."[548] Possibly, the same or a similar eagle plume was once tied to the shoulder of the Crazy Horse's scalp shirt which, lacking elaborate porcupine quill and beadwork, ermine tails, and eagle feathers, as we said reflected the war chief's modesty. A color plate of the same war shirt was published by Capt. John E. Bourke in his classic *The Medicine-man of the Apache.* Captioned "Scalp Shirt of 'Little Big Man' (Sioux)." It was said to have belonged to Crazy Horse and it shows, on the right shoulder, the Mnicojou white eagle plume.[549] The shirt is now in the National Museum of the American Indian, the plume decoration long lost, and no claim for repatriation has yet been filed by Crazy Horse descendants.

A close examination of the pictograph No. 103 for 1877-78 in the American Horse Winter Count, previously cited, reveals an interesting detail. The small design portrays Crazy Horse struck by a bayonet causing a wound in the victim's lower abdomen from which blood gushes. In the back of Crazy Horse's head, between the two braids, is visible a small white "clove," possibly symbolizing a feather, hanging upside down.[550] We cannot positively say whether the one represented is the single, spotted eagle tail feather, or the white plume we just discussed. If we are to believe Horn Chips, and there is no reason not to, we do know that Crazy Horse was indeed wearing an eagle feather when he was killed: "Chips [sic] made Medicine to Crazy Horse and gave him a feather, and he now has the feather; it is not the feather he was wearing when he was killed."[551] American Horse's crude pictograph supports the single feather testimonies. American Horse was there, so it is safe to assume that he sketched a detail he actually saw. We suggest that when Crazy Horse left for Spotted Tail agency with his sick wife on the morning of September 5th, he likely wore his single eagle feather, aware confrontation could ensue. It is obvious that for American Horse the single feather tied tip-down was distinctive of Crazy Horse's identity. In its artistic, almost naive simplicity, the American Horse pictograph is telling.

Conversely, Amos Bad Heart Bull's elaborate and detailed drawing of the stabbing of Crazy Horse, while showing the dynamics of the mortal wound he received and those directly involved in the scuffle, does not include any feather on the war chief's head. In Bad Heart Bull's color drawing, Crazy Horse, his hair braided like in the American Horse's glyph, wears stroud leggings, white shirt, blanket wrapped around the waist, and a revolver tucked in his belt. He is being held strongly on one side by Little Big Man, dressed about the same, and on the other by an army sergeant, while a mustached private, carbine in hand, is rushing forward and is about to thrust his bayonet into Crazy Horse's back (or side).[552] Again, the Bad Heart Bull drawing matches the tintype, beaded moccasins included. In 1955, shortly before his death, Dewey Beard told Moses Two Bulls and Ben Reifel, that "Crazy Horse [...] never wore more than two feathers."[553]

With regard to Crazy Horse's hair decoration, for comparison we cite additional interpretations; one written, others iconographic. The white eagle down plume was addressed in an email to the Custer Museum by Michael Samuel who suggested the Crazy Horse tintype "was taken just outside o[f] Fort Laramie in 1862. [...] The eagle plumb [sic. read plume] in his hair on the left side of his head was given to him just prior to this photo being taken for being wounded in battle. He had been shot just above the left knee on the outside of his leg with a stone tipped arrow during a fight about 10 days before that. This occurred someplace north west of there with a people whose language they did not understand. [...] Hump removed the arrow. It was not much of a wound, but enough for him to favor that leg for a month or so, as you will notice in the photo." Samuel recognizes that an eagle feather is shown in the tintype, hanging in front of the left thigh of the Indian he maintains is Crazy Horse. But he does not see the chief's wotawe held in his left hand. Instead, according to Samuel, "Held in his right [i.e. left] hand you can see the end of the barrel of a 45.70 breech loading short carbine rifle that he had got from 'Alights on the Cloud' the son of Dull Knife. [...] The butt of the rifle was sitting in the seat of the chair next to him. Attached to the barrel of that carbine was an eagle feather."[554] We disagree with such reading of the tintype, as we do not identify any weapon, let alone the barrel of a gun, held in the subject's left hand.

Some modern portraits of Crazy Horse combine both conjecture and free interpretation of evidence that has surfaced in later years. Richard Hook's "Crazy Horse" for example, is seated crossed legged in the Oglala tribal council lodge during his investiture as a Shirt Wearer, hence before he was shot in the face by No Water.[555] The face is that of a handsome young Indian, vaguely reminiscent of the tintype. On the other hand, David Shanahan's "A Victory for Crazy Horse" celebrates the Greasy Grass win. Shanahan's Crazy Horse is on horseback, wearing a full bird decoration on his light hair and showing a victorious and "brutal" expression while raising a repeating rifle. There is no easily detectable, visible scar on the harsh-looking, square-jawed, highly fictional Indian face.[556] The bird decoration in Shanahan's portrait of Crazy Horse reflects the red-tail hawk testimonies. Edward and Mabell Kladececk were told by Frank White Buffalo Man that, when young, Crazy Horse "dreamed of the red [tail] hawks and received [their] power."[557] As messengers of Thunder, red-tail hawks are very sacred and powerful birds for the Lakota who, in the words of Luther Standing Bear, "Believe that the [red-tail] hawk was his [Crazy Horse's] protecting power."[558]

Also inspired by the red-tail hawk and the day at the Greasy Grass is the artistic rendering of an exulting Crazy Horse on horseback in his war attire, titled "Red Victory" (2001) by Michael Schreck. It depicts "victorious warriors after the Battle of the Little Big Horn. Leading the group is Crazy Horse, painted with hail stones and wearing a [complete, embalmed] red-tail hawk in his light sun-bleached hair."[559] The single white feather is partially visible in a conjectural close-up, front portrait of the "Strange Man of the Lakota" (2006) by Kenneth Ferguson. Standing in front of a buffalo robe painted with the sun-bust/war bonnet design, here too Crazy Horse is shown in his war attire: chest and right arm are covered with white hail dots, a wide red streak of lightning runs length-wise on the right side of his face, and a single white eagle feather stands up, behind his head, from his brownish, relatively short, loosened hair. On the left side of his face, a small scar is visible just between the left nostril and the upper lip. Crazy Horse's stone wotawe adorns his left earring, and an eagle wing-bone war whistle hangs around his neck. Crazy Horse is partially wrapped in his red blanket, covering his left arm that cradles a stone-head war club. The Oglala war chief's piercing brown eyes look straight at the viewer.

Breastplate

One of the main arguments against the identification of the Indian in the tintype as Crazy Horse focuses on the typology and length of the breastplate. Jack Heriard argued strongly against the tintype, publishing for comparison two historical photographs. The first, courtesy of Richard Green is titled "Group of Sioux Indian Chiefs" and portrays five Sioux men all wearing long breastplates, elaborate war bonnets, holding war shields and lances, or warrior society staffs heavily decorated with eagle feathers. They represent, in Heriard's words, "typical Sioux outfits worn for *Wild West* shows. These men have waist length breastplates, neck scarfs, wrist and arm bands of nickel silver or brass; circa 1900." The other photograph is a famous group portrait by Mathew Brady of some Sioux and Arapaho members of the October 1877 delegation to Washington and their interpreters. "Note," writes Heriard, "the short breastplates, typical of this period."[560] The "excessive" length of the breastplate and allegedly "modern" dress style of the Indian in the tintype is therefore, for Heriard and others, "proof" against the Crazy Horse identification. John S. Bishop agrees with Heriard that the greatest anti-evidence is the apparent lateness of the "costume" worn by the subject in the tintype, and in particular the length of the breastplate, datable according to him to 1890+; the turned bone hair-pipes, arguably dated after 1880, combined with the 'Ascot' tie, or scarf, fashionable around the turn of the century, would make an anachronistic dating for the proper identification.[561]

It is true that most breastplates seen in the 1877 Sioux delegation photographs are shorter than the one in the tintype, but there are other period images where similar, two-row breastplates are not much shorter, and one actually longer. There are three photographic portraits of Low Dog (Šunke Kucigala, c. 1847-after 1920) by D.F. Barry taken at Fort Buford in May 1881 after the return of Low Dog and other diehard Northern Indians from the Canadian exile. As a leading warrior of the Fast Bull thiyóšpaye (Fast Bull having succeeded his father, Mnicojou chief Old Lame Deer, killed in May by a trooper of Gen. Miles), Low Dog had originally surrendered at

Spotted Tail Agency in early September 1877. The parentage of Low Dog is uncertain, alternatively given as either Oglala, Mnicojou, Wazhazha/Brule, or Sihasapa. After his second surrender, Low Dog settled with the Mnicojou at Cheyenne River where he lived the rest of his life except for a brief imprisonment at Fort Snelling, Minnesota, in 1891, where he was probably photographed (his hair cut short) by Edward A. Bromley.

The three photographs previously referred to portray the Lakota head warrior wearing the usual white shirt, a wide nine row dentalium chocker similar to those worn by Sioux and Cheyenne in many contemporary photographs, and a bone hair-pipe breastplate. Its typology is similar to the one in the tintype with two long, wide parallel rows of turned bone hair-pipes separated by a center leather strip. In two Barry images, Low Dog is seated, the bottom part of the breastplate partially covered by a blanket wrapped around his waist and by his left arm holding a pipe tomahawk. In another image, Low Dog is standing and the breastplate is clearly visible; the two parallel rows count approximately 33 hair-pipes each. He wears the same hair-pipe breastplate and holds the same pipe tomahawk in the Barry group picture, referred to earlier, where Low Dog is seated next to Major Brotherton, flanked by Crow King. The comparison between Crow King's short, so-called Cheyenne-style ("chevron" or "fish-scale" pattern) breastplate with German silver ring pendant, and Low Dog's own breastplate, whose typology is very similar to that of our tintype is interesting. There is yet another elusive single image of Low Dog. David Shanahan suggests this recently uncovered "photograph of a younger Low Dog was taken some 5/6 years previous to those that we are all now so familiar with, those taken around the time of his surrender."[562] Date, location, and photographer of this earlier portrait are unknown. Here, a young-looking Low Dog wears the same dentalium necklace, and a shorter, two-row breastplate. He wears armbands, probably brass.

Metal armbands are worn by Spleen headman Yellow Bear (ca. 1844-1913), who also wears a long double-row bone hair-pipe breastplate – very similar to that of the Indian in the tintype – over his white cotton shirt in two Mathew Brady group photographs of the famous October 1877 Sioux

Delegation to Washington.[563] The relative length of Yellow Bear's breast-plate can be appreciated in comparison to the shorter breastplate worn by American Horse, shown seated in front of the Tapisleča headman in another famous, larger group photograph taken by Alexander Gardner that same October 1877 at the Corcoran Gallery of Art.[564] In these images, the two-row Lakota breastplates made with the same kind of long bone hair-pipes as the ones in the tintype, differ from the multiple-row breast-plates, made with shorter hair-pipes, worn by Arapaho chiefs Sharp Nose and Black Coal. John C. Ewers pointed out that there was a transition among the Lakota from shorter dentalium shell to longer bone hair-pipe breastplates, a transition that occurred in Crazy Horse's time: "The earliest photographs of Teton [Lakota] men wearing hair-pipe breastplates appear in the pictorial record of delegations to Washington in 1872. Of the 15 men in Red Cloud's Oglala delegation in that year, two wore the hair-pipe breastplate. [...] Photographs of the Teton [Lakota] delegation of 1877 depicts no use of dentalium-shell breastplates, while the hair-pipe breast-plates worn are not only more numerous but larger and more elaborate than the ornaments worn by delegates from these tribes five years earlier. It appears, therefore, that during the period 1872-77 the hair-pipe breast-plate supplanted the one of dentalium shell as a popular ornament among Teton [Lakota] leaders."[565]

In a similar article on trade goods seen in early American Indian photo-graphs, James A. Hanson published a sample of images from the set of unusually large (size 11" x 14") original glass plates found in the 1950s in a second hand store in Montana. The photographs, made by Iowa-native L.A. Huffman (1854-1951) at Fort Keogh in early 1879, are significant because, Hanson wrote, the remote military post was "still very much on the fron-tier. Little Wolf's band of Cheyennes was finally captured by troops from the fort on March 25, 1879. Fights with small bands of hostile Sioux were frequent and the first big surrender of 585 Sioux Indians at Keogh did not take place until June 1880. There were still traders actively buying buffalo robes from the Indians and the final buffalo slaughter by white hunters was just getting underway." One of the subjects photographed by Huffman is "a fine young dandy with a handsome otterskin necklace. [...] He is also wearing a profusion of brass or German silver trade goods, including bracelets, an armband [...]. A small chocker with ribbon streamers hangs at his throat. The typical breastplate contains brass beads and he is also wearing a string of them in his scalp-lock. His braid tie is a strip of wool stroud with interesting scallops and cut-outs. He is wearing two commercial shirts and note also his beaded was club handle."[566] The author did not mention the standing eagle feather and the hanging eagle plume on the subject's hair. What is interesting, besides the reference to the metal armbands and bracelets, is the length of the double-row breastplate, each row counting about 40 bone hair-pipes.

Echoing Jack Heriard, the overall dress and seemingly "excessive" length of the tintype breastplate has been invoked also by the specialists cited by Angela Aleiss in her article. "Experts," wrote Aleiss, "believe that the image could be an Indian performer from *Buffalo Bill's Wild West*, which operated from 1883 to approximately 1917. 'This 'Crazy Horse' photo definitely looks like an individual who is dressing up for a photo or a performance' says Jeremy Johnston of the Buffalo Bill Center of the West in Cody, Wyoming. [...] He says the 'cross-cultural' attire of the man is consistent with the Indian performers who often posed in both Western and Native clothing for *Buffalo Bill's Wild West* shows. To me, this' Crazy Horse' photo looks like some of those that were sold as souvenirs and postcards in Germany,' Johnston says by telephone. 'The attire just doesn't fit the [1870s] era.'"[567] Of a similar opinion, tribal historian Donovin Sprague, also quoted by Aleiss. "'The person in the photo is dressed in a flamboyant manner unlike how Crazy Horse dressed,' he says. Sprague teaches history at the Black Hills State University [...] and is related to Crazy Horse through High Backbone (Hump), the brother to the biological mother of Crazy Horse." Specifically regarding the breastplate, Aleiss again turned to Sprague: "During 1877 or earlier, there were smaller breastplates with double rows of between 14 and 25 hair-pipes compared to the one in this photo which has 51 per row." This statement is inconsistent with Sprague's own date attributed to the "debated" tintype as: "No Neck? 'Tahu Wanjini'

(Hunkpapa) 1877." Identity aside, Sprague implicitly confirmed the long breastplate worn by "No Neck" (or whomever) did fit the period.[568]

As just noted, the breastplate in our tintype shows two rows, counting some 51 bone hair-pipes each, the two rows separated by a much shorter center-row of what seem to be, by their uneven shape, dentalium shells. Of this same type, long double-row with central divider, is the even longer breastplate worn by Sam Little Bull, Jr., in an undated photograph, possibly a tintype, by an unknown photographer. This rare portrait of a young Little Bull was originally published in an article by Charles Hanson precisely on Oglala hair-pipe breastplates: "The Sioux expanded the use of long hair-pipes and the breastplates became fantastically long. On page 9 is a 19th century photo of young Sam Little Bull resplendent in a very long breastplate of two rows separated by a centre strip of large beads, a fine robe of stroud with list edges joined in the middle and a wide beaded strip, an otterskin necklace with mirrors, otter braid wrappings, bracelets, armbands, chain dangles on his leggings and a wampum moon on his throat."[569]

According to a reliable biographical sketch by Emil Afraid of Hawk, "Samuel Little Bull, one of our oldest Oglala Sioux Indians, was born somewhere near the Laramie Peaks in Wyoming in the spring of 1861."[570] Sam and his older brother White Eagle (or Lone/One Eagle), fought against the Reno soldiers at the Little Bighorn, where White Eagle was killed.[571] Their father was (Old) Little Buffalo Bull (Little Bull, Tatanka Čikala), as noted earlier also known as Horned Horse (Tašunke Heton). Sam was about sixteen years old when his father surrendered with other Oglala at Red Cloud Agency a couple of weeks before Crazy Horse. Lieut. John G. Bourke who was with Gen. Crook at the agency, met with Old Little Bull, whose alternative name was dubiously rendered by a translator as "Horney Horse," the handwriting later mistakenly given as "Hardy Horse." The Oglala headman gave Lieut. Burke details of the battle where Custer was whipped. Burke used the information to draw a sketch map of the Indian village and the sites of the Custer massacre and the Reno-Benteen entrenchment.[572]

Like Crazy Horse and other leading Northern Indians, Horned Horse/ Little Bull (Sr.) also enrolled as an Army scout. Again, as noted, it was the elder Little Bull who, present Crazy Horse, did most of the talking, also using sign language, both interpreted by Billy Garnett, when a Chicago newspaperman accompanied by Lieut. Clark came to the recently arrived Northern village with more questions about the famous Custer battle. After the killing of Crazy Horse, Horned Horse fled to Canada and surrendered again in 1881 at Fort Buford with He Dog's Soreback band, along with Oglala loyalists Short Bull, Iron Hawk, Bad Heart Bull, Iron Crow, and others.[573] Little Bull and his family were first sent to Standing Rock, and in the spring of 1882, transferred definitively to Pine Ridge. We do not know if the photograph, or tintype of his son Sam Little Bull, was taken at Camp Robinson in 1877, or later at Standing Rock. Given his apparent age, it is unlikely it was taken after the family returned to Pine Ridge, where Horned Horse later died in 1897.

What the photograph clearly shows, and an expert like Charles Hanson also acknowledged, is that the features of Sam Little Bull, Jr., are clearly young, those of a teenager. Very close in time to when Crazy Horse was still alive or shortly after he was killed. Sam Little Bull's breastplate reaches well

Sam Little Bull, Jr., (b. 1861) Oglala, by unknown photographer, no date, ca. late 1870s-early 1880s. Likely a tintype, originally published by Charles Hanson, Jr., 1976.

below the youth's waist and is admittedly of considerable length for the time, even if the picture were taken in the early-1880s, when Sam would have been in his early-twenties. In this rare photo, Sam's entire attire, long double-row breastplate, stroud leggings, long cotton shirt, arm and wrist bands, braids wrapped in otterskin, even the eagle plume, resembles that of the Indian in our tintype. It is to wonder whether this is a coincidence, being common Indian dress for the photo sitting, or whether it was purposely chosen by Sam Little Bull, Jr., to look like, hence in honor of the late Crazy Horse. Either way, this image and others previously discussed disprove the generally held view that such a dress was typical only of the 1890s-1900s. By then, Sam himself would have been too old for the picture he is in. He died in 1943.

There is also a full length portrait of a mustached Baptiste "Little Bat" Garnier with long breastplate. This rare photo was originally published by De Barthe in his biography of Frank Grouard, unfortunately without any information on the photographer, date, and place where the picture was taken.[574] Little Bat, donning an eagle feather war bonnet and holding a Lakota-style, single curve bow and arrows, is wearing a typical Indian dress of the time, ca. the 1880s: long white shirt, stroud leggings with light border, long and richly beaded dark (stroud) breechcloth, beaded moccasins (barely visible), and a long, double-row hair-pipe breastplate reaching below the waist. The type and length of Little Bat's breastplate is very similar to the breastplate in the Sam Little Bull's photograph, and the tintype.

Again, speaking of long breastplates, there is yet an unidentified portrait auctioned a few years ago as an "early tintype of a Native American Indian 1860's." The lack of information invites caution, but the image is interesting. Standing in a pose clearly inspired by the anonymous photographer, it shows the almost full length profile a young adult Indian male with his right arm (if a tintype/mirror-image) resting on his stomach, the left one with the hand touching the forehead as to protect the eyes from the sun while scouting the horizon. The hair is short, with a roach-style decoration; his shirtless chest is partially covered by long hair-pipe breastplate that reaches well below the waist; metal wristbands and armbands

Baptiste "Little Bat" Garnier, by unknown photographer,
no date, ca. 1880s.

on his bare arms are clearly visible. Finally, the subject appears to be wearing dark stroud leggings, breechcloth, and a large belt from which hangs a long sash.[575]

Michael Samuel sees no problem with the tintype breastplate, which, he wrote, was actually a war trophy. According to Samuel, earlier in the spring of 1862 Crazy Horse "had fought with a group of Crow on the flats just east of where the Custer Fight was [later] held. The blue leggings with beads down the sides, and bone breastplate he is wearing came from one of the Crow warriors he shot in that fight. If you look closely you may notice the broken end of one of the hair-pipe bones where the slug entered the center left of that Crow." Crazy Horse led many raids, skirmishes, and full battles with the Crows and there is a curious, perhaps conjectural but interesting iconographic representation of one such raid that relates precisely to the breastplate issue, if not the very battle referred to by Samuel. It is found in the so called *Red Hawk Ledger*, held at the Milwaukee Public Museum. The ledgerbook was apparently captured from Red Hawk's camp near Wounded Knee by Capt. R. Miller a few days after the infamous Big Foot affair. The ledger contains over one hundred ink and crayon color drawings depicting the war exploits of several prominent Lakota. Six such drawings are dedicated to Crazy Horse, who is identified by name in both Lakota and English.

One in particular, on page 55 of the *Ledger*, shows the Oglala war chief on horseback spearing a Crow with a lance; the Crow had just dismounted his pony that Crazy Horse himself had wounded with an arrow from the bow he is holding in his left hand. The encounter must have taken place during the cold months, as the Crow is shown wearing long dark (blue) stroud leggings and a white-wool, red fringed, blanket coat, not typically naked except a loincloth. Crazy Horse, his long hair as usual lose in the wind (no decorations), wears instead a long dark (blue) military-style jacket tied at the waist by a sash. From the jacket's tail emerges the insignia of warrior society chief, a red stroud double trailer decorated with eagle feathers. On his neck Crazy Horse wears a dentalium chocker (like the one worn by Low Dog) and on his chest, covering the front of his jacket from the neck almost to the waist, a white, double-row breastplate. The drawing is obviously evocative, but the detail is interesting as the author of the drawing, Red Hawk, had known Crazy Horse and fought alongside him at the Little Bighorn. That he chose a specific "winter" scene in which Crazy Horse wore a hair-pipe breastplate may suggest that Red Hawk himself had been in that battle with the Crow and witnessed Crazy Horse's war exploit.[576] With regard to the actual breastplate allegedly captured from the Crow, again according to Michael Samuel, Crazy Horse "gave Alights the bone hair-pipe breastplate as a gift. Alights was later killed at the Rosebud fight with Crook not long before the Custer fight in June of 1876. At that fight Crazy Horse inherited [sic] the Henry 44 repeating rifle from Alights as he died in his arms."[577] In another scene, on p. 31 of the same *Red Hawk Ledger*, again Crazy horse is shown wearing a long breastplate as he drives off three ponies and a mule from a Crow camp. Likewise, Crazy Horse wears a breastplate while he lassoes a Crow woman from her pony on p. 57 of the *Ledger*. [578]

Old Red Hawk (ca. 1824-1896) and his son Red Hawk (CetanLuta, ca. 1856-1928) fought with Crazy Horse at the Little Bighorn, June 25th, 1876, and surrendered with him the following May. In this autobiographical scene, Red Hawk shoots a Crow scout who had mortally wounded Black Whiteman (WasicuSapa), a Lakota warrior shown with long breastplate and armbands. Redrawn in the 1930s by W. Ben Hunt from the original no longer in the collection of the Milwaukee Museum.

Bad Heart Bull's drawing of Crazy Horse (body painted with dots representing hail) on his war-pony at the Little Bighorn, June 25th, 1876, chasing Reno's soldiers in the valley fight. In the foreground is a warrior with long breastplate and armbands.

Billy Hunter Garnett (b. 1855), by unknown photographer, no date (ca. 1880-1885), donning an eagle-feather war bonnet with ermine-tail pendants, revolver and painted war shield. He wears a long double-row bone hair-pipe breastplate with divider, armbands, Ascot tie, stroud leggings with light trim, and beaded moccasins. Like American Horse, He Dog, Touch the Cloud, and Little big Man, Billy Garnett too was photographed by Charles M. Bell in 1877 wearing full Lakota regalia.

Sioux delegation, by Mathew Brady, Washington, late Sept.-Oct. 1877. Yellow Bear, sitting first from the left, wears a blanket, stroud leggings, beaded moccasins, white shirt, long double-row breastplate, and metal armbands. Standing from the right is Spotted Tail, Jr., with war bonnet, cotton shirt and breastplate with 32 hair-pipes, more than the 14-25 pipes said to be typical of the time. Young Man Afraid, made a shirt wearer with Crazy Horse, sits first from the right, with white shirt and Ascot tie under a large German-silver cross. [579]

Armbands, Wristbands, Neckerchiefs/Ascot Ties

Like the breastplate, the armbands and wristbands of nickel silver or brass of the subject in the tintype are also regarded by "nay" supporters as diagnostically "too early" for Crazy Horse's times. Critics have argued that the adoption of these accessories by the Lakota took place at least a decade after the death of Crazy Horse and, therefore, the Indian in the tintype could not possibly be the famous war chief. To the contrary, there is ample photographic evidence of the use of such male accessories among the Sioux and other Plains tribes prior to, and certainly during, Crazy Horse's time. We already mentioned a group photograph of the 1875 Sioux delegation to Washington in which some Lakota wear armbands and neckerchiefs. Even earlier, for example, there is the portrait of Hunkpapa chief Broken Bear Rib (Mato Čuwiyuska), a signer of the 1868 Treaty, photographed by Alexander Gardner in Washington in 1872. In this classic studio portrait, Bear Rib (Bear's Rib, Bears Rib, and the like) is seated, wears a fur turban decorated with feathers, a long sleeve white shirt under a dark vest, and shiny metal armbands.

By 1872, neckerchiefs/Ascot ties were also common among the Lakota. That year, Slow Bull was photographed by Gardner wearing a Crow-style scalp/war shirt, similar to, if not the same as, the one he had at Fort Laramie in 1868, and a very large neckerchief. There are early photos of Red Cloud wearing both small and large white neckerchiefs/Ascot ties, including a

Red Cloud, shaking hands with William Blackmore, by Alexander Gardner, Washington, May1872. The Oglala chief wears a large white neckerchief/Ascot tie; he also dons a (red) trade blanket with large beaded strip and light-color trim over stroud leggings and beaded moccasins.

famous photograph by Gardner in which the Oglala chief is shaking hands with his English friend William Blackmore in May 1872.

Several other members of the Oglala and Brule 1872 delegation to Washington, including Spotted Tail, had Ascot ties. Brule chief Two Strike (Numkahpa, ca. 1822-1909), too, was photographed by Gardner in 1872, in at least two poses alone and one with his wife, with war shirt and white neckerchief.[580] Again regarding metal armbands, previously mentioned photographs by James H. Hamilton, taken in 1877 at Red Cloud Agency right in front of the log-cabin studio, "154. Family Group at Red Cloud" – as noted – show chief American Horse wearing brass armbands over white cotton shirt. Also, "160. Two-Strike and Family", where the Brule chief's son is wearing precisely the same-type metal armbands over long sleeves of white cotton shirt as our tintype Indian. Oglala warrior Stands First (Toka Najin) was photographed by D.S. Mitchell in 1877 and listed as "No. 16" in Mitchell and McCowan's Western Stereoscopic Gems. Stands First, too, wears shiny metal armbands over his long sleeve white shirt. Still with regard to armbands, there is a classic photographic portrait of Hunts the Enemy (ca. 1847-1910), later known as George Sword. His photo, taken in Washington in 1877 by Charles M. Bell in the same staged studio setting as Little Big Man (with side display of a long-tailed, eagle feather "black" war

Hamilton photograph #154, "Family Group at Red Cloud." Photograph shows chief American Horse, who was made shirt wearer together with Crazy Horse, wearing armbands over a white shirt just like the Indian in the tintype.

bonnet), was reproduced by Sprague,[581] and by Bray who captioned the image: "Nephew of Red Cloud and later captain of Pine Ridge Reservation Police, Hunts the Enemy's diplomacy was crucial in effecting the surrender of Crazy Horse's followers."[582]

Sword, too, wears metal armbands over his candid white cotton shirt. Shown sitting, his legs covered with his trade blanket with lighter border trim, Hunts the Enemy is holding in one hand a long, flat stem with big t-shape bowl catlinite pipe, and in the other a richly beaded, fringed, buckskin pipe bag, both the same pipe and bag shown leaning against a papermaché rock in the Little Big Man photograph.

German silver or brass armbands and wristbands were certainly not the prerogative of the Sioux among the Plains tribes. In yet another photograph of the Sioux delegation, taken by Mathew Brady in Washington in 1877, reprinted by Bray[583] and Heriard,[584] we see Touch the Clouds, sitting

Sioux and Arapaho delegation to Washington, late Sept. - Oct. 1877, photographed during a visit at the Corcoran Gallery of Art.

resplendent in a long-tailed war bonnet (difficult to say whether the same one seen in other contemporary Sioux photographs), flanked by three noted Arapaho chiefs, Sharp Nose, Black Coal, and Friday, all three also referenced in individual portraits in Mitchell and McCowan's *Stereoscopic Gems*. In the Brady photo, Black Coal is wearing metal armbands. So does the Oglala Three Bears, head warrior of the Kiyuska band friendly to the Americans, protagonist a few months earlier of his violent altercation with Crazy Horse in Lieut. Clark's office at Camp Robinson.

Three Bears, a member of the 1877 delegation to Washington, is portrayed in another classic C.M Bell group photo.[585] Sitting to the extreme right, next to interpreter Leon Pallady (Pallardy), Mato Yamni wears brass or nickel silver armbands over long white shirt sleeves, Ascot tie, and a medium length breastplate of two large row hair-pipes, separated by a center row of dentalium shells, same typology as the one worn by the

Most if not all wearing white cotton shirts, trade blankets, stroud leggings and beaded moccasins; Ascot ties are worn by some, see Spotted Tail, and armbands are also worn by some others including George Sword, first seated from right, who was made shirt wearer together with Crazy Horse.

Taken only about one month after the death of Crazy Horse, the studio portrait shows Three Bears, the rival of the Oglala war chief wearing (red) blanket with light border trim over stroud leggings, beaded moccasins, white shirt, two-row hair-pipe breastplate, neckerchief/Ascot tie, and metal arm bands.[587]
Three Bears (Mato Yamni), by Charles M. Bell, Washington, Oct. 1877.

He Dog (Shunka Bloka), by Charles M. Bell, Washington, Oct. 1877. He Dog, Oglala shirt wearer and Crazy Horse's long-time best friend, is dressed like other Lakota, 1870s style. Except for the war bonnet and the missing breastplate, his basic clothes are just like those of the Indian in the tintype: long white shirt over dark stroud leggings, beaded moccasins, and long neckerchief/Ascot tie.[586]

Indian in the tintype. There are other examples in period photographs of individual and group Sioux, Northern Cheyenne, and Northern Arapaho. As with the presence of photographers at Camp Robinson - Red Cloud Agency in 1877 the comparative evidence specifically on clothing and accessories, in this case the armbands and wristbands of the subject in the tintype, in addition to white shirt, neckerchief/Ascot tie, stroud leggings, and beaded moccasins, is supportive of the Crazy Horse identification.

Wrist Bone

The Indian in the tintype shows a distinctive anatomical trait, a very pronounced wrist bone, visible below his right wristband. In modern medicine, this trait is called "Madelung's deformity." It is characterized to varying degrees by a small protrusion up to a major upward displacement of the distal end of the radius (forearm) bone. Its origin can be either congenital or traumatic, or a combination thereof. The Indian in the tintype appears to be affected by a moderate to major deformation. This trait was said to be typical of the Mnicojou maternal side of Crazy Horse's family. Lakota oral tradition relates that Crazy Horse's mother Rattling Blanket Woman was notorious for the prominent bone sticking out of her wrist. Sonya Holy Eagle, who lived on both the Cheyenne River and Pine Ridge reservations and has the same prominent feature, whose own mother was Mnicojou and a blood relative of Rattling Blanket Woman, hence related to Crazy Horse, reported that her Grandmother said that at family gatherings they watched for what she called "the dewclaw," the wrist bone sticking out more than in other people. The feature of the prominent wrist bone has long been regarded a distinctive family trademark to identify relatives on Crazy Horse's side. That this peculiar feature is not mentioned in the classic testimonies about Crazy Horse is not surprising. It pertained to an inherited, secondary physical trait, which no one but the very close relatives paid attention to. And, perhaps, because until now those who knew preferred to keep quiet about it.

Crazy Horse's protruding wrist bone. Enlarged detail from tintype.

Testimonies

The Tintype

One key element in support of the Crazy Horse identification, is that the tintype itself as well as much of the circumstantial evidence and testimonies accompanying it come expressly from <u>within</u> the Lakota Indian community. The significance of this fact has generally been overlooked or altogether downplayed by critics of the tintype. We saw earlier that while searching for a likeness of Crazy Horse, Feraca reported that at Pine Ridge a number of tintype portraits of Indians circulated, and that Jake Herman had access to one such tintype he strongly believed to be that of Crazy Horse. [588] Francis White Lance, on the basis of his father-in-law's testimony, related the same information in the Foreword. We know that tintype photography was common out West before and during Crazy Horse's time. From a strictly technical perspective, we also know that the technology of the time made it possible to produce a tintype with a regular camera, but that there were also specially-made tintype cameras. Contemporary historical accounts reported that some photographers used four-lens cameras to produce four tintypes per setting, as in our case.

The Smithsonian has in its photographic history collections a sample of such a four-lens tintype camera, complete with bellows, fixed front, and rear focusing, attributed to maker Benton Pixley Stebbins (1825-1906). The caption accompanying this museum specimen of photographic wonder explains why the tintype became a favorite in the mid-1800s and after: "Tintype photography became popular in the mid-1850s with the advent

of wet-plate collodion photography and continued being produced into the early twentieth century. Cheaper and more durable than the earlier daguerreotypes or the ambrotype (glass) photographs, the tintype was a [positive, mirror image] photograph made on japanned iron coated with collodion. Tintypes were very popular during the Civil War-era, providing soldiers and their distant families with images of their loved ones to carry with them." Specifically, the four-lens camera, the same-type camera utilized in the making of our tintype, "allowed four of the same images to be made at one time on one sensitized metal plate. The plate was then cut to provide four individual photographs."[589]

Photo historian George Gilbert pointed out that like any other photographic format, tintypes, too, modified over time. Based on Gilbert's typology, our tintype belongs to the so-called "brown period," about 1870-1885. "In 1870, the Phoenix Plate Co. began making plates with a chocolate-tinted surface. They created a sensation among ferrotypists throughout the country, and the pictures made on the chocolate-tinted surface soon became all the rage."[590] Paula Fleming also noted that "because of the difficulties with wet plate photography, photographers in the 19th century tended to be professionals. They made their money in studios, and/or as traveling photographers. Some specialized in tintypes, making quick money from an inexpensive format. [...] With respect to Native Americans [...] the photographer took their portraits with the aim of making a profit from selling copies of the image. As such, a negative was required so that multiple copies could be made. Why would a photographer take a tintype – a 'one-of' format – of an Indian? As tintypes do exist, including the one identified as being Crazy Horse, obviously this did happen, but the circumstances would have been uncommon."[591]

Unfortunately, Mari Sandoz's presumptuous denial of a possible photograph of Crazy Horse, resulting from her deficient knowledge of 19th-century photography, had a negative influence on objective research. In a 1955 letter to J.W. Vaughn, congratulating the author for his soon-to-be-published book on the battle of the Rosebud, Sandoz confused the issues and claimed an expertise she did not have, coming down against the tintype.

"Dear Mr. Vaughn," she wrote, "Hurrah for Stackpole and the book! I'll watch for the result. [...] About the Crazy Horse picture that Jake Herman has: Crazy Horse was neither important enough [!] or available [!] at the time the tintypes were at their height, around the Civil War period. If there is a tin type of an Oglala Crazy Horse it would be the father [!]."[592]

Contrary to her wrong assumption, we saw earlier that Judge Charles Hamilton himself explained why on occasion his father, while at Red Cloud Agency and elsewhere on the Frontier would use the simpler tintype instead of the more involved and longer process of the negative wetplate. Other Western photographers did the same at the time. That Crazy Horse would agree to have his picture taken, especially if indeed he had previously refused to, could certainly qualify as an uncommon circumstance, and a good reason for the utilization of the tintype technique. This, of course, would not exclude that regular photographs were taken, as implied by the listing of the "No. 104. Crazy Horse" stereoscopic portrait in James H. Hamilton's *Catalogue*. Unless "No. 104" will turn out to be similar or identical to the tintype given to Little Bat Garnier. Unlike the stereoview, it was often the occasion of the moment and simpler technique to determine the choice of a tintype over a glass plate negative. In his article "Faces of War," historian Jerome Greene[593] discussed a rare photograph: "One of the few known portrait-style contemporary images of enlisted men who served on Brig. Gen. Crook's Big Horn and Yellowstone Expedition, August-October 1876" in pursuit of the Lakota and the Cheyenne bands who had scattered after the Little Bighorn victory.

The photograph, Green wrote, "is a ferrotype (commonly called a tintype). Thus it is an in-camera original, not a print made from a negative, and the image is reversed by the camera lens." The maker of the tintype remains to be determined – probably either Stanley J. Morrow or Daniel S. Mitchell – as are the exact circumstances of the sitting. With regard to the use of tintypes, Morrow's biographers Wesley Hurt and William Lass noted that "two of the most popular photographic types produced by the wet plate process were the ambrotype and the ferrotype. Ambrotypes were thin collodion negatives on glass. [...] Ferrotypes or tintypes were a

modification of the ambrotype. A thin plate was covered with a brown or black varnish to take the place of the ambrotypes' black background [...]. Ferrotypes were sometimes mounted under glass [to prevent scratching]. [...] Among their advantages were economy, durability, and portability. For example, [in] 1880, Morrow advertised the rate of 50 cents for four pictures on tin. The tintype was extensively used for personal pictures [...]. Since ferrotypes could be rapidly produced, they were popular with those who desired 'rush pictures' or reproductions while they waited."594 As we saw, tintypes were made by Private Charles Howard, again the technique being simpler, faster, less intrusive.

It is interesting that Billy Garnett, in the previously cited 1927 letter to Dr. McGillycuddy, came down against a photograph said to be that of Crazy Horse, correctly because it showed an old man, but also erroneously because it was a printed image. "If I am not mistaken," he wrote, paradoxically, "there was nothing in the picture line but tin types up to the time of his death, the photograph prints having been invented later. The photograph is of a Rosebud Indian named Goes to War, a brother of Hollow Horn Bear [etc.]."595 Obviously, Garnett was incorrect on the issue of printed photographs, basing his non-expert opinion on the fact that, evidently, what he had seen personally out West in the 1870s, especially during Crazy Horse's stay at Red Cloud, were mostly tintypes.

Again, contrary to an old Crazy Horse tell-tale, strictly with regard to the technology of the time, it would have been perfectly possible for a photographer to produce during a rapid and less intrusive sitting, a tintype of the Lakota war chief. It is also very interesting that there are no reports, testimonies, or accounts by contemporary photographers or journalists who were at Camp Robinson-Red Cloud Agency in 1877, specifically discussing Crazy Horse's alleged refusal to be photographed. The question of whether or not the famous Oglala had ever agreed to have his picture taken during the four months following his surrender, was raised by White people only after his death. Embracing the McGillycuddy-Barry "no picture" tales, many who followed took the dubious liberty of putting their own words in Crazy Horse's month.

J.W. Vaughn, too, discussing the background information on the broader issue, began with this very line of thinking. "Crazy Horse is said to have made his boast that his image would never be taken by the white man's little black box," he wrote, and he noted that "It has long been a question of controversy as to whether his picture was in fact ever taken."[596] Vaughn, like Robinson and others, hoped for a definitive answer and published sample statements to that effect, including D.F. Barry's authoritative verdict against the famous photograph of the old Indian with war bonnet. It was originally published in 1914 by Lieut. Jesse M. Lee and Lieut. Henry R. Lemly in their accounts of the capture and death of Crazy Horse. Why the two senior officers, who had known Crazy Horse personally, would publish a wrong photograph of the Lakota chief is puzzling; most likely it was the printer's choice.

Lee actually did not think Crazy Horse had ever been photographed, but Lemly thought otherwise.[597] In any case, significant testimonies against the Crazy Horse identification of a "very dark little Indian man with war bonnet" were collected at Pine Ridge by local Superintendent Ernest W. Jermark who, in 1926, wrote to Gen. Hugh L. Scott: "Interviewed your friend 'He Dog' and other old timers re picture. These Indians are agreed that the picture is not a likeness of the Oglala Chief Crazy Horse." Later in 1955, a letter was written by Ben Reifel, then Superintendent also at Pine Ridge who, together with Moses Two Bulls, President of the Oglala Sioux Tribe, interviewed Dewey Beard, the only living participant in the Custer Battle: "Mr. Beard was positive that no picture was ever taken of Crazy Horse. And, certainly, he said, 'with war bonnet and other colorful regalia such a picture could not be one of Crazy Horse. He never wore more than two feathers.'" But once he was shown the tintype Dewey Beard changed his categorical 'ever,' and indeed recognized in the Garnier-Howard tintype the likeness of Crazy Horse.

Returning to the old, war-bonneted Indian, he was identified alternatively as Flat Iron by Stanley Vestal, as Race Horse by D.F. Barry, and as Greasy Head by Mari Sandoz who wrote: "The Indians told me this is of Greasy Head, known as Crazy Horse No. 2 after, by good Sioux custom,

he took the name of his illustrious predecessor [as Albert Crazy Horse, below] when he married Crazy Horse's widow, the Larrabee woman." Jake Herman, who had shown to a young and skeptical Feraca the tintype soon to be published by Vaughn, sought to verify too the identity of the old Indian with the war bonnet, and come out with yet another identification: "This picture I showed a few older Indians and they identified him as a man by the name of Bald Eagle from Pine Ridge who at one time travelled with Buffalo Bill show. It is not the authentic picture of Chief Crazy Horse."[598] Donovin Sprague reproduced the old photograph, listing the many names by which this Indian was identified. Suggesting also that Sandoz's "Greasy Head" may be a mistranslation of "Greasing Hand," as "Albert Crazy Horse used the name Race Horse and Greasing Hand. There was also the name Greasing The Fingers," Sprague continued, "which could be a translation variation of the same name. Some family members of Albert say it is not him."[599]

With so many erroneous identifications, the tintype owned by Ellen Howard became the subject of serious discussion among the Pine Ridge Sioux, especially because Mrs. Howard's case was very different. She could claim a long-standing family oral tradition and an uninterrupted line of ownership directly from her father, the late Little Bat Garnier, as original owner of that photograph impressed on a small piece of metal. The good condition of the image corroborated her story, that it had been carefully kept in the family as an heirloom. Mrs. Howard's tintype and accompanying testimony were embraced by Ethel Merrival (1906-2001), at the time a member of the Oglala Sioux Tribal Council and later a prominent tribal attorney at Pine Ridge. This was only months before Dr. Robert H. Ruby (1921-2013), accompanied by wife Jeanne, took-up residence at Pine Ridge as medical officer in charge of Pine Ridge Hospital in 1953-1954.

Dr. Ruby described Ethel Merrival as a feisty "troublemaker" deeply involved in tribal politics: "Everybody around here knows Mrs. Ethel Merrival. She calls herself a champion of Indians, and she is bucking the council, the Bureau Office, and whatnot." Admittedly, not without a good reason, as her opposition was to Norwegian-born educator Ole R. Sande, then Pine Ridge Superintendent. "Mr. Sande," wrote Ruby in January 1954, "announced that he was going to be fired. Or perhaps I should say transferred. [...] Mr. Sande laid the blame [...] on Ethel Merrival. But in a huddle later with Elizabeth Forshey, she says it is not Ethel Merrival directly but rather his gross mishandling of so many situations here. Anyway, Mr. Sande blames it all on Ethel Merrival."[600] She also opposed Dr. Ruby, and this too is discussed in the doctor's letters that reflect the great cultural divide between Oglala traditional culture and Anglo outlook. "I just finished reading McGillycuddy – Agent [...] written by his second wife," wrote Ruby in March 1954. "It is a book that one year ago would not have been interesting [...], but today I was absorbed in it. [...] And I reveled in McGillycuddy's circumstances because I find myself in them. That impressed me more than anything else. I don't think these people have changed a bit. McGillycuddy remarks [...] that the troublemakers were always making complains [...] just as they do now. [..] he quotes Red Cloud as saying, 'Father, the Great Spirit did not make us to work' [...] 'the white man can work if he wants to, but the Great Spirit did not make us to work.'"[601]

Despite his interest in photography, Robert Ruby said nothing of McGillycuddy's allegations regarding his attempts to photograph Crazy Horse. Dr. Ruby himself owned a camera at Pine Ridge, and took several photographs, including at a sun dance camp in early July 1954: "Joe Red Bear of Oglala is giving a Sun Dance as a wow he made to the Great Spirit if his wife could again see. [...] Dr. [Joseph] Walters and I went out today to take pictures. When we got to Oglala [community] and saw the camp groups, there were perhaps not more than a dozen or so tents. [...] In a couple of tents down, the grandma brought over the two Swimmer twins. She asked us if we wanted to take a picture of them."[602] The doctor also recalled that "Steve Ferraca [sic], who is from Scarsdale, New York, was here Sunday night to ask for copies of my 35 mm Kodachromes taken at the Sun Dance."[603] Busy as he was with his professional preoccupations for the greater medical needs the Oglala, Dr. Ruby apparently had no knowledge of, or interest in, the ongoing discussion on the "Crazy Horse"

tintype. His biographical sketch of the Lakota hero was very approximate and impressionistic.[604]

For her part, Ethel Merrival was determined to support Mrs. Ellen Howard's family history of the "Crazy Horse" tintype, and decided to make the case for a tintype portrait of the great Lakota chief known outside the reservation community. Merrival drafted a typescript letter in three copies, sending them, respectively, to historian Will G. Robinson, to the Washington, D.C., Museum (the Smithsonian), and to Bob Lee of the *Rapid City Daily Journal*. Despite inaccuracies, her long letter is of great significance in support of the tintype as a true photo of the Lakota patriot:

Pine Ridge, South Dakota, February 3, 1953

Dear friends:

It seems as if I may have run on to a picture of "Crazy Horse." This would seem illogical in view of the fact the so many have said that they have had his picture. However, be that as it may, I have every reason to believe that there is good argument to substantiate that this is truly a picture of Crazy Horse. It would bear investigating. This picture is of the tin-type and it has been put away for many years now where no one has seen it since the owner of the picture died at least [sic]. It is known that two scout guide interpreters of whose names I will not disclose now were given the undertaking of going after Crazy Horse. They were half-breeds and particularly one was chosen because he was a very close friend of Crazy Horse. He was a little fellow and the other fellow was of the big strapping strong type of man. Well, these two accomplished their mission in bringing Crazy Horse back and upon the arrival at the fort these two scouts and friends of Crazy Horse were about to induce Crazy Horse to enter the cellar which was used as quarters for prisoners, etc. when soldiers intervened resulting in the fatal wounding of Crazy Horse. The little fellow who was particularly close to Crazy Horse had been able to have Crazy Horse agree to have his picture taken promising him that this picture would never be disclosed as long as he lived but that he only wanted it for himself as a precious likeness of his friend. That word was kept honorably by the little man as well as his widow and just the other day his daughter who is a very dear friend of mine showed me the picture as well as another tintype of her father and this other scout with the pack-horses they used when they went after Crazy Horse.

I talked with this friend of mine and explained to her that if this was a picture of Crazy Horse she owed it to her tribe and historical events to make it possible for the right parties to get this picture in order to further the cause of Crazy Horse as a great Warrior. She said that she would be willing but I feel that she should get something out of it and that no pictures should be sold to the public unless she got a certain percentage out of it which is no more than business. If the father of this lady had not actually been the man to go after Crazy Horse I would never give it another thought but there are witnesses living today who can substantiate this as well as records. He is also the man that had the gun of Sitting Bull of which the Department of the Interior or War Department sent his widow one hundred dollars for the gun which is now hanging in the Museum in D.C. of which she beaded a holster for it. I also have some other pictures that may be of interest to you and as soon as I gather them up I will make arrangements to send them to you for reproductions but I would want the picture and negative back.

[signed] Ethel Merrival.[605]

As we know, the tintype Ethel Merrival was referring to had been stored away with other family heirlooms in a trunk since the death of the original owner, Little Bat Garnier. Tribal historian and publicity-man Jake Herman, too, supported the Crazy Horse identification of the tintype, and shared his evidence with J.W. Vaughn, who first published the image and accompanying documentation in 1956, the 80th anniversary of the Rosebud fight that had seen Crazy Horse victorious. "New evidence has recently been brought to light," wrote Vaughn. "Ellen Howard, Pine Ridge Agency,

one of the daughters of Baptiste Garnier, the famous scout Little Bat, dug up from her mother's trunk some old tin types taken near Fort Laramie, Wyoming, about 1870. One was the picture of Little Bat's wife, who was a cousin of Crazy Horse. Another was of Frank Grouard, the Grabber, and Little Bat. The third was to cause instant excitement and speculation. It was a picture of an Indian of medium height and build, with light complexion, and long hair coming down to his waist. The picture answered the description of Crazy Horse, but how came it here? Ellen Howard tells the story as it was told to her by her mother and father. One day Little Bat and Frank Grouard coaxed Crazy Horse into having his picture taken and – as a family lark – they all went together and had their picture taken. The fact that it was found among the effects of a close relative was significant. Yet the Sioux were cautious. Only after careful study of the picture and much checking among older Indians at the Agency, did Jake Herman, the Fifth Member of the Sioux Tribal Council, announce the he believed it to be the authentic picture of Chief Crazy Horse who led the Sioux at the Battle of the Rosebud and Custer's massacre at the Little Big Horn."

Ethel Merrival, J.W. Vaughn, Jake Herman, and Fred Hackett, all valued the sincerity of Ellen Howard, an Oglala, her loyalty to her father and mother's memory, and the careful consideration she had given to making the Crazy Horse tintype known. As additional proof of Mrs. Howard's good faith, Vaughn published an undated affidavit he had received from her through Jake Herman. Vaughn advised the reader that "a signed copy of this statement which is in the possession of the writer, attests to the authenticity of the picture of Crazy Horse." In its original misspellings and punctuation, the affidavit read:

Pine Ridge, S,D, Statement.

I Ellen Howard A member of the Ogalla Sioux tribe of Pine Ridge S,D, Certify that i am the daughter of Bat Garnier an Ogalla Sioux, Who was an Indian Scout Station

At Fort Robinson. Neb in 1876 and 1877 And my father and mother are dead. My father left a tin type picture and always told me that it was the picture of Chief Crazy Horse

And i am letting Jake Herman giving him the rights to have him printed in a book or to Whom ever he degnigated [designated] it to. I further state that my mother is dead and she left the picture to me.

Signed, Ellen Howard[606]

In Vaughn's book, the tintype photograph of "Crazy Horse," cropped from the original small "quarter tintype" had a caption that read: "This rare old tintype of Crazy Horse, never before published, is believed by Jake Herman, 5th Member of the Oglala Sioux Tribal Council to be the only existing, authentic picture of the great Oglala chieftain [...]."[607] Vaughn also published an undated and unattributed photo (possibly also a tintype, by either Morrow or Mitchell) of Gen. George Crook. A couple of years later, Mrs. Ellen Howard signed a second typed affidavit, also undated, with similar content as her previous one, to accompany the story of her father and "the old time Indian pictures" she mailed to Fred H. Hackett in Chicago in 1958.[608] In addition to Mrs. Howard's signature, this second affidavit had that of C. Bear Robe as witness to the signing; Hackett added his own signature under that of Bear Robe:

> This is to certify that the tintype of Crazy Horse has been in our family since it was taken; first it was owned by my father, Little Bat Garnier, then by my mother, and then it came to me by inheritance. Many times did my father tell us in the family that this was truly a picture of Crazy Horse. Signed Mrs. Howard Pine Ridge, South Dakota. Witness: C. Bear Robe Fred B. Hackett

From Fred Hackett, the tintype and the second affidavit were acquired by Carroll Friswold (1897-1969) while he drafted the text and assembled the illustrations for his book on the killing of Crazy Horse, published posthumously in 1976. Friswold was positive of the identity of the Indian in the tintype: "From the people involved and my research I firmly believe

This is to certify that the tintype
of Crazy Horse has been in our family since it
was taken; first it was owned by my father,
Little Bat Garnier, then by my mother, and then
it came to me by inheritance. Many times did
my father tell us in the family that this was
truly a picture of Crazy Horse.

Signed *Mrs. Howard*

Pine Ridge,
South Dakota.

Witness:

C. Bear Robe
Fred B. Hackett

Mrs. Ellen Howard's second affidavit, ca. 1958.

this is an authentic likeness of Crazy Horse." Friswold calculated that both Grouard and Little Bat would have still been too young in 1870, and he corrected Vaughn on the location and date of the tintype sitting, placing it at Camp Robinson seven years later, in the summer 1877.[609] While during the earlier research conducted by Will Robinson the intermediary in the Crazy Horse picture taking was thought to have been his mixed-blood wife Nellie Laravie, now the focus shifted to the key protagonist in Mrs. Howard's affidavits, her late father Little Bat Garnier.

Baptiste "Little Bat" Garnier and Julie Mousseau

Baptiste Garnier was a most colorful character, an unsurpassed hunter and scout, well-liked by both Indians and Whites. A personal friend of his, scout and ranchman James H. Cook (1857-1942), drew the following sketch of the legendary little fellow, correctly identifying him as a mixed-blood Sioux of exceptional physical abilities and good character. A modest, reserved man, a man the same Crazy Horse would have trusted. "Two of the best-known army scouts and interpreters in the land of the Sioux

[...] were Baptiste Garnier, a half-blood Sioux whose father was of French descent, and the Baptiste Pourier already referred to. Both lived at Fort Laramie during Little Bat's early manhood. Each had the same given name, shortened into 'Bat' by the soldiers, the older man being called 'Big Bat' and the younger 'Little Bat.' At the outbreak of the Spanish-American War [1898], Little Bat was employed at Fort Robinson, Nebraska, as post guide and interpreter. We were close friends from the year 1876 up to the day of his death, which occurred soon after the troops of the Ninth Cavalry were ordered to Cuba. Little Bat," Cook continued, "was well thought of by both officers and men of whatever regiment he was associated with. Good-natured, even-tempered at all times, he was a fine specimen of physical manhood. He was considered by such men as General Crook [...] as being one of the best big-game hunters in the Rocky Mountains. [...] During all the years in which Little Bat and I were such close friends, I never knew him to have a quarrel with anyone. He was murdered by a barkeeper at Crawford, Nebraska, [...] who [...] was drinking quite heavily at the time when he took the life of my friend."

Cook recounted the sad details of the dastardly murder, and the last moments between Little Bat and his wife, Julie Mousseau who had rushed into town from Fort Robinson. Like her husband, she was part-French Canadian and part-Oglala. Julie was a first cousin Crazy Horse's first wife Black Shawl, hence she was considered also a second cousin of Crazy Horse. Little Bat died in the arms of his wife Julie and spoke to her in Sioux, wrote again Cook: "He told her, when dying, that he thought Haguewood [the bartender] was his friend, and he could not see why a friend should shoot him. [...] To many persons about Crawford, Little Bat was seem-ingly 'nothing but an Indian.' He was killed by a 'white' man." Cook also pointed out that Little Bat had been present, as a scout and interpreter, at the "Wounded Knee Affair" during which he was also severely injured.

Bat himself later confided to Cook that "the sights he had witnessed during the killing of women and children would never be effaced from his memory. He had a family – a wife, one son, and six daughters. His wife," explained Cook, "was a daughter of M.A. Mousseau, a French Canadian

who was one of the very early traders and trappers in the Rocky Mountain country. Little Bat was a man possessed of more than ordinary intelligence. […] His honesty and fearlessness never were questioned. […] He was a most modest and unassuming type of rugged frontier manhood. His home and family and the simple life of the western pioneer were the things which he most desired."[610] Despite obvious differences, there are symbolic similarities between the murders of the mixed-blood scout and that of the Oglala war chief: both had trusted their killers, thinking they were their friends; both staggered into the open air, were then carried indoors, and died in the arms and spoke their last words in Lakota to their closest relatives. Both, as Cook put it "certainly met an undeserved death"; and finally, in both cases, no one paid for their murder.

Details on Little Bat are also found in the diary of his brother-in-law John Hunton (1839-1928), rancher and post trader at Post Laramie who married and later divorced Eulalie (LaLe) Garnier. Hunton's biographical sketch of Little Bat first appeared in the *Fort Laramie Scout* of December 9, 1926, and was later reprinted in condensed version by Flannery in the first volume of the *Hunton Diary*: "Baptiste Garnier (Little Bat) was born in the neighborhood of Fort Laramie, Nebraska territory in 1854. His father was a Canadian Frenchman, his mother a Sioux Indian. His father was killed by Cheyenne Indians in […] 1856, at the mouth of Deer Creek where Glenrock now stands. When about 8 years old, his mother having died, he was taken to the family of E.W. Whitcomb, whose wife was a relative. In 1872 he commenced making his home at Hunton's Ranch aT Bordeaux on Chugwater Creek […] he developed into a fine worker […] and extraordinary fine huntsman. […] In March, 1876 he was (a guide) with the Crook expedition against the Sioux and was in the fight with Crazy Horse's band of Indians. [This is probably what Ethel Merrival was referring to, when she stated that they went after Crazy Horse.] After returning from that lamentable fiasco he went (back) to Hunton's Ranch. In May, 1876 he joined the command of Col. Merritt as scout for the 5th U.S. Cavalry … attracted the special attention of General Crook and his officers … gained their respect and confidence. He was at Hunton's Ranch at the time the Indians killed

Jim Hunton and ran off all of Hunton's mules and horses. In June and July 1877 he was with Hunton, only two of them, riding over the country adjacent to Camp McKinney, looking for hay, extending their ride as far as where Sheridan now stands. He married a daughter of M.A. Mous[s]eau ... made his home in camps in the Fort Fetterman neighborhood and worked on wood and hay contracts for Hunton ... until 1880. His last service at Fort Laramie was a courier between that place and Fort Robinson and Bordeaux in 1890. I could write a great deal more concerning his life ALL commendatory. He was called 'Little Bat' to distinguish him from Baptiste Pourier. Both lived in the family of John Richard (Reshaw) for several years. One was 'Big Bat' and the other 'Little Bat.' General Crook considered Little Bat as one of the most valuable scouts and best hunter. He met an untimely death at the hands of an assassin at Crawford, Nebraska."[611]

Little Bat's presence at Red Cloud Agency during the months of May to September, 1877, appears to have been sporadic, according the entries in the diary kept Hunton. This fact alone, argued by some as proof against the Little Bat trail, should be regarded objectively like the proverbial "glass" as being not just half empty but also half full. Little Bat was known to be a hard rider and a free spirit. Nothing prevented Baptiste Garnier from visiting Camp Robinson and nearby agency, where he and his wife had relatives, including in Crazy Horse's own camp.

Particularly revealing is an editorial comment by Pat Flannery specifically relating to Little Bat's movements during the summer 1877 which contradicts the "perfect chronology" attributed to Hunton by critics of the tintype: "In his history of the life of Little Bat (Baptiste Garnier) ... Mr. Hunton writes that this search for hay across the entire north half of the Territory of Wyoming, from Ft. Fetterman to the present site of the City of Sheridan, took place 'In June and July 1877.' Although he was extremely accurate and meticulous in such matters the above entries establish that the trip was actually made in August 1877. During June and July of that year Hunton's time was largely taken up with the 'lower roundup' on the Platte, [...] the aftermath of domestic upheaval and that serious illness which laid him low shortly after Lallee [Bat's sister] left Bordeaux with her

bed and clothing."[612] Another important discrepancy regards Little Bat's age. Contrary to Hutton's diary, the Pine Ridge 1896 Census listed Baptiste Garnier as being 49 years old, which would place his birth in the year 1847 rather than the generally accepted 1854.[613] The earlier date makes more sense. Little Bat would have been about thirty when Crazy Horse surrendered, and clearly in the position to interact with the Oglala war chief.

More problematic is the age determination for Baptiste's wife Julie Mousseau, listed in the same census erroneously as "Julia, 32." This would make her born in 1864, hence about thirteen years old in 1877, and only ten when, according to some records, Julie married Little Bat. Other records however indicate that Julie was born in 1861, thus making her about sixteen years old in 1877, and about fifteen when, according to John Hunton, the previous year she married Bat.[614] Still young, but not uncommon then for American Indian and mixed-blood women. Another source provides an earlier date of birth for Julie Mousseau, ca. 1855, placing her in her early twenties at time of marriage. Which sounds more reasonable. As noted, Julie was the daughter of Alexis Magloire Mousseau (ca. 1820-??) and Ellen Yellow Woman (ZiWiyan/Waštewin, ca.1830-??), a second cousin of Crazy Horse's biological mother.[615] Alexis and Ellen had married in the mid-1840s, which again, by today's standards, would seem quite young for a woman, but not in traditional Lakota culture. Their marriage was blessed with six children, four boys and two girls, the youngest of the latter being Julie. Julie and Little Bat will have eight children of their own: John, born in 1880; Elizabeth, 1881; Lucy, 1882; Ellen, 1884; Emma, 1887; Sophia, 1889; Sallie, 1890; Baptiste Jr., 1894.[616]

The year daughter Sallie was born, as Cook recalled Little Bat found himself right in the middle of the Ghost Dance crisis. Together with his brother-in-law Louis Mousseau, Little Bat was at Wounded Knee that tragic day of December 29th, and he too was wounded in the cross-fire. Years later, in 1906, Judge Ricker recorded the following notes from Louis's testimony: "Little Bat was at the upper end of the camp up the ravine with a party [of soldiers] who were disarming [the Indians] There were two parties disarming at the same time – both started together. [...] He tells of a woman close to the road crossing the ravine; he and Little Bat heard some hollering (after the battle was over) down by the ravine – heard words like these 'Shoot him again!' A wounded woman [was] lying in a washout right in the road and at her feet was a little baby swathed as is their custom, and it was alive; somebody took it (he thinks was the one that went east or was the one Charley Merrivall's mother took) and it was saved; a little boy about two years old was lying against the bank half sitting as though it was yet alive, and four soldiers were standing right above it. Louie & Bat went down, drawn by what they had heard and found the woman and asked if she was hurt much & if she could get up. She did not want to be moved, and said 'Those soldiers just now killed my two children (she thought both were dead) and I want to lie here and die with them.' Bat went up to them and in his forcible way gave them a berating and made them go away. He says as Horn Cloud does that the soldiers encircling the council fired toward the center at the Indians inside [...]. He says it was a bungle and batch – no need of anybody being injured if it had been properly managed. He talked to Big Foot that morning and B.F. said he did not want any fight – no trouble. He said it was surprising that they should come out with cannon to meet him."[617]

Little Bat was a family man. His positive attitude and peaceful nature clashed ten years later, on the 15th of December, 1900 (ten years to the day from the killing of Sitting Bull), with yet another episode of racial prejudice and violence that cost him his own life just for being "nothing but an Indian," as his friend Crook tragically stated. Baptiste "Little Bat" Garnier, Chief of Scouts at Fort Robinson, was shot to death by James Haguewood, bartender in a Crawford saloon. Pleading "self-defense," the assassin was acquitted a few months later by a White jury. And so ended the life of a good man, a iyeška, a mixed-blood, an Oglala who had proudly posed for a photograph dressed the traditional Indian way, leggings and long breastplate, war bonnet, bow and arrows.[618]

Little Bat was an honest and fearless man; in many ways, very much like Crazy Horse. We do not know exactly where and when the tintype of Crazy Horse was taken, although the circumstantial evidence, substantiated

Little Bat Garnier and his family, Camp Robinson. Ellen Howard, here a teenager wrapped in a blanket over her traditional Lakota dress, stands between her father and her mother. Photographer unknown, ca. 1898-1900.

also by related photographs, suggests it was in the log cabin studio with a skylight at Red Cloud Agency temporarily used by James H. Hamilton in the summer 1877. Little Bat's life was suddenly cut short, so we do not have his autobiographical statement regarding the tintype itself. But given Little Bat's legacy, there is no reason to doubt the story narrated and the affidavits signed by his daughter Ellen. Ellen would not tarnish the good memory of her father and mother with an invented story, especially regarding an issue, the photographic portrait of Crazy Horse, so meaningful to her personally and to her People, the Lakota.

Ethel Merrival, Jake Herman, and Charles Bear Robe knew Ellen Howard and her good standing at Pine Ridge. After consultation with tribal elders they corroborated her family tradition of the tintype being a portrait of Crazy Horse; they were themselves all members of the Oglala community. The fourth, Fred Hackett, though a not an Indian, was closely associated with the Sioux and had been adopted as his son by Oglala Chief Iron Tail. Of the four, Jake Herman in particular was actively involved in the preservation of Oglala history, traditions, and ceremonies at a time when termination and relocation were once again undermining the already beleaguered, socially and politically polarized Pine Ridge Reservation. Remarkably, it was Jake Herman who obtained the crucial validation of octogenarian Lakota elder Dewey Beard/Iron Hail in favor of the Crazy Horse identification of the tintype. Iron Hail, Mnicojou (Wasu Maza, ca. 1858/1862-1955), who as noted took the Anglo name of Dewey Beard,[619] has at times been confused with the older Oglala Iron Tail (Sinte Maza, ca. 1847-1916).[620]

Fortunately, Dewey Beard was able to play a crucial role in Fred Hackett and Jake Herman's search for evidence in support of the tintype as a photographic portrait of Crazy Horse. Dewey Beard, too, though still a teenager, had fought at the Little Bighorn killing a trooper on Custer Hill. He "called Crazy Horse his uncle," and was later involved in early identifications of various purported photographs of Crazy Horse, which he all denied, until shortly before his death, when Jake Herman showed Dewey Beard the Garnier-Howard tintype. Despite his venerable age, the old Lakota this time recognized that the Indian in the tintype actually looked like Crazy Horse! No doubts on his part. Was Dewey Beard senile? No, as his granddaughter Marie Fox Belly later testified: "He was tough, healthy [...] I guess that's because my grandfather was born free."[621] Dewey Beard's identification corroborated Short Bull's certainty that Crazy Horse had indeed been photographed. To the point, Dewey Beard's critical endorsement of the tintype as a photographic portrait of the Oglala war chief has never before been taken into full account.[622]

Jake Herman

Jake Herman was a pivotal figure in support of the tintype. A tribal historian, Herman searched for corroborating evidence and shared the little photographic portrait with the last surviving tribesmen who could attest with a degree of certainty, despite old age and fading memories, to the likeness of the famous chief. Herman's research methodology was limited to the verbal testimony and informal historical validation typical of the time

among old reservation Indians, many of whom spoke little or no English. Jake's own Indian family history began with his paternal grandfather Jacob Herman (1827-1874) who in 1844, at age 17, immigrated to the U.S. from Germany. Grandpa Jacob moved west and landed a job as a blacksmith at Fort Laramie. There he married Mary Tesson White Cloud, a mixed-blood woman from Kansas. Their son, Antoine Herman, born in 1860, later married Lizzie Clifford, also a mixed-blood, and the two settled on the Pine Ridge Reservation. There Jacob (Jake) Herman was born in 1890, the tragic year of Wounded Knee; other sources, including the 1896 and 1904 Indian census at Pine Ridge, give 1891 as Jacob's birth. He was the youngest of five children, attended mission school at Pine Ridge, and was later sent to boarding school at Carlisle, Pennsylvania, where he distinguished himself for his athletic abilities, especially in basketball and as a member of the school football team.[623] After graduation, Jake worked at the naval shipyards in Philadelphia before returning to Pine Ridge where he married Alice Janis, a mixed-blood Oglala of the large Janis kindred. Jake and Alice had four children.

In 1967, Joseph H. Cash interviewed Herman and described him posthumously as "one of America's most famed rodeo clowns. A Brule Sioux, he married an Oglala girl and was selected as a member of the Oglala tribal council. He ran his own museum, painted pictures, made artifacts, and talked endlessly about tribal history before his death in 1970." Jake quit his rodeo activities in 1943. "I was up in age then," he confessed to J.H. Cash, "and I couldn't fight those bulls out […] I thought before I got killed I better quit. […] I never was crippled, but it got pretty rough."[624] Jake Herman served as Oglala Tribal councilman from 1952-1956, and again between 1964 and the year of his death. He was very much involved in the preservation of Sioux tribal history and traditional knowledge at a time when life on the reservation was undergoing major changes with the passing of the last generation of elders who had had direct contact with the great tribal leaders of the previous century. Herman feared many things would be forgotten. Despite contradictions, some intrinsic to his mixed-blood background, he felt his strong Sioux identity. His relationship with

Dr. Ruby was more cordial and collaborative than Ethel Merrival's, sharing with the "green" doctor traditional stories and insights on tribal affairs. And, as the doctor himself recalled, "At the going-away party Jake Herman presented us with beaded moccasins for [our young daughter] Edna. [...] the first time in the history of Pine Ridge in which any group of Indians has come to send off a white government official."[625]

Herman produced mimeographed pamphlets on Sioux traditional culture and history, and concluded an article on the Sacred Pole – reprinted shortly before his death – with the following words: "These are some of the stories that are getting to be a last chapter of our forefathers. This writer is attempting to keep them alive. They are certainly worth preserving – that is why I thought I would pass them along to you."[626] While he acknowledged his mixed-blood ancestry, Herman regarded himself also a Lakota. "I was born on the Pine Ridge Indian Reservation in South Dakota," he wrote in an autobiographical sketch. "The census roll here at the Agency shows that I am recorded as one-half Sioux and one-half a white. Half of my ancestors came over the Big Pond, and my other half were hunting the big buffalo when they met. My father was a roundup foreman; he taught me how to ride and rope. [...] Never in my kid days did I think of becoming a *Wild West* Rodeo Clown, as in those days there was no such animal. I probably attended more governmental Indian schools than any other Sioux alive. [...] I am now retired and I live here at Pine Ridge [...]. For a hobby, I write legends, folklore, and history of the Oglala Sioux."[627]

In 1985, Herman was inducted under the category "professional cowboy" in the South Dakota Hall of Fame at Chamberlain: "Jake Herman of Pine Ridge was an artist, writer, trick rider, fancy roper and most of all, a great rodeo clown. His rodeo career began with *Jack King's Wild West Show* and the Rodeo Royal Circus." The rodeo clown was considered the most dangerous of the rodeo circus jobs, requiring great courage and athleticism: "Clad in baggy pants, a swallowtail coat and derby hat, he entertained with the help of a pet skunk named 'Stinky,' his devoted dog 'Tag,' and a trick mule called 'Creepy Jenny.' Jake himself was quoted as saying, 'There is one thing about rodeo fans, if a cowboy gets bucked off or gets

hooked by a bull, he gets their sympathy, but if a rodeo clown encounters the same type of situation, everyone gets a big laugh out of it.' The old rodeo clown had to have the ability to ride broncs, ride bareback, trick ride and rope, fight bulls, as well as be an outstanding comedian. After many years [... Jake Herman] became a rodeo announcer and wrote articles on rodeo, cowboys and Indians for such national publications as 'True West,' 'The Western Horseman' [etc.]. He took up painting and produced many works including scenes depicting traditional legends of the Oglala Sioux. During his 79 years, Jake also worked for the federal government and the Pine Ridge police [...] Relatives, friends and acquaintances remember him as a man of many talents, interests and achievements."[628]

Jesuit priest Paul B. Steinmetz who served at Pine Ridge between 1961 and 1981, remarked that Jake Herman, recognized by the Oglala as a tribal historian, helped foster harmony between Sun Dance traditionalists and Christian tribal members. "He was influential in the decision to have Mass celebrated on the Sun Dance grounds. I was asked to do this from 1965 to 1970," wrote Steinmetz, recalling also that the opposition of a young militant brought an end to the practice the year Jake Herman passed away.[629] It may be a forced reading of the events by Father Steinmetz, but in the context of the time, clearly Herman's intentions were good.

Jake Herman took a keen interest in the Crazy Horse picture question. He admitted that he himself, like many Indians, had long believed that no picture of Crazy Horse existed, until he was shown the tintype and he began searching for evidence within the Lakota community in support of Ellen Howard's story. He tried unsuccessfully to convince young Steve Feraca that the tintype owned by Little Bat's daughter was truly a likeness of Crazy Horse. He was more successful with J.W. Vaughn, and did so by presenting him uncompromising testimonies of a few Lakota elders, that of Dewey Beard in particular, who validated the likeness of Crazy Horse in the tintype. In his long, at times cryptic 1956 letter to Vaughn, Herman challenged "the experts" and gave instead weight and credence to the opinion of those he called "my people":

Dear kola (friend) J.W. Vaughn.

Received your letter dated Oct 16/56 and I am glad to give you all the information of the picture that I sent you, of Chief Crazy Horse. In fact many of the Sioux Indians have repeatedly told me that Crazy Horse never had his picture taken or did attend any council. This became legendary among the Sioux. My wife[']s Aunt Phyllis Janis Garnettee who is now dead left a picture of some teepees with the Sioux holding a council around the year of 1850. The picture is rather small impossible to identify the men. She told me that Chief Crazy Horse was at that council. She described to me what Crazy Horse looked like. Light brown reddish hair rather straight nose. Light complexed looked more like a breed Indian about 5 ft 10 inches. I showed the picture to Dewey Beard just before he died. He looked at a long time. And said it looks like Crazy Horse. […] Yes I also believed at one time there was no picture of him until I heard the rumors that Ellen Howard the daughter of Ba[p]tiste Garnier had one. She herself came to me and asked me to come down to her place and she would show me the picture of the Chief Crazy Horse, which I did. And you know the rest [..]. Remember I am a free lance writer trying to be a Sioux historian is my hobby. With one that in mind to preserve the Indian history[,] folklore[,] legends. As I know I lived it for 65 years and as the old Sioux warriors who told me as they lived it. Recently Jim Red Cloud age 76 received a letter from a man by the name Joseph Balmer […], Switzerland, who stated that I was unreliable and that the Photo of Chief Crazy Horse was not so. I do not know the man from Adam and don[']t care to know him if he feels that way to condemn me. Even Will Robinson the State Historian of S.D. said in an article that there was a serious doubt that Dewey Beard was not at Custer Battle as he was to[o] small at that time to take scalps. I[']d rather stick to my people as to what they tell me, and as long as Grandma Dirt Kettle who is alive tells me I know it so. She knows. She can't see nor hear but she can talk.

She told me Dewey was at Custer Battle [,] she stood on the hill [,] watched the battle ['] walked among the Dead. [...] She convinced me that Crazy Horse was great war chief and also know my Grand Mother Mrs. Hard Ground both same age.

Sincerely Your Kola, Jake Herman (Pta-Sun-Wacta). [630]

Jake Herman was right to trust his own people. As we saw earlier, a teenager Iron Hail had indeed fought at the Battle of the Little Bighorn. After the victory over Custer, his father's thiyóšpaye followed Sitting Bull in Canada, then re-crossed the medicine line and settled with fellow Mnicojou tribesmen on the Cheyenne River Indian Reservation. Like many other Lakota, Iron Hail and his family embraced the Ghost Dance, and in the wake of Sitting Bull's assassination, they joined Big Foot/Spotted Elk's desperate attempt to seek refuge at Pine Ridge, under the protection of Red Cloud, the last of the great Lakota chiefs who was still alive. In the Wounded Knee Massacre, Iron Hail lost his father, mother, wife, and child, while he managed to survive, though severely wounded. He later converted to Roman Catholicism taking the name of Dewey Beard – the former in honor of Admiral George Dewey who he had befriend in Washington, the latter a Lakota nickname. Like Iron Tail, Iron Hail also joined *Buffalo Bill's Wild West* show. Dewey Beard died nearly a centenarian in 1955 in Kyle, Pine Ridge Reservation, and was buried in an unmarked grave in the local Saint Stephen Catholic Cemetery.[631]

Charles Bear Robe

The signature of C. Bear Robe accompanies the second Ellen Howard affidavit. Charles Bear Robe was a descendant of Bear Robe, one of the signatories of the 1868 Laramie Treaty. The last entry in the Oglala signatories shows "Moh-to-ha-she-na, his x mark, The Bear Hide."[632] Bray suggests that since Bear Robe appears at the end of the Oglala list, he might have been one of the headmen who signed the treaty at the Upper Platte Agency in

Nebraska around June 1, 1868. Bray also states that Bear Robe was a head soldier in 1875. The name, spelled Bears Robe, with the Lakota equivalent Mato ha xina and the rank of "Soldier" is shown with that of Little Wound, Pawnee Killer, Red Dog, and others who were induced or actually forced to "touch the pen" on the fraudulent Black Hills Agreement of September 1876. This could be an indication that he was not at the Little Bighorn, as in fact his name does not appear in the current listing of warriors who fought against Custer. On the other hand, we find an Anglicized "Robe Hair Outside" in the 1877 Surrender Ledger.

At the present time, it is not clear whether the latter was indeed the same signatory of the 1868 and 1876 documents. Specifically regarding Charles Bear Robe, he was the youngest son of Paul Bear Robe (b. 1869) and Jessie Bear Robe (b. 1875). A photographic portrait of Paul Bear Robe donning an eagle feather war bonnet with a long trailer, his braids wrapped in otter furs, was made by James H. Brown, Jr. in the early 1900s.[633] Charles himself was born in 1912 and is listed with his parents and siblings in the Pine Ridge Reservation census of 1913, where the mother's name is "Nellie," possibly an error in transcription. Charles appears again in the same reservation 1915 census, living with his large family at Wakpamni District. He is listed in the 1924 Pine Ridge census, with siblings and mother Jessie as head of family. Charles appears separately, as a full blood Oglala, age 22, widowed, head of family, no children, in the Pine Ridge census taken by James H. McGregor in 1934.[634] Given that we are dealing with the same person, Bear Robe probably remarried and had children, as he resurfaces in the early and mid-1950s, in the narrative of Dr. Robert Ruby. We learn from the doctor that Charles, or Charlie Bear Robe was a member of one of the two branches of the Native American Church, the syncretistic religion that centers around the sacramental use of peyote.[635]

Indicative of the factionalism that pervaded all aspects of life among the Oglala, "at the Pine Ridge Reservation," Dr. Thomas H. Lewis (himself a psychiatrist) observed later in the 1960s, "the Native American Church Division called Cross Fire emphasizes Bible readings. The Half-Moon

Group was conducted in a 'more Indian tradition' with meetings held in tipis. Both rituals begin at dusk and extent through the night to daylight or beyond, with drumming, singing, prayers, confession, and meditation. Peyote buttons are chewed, consumed in the form of past, or taken as a tea from a communal pitcher. Since it is considered a supernatural and literally contains wak'an attributes, it is taken in four doses, the required sacred number."[636] Charles Bear Robe belonged to the first group and tried to win Dr. Ruby over to their side. "Mrs. Elizabeth Forshey [the Agency social worker]," Dr. Ruby wrote in May 1954, "told me that the Half Moon peyote followers are holding a big prayer meeting this Saturday in expectation of our visit. […] Less than fifteen minutes later Charlie Bear Robe, a Cross Fire practitioner, came to the hospital and said […] that both groups, the Half Moon and the Cross Fire were going to meet at Porcupine and he was supposed to take me to the place."[637] During the summer, the two groups held other concomitant but separate midnight meetings and on one occasion, upon leaving a Half Moon ceremony, the doctor recalled that "on the way out we looked into the nearby house. […] Charles Bear Robe was in there. He is the one that tried to kidnap me and Mrs. Forshey the other time. I was afraid he was coming in the tepee, but he went to the house meeting. He is such a crook according to Mrs. Forshey. Now he will probably spread a lot of malicious stuff about how peyoted-up Mrs. [Nell] Coker [acting director of nursing at Pine Ridge Hospital] and I were."[638]

This would seem to cast a shadow of doubt on Charles Bear Robe, but again we need to read Dr. Ruby's statements in context. His words were spontaneous, unfiltered, often impressionistic, as he reported on the state of affairs at Pine Ridge during his limited stay; both a strength and a limitation, from a historical perspective. The doctor addressed his letters to his sister Marion, and he also candidly commented on the same Mrs. Forshey. As it often happened, given the very nature of their work, reservation doctors found themselves caught in the middle: "Mrs. Forshey hates Mr. Sande. […] Mrs. Forshey soft-peddles Communism and admitted that some of her best friends were Communists at one time. […] Naturally she hates McCarthy. But she does not speak well of [F.D.] Roosevelt [democratic]. She speaks nastily of this [D. Eisenhower- republican] administration. I can't figure out just what she might like. She seems like Gerald K. Smith [the evangelist leader of Share Our Wealth Society]. She simply gives her disapproval of everything."[639] Still with regard to Charles Bear Robe, Dr. Ruby related that at a Cross Fire meeting attended also by Edgar Red Cloud (1897-1977), the famous Oglala chief's great-grandson, "they all ate too much peyote [...]. So that group of Cross Fire is quite a peyote-eating bunch. Charles Bear Robe was at that meeting. He came to the house Monday, Bear Robe did, and asked Jeanne for something to eat for his kids. She fixed him a stack of sandwiches."[640]

Fred B. Hackett

The fourth and only non-Indian witness to the Ellen Howard testimonial is Fred B. Hackett. Hackett was a fairly well-known figure among amateur historians of the West and the multi-faceted world of Buffalo Bill. Hackett is mentioned in a classic book on Plains Indian feathered headdresses published in Germany by the late Colin F. Taylor, who wrote, "I first became really interested in Plains Indian headgear [...] when I acquired a magnificent eagle feather bonnet from Tex McLeod who was with Buffalo Bill's circus. Tex McLeod told me that the headdress had once belonged to Chief Iron Tail. [...] Fred Hackett told me that Iron Tail was considered a very fine Indian, always smiling and very fond of jokes upon himself as well as others." Taylor accompanied the text with several illustrations relating to Iron Tail, including a rare photograph taken by Fred Hackett himself, about 1911, depicting "Iron Tail in beaded shirt and leggings wearing a feathered head-dress of mixed white and brown feathers and mottled feathers from the golden eagle." In a footnote, Taylor also provided some basic biographical information on the photographer: "Fred Hackett worked with the Buffalo Bill Show in the early 1900s and was in charge of the Indians with whom he formed many strong relationships. He was the adopted son of

Iron Tail and arranged his funeral when Iron Tail died on 29 May 1916 (he is buried at Pine Ridge). Fred Hackett died 16 February 1975 at the age of 92 and is buried in Graceland Cemetery, Chicago."[641]

Drawing from Taylor's early correspondence with Hackett, Richard Green recently expanded on the life of this elusive Westerner who had acquired Sinte Maza's painted muslin dance shield: "Frederick B. Hackett (c.1884-1975) was born and raised in Boston [...] the son of a Western scout. As a boy, he had listened [...] to conversations between Colonel Cody and his father. Tantalized by colorful stories of the American West, he ran away from home at the age of sixteen and spent a period working as a cowboy and guide on a ranch in Cheyenne, Wyoming. Some years later, he is reported as having worked as a ration clerk at Pine Ridge Agency [...]." According to the biographical sketch drawn by Green, "In 1905, Hackett married his wife Lila and settled in Chicago, working as an elevator safety engineer, a career he maintained for many years until retirement. Through his early contact with the legendary *Wild West* showman, Hackett finally took up Cody's offer of working for his *Wild West and Congress of Rough Riders of the World*. Both Hackett and his wife Lila signed up for the 1914, 1915, and 1916 seasons. Hackett chased Indians around the show arena in rough-riding exhibitions, and also managed the Sioux performers, while Lila performed in riding and shooting acts. Over the years, Hackett built up a sizeable collection of historical Indian and Western artifacts, photographs, and ephemera. In 1944, he was among the founders of the Westerners' Chicago Corral. His summers were usually spent at Pine Ridge, where he had many Sioux friends. [...] By 1914, when Fred Hackett was first recruited to work with Cody's show, it seems he had already known the celebrated Oglala Sioux chief, Iron Tail for nearly twenty years. During the three seasons he and Lila spent working with Cody's *Wild West*, the two men became close friends and the chief eventually adopted Hackett as his son. [...] A fascinating collection of photographs of Iron Tail and other Sioux *Wild West* performers was taken by Fred Hackett while touring New York around 1915."[642]

Some of these photographs were later published by Don Russell in his classic Buffalo Bill biography.[643] Like Jake Herman, whom he befriended, Hackett was also very much interested in Sioux history. Somewhat conversant in Lakota, Hackett established a rapport of trust with the Lakota at both Pine Ridge and Rosebud reservations where he collected objects, winter counts,[644] old documents and photographs, and testimonies especially on Crazy Horse. It was Fred Hackett who added a cover letter to a copy of the report Billy Garnett had written in the 1920s on the death of Crazy Horse. Writing in 1958 to his friend Thomas W. Wright, Hackett informed him that while at Pine Ridge he "set about talking to all the old timers a few still live there. While talking, a grandson of Billie Garnett the interpreter who was at the side of 'Crazy Horse' when he was stabbed said 'Fred I have my grandfather [']s written report [...] I will let you take and copy it." And he also told him that he was going to return soon to Pine Ridge, "as the Sun Dance will be held on 8/21-22-23."[645]

Hackett himself authored a number of ephemeral publications on the Sioux.[646] His special interest in photography, both his own production and old vintage Sioux photographs, and in the life and death of Crazy Horse, motivated his search for a true likeness of the Oglala hero. Hackett established a close friendship with Ellen Howard, who eventually shared with him the "forgotten" tintype and her father's story of that image. Their friendship continued while Hackett lived in Chicago, as we infer from two letters Mrs. Howard sent Hackett in late 1957. The first piece of correspondence read:

Pine Ridge, S. Dak Nov-29-[19]57

Fred B. Hackett, my dear friend [,] I thought I would write to you & let you know that we have [had] bad luck last month [.] We lost our grandson 18 years old on Oct. 14. He got sick & died so we were sure are takening [taking it] pretty hard. his [He is] the boy you was talking to him [&] told him learn all he can. He was with me when you was at hotel & besides we need clothes bad & also we went

broke [on] account of the poor boy. I also spend lots of money for coffin & suit & I'll have them paper sent out on my father story & some other Indians. I wish you could send me some clothes for us we are pretty hard up since we lost our boy. You know Doctor bill & Hospital. I hope we hear from you soon. yours friend Mrs Helen [sic] Howard North Route[647]

The second letter was written a month later in reply to the answer Fred had sent Ellen. It specifically mentioned the "old time Indian picture" she would soon send him:

Pine Ridge, S. Dak, Dec 30 – 57

Mr Fred B. Hackett

Dear friend, I just got your letter the other day & I was glad to hear from you. Well first of all we are felling [feeling] pretty bad over our grandson yet it seems like we could not forget our grandson & also I don't fell like do any thing yet but soon as I am better I'll have the story about my father's history & also the old time Indian picture and I'll send it to you soon [.] besides I would like to have blanke[t] its pretty cold out here & my husband would like to have dress pants size waist 36 – leg 31 or 32 [.] besides my little grandson sure need shoes brown size shoes 7 ½ [.] I hope you are getting along good like we are hoping you are in good health [.] we must say good by & God Bless you[.] your friend Ellen Howard[.]

The "dear friend," indicative of mutual trust, the simple language, the reference to the hardships and sorrows of reservation life, the request for clothing, and the blessings, together point once again to the sincerity of the person, the veracity of her narration, and the authenticity of the tintype. As Thomas Wright later related in his unpublished study of the various photographs identified as Crazy Horse, the tintype was indeed acquired by Fred Hackett, whom he called "a long-time friend of the Sioux at Pine Ridge. Hackett," explained Thomas Wright, "was a range rider in

South Dakota in his youth and later was a rodeo rider with Buffalo Bill's circus. In his yearly visits to Pine Ridge, Hackett heard much talk about Crazy Horse from old timers then living such as Chief He Dog, brother-friend of Crazy Horse. Everybody first said that Crazy Horse had no picture taken; then after a while Hackett learned that someone might have a picture of the chief. 'I was told,' Hackett said, 'that a daughter of Little Bat Garnier had one she said belonged to her father, a great friend of Crazy Horse, but I was never able to obtain it. Then some friends told her of my interest in the Sioux. She said she would sell it to me with other old-time photos of the tribe. In 1957 on my fifty-first visit among them, she came and offered them to me and I bought them from her.'"[648]

Epilogue

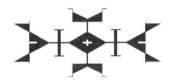

In late summer 2012, Pietro and I intended to travel together to Fort Robinson, Nebraska, to honor the memory of Crazy Horse on the 135th anniversary of his death. Disappointingly, due to conflicting personal circumstances, we were unable to do so. For my part, finding myself in Washington that early September day, I sat silently on the banks of the Potomac River thinking about Crazy Horse. It occurred to me that a visit to the exhibit *A Song for the Horse Nation* at the National Museum of the American Indian – the exhibit running from Oct. 2011 to Jan. 2013 – would be a good way to remember the great Lakota patriot. I thought that for certain, given the historic date, in conjunction with the museum displays and the lectures on the return of the horse to North America after thousands of years, and its impact on Indian life especially on the Great Plains, Crazy Horse would be remembered with a ceremony, a honoring song; perhaps, even a special viewing of the DVDs recently produced by his Mnicojou descendants. I was wrong. Crazy Horse was not publicly remembered in the Native People's home in the Capital City.

The following year, Pietro and I revisited the many sites so closely linked to Crazy Horse in Montana, Wyoming, Dakota, and Nebraska. In early June 2013, we were at Fort Robinson, where two meaningful episodes greatly inspired us. The first "sign" came as we stood, in silence, at the small stone monument marking the spot where Crazy Horse was mortally wounded in front of the (now reconstructed) guard house. A large white cloud formation distinctively shaped like an Indian warrior on horseback slowly passed over our heads in the bright blue Nebraska sky. That the "warrior-cloud" was not the fruit of our separate imaginations rests on the fact that we both noticed it simultaneously, identified as such, and then clearly and distinctly observed it hover in the sky. We stared at the cloud and looked at each other in amazement, almost in disbelief, incredulous at the sight. As we stood there, heads up, we contemplated the slow moving cloud shaped like a warrior on a horse that lasted several minutes, until a gentle breeze pushed away and dispersed the white-cloud warrior.

Still moved by the experience, we silently resumed our walk through the grassy parade ground and its wooden buildings. Hallowed ground. There the life of Crazy Horse had come to a tragic end, and there many proud Northern Cheyenne had died in their heroic break-out for freedom. While we were both absorbed in thoughts, the prolonged silence that embraced the wide open space was suddenly interrupted by a second "sign." A park custodian approached and greeted us. We exchanged a few words, telling him of our interest in Crazy Horse. He asked us if we had come to historic Fort Robinson expressly for the Crazy Horse Memorial Ride ceremony scheduled to take place the following day on those very same grounds. Again, we were greatly surprised. Although we vaguely knew of the yearly event, neither Pietro nor I had thought of it then. We admitted our oversight. The custodian smiled and assured us that our presence at the Fort was more than just a lucky coincidence; it coincided with the arrival of the Indian riders who were already camped nearby. An added bonus, good weather was also expected the next day for the ceremony and the departure of the Memorial Ride back to Pine Ridge.

So it was that, unaware of the rendezvous with the Lakota Riders at Fort Robinson, Pietro and I had driven for days, with sweet-grass and a copy of the Crazy Horse tintype on our dashboard. We had come all the way from the Little Bighorn Battlefield, through the Northern Cheyenne Reservation and the Black Hills, to the Crazy Horse Memorial, where we met with Francis White Lance. We then traveled together across the Badlands to Allen for much needed food and rest at Francis and Suzanne's welcoming home. After visiting the sun dance ground, now powerfully silent in

the bright sunlight, we resumed our journey. On the way, we picked-up a nephew of Hollow Horn Bear who, badly dehydrated from the heat was hitch-hiking a ride, gave him plenty of water, and dropped him off at a relative's house. We stopped at Wounded Knee and passed through Pine Ridge. Saw the desolation of the infamous border town of White Clay. Drove into Crawford, where Little Bat was murdered, ten years to the day after the killing of Sitting Bull at Standing Rock. Finally, with no planning, we had arrived at Fort Robinson with perfect timing to attend the Crazy Horse Memorial Ride. The theme was "Year of Renewal." By the time we returned to the Battlefield, we had completed a large clockwise circle, which we dedicated to Crazy Horse.

For those who will welcome the evidence presented herein as sufficient proof for the identification of the Indian in the tintype as Crazy Horse, the name and memory of the Lakota patriot will henceforth be associated with his likeness with a degree of humble certainty. To the skeptics, we offer the olive branch of friendly discussion and fair confrontation. Once again, we should always keep in mind that the existence of one or more Crazy Horse photographs was suggested by no less a true Lakota than Short Bull in his July 13, 1930 interview with Eleanor Hinman: "I have seen two photographs of Crazy Horse that I think were really he, both showing him on horse-back. One showed him on a buckskin horse he owned, one on a roan. I have seen a third photograph that I am sure was he, because it showed him on the pinto horse he rode in the Custer fight. I could not possibly make a mistake about that horse, and nobody rode it but Crazy Horse. The man who owns these pictures got them from the soldiers who used to be at Fort Robinson. He [sic] was quite a collection of pictures of chiefs. I think he lives in California now, near the National Park there. I do not remember his name."[649]

Short Bull did not bring up the "fear" of "soul loss," "stubborn refusal," "hate of the White man" stories long argued by "nay" supporters. These second-hand accounts of "stubborn refusal" and the like, attributed to Crazy Horse and embraced as historic truths, were not even considered by Tatanka Ptečela. If Crazy Horse truly held such beliefs, Short Bull would have known and said so. He did not. He Dog, who was present at the interviews, did not contradict his brother either. There is another puzzling side to Short Bull's comment regarding those possible Crazy Horse photos and why he was sure they were the Oglala war chief. Short Bull did not bring up the famous scar on Tašunke's face as a distinctive mark for his identification. Evidently the subject in the photo(s) he remembered was too far, hence too small for such a detail. Short Bull did recognize something bigger and easily distinguishable, the chief's war horse. The same distinctive element was used by Short Bull's own brother He Dog in one of his now lost 21 pictographs, previously mentioned. The accompanying text written by He Dog's nephew Joseph Eagle Hawk (1870-1951), a Carlisle Indian School graduate, read in part, "[Pictograph No.] 7. This represents the soldiers, and this represents White Hat [...] and the one to the left, on the spotted horse, is Crazy Horse."[650] Tašunke Witko's favorite war horse aside, what matters in Short Bull's testimony, supported by He Dog's recollection, is precisely the open mind Marshall hoped for and we, too, invoked at the beginning.

Does this mean we can be absolutely positive that there is, out there, a photograph of Crazy Horse on a spotted or other horse? Of course not, but we ought to be open to the possibility there may be. The other question, as in the characterization of Little Bat and his daughter Ellen as reliable sources, is the extent to which Short Bull, who was "in his early twenties at the time of the events," can be regarded as trustworthy. The answer to this rhetorical question was given by Eleanor Hinman herself: "Short Buffalo [...] is the youngest brother of He Dog and shares the remarkable memory which seems to be a family characteristic. Anyone who will take the pains to compare his account of the John Brughier incident or of the surrender of Crazy Horse with accounts by white officers published thirty-five years or more ago will be struck by Short Buffalo's accuracy after so many years. None of the men interviewed had any means of access to the published accounts. In certain other instances Short Buffalo's version of events differs sharply from the published accounts but in such a way as to suggest that the Indian version deserves at least consideration."[651]

Short Bull was not the only one to believe a photograph of Crazy Horse (perhaps more than one) existed. Again, the Hinman *Interviews* provide indirect evidence to support the claim. And again the bone of contention centers around the old McGillycuddy-Barry tale of Tašunke Witko never consenting to a photograph for fear of losing his soul. Unfortunately, the story stuck. In the Editor's "Introduction" to the new (1976) edition of the *Interviews*, distinguished Custer historian John M. Carroll addressed specifically the question "On a Photo of Crazy Horse:" "It is impossible at this late date to ever confirm the existence of a photo of Crazy Horse; it is a repeated story that Crazy Horse never wished his 'shadow to be captured." After touching upon the Short Bull pro-photo testimony and the Barry no-photo (invented) story, Carroll quoted a 1954 letter by Harry Anderson to Col. W.A. Graham stating that "there was a photographer at Ft. [Camp] Robinson in 1877, plus an officer with a camera, and that one of the two correspondents from Harper's Weekly had a camera." A seasoned, open-minded scholar, Carroll came to the logical conclusion that "it seems possible that a photo could have been taken then either with or without the knowledge of Crazy Horse." More crucial was yet another note by Will G. Robinson on the Crazy Horse picture question. "Robinson claims," wrote Carroll, "that, second-hand, he has it that Billy Garnett told an old Indian named Fairweather that McGillicuddy [sic] was wrong about there being no picture of Crazy Horse."[652]

With the same open mind, we began our journey. We keep searching for another image showing the same identical backdrop (and carpet), and possibly also the elusive James H. Hamilton "No. 104. Crazy Horse" stereoscopic view. We are satisfied with the circumstantial evidence, the comparative analysis of the tintype, the affidavits and the testimonies we presented in support of the tintype as a true likeness of Crazy Horse. There are some modern Lakota who also believe that the Indian in the tintype is without question Crazy Horse. Writing little over a decade ago on the recently acquired small picture, Carl Rieckmann reported James "Putt" Thompson's "first chilling moment after obtaining the portrait – the time he showed it to his friends, Oglala Sioux artist Ed Two Bulls and his wife,

Lovey, descendants of the great chief. He says he figured they would be quite dubious about the tintype being Crazy Horse. First engaging them in conversation, he asked what they thought about the story the chief was afraid of what cameras might do to him and thus rejected ever having a photograph taken. 'He wasn't scared of a camera. He wasn't scared of anything,' the curator reports the couple told him. Then, Thompson drew the treasured portrait from its protective sleeve and showed it to them. 'It's him! It's him!' he says they both exclaimed."[653]

More than once, many years ago Steve Feraca said "no!" Knowing Steve, he certainly would have enjoyed reading these pages with his usual, critical eye. Perhaps, at long last he might have agreed with the case we presented. If not, he would have at least given the tintype the benefit of the doubt, softening his entrenched "nay" to a more open-minded "maybe." After all, as Dean O'Bannon once wrote, and Steve himself often stated, "Crazy Horse, in my opinion he was the greatest Sioux of them all, bar none."[654] Our book began with the supportive and encouraging words of Francis White Lance, Lakota historian and educator, author, and spiritual leader. A descendant of Crazy Horse, White Lance himself believes the tintype is indeed a photograph of the great Lakota patriot chief. And that is good enough for us. Crazy Horse, the quiet, modest, good looking Oglala war chief with piercing hazel eyes, light-skin, and long brown-hair, finally agreed to have his picture taken. The tintype is a picture of Crazy Horse.

"It does not matter where his body is now, for it is grass.
But where his spirit is, that is a good place to be."
Black Elk, speaking of Crazy Horse

About the Authors

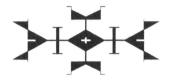

Cesare Marino is a veteran of the Italian Army, holds a Ph.D. in anthropology, and is retired from the *Handbook of North American Indians*, where he worked as a researcher, writer, and bibliographer. Has contributed articles to the Little Big Horn Associates *Research Review*, and published books on the Italians and the American Indians, including: *Dal Piave al Little Bighorn* (1996, 2010); *The Remarkable Carlo Gentile: Italian Photographer of the American Frontier* (1998); and *Along the Hudson and Mohawk* (2006, with Karim Tiro). A life-long student of Shotokan karate, he was senior instructor at the Alexandria YMCA, and taught a special karate course to youths at St. Francis Indian School, Rosebud Sioux Reservation, South Dakota. In 2014, he was a guest lecturer on American Indian history and culture at Rikkyo University, Tokyo. Cesare lives in Alexandria, Virginia.

Pietro Abiuso is a veteran of the Italian Army, and an engineer technician, retired from the U.S. Postal Service. As an amateur historian long interested in the American Indians, he conducted extensive archival and library research on Crazy Horse and the Plains Indian wars for more than thirty years. He has visited the West and the Crow and Sioux reservations many times and is particularly interested in their culture and the Battle of the Little Bighorn. His interview on the Crazy Horse tintype appeared on numerous newspapers, including *The Billings Gazette*. Pietro lives with his wife Teresa in West Palm Beach, Florida.

Francis White Lance (*Wapaha Ska*) is a member of the Oglala Lakota Sioux Tribe and a veteran of the U.S. Air Force. A tribal historian, he holds an Honorary Doctor of Letters degree, and a Master's of Theological Studies. Dr. White Lance is an associate instructor at Oglala Lakota College in Kyle, and serves as Cultural Coordinator and teacher at American Horse School in Allen. He has lectured extensively on Lakota history and culture, thought and philosophy. His publications include: *Why the Black Hills Are Sacred: A Unified Theory of the Lakota Sun Dance* (2004); *Tasunke Witko Woihamble: The Vision of Crazy Horse* (2007); and, *The Genealogy of Chief Crazy Horse* (2013). White Lance is a respected spiritual leader, Sun Dance leader, and *yuwipi* man. A descendant of chief Crazy Horse, he is the grandson of Daniel White Lance, a survivor of Wounded Knee. He is also the current leader of Crazy Horse's *Hoksi Hakata* (Last Born Child) Warrior Society. Francis lives with his wife Suzanne Fire Thunder and their children in Allen, South Dakota.

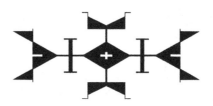

Endnotes

1   This introductory chapter is written in the first person by Cesare Marino, to relate how he crossed paths with Pietro Abiuso and why he wrote this joint-effort book.

2   Feraca retired from the BIA in 1985 after twenty five years of passionate and at times turbulent service. He died of lung cancer in Arlington, Virginia, shortly before his sixty-fifth birthday: C. Marino, "Stephen E. Feraca (1934-1999)." *European Review of Native American Studies*, Vol. 14, No. 1, 2000 p. 56. A more personal view is Jean Feraca, "My Brother/The Other." *The North American Review*, Vol. 292, No. 3 / 4, 2007, pp. 63-70.

3   Wounded Knee 1973, the tragic sequel of deaths, and the incarceration of Leonard Pelletier (Michael Apted's *Incident at Oglala*, 1992) evoke strong emotions among the Lakota and the wider American Indian community, generally sympathetic to the takeover: [The Editorial Collective], *Voices from Wounded Knee 1973 - In the Words of the Participants*. Akwesasne Notes, Mohawk Nation, N.Y., 1974. Among the dissenting voices, JoAnn Gildersleeve Feraca and others signed a letter against inaccuracies in Stanley Nelson's *Wounded Knee* documentary (2009), part of the PBS series *We Shall Remain*. A vast literature covers the event from different perspectives, and there is plenty on the web: Michael Getler, "Burying Some Questions at Wounded Knee." *PBS Ombudsman*, May 20, 2009. The historic site, owned by James A. Czywczynski who had bought it from the Gildersleeves in the 1960s, was recently offered for sale for some $4 million. The media had it that actor Johnny Depp, claiming Cherokee ancestry, was considering helping the Oglala Sioux Tribe with the purchase to ensure the site and surrounding lands return to the Lakota. As this book goes to press, no final sale has been made.

4   Charles "Chuck" Emery passed away in early 2009. He was born in 1930 on the Cheyenne River Indian Reservation. A former Marine and Korean War

veteran, Charles was married to Marie Janis Emery (Oglala). He is remembered as a kind and generous man who devoted his professional life to promoting American Indian education. An obituary appeared in the *Rapid City Journal*, Jan. 8, 2009.

5   Especially, by Feraca alone, "The Yuwipi Cult of the Oglala and Sicangu Teton Sioux." *Plains Anthropologist*, Vol. 6, No. 13, 1961, pp. 155-163; and, *Wakinyan: Contemporary Teton Dakota Religion*. Museum of the Plains Indian, Browning, Mont., 1963, based on his M.A. Thesis; revised and updated in 1998. And by Feraca and James H. Howard, "The Identity and Demography of the Dakota or Sioux Tribe." *Plains Anthropologist*, Vol. 8, No. 20, 1963, pp. 80-84; see also Steven E. Feraca, *Why Don't They Give Them Guns? The Great American Indian Myth*. University Press of America, Lanham, Md., 1990; S.E. Feraca, ed. *The Wounded Bear Winter Count, 1815-1816 [to] 1896-1897*. With Notations in Lakota. Lakota Books, Kendall Park, N.J. 1994.

6   The late Beatrice (Bea) Medicine (1924-2006) gave a poignant insider's view of the problem in *Drinking and Sobriety among the Lakota Sioux*. AltaMira Press, Lanham, Md., 2006.

7   Randy Emery is a CRM specialist and former Instructor in the Lakota Studies Department at Sinte Gleska University, Rosebud Indian Reservation, S.Dak. In 2007 Randy, with his father Chuck and other family members, donated to Oglala Lakota College some 300 audiotape recordings of Lakota songs, powwow music, and conversations with elders including Black Elk, Dewey Beard, and Fools Crow, collected by the late Jim Emery, Randy's grandfather, in 1950-1960.

8   [Comparative shapes and heights] in: *Progress: News from Crazy Horse Memorial Foundation*, Vol. XXVII, No. 1, April 2005, [p. 1].

9   Means cited by Chris Roberts, "The Progressive Interview: Russell Means." *The Progressive*, September 1, 2001.

10   Korczak Ziolkowski "Letter to Charles Dettborn, [dated] Oct. 5, 1955." Typescript, in Crazy Horse File, South Dakota State Historical Society, Pierre; copy in authors' possession.

11   Charles Dettborn, "Letter to Korczak Ziolkowski, [dated] Aug. 30, 1955." Handwritten, in Crazy Horse File, South Dakota State Historical Society, Pierre; copy in authors' possession.

12   Charles Dettborn, "Letter to Korczak Ziolkowski, [dated] 10/24/55"; handwritten, in Crazy Horse File, South Dakota State Historical Society, Pierre; copy in authors' possession.

13   Julie Schimmel and Robert R. White, *Bert Geer Phillips and the Taos Art Colony*. University of New Mexico Press, Albuquerque, 1994.

14   Korczak Ziolkowski "Letter to Charles Dettborn, [dated] Oct. 31, 1955"; Typescript, Crazy Horse File, South Dakota State Historical Society, Pierre; copy in authors' possession.

15   [USA 13c Crazy Horse] in: *Progress: News from Crazy Horse Memorial Foundation*, Vol. XXVII, No. 1, April 2005, p. 6.

16   As shown in a photograph in: *Progress: News from Sculptor Korczak Ziolkowski's Crazy Horse Mountain*, Vol. VIII, No. 1, 1986, p. 3.

17   Charles Trimble, "'What Did Crazy Horse Look Like?' With Sketch by Andrew Standing Soldier." *Indian Country Today*, July 28, 2005.

18   Editorial, "Praise of an epic dreamer still meaningful." *Progress: News from Crazy Horse Memorial Foundation*, Vol. XXXIV, Issue 2, Fall 2012, p.2.

19   Larry McMurtry, *Crazy Horse*. Viking, New York, 1999; Joan Morrison, "Crazy Horse: We May Never Know the Truth." *The Lakota Times*, Wed., Nov. 19, 1986, p. 3. As we discuss below, only now Crazy Horse's Mnicojou descendants have come forward, not without controversy *within* the Lakota community itself.

20   S.B.Oates on back cover of the Bison Books edition of Sandoz's *Crazy Horse*, 1961. Jack Heriard, "Debating Crazy Horse. Is this the photo of the famous Oglala?" *Whispering Wind*, Vol. 34, No. 3, 2004, p. 16, expressed similar praise: "Mari Sandoz [...] wrote the definitive biography of Crazy Horse." In 2007 her classic work was selected for the celebration "One Book One Nebraska" held at the Mari Sandoz High Plains Heritage Center, Chadron State College. Of value are Sandoz's historical and biographical manuscript notes now in the Special Collections at Oglala Lakota College. Together with the Eli S. Ricker and Eleanor H. Hinman papers at the Nebraska State Historical Society, Sandoz's notes form what Kingsley Bray, in the introductory pages of his *Crazy Horse: A Lakota Life*, University of Nebraska Press, Lincoln, 2006, calls "the tip of an iceberg of Lakota testimony on the man and his times." That testimony, which relied on the mediation and contribution of mixed-blood tribal members, was also utilized by Thomas Powers, *The Killing of Crazy Horse*. Alfred A. Knopf, New York, 2010.

21   Ibid., pp. 462, 534, Note 17.

22   JW Vaughn, *With Crook at the Rosebud*. Stackpole Books, Mechanicsburg, Pa., 1956; the "rare old tintype of Crazy Horse, never before published" is on plate facing p. 132; the transcript of Ellen Howard's affidavit of authenticity and permission to publish is on p. 46; see also pp. 40-43.

23 Steve Feraca, "Crazy Horse: The Enigmatic Sioux." *Frontier Times*, Dec. [1963]-Jan. 1964, p. 62 [pp. 14-15, 62-64.]

24 Ibid. p. 63.

25 Specifically, on the knife, an interesting sequel is: John P. Scheiwe and Karin A. Scheiwe, *Crazy Horse's Knife: Background and Provenance*. [Privately printed], Canyon Lake, Tex, 2006. Camp Robinson was renamed "Fort" in 1878; see Roger T. Grange, Jr. "Fort Robinson, Outpost on the Plains." *Nebraska History*, Vol. 39, No. 3, 1958, pp. 191-240; Thomas R. Buecker, *Fort Robinson and the American West, 1874-1899*. Nebraska State Historical Society, Lincoln, 1999; Ephriam D. Dickson, III, *Fort Robinson*. Arcadia Publishing, Charleston, S.C., 2010.

26 Carroll Friswold, *The Killing of Chief Crazy Horse: Three Eyewitness Views by the Indian, Chief He Dog, the Indian-white, William Garnett, the White Doctor, Valentine McGillycuddy*. Edited, with an Introduction, by Robert A. Clark, The Arthur H. Clark Co., Glendale, Calif., 1976; reprinted, University of Nebraska Press, Lincoln, 1988: this latter edition we cite throughout.

27 Ibid. pp. 46-47.

28 In 1976, a commemorative medallion, 2.75 inches in diameter, was issued by the Medallic Art Company of Danbury, Conn., to mark the 100th anniversary of the Battle of the Little Bighorn. The medal featured on the obverse the idealized profiles of Sitting Bull and Crazy Horse, and full face of Gall; on the reverse it showed two victorious Indians on horseback, one holding a broken 7th Cavalry guidon, and the writing (top) "Cheyenne * Sioux * Arapahoe," and (bottom) "1876-1976 Defeated the 7th Cavalry Lt. Col. G.A. Custer Comdr. June 25 Greasy Grass Mont. Terr."

29 Edward Kadlececk and Mabell Kadlececk, *To Kill an Eagle: Indian Views on the Death of Crazy Horse*. Johnson Books, Boulder, Colo, 1981.

30 Jason Hook, *American Indian Chiefs: Tecumseh, Crazy Horse, Chief Joseph, Geronimo*. Plates by Richard Hook. Firebird Books, Poole, Dorset, U.K., 1989.

31 Ibid., pp. [50], 93.

32 Editorial, "Is This Crazy Horse?" *Indian Country Today*, July 2-15, 1996, p. B1. Tom Buecker, "Crazy Horse: The Search for the Elusive (and Improbable) Photo of Famous Oglala Chief." *Greasy Grass Magazine*, Vol. 14, May 1998, pp. 33-34, Fig. 6.

33 Frank H. Goodyear, III, *Red Cloud: Photographs of a Lakota Chief*. University of Nebraska Press, Lincoln, 2003, pp. 19-27. The portraits were collected in: Photographs of Red Cloud and Principal Chiefs of Dacotah [sic]

Indians taken on their Visit to Washington, D.C., May 1872, by Alexander Gardner for Trustees of Blackmore Museum, Salisbury, England; see Anthony Hamber, *Collecting the American West: The Rise and Fall of William Blackmore*. The Hobnob Press, East Knoyle, Salisbury, U.K., 2010.

34   Richard Jepperson, "A Portrait of Chief Crazy Horse: The Challenge"; posted on Monday, June 04, 2001: *http://www.authorsden.com/visit/viewArticle. asp?id=1358.*

35   Vittorio Zucconi, *Gli spiriti non dimenticano*. A. Mondadori, Milano, 1996. To be noted that there is no mention in Zucconi's recounting of the ceremony held by Marvin Helper, of the key element of a truly *yuwipi* ritual, the tying-up and freeing of the *yuwipi wičaša* by the spirits.

36   James Hagengruber, "Man without a face: Mystery continues in hunt for image of Chief Crazy Horse." *Billings Gazette*, Sunday, Nov. 16, 2003.

37   Paula Richardson Fleming and Judith Lynn Luskey, *The North American Indians in Early Photographs*. Harper and Row, New York, 1986; by the same co-authors, *Grand Endeavors of American Indian Photography*. Smithsonian Institution Press, Washington, 1993; and by Paula R. Fleming, *Native American Photography at the Smithsonian: The Shindler Catalogue*. Smithsonian Books, Washington and London, 2003.

38   The Edward Clown Family, as told to William B. Matson, *Crazy Horse: The Lakota Warrior's Life & Legacy*. Gibbs Smith Publ., Layton, Utah, 2016.

39   David Melmer, "New DVD Release Presents the Contested Story of Crazy Horse." *Indian Country Today*, May 21, 2007.

40   Francis White Lance, *Tasunke Witko Woihanble – The Vision of Crazy Horse*. [Pine Ridge, S.Dak., privately printed], 2007, [unpaged, pp. 2-3].

41   Jack Heriard, "Debating Crazy Horse. Is This the Photo of the Famous Oglala?" *Whispering Wind*, Vol. 34, No. 3, 2004, p. 16.

42   Earl A. Brininstool, *A Trooper with Custer*. Hunter-Trader-Trapper Co., Columbus, Ohio, 1925; revised and expanded under new title: *Troopers with Custer*. Stackpole Co., Harrisburg, Penn., 1952, 1989.

43   Editorial "Is There a Picture of Crazy Horse?" *Wi'iyohi*, Vol. I, No. VI, Sept. 1, 1947, pp. 1-2. Pierre, S.Dak.

44   Will G. Robinson, "Letter to Mr. Olson, Oct. 4th, 1947." Typescript, in Crazy Horse File, South Dakota State Historical Society, Pierre; copy in authors' possession.

45   Rudy White Buffalo, "Letter to Mr. Robinson, La Plant, S.D., November 29-47." Handwritten, in Crazy Horse File, South Dakota State Historical Society, Pierre; copy in authors' possession.

46   Henry Standing Bear, "Letter to Mr. Will G. Robinson, Tulsa, Okla. Dec. 1ˢᵗ, 1947." Handwritten, in Crazy Horse File, South Dakota State Historical Society, Pierre; copy in authors' possession.

47   Will G. Robinson, "Letter to: Ethel Merrival, Pine Ridge, S.Dakota, 2/27/53." Typescript, in Crazy Horse File, South Dakota State Historical Society, Pierre; copy in authors' possession.

48   Will G. Robinson, "Letter to Charles Dettborn of Tacoma, Wash., March 3, 1956." Typescript, in Crazy Horse File, South Dakota State Historical Society, Pierre; copy in authors' possession.

49   Robinson to Bordeaux, *Letter.*

50   Feraca, "Crazy Horse," p. 14.

51   Buecker, "Crazy Horse," p. 32; also, Heriard, "Debating," p. 23.

52   Martin Knifechief in "Debating Crazy Horse: Commentary." *Whispering Wind*, Vol. 34, No. 4, 2004.

53   Cited by Will G. Robinson, "Letter to Miss Marie [sic] Sandoz, Sept. 30, 1947"; typescript, in Crazy Horse File, South Dakota State Historical Society, Pierre; copy in authors' possession. Zoe "Geo" Laravie (1862-1950) married noted cattleman and rancher James E. "Cornie" Utterback in 1879; a photograph and biographical sketch of Zoe 'Geo' Utterback is in Donovin A. Sprague, *Rosebud Sioux.* Arcadia Publ., Charleston, S.C., 2005, p. 11.

54   Mari Sandoz, *Crazy Horse. The Strange Man of the Oglalas.* University of Nebraska Press, Lincoln, 1961 [1942], p. 370.

55   Bob Lee, "Historian: Crazy Horse Was Scout for the Cavalry." *Capital Journal*, July 28, 1992.

56   V.T. McGillycuddy, "Letter to Wm. Garnett, February 28, 1922," in C. Friswold, *The Killing*, p. 108.

57   [William Garnett] "Letter to Mr. V.T. McGillicuddy [sic], March 6, 1922," in C. Friswold, *The Killing*, pp. 109-110.

58   V.T. M'G., "Letter to Friend Garnett, May 10ᵗʰ, 1926," in C. Friswold, *The Killing,* pp. 117-118.

59   Candy Moulton, *Valentine T. McGillycuddy: Army Surgeon, Agent to the Sioux.* University of Oklahoma Press, Norman, 2011, p. 104.

60   V.T. M'Gillycuddy, "Letter to Friend Garnett, April 15th, 1926," in C. Friswold, *The Killing*, p. 113.

61   "Letter from Dr. V.T. McGillycuddy, Physician Who Attended Crazy Horse at Ft. Robinson [etc.]," in: "Crazy Horse Photo at the Custer Museum," *http://lbha.org.proboards*, 2005.

62   Julia B. McGillycuddy, *McGillycuddy Agent: A Biography of Dr. Valentine T. McGillycuddy*. Stanford University Press, Stanford, Calif. 1941; especially the chapter "The Killing of Crazy Horse," pp. 65-87; also, Candy Moulton, *Valentine T. McGillycuddy*, especially the chapter "Crazy Horse," pp. 119-141.

63   Denis McLoughlin, *Wild and Woolly: An Encyclopedia of the Old West*. Doubleday, Garden City, 1975, p. 118, Note 78.

64   Thomas Powers, *The Killing*, p. 439.

65   Thomas Buecker, "Crazy Horse," pp. 29-30.

66   "No Picture of Crazy Horse Exists," McGillycuddy in Brininstool, "Chief Crazy Horse, His Career and Death," p. 42.

67   Ibid.

68   Brininstool, ed., *Crazy Horse*, p. 11: "Crazy Horse was never photographed. He steadfastly refused to allow any pictures of himself to be taken. D.F. Barry, the noted photographer of Indian life, *told me in 1926 he had repeatedly tried to bribe Crazy Horse to sit for his photograph, but the chief could not be bribed*. It is regrettable that no photograph of this mighty warrior and great Sioux leader is in existence" [emphasis added].

69   "E.A. Brininstool letter to Will Robinson, [dated] Los Angeles, August 1st, 1947"; typescript, Crazy Horse File, South Dakota State Historical Society, Pierre; copy in authors' possession.

70   Buecker, "Crazy Horse," p. 29.

71   Thomas W. Wright, *The Evidence on the Photographs "Identified" as Crazy Horse*. Typescript, [1962], p. 7. Thomas W. Wright Papers, R.G. 1578.AM, Nebraska State Historical Society, Lincoln; copy in authors' possession.

72   John S. Gray, "Itinerant Frontier Photographers and Images Lost, Strayed or Stolen." *Montana: The Magazine of Western History*, Vol. 28, No. 2, 1978, p. 15.

73   Thomas M. Heski, *'Icastinyanka Cikala Hanzi': The Little Shadow Catcher. D.F. Barry, Celebrated Photographer of Famous Indians*. Superior Publ. Co., Seattle, Wash., 1978, p. 21.

74   "Will G. Robinson, Letter to William J. Bordeaux, [dated] October 26th, 1951"; typescript, Crazy Horse File, South Dakota State Historical Society, Pierre; copy in authors' possession.

75   Robert R. Wellington, quoted in: Thomas W. Wright, *The evidence,* pp. 13-14.

76   John L. Smith, in "Debating Crazy Horse: Commentary." *Whispering Wind*, Vol. 34, No. 4, (July-August) 2004.

77   Amos Bad Heart Bull, *A Pictographic History of the Oglala Sioux*, edited by Helen H. Blish. University of Nebraska Press, Lincoln, 1967.

78   "Alleged Ta'Sunke Witko Photo": *http://www.dckshovel.com/Allegedphoto.html*

79   "Welcome from Joseph M. Marshall, III": *http://www.thunderdreamers.com*

80   Joseph M. Marshall, III, "A Battle Won and a War Lost: A Lakota Perspective," in *Legacy: New Perspectives on the Battle of the Little Bighorn*. Charles E. Rankin, ed. Montana Historical Society Press, Helena, 1996, p. 115.

81   [Wm. Garnett], "Letter to Dr. V.T. McGillycuddy, dated April 21, 1926," in C. Friswold, *The Killing*, p. 115.

82   For example, "Alleged Ta'Sunke Witko Photo": *http://www.disckshovel.com/Allegedphoto.html*

83   Eleanor Hinman, comp. "Oglala Sources on the Life of Crazy Horse." *Nebraska History*, Vol. 57, No. 1, 1976, p. 41; frontispiece, the Brule He Dog, *supra,* is mistakenly identified as the Oglala.

84   *Crazy Horse Memorial Progress*, Winter 2015, p. 12.

85   Will G. Robinson, "Letter to Mrs. Helen A. Bowser, dated April 29, 1957." Original in State Historical Society Memorial Hall, Pierre, S.Dak.; copy in authors' possession.

86   Joseph M. Marshall, III, "Great Chiefs: Tasunke Witko (His Crazy Horse)." *Native Peoples, Arts & Lifeway*, Vol. 20, No. 1, 2009, pp. 76-79.

87   Alice Beck Kehoe, *The Kensington Runestone: Approaching a Research Question Holistically*. Waveland Press, Long Grove, Ill., 2005.

88   Paul I. Hedren, *After Custer: Loss and Transformation in Sioux Coutry*. University of Oklahoma Press, Norman, 2011.

89   There is a posthumous portrait of Tecumseh by Benjamin J. Lossing based on sketch of the Shawnee chief made from life in 1808 by Pierre Le Dru, a young French fur trader of Vincennes. Notable exceptions to the faceless theme

include, prominently, Joseph Brant (*Thayendanega*, 1742-1807), leader of the Iroquois loyalists in the Revolutionary War, portrayed by famous artists of his time, partly because of his political and military fame and partly because he had adopted much of British colonial culture. There is also a portrait by George Catlin of Osceola (a.k.a. Billy Powell, 1804-1838), the mixed-blood Seminole chief who in 1835-1837 waged a war of resistance against the removal of his people to Indian Territory. Osceola was captured by deceit during a peace parlay with Gen. Thomas S. Jesup and died in prison of malaria shortly thereafter.

90   Charles A. Eastman, *Indian Heroes and Chieftains*. Little, Brown, Boston, 1918, p. 95.

91   Photographed in his old age at Rosebud by John Anderson; Claes H. Jacobson, *Rosebud Sioux: A Lakota People in Transition*, Jacobson Produktion, Stockholm, Sweden, 2004, pp. 134-137; see also Jacobson's article in *Wild West*, October 2009.

92   "He Dog. Photo taken in Washington, DC in 1877," in Hardorff, *The Death*, p. 116.

93   J. Hook, *American Indian*, p. 85.

94   No. 61 "Rare, unpublished Alexander Gardner cabinet card of Big Foot and Wife, Miniconjou Sioux," *Cowan's Auctions, Dec. 6th and 7th, 2007*, prev. cit.; already known were individual portraits of Big Foot and his wife in the same sitting.

95   W.H. Jackson, comp., *Descriptive Catalogue of Photographs of North American Indians*. Miscellaneous Publications No. 9. Government Printing Office, Washington, 1877.

96   "Eagle Hawk Narrative," in Hardorff, *The Death*, p. 134.

97   There are several editions, with slightly different titles, of Catlin's original 2 vols., *Letters and Notes on the Manners, Customs, and Condition of the North American Indians*. Published by the Author, London, 1841, 1844, etc.: One Horn's story and portrait are on p. 211 and Plate 86. See also William H. Truettner, *The Natural Man Observed: A Study of Catlin's Indian Gallery*. Smithsonian Institution Press, Washington, 1979.

98   Feraca, *The Wounded Bear*, p. 9.

99   Hinman, "Oglala Sources," p. 40.

100   Robert H. Ruby, *The Oglala Sioux: Warriors in Transition*. New Introduction by Cary C. Collins. University of Nebraska Press, Lincoln, 2010, p. 98. Originally published in 1955.

101   Catlin, *Letters and Notes*, Vol. 2, pp. 193-194.

102   Compare the testimonies of True Clown, Sr., Elaine Quick Bear Quiver, Ellen in the Woods, and Joe Swift Bird in Mario Gonzalez and Elizabeth Cook-Lynn, *The Politics of Hallowed Ground: Wounded Knee and the Struggle for Indian Sovereignty.* University of Illinois Press, Urbana, 1999, pp. 188-190.

103   Ephriam D. Dickson, III, "Crazy Horse's Grave: A Photograph by Private Charles Howard, 1877." *Little Big Horn Associates Newsletter*, Vol. XL, No. 1, Feb. 2006, pp. 4-5; and, "A New Photograph of Crazy Horse's Grave." *Little Big Horn Associates Newsletter*, Vol. XLIII, No. 3, April 2009, pp. 4-5.

104   T. Powers, *The Killing*, p. 436.

105   Hardorff, *The Death*, p. 87.

106   "Nebraska – The Late Chief Crazy Horse – The Elevated Grave Near Camp Sheridan." *Frank Leslie's Illustrated Magazine*, October 20, 1877, p. 108.

107   Marc H. Abrams, "St. George Stanley and the Great Sioux War." *Research Review: The Journal of the Little Big Horn Associates*, Vol. 23, No. 1, 2009, p. 5 [pp. 2-10, 29-31].

108   Bray, *Crazy Horse*, pp. 393-394.

109   "The Death of Crazy Horse." *The New York Sun*, Sept. 14, 1877, in Handorff, *The Death*, p. 243.

110   A large reproduction of this second photo, captioned "Crazy Horse Grave. October 1877. Another view by photographer Charles Howard" is in Paul L. Hedren, "Camp Sheridan, Nebraska: The Uncommonly Quiet Post on Beaver Creek." *Nebraska History*, Vol. 91, No. 2, 2010, p. 87 [pp. 80-93]. In Thomas R. Buecker's book, below, Pvt. C. Howard's second view captioned "Grave of Crazy Horse" is reproduced with editorial notes at pp. 194-195.

111   Thomas R. Buecker, *Last Days of Red Cloud Agency. Peter T. Buckley's Photograph Collection, 1876-1877.* Nebraska State Historical Society, Lincoln, 2016.

112   Goodyear, *Red Cloud*.

113   Grahamew, "John Hauser," posts, Jan.-Dec. 2011 *http://amertribes. proboards.com/index.cgi?board=artists&action=display&thread=1154*

114   Grahamew, "John Hauser," posts cited.

115   Dickson, "Photographers," p. 4.

116   In 1847 Easterly took a daguerreotype of Sac and Fox Chief *Keokuk* (The Watchful Fox, 1767-1848), who had been painted by Catlin in 1835. Twelve

years separate the two images, so at first the facial features seem hardly a match. At a closer look, however, the similarity is there, thanks also to the presence in both the portrait and the photo of the chief's goatee, ear decorations, and an impressive bear-claw necklace. Both likenesses were taken in St. Louis, Missouri. Later photographed in a daguerreotype also by Easterly. For side by side comparison see John C. Ewers, "Thomas M. Easterly's Pioneer Daguerreotypes of Plains Indians." *Bulletin of the Missouri Historical Society*, Vol. 24, No. 2, 1968, pp. 329-339. Easterly also photographed Iowa chief No Heart of Fear (*Notchimine*, 1797-1862) whose portrait had been painted by Charles Bird King in Washington in 1837.

117   W.H. Jackson joined the U.S. Government Survey of the Western Territories led by Ferdinand Vandeveer Hayden, and later published his *Descriptive Catalogue of Photographs of North American Indians.* Miscellaneous Publications No. 9. Government Printing Office, Washington, 1877. For this important compilation of early American Indian photographs, many of them Sioux, Jackson tapped both government and private sources, including the large collection of images assembled by English philanthropist and amateur ethnologist William Henry Blackmore. Blackmore's collection included works by Jackson himself, and the other photographers just mentioned.

118   In an anthology of pioneer photography in the West from the early daguerreotype "only" to the end of the Civil War, Peter Palmquist and Thomas Kailbourn compiled biographical sketches of several hundred photographers and individuals associated with photography; Peter E. Palmquist and Thomas R. Kailbourn, *Pioneer Photographers from the Mississippi to the Continental Divide: A Biographical Dictionary, 1839-1865.* Stanford University Press, Stanford, Calif., 2005. A truly impressive listing.

119   Quoted by Fleming and Luskey, *The North American Indians*, p. 16.

120   Paula Fleming, "Ridgway Glover." *Annals of Wyoming*, Vol. 74, No. 2, 2002, pp. 17-27.

121   For example, Feraca, *The Wounded Bear*, p. 13.

122   Citations are from Paula Fleming's article that quotes extensively from Ridgway Glover's own, "Photography among the Indians, Fort Laramie, June 30, 1866." *Philadelphia Photographer*, No. 3, August 1866, pp. 239-240, and other Glover's letters to the same professional magazine.

123   *Pejuta sapa*, herbal roots, "medicine"; "black" hence poisonous or "bad," as in the text.

124   Fleming, "Ridgway Glover," p. 23.

125   "Obituary." *Philadelphia Photographer*, No. 3, August 29, 1866, p. 371, in Fleming, "Ridgway Glover," p. 24.

126   Fleming, ibid. p. 27.

127   Bray, *Crazy Horse*, p. 97.

128   Dee Brown and Martin F. Schmitt, *Fighting Indians of the West*. Ballantine Books, New York, 1974/75, p. 30.

129   Raymond J. DeMallie, "Scenes in the Indian Country." *Montana: The Magazine of Western History*, Vol. XXXI, No. 3, 1981, p. 48; also, D. Mark Katz, *Witness to an Era: The Life and Photographs of Alexander Gardner*. Viking, New York, 1991.

130   DeMallie, "Scenes," p. 48.

131   Reproduced in Brown and Schmitt, *Fighting Indians,* p. 94; the caption refers to Custer, "the Thieves' Road," and monetary compensation for the Black Hills, all subsequent to the Laramie Treaty of '68, where the picture was taken.

132   DeMallie, "Scenes," p. 48.

133   Ibid., pp. 57-59, figs. 21-24.

134   Catherine, again, points out that Roman Nose was in fact "Roaming Nose," also known as "Frog," hence one and the same, as previously Worm and Woman Breast. Catherine, re: "Crazy Horse Genealogy," post on Dec. 19, 2006: *http://www.lbha.proboards12.com*

135   Kingsley M. Bray, "Lone Horn's Peace: A New View of Sioux-Crow Relations, 1851-1858." *Nebraska History*, Vol. 66, No. 1, 1985, pp. 28-47.

136   Reproduced, partially cropped, as front and half-back covers in Donovin A. Sprague, *Cheyenne River Sioux, South Dakota*. Arcadia Publishing, Charleston, S.C., 2003, and in full on p.16. In another 1868 Gardner photograph, Lone Horn is with Pipe, Grass, and Young Elk.

137   An interesting on-line exchange in the already cited "Crazy Horse Genealogy" thread deals with the origin, mistranslation, etc., of the name "Roman Nose." Echoing what Catherine had said, Brock wrote on Jan. 23, 2007: "I can't believe that a Lakota would choose a name that says he has the same nose as the people who live in the capital of Italy [...] the name makes no sense for a Lakota or even a Cheyenne. [...] The name was Roaming Nose, meaning going to other camps [...] and sticking your nose in their business. How do I know? I went to the rez and asked." Shatonska, same day, replied: "Roman Nose is related to the aquiline shape of the nose, ancient Romans had a big curved nose, that's the origin of that word, in Italy we use the word aquiline not

Roman for such noses. Probably the translators used Roman to explain [etc.]." Brock remained unconvinced on account of what he claimed was widespread illiteracy among mixed-blood translators, and Shatonska came back with other anatomical names such as Big Foot, the use of sign language, and the Cheyenne Roman Nose's own native name, meaning "aquiline or maybe big." The latter statement is supported by the pictographic list of Northern Cheyenne names drawn by Daniel Little Chief in 1891 in which *Vooxénéhe* is translated as "Roman Nose" with the corresponding pictograph showing a profile aquiline nose; see *HNAI*, Vol. 17 "Languages," Ives Goddard, vol. ed. Smithsonian Institution, Washington, 1996, p. 28, Fig. 3. Roman Nose, *"Pa-sko-pe-win,"* as a woman's name, was also reported in Ephriam D. Dickson, III, ed., *The Sitting Bull Surrender Census: The Lakotas at Standing Rock Agency, 1881*. South Dakota State Historical Society Press, Pierre, 2010, p. 144.

138   John H. Monnett, *The Battle of Beecher Island and the Indian War of 1867-1868*. University Press of Colorado, Boulder, 1992.

139   John Koster, "Roman Nose, Knight-Errant in a War Bonnet." *Wild West*, Vol. 23, No. 2, Aug. 2010, p. 31 [pp. 28-35].

140   White Lance, *Tasunke Witko*, [unpaged, p. 4].

141   "The White Bull Interview," in Richard G. Hardorff, comp. and ed., *Cheyenne Memories of the Custer Fight*. University of Nebraska Press, Lincoln 1998, p. 37 [pp. 37-40].

142   After the great village was forced by logistics and the approaching column of Gen. Alfred H. Terry and Col. John Gibbon to disperse, the Cheyenne crossed into Wyoming. There, in late November 1876, the large camp of Dull Knife and Little Wolf, totaling some 173 lodges, was attacked by Col. Ranald S. Mackenzie. Under constant pressure, in April 1877, Two Moon and his band surrendered at Fort Keogh, Montana, while Little Wolf and Dull Knife preceded Crazy Horse at Camp Robinson. Little Wolf, Dull Knife, and their bands soon experienced a great ordeal. Forcibly removed to Indian Territory, they found unwelcoming southern kinsmen, unhealthy climate, disease and hunger. A year later, in early September 1878, they escaped back north, traveling some 400 miles with the soldiers in hot pursuit. The two bands split. Little Wolf headed towards Montana where he surrendered in March 1879 and was eventually allowed to remain there. Dull Knife's people fared the worst. They surrendered at Fort Robinson in October 1878, but upon their refusal to return to Oklahoma they were imprisoned under harsh conditions. In early January 1879, Dull Knife and his people tried to escape; in the attempt, many women and children were killed and others recaptured. Dull Knife himself and a handful of his immediate

family were able to reach the newly established Red Cloud's Pine Ridge Agency, where descendants still live. Only after American public opinion rose in their defense, were some eighty remnants of this once powerful band permitted to rejoin their northern kinsmen on the Tongue River Reservation, Montana, established in 1884. The *Tséstsestahse* heroic struggle for survival was later recounted in *Cheyenne Autumn*, another epic work by Mari Sandoz.

143   Hardorff, *The Death*, pp. 79, 196, 199; Bray, *Crazy Horse*, pp. 177-178.

144   Garrick Mallery, "Picture-writing of the American Indians." *10th Annual Report of the Bureau of Ethnology*, 1888-'89. Government Printing Office, Washington, 1893, pp. 445-446, 450.

145   Mari Sandoz, "There Were *Two* Sitting Bulls." *Blue Book Magazine*, Vol. 90, Nov. 1949, pp. 58-64. C.J. Kappler, comp., *Treaties*. GPO, Washington, 1904, pp, 1004, 1006.

146   Dickson, *The Sitting Bull Surrender*, p. 24.

147   Ibid.; see also Diane Merkel and Dietmar Schulte-Möhring, "Crazy Dog," 2009: *http://www.American-Tribes.com*

148   Harry H. Anderson, "The War Club of Sitting Bull the Oglala." *Nebraska History*, Vol. 42, No. 1, 1961, pp. 55-62; reprinted in: R. Eli Paul, ed. *The Nebraska Indian Wars Reader, 1865-1877*. University of Nebraska Press, Lincoln, 1998, pp. 122-127.

149   "Julius Meyer in front of his store at 163 Farnam Street, Omaha, Nebraska, about 1875"; photograph No. 4924, Nebraska State Historical Society, Lincoln.

150   "Indian Wigwam" advertisement: *http://www.antiquephotographics.com/images/ForSale/Indians2*

151   William Garnett was born in 1855 and died in 1930; see John Koster, "The Son of a Confederate General and a Lakota Woman, Billy Garnett Was a Man in the Middle," *Wild West*, Vol. 27, No. 2, August 2014, pp. 18-19.

152   Goodyear, Red Cloud, pp. 26-29, figs. 10, 11; Jim Linderman, *The Painted Backdrop: Behind the Sitter in American Tintype Photography 1860-1920*. Dull Tool Dim Bulb Books, 2010.

153   Grange, "Fort Robinson," p. 204; Charles W. Allen, "Red Cloud and the U.S. Flag." *Nebraska History*, Vol. 21, No. 4, 1940, pp. 293-304; reprinted in: R. Eli Paul, ed., *Indian Wars*, pp. 113-121; see also Randy Kane, "The 'Flagpole Affair' at Red Cloud Agency. An Incident in the Cultural Transition of the Oglala Lakota." *Nebraska History*, Vol. 97, No. 3, 2016, pp. 117-126.

154   The effigy weapon was identified by John Ewers as "a long wooden war club bearing the carved head of a snake, and the pattern of a writhing snake's body executed in brass tacks is carried down the handle. This snake effigy may be unique, but the wooden war club armed with three parallel knives set into the side of the handle was not. Because of its deadly striking power, the snake effigy made a very appropriate war medicine." John C. Ewers, *Plains Indian Sculpture: A Traditional Art Form from America's Heartland*. Smithsonian Institution Press, Washington, 1986, p. 134.

155   Sprague, *Pine Ridge*, p. 61; Dickson, *Fort Robinson*, p. 24.

156   Dickson, ibid. photo and quote; also Ephriam D. Dickson, III, "Capturing the Lakota Spirit: Photographers at the Red Cloud & Spotted Tail Agencies." *Nebraska History*, Vol. 88, Nos. 1-2, 2007, p. 6.

157   Fred Eggan and Joseph A. Maxwell, "Kinship," in *HNAI*, Vol. 13, "Plains," Pt. 2, pp. 974-982.

158   Hassrick, *The Sioux*, p.106; we inserted the Lakota equivalents from James R. Walker, "Oglala Kinship Terms." *American Anthropologist*, Vol. 16, No. 1, 1914, pp. 96-109.

159   Kingsley Bray, "'We Belong to the North': The Flights of the Northern Indians from the White River Agencies, 1877-1878." *Montana: The Magazine of Western History*, Vol. 55, No. 3, 2005, pp. 28-47.

160   Cowan's Auctions "CDV of Red Bear, Sioux Chief, Probably Oglala." Auction, June 5-6, 2008. With note: *http://www.cowanauctions.com/auctions/itemn. aspx?Itemid=60459*. The same image was originally listed as "No. 71. Red Bear and family" in C. Howard's *Views: In the Black Hills, Military Posts, Department Platte and Indian Camps, &c.*, ca. 1878. Since the auctioned image bears the imprint "Howard, Fort Sanders, Wyoming Ty." Dickson thinks "it would have been printed between 1878, when Howard arrived at Fort Sanders, and 1880, when he was discharged from the army."

161   Side-by-side reproduction of silver certificate and Running Antelope in Raymond J. DeMallie, "Sioux Until 1850," *HNAI* Vol. 13 "Plains," Vol. 2, p. 732; see also Forrest W. Daniel, "Running Antelope – Misnamed Onepapa." *Paper Money*, Vol. 8, No. 1, Whole No. 29, 1969, pp. 4-9.

162   Ironically, the headdress used as a model was actually a Pawnee museum specimen. Both the buffalo nickel and the $5 silver certificate are today eagerly sought by numismatic and Western Americana collectors. As is also the old $10 gold coin featuring an eagle feather war bonnet adorning a non-Indian female face profile.

163   John Neihardt, *Black Elk Speaks: The Complete Edition.* University of Nebraska Press, Lincoln, 2014, p. 54.

164   "Billy Hunter Garnett Interview," typescript to Gen. Hugh L. Scott and Maj. James McLaughlin, signed by Garnett dated Pine Ridge Agency, S.D., August 19, 1920.

165   "Battiste [Baptise] Good's Winter Count": in Garrick Mallery, "Picture-writing," p. 327.

166   "Chips Interview," in Hardorff, *The Death*, p. 77.

167   Allen C. Ross-Ehanamani, *The Hero: A Comparison of Chief Crazy Horse and Field Marshal Rommel.* Wiconi Waste Publ., Denver, 2003.

168   DeMallie, "Teton," *HNAI*, Vol. 13, "Plains," Pt. 2, p. 803. Women too had their own sodalities; Marla Powers, *Oglala Women: Myth, Ritual, and Reality.* University of Chicago Press, Chicago, 1986.

169   Eli S. Ricker, "[Charles A. Eastman's Interview, Tablet 11, Tuesday, August 20, 1907]." *The Indian Interviews*, p. 286.

170   White Lance, *Tasunke Witko*, [unpaged, p. 35].

171   Juri Abe is History Professor at Rikkyo University, Tokyo. She has visited Fort Robinson and done extensive fieldwork among the Lakota, especially at Rosebud. Here we quote from her article, originally written in Japanese: "Do You Know General Nozu? To a Far Away Land, Fascinated by the Hero of the Native Americans." *Asai Shinbun*, 2d ed., 25 September 2001 (Heisei 13), Tokyo.

172   Candace S. Green and Russell Thornton, eds., *The Year the Stars Fell: Lakota Winter Counts at the Smithsonian.* Smithsonian Institution, 2007, pp. 126, 136, 232.

173   S. Vestal, *Sitting Bull*, p. 84.

174   Michael Samuel, "Crazy Horse Info." Email to Custer Battlefield Museum, [dated] March 12, 2006; copy in authors' possession.

175   Hardorff, *The Death*, p. 85.

176   These *wičaša yatápika*, "men praiseworthy" were to embody the principles of rectitude, generosity, altruism, courage and wisdom, pillars of the Lakota ideal of manhood. Their badge of office were human hair-decorated buckskin shirts. In the summer 1868, Crazy Horse moved his lodge from the Bad Face and Oyuhpe militant camps under Red Cloud and Red Dog, who had not yet signed the Laramie Treaty, to the village of the more conciliatory Old Man Afraid of His Horse, on the south fork of the Cheyenne River. There, *Tašunke Witko*, son of Worm, along with American Horse, son of Sitting Bear and son-in-law of

Red Cloud; Young Man Afraid of His Horse, son of Old Man; and Sword Owner, son of Brave Bear, were chosen as Shirt Wearers (*OgletankaUun*) of the Oglala; see Sandoz, *Crazy Horse,* pp. 176-178; Bray, *Crazy Horse,* pp. 119-125; see also Hassrick, *The Sioux,* pp. 7, 26-28, et seq.; Hyde, *Red Cloud's,* pp. 309-310.

177   He Dog in Hinman, "Oglala Sources," p. 18.

178   Bray, *Crazy Horse,* pp. 172-173.

179   Photo reproduced in Sprague, *Pine Ridge,* p. 15.

180   Bray, *Crazy Horse,* p. 424, note 3.

181   Jesse Lee in E.A. Brininstool, *Crazy Horse,* pp. 39-40.

182   William J. Bordeaux, *Custer's Conqueror.* Sioux Falls, S.Dak., Smith and Co., 1952, p. 94.

183   Major H.R. Lemly cited in Brininstool, *Crazy Horse,* p. 51.

184   On Victoria Standing Bear Conroy see Sprague, *Rosebud Sioux,* pp. 68, 118; "The Conroy Letter, 1934," in Hardorff, *The Death,* pp. 265-267, 270-271.

185   Richard G. Hardorff, *The Oglala Lakota Crazy Horse.* J.M. Carroll, Mattituck, N.Y., 1985, p. 30.

186   "The Second Chips Interview," in Hardorff, *The Death,* p. 86.

187   Eli S. Ricker, *The Settler and Soldier Interviews of Eli S. Ricker, 1903-1919.* Richard E. Jensen, ed., University of Nebraska Press, Lincoln, 2005, p. 271.

188   Ibid.

189   Eli S. Ricker, *The Indian Interviews of Eli S. Ricker, 1903-1919.* Richard E. Jensen, ed., University of Nebraska Press, Lincoln, 2005, p. 117.

190   R.A. Clark in Friswold, *The Killing,* p. 27.

191   White Bull in Stanley Vestal, *Warpath: The True Story of the Fighting Sioux Told in a Biography of Chief White Bull,* Houghton Mifflin Co., Boston, 1934, p. 182; White Bull, instead, was "a tireless talker."

192   Joe DeBarthe, *Life and Adventures of Frank Grouard.* Combe Printing Co., St. Joseph, Mo., 1894.

193   Thomas R. Buecker and R. Eli Paul, eds., *The Crazy Horse Surrender Ledger.* Nebraska State Historical Society, Lincoln, 1994.

194   Editorial, "The End," in Hardorff, *The Death,* p. 210; more accurate the *New York Herald,* May 8, 1877, also in Hardorff, ibid., p. 213.

195   Sprague, *Cheyenne River Sioux,* p. 27.

196   All of the above is summarized from threads in "Crazy Horse Genealogy": *http://www.lbha.proboards12.com*; "Notes on the Crazy Horse Genealogy": *http://www.christianforums.com*; and "Crazy Horse and Relatives": *http://amertribes.proboards.com/threads/107/crazy-horse relatives?*

197   Francis White Lance, comp., *The Genealogy of Chief Crazy Horse*. Poster-size. [Pine Ridge, S.Dak., privately printed, 2013]; color copy in authors' possession.

198   Luther Standing Bear, *My People the Sioux*. University of Nebraska Press, Lincoln, 1975 [1928], p. 83.

199   Then Superintendent at Pine Ridge Agency; see Gordon Macgregor, *Warriors Without Weapons: A Study of the Society and Personality Development of the Pine Ridge Sioux*. University of Chicago Press, Chicago, 1946.

200   Hinman, "Oglala Sources," pp. 20, 24.

201   [Pictograph] 3, "The Eagle Hawk Narrative [Circa 1840]," in Hardorff, *The Death*, p. 134.

202   Addison E. Sheldon, "Appendix" to E.A. Brininstool, "Chief Crazy Horse, His Career and Death," pp. 45-46.

203   Ricker, "George Sword's Interview," *The Indian Interviews*, p. 328.

204   He Dog quoted by interpreter John Colhoff in Hinman, "Oglala Sources," p. 24.

205   Garnett in Friswold, "William Garnett's Account," *The Killing*, pp. 75-77; based on the William Garnett interview of August 19, 1920, previously cited.

206   Garnett in Ricker, *The Indian Interviews*, pp. 58-59, et seq.; also Hardorff, *The Death*, p. 27, with occasional misprints.

207   T. Powers, *The Killing*, p. 277.

208   Ricker, "[Louis Bordeaux's Interview, Tuesday, August 30-31, 1907]." *The Indian Interviews*, p. 295.

209   Ibid. p. 296.

210   Red Feather interview of July 30, 1930, in Hinman, *Oglala Sources*, p. 29; *Denver Daily Tribune*, May 18, 1877, in Hardorff, *The Surrender and Death*, p. 209.

211   [Charles Diehl], "Doves and Devils: Before the Big Talk" [Special Telegram], Camp Robinson, Neb., May 24, *Chicago Times*, May 26, 1877, in Hardorff, *The Death*, pp. 221-224.

212   Charles M. Robinson, *General Crook and the Western Frontier*. University of Oklahoma Press, Norman, 2001, pp. 165-166, 174-175.

213   Editorial, "Crazy Horse and Gen. Crook: Indian Warriors at the Camp Robinson Agency—Speeches by the Chiefs," *The New York Times*, May 27, 1877; also, "The Great Council" [Special Telegram], Camp Robinson, Neb., May 25, *Chicago Times*, May 26, 1877, in Hardorff, *The Death*, p. 226.

214   W.J. Bordeaux, *Custer's Conqueror*, p. 39.

215   Grange, "Fort Robinson," pp. 191-240.

216   Bray, *Crazy Horse*, p. 397.

217   "Story of Gen. Jesse M. Lee," in Brininstool, "Chief Crazy Horse," p. 31.

218   Reprinted in Hardorff, *The Death*, 203- 207.

219   *Cheyenne Sun*, October 29, 1876, Cheyenne, Wyoming Terr.

220   Markus H. Lindner, "Goggles, Family, and the 'Wild West': The Photographs of Sitting Bull." *European Review of Native American Studies*, Vol. 15, No. 1, 2001, pp. 37-48.

221   Goodyear, *Red Cloud*, p. 5.

222   Ibid. pp. 4, 7.

223   Editorial, "Sioux Chiefs and Warriors". *Frank Leslie's Illustrated Newspaper*, Vol. 30, July 9, 1870, p. 261.

224   Hyde, *Red Cloud's*, p. 182. Goodyear, *Red Cloud*, pp. 11-12, et seq., does not mention the episode and writes that "Red Cloud was forty-nine years old when he first encountered the visual medium of photography in the spring of 1870."

225   Martha A. Sandweiss, *Print the Legend: Photography and the American West.* Yale University Press, New Haven, Conn. 2002, p. 329

226   Goodyear, *Red Cloud*, pp. 6-7.

227   T. Powers, *The Killing*, pp. 262-263.

228   Sandoz, *Crazy Horse*, p. 370.

229   Mangas Coloradas was murdered during a peace parlay in New Mexico with Gen. J.R. West. Soldiers decapitated him, boiled his head and sent the skull to a phrenologist in New York who featured it in a book.

230   "Cochise's Physical Appearance" in: The Land of Cochise"; *https://www.landofcochise.com*

231   Terry Mort, *The Wrath of Cochise: The Bascom Affair and the Origins of the Apache Wars*. Pegasus Books, New York, 2013; side by side photographic portraits of Naiche and Taza in inset between pp. 150-151.

232   National Anthropological Archives: NAA Inv. 02090400.

233   National Anthropological Archives: NAA Inv. 02086300, Naiche alone. NAA Inv. 02004700 and NAA Inv. 02039200, both Naiche and wife.

234   Inkpaduta, the Scarlet Point, in Mark Diedrich, *Famous Chiefs of the Eastern Sioux*. Coyote Books, Minneapolis, 1987, pp. [42] 43-60; also, Maxwell Van Nuys, *Inkpaduta: Sitting Bull's Predecessor*. Privately Printed, Denver, rev. ed. 2004. Peggy Rodina Larson, "A New Look at the Elusive Inkpaduta." *Minnesota History*, Vol. 48, No. 1, Spring 1982, pp. 24-35; a more recent, balanced assessment is Paul N. Beck, *Inkpaduta: Dakota Leader*. University of Oklahoma Press, Norman, 2008.

235   Diedrich, *Famous Chiefs*, p. 43.

236   "Eastman knew Inkpaduta who was in the battle of the Little Big Horn. Says he was a good man": Eli S. Ricker, "[Charles A. Eastman's Interview, Tablet 11, Tuesday, August 20, 1907]." *The Indian Interviews*, p. 286.

237   Van Nuys, *Inkpaduta*, p. 7.

238   The present writer was told by an American Indian friend who wishes to remain anonymous that, to his knowledge, a Gros Ventre from Fort Belknap had actually killed Inkpaduta in a dispute.

239   See Little Crow's photograph No. 48 in Fleming, *Shindler Catalogue*; also, Diedrich, *Famous Chiefs*, p. 61. A biography is Gary Clayton Anderson, *Little Crow, Spokesman for the Sioux*. Minnesota Historical Society Press, St. Paul, 1986.

240   Diedrich, *Famous Chiefs*, p. 42.

241   Van Nuys, *Inkpaduta*, frontispiece.

242   Bray, *Crazy Horse*, p. 201.

243   Quoted by Joan Morrison, *Lakota Times*, Wednesday, Nov. 12, 1986, p. 3.

244   Mrs. J.M. Lee in Brininstool, *Crazy Horse*, pp. 69-70.

245   Bray, *Crazy Horse*, p. 403, note 33.

246   C.A. Eastman, *Indian Heroes*, p. 83.

247   Quoted by interpreter Samuel Stands, in Hinman, "Oglala Sources," p. 6.

248   Bray, *Crazy Horse*, pp. 395-396, 475, note 19; see also, Cleve Walstrom, *Search for the Lost Trail of Crazy Horse*. Dageforde Pub., Crete, Neb., 2003.

249   Robert K. Wilcox, *The Truth about the Shroud of Turin: Solving the Mystery*. Regnery Publ., Washington, 2010; Thomas de Wesselow, *The Sign: The Shroud of Turin and the Secret of the Resurrection*. Dutton, New York, 2012.

250   R. Eli Paul, ed., *Autobiography of Red Cloud: War Leader of the Oglalas*. Montana Historical Society Press, Helena, 1997, p. 206, note 53.

251   Thomas W. Dunley, *Wolves for the Blue Soldiers: Indian Scouts and Auxiliaries with the United States Army, 1860-90*, University of Nebraska Press, Lincoln, 1982.

252   Garnett in Ricker, *The Indian Interviews*, pp. 46-47.

253   Hardorff, *The Death*, p. 214; also Bray, "We Belong," pp. 28-29; and Bray, *Crazy Horse*, pp. 299-300.

254   Ambrose, *Crazy Horse*, p. 467.

255   Russell Freedman, *The Life and Death of Crazy Horse*. Holyday House, New York, 1996, p. 143.

256   Sandoz, *Crazy Horse*, p. 372.

257   Garnett in Ricker, *The Indian Interviews*, p. 49.

258   William Philo Clark, *Indian Sign Language*. L.R. Hamersly & Co., Philadelphia, 1885.

259   Friswold, *The Killing*, p. 139.

260   Bray, *Crazy Horse*, p. 339.

261   Ricker, [Mrs, Stirk Interview], *The Indian Interviews*, pp. 287-288.

262   Louis Bordeaux Interview, in Hardorff, *The Death*, p. 111.

263   Ibid. p. 68; tribes here meaning the several *thiyóšpaye* comprising the Oglala tribal village under Red Cloud, and possibly also the loyal Brule followers of Spotted Tail.

264   Bray, *Crazy Horse*, p. 356.

265   Ibid. p. 463, Note 5; Eddie Herman, "Betrayer of Crazy Horse Disgraced." *Rapid City, S.D. Daily Journal*, December 10, 1950; also, Billy Garnett in Ricker, *The Indian Interviews*, pp. 60-61, 66-67.

266   Turning Bear quoted in W.J. Bordeaux, *Custer's Conqueror*, pp. 89-90.

267   Major H.R. Lemly quoted in Brininstool, *Crazy Horse*, p. 57.

268   Feraca, "Crazy Horse," p. 15; the medal is discussed by Paul L. Hedren, "The Crazy Horse Medal: An Enigma from the Great Sioux War." *Nebraska History*, Vol. 75, No. 2, 1994, pp. 195-199.

269   "The Baptiste Pourier Interview, March 6, 1907," in Hardorff, *The Death*, p. 93. On this very point, in his email Michael Samuel was firm: "You should note that it was not the White Soldier 'Private Gentles' that took the life of

Tasunke Witko! Even though 'Private Gentals' [sic] tried his best to stab, and kill Crazy Horse with his bayonet at the door of the Guard House, and also across the grounds, he was only able to inflict a very small wound in his right side just above his hip, but it was that small injury that caused Crazy Horse to lose what remaining strength he had which allowed Little Big Man to thrust the final blow into his right kidney. [...] [Crazy Horse] did not want to kill anyone, that's why he was slashing instead of thrusting. Thrusting is to Kill, while Slashing is to make people get away from you. [...] This was the second time Little Big Man had held his hand, and held him back, causing him harm, this time ending in his death. Was the first time intentional? We do not know, but the second time was."

270   L.P. Bradley, "The Arrest and Death of Crazy Horse," p. 51 [pp. 50-52] in Addison E. Sheldon, "Appendix" to E.A. Brininstool (and others) "Chief Crazy Horse, His Career and Death."

271   Bray, *Crazy Horse*, p. 472, Note 67.

272   Ephriam D. Dickson, III, "Crazy Horse: Who Really Wielded Bayonet That Killed the Oglala Leader?" *Greasy Grass Magazine*, Vol. 12, May 1996, pp. 2-10.

273   "Newspaper Account of the Murder of Chief Crazy Horse, Written by Mrs. Lucy W. Lee, Wife of General Lee, from Camp Sheridan," in Brininstool, *Crazy Horse*, pp. 67-68 [62-71].

274   "Wm. Garnett to Dr. V.T. McGillycuddy, April 21, 1926," in Friswold, *The Killing*, p. 114.

275   Grange, "Fort Robinson," p. 214.

276   Bruce Brown, *Conversations with Crazy Horse*, 2006: *http://astonisher.com/Archives/cwch/cwch_ch1.htm*

277   Buecker, *Last Days*, p. 6.

278   Michelle Dulaney, *Buffalo Bill's Wild West Warriors: A Photographic History by Gertrude Käsebier*. Smithsonian Institution and HarperCollins, New York, 2007, pp. 60-61.

279   The tragic epilogue to the Little Crow's War of 1862 and President Lincoln's shameful decision is the subject of the documentary directed by Silas Hagerty, *Dakota 38*. Smooth Feather Productions, Portland, Maine, 2012.

280   Dust jacket, Vestal, *Sitting Bull*, 1972 ed.

281   James Dowd–Bookseller, letter to Mrs. Bonnie Gardner, [dated] June 21, 1979; typescript, Crazy Horse File, South Dakota State Historical Society,

Pierre; copy in authors' possession. Front cover, Brenda Hagen, *Crazy Horse: Sioux Warrior*. Compass Point Books, Minneapolis, 2006 [juvenile literature].

282   Kay Bischoff and Delphine Hewitt, *Famous American Indian Chiefs. Read and Color*. Eukabi Publ., Albuquerque, 1951, [p. 13], "Crazy Horse," by E.H. Bischoff; [juvenile literature].

283   The late Crow elder and historian Joe Medicine Crow (1913-2016) stated that it was the name the Crow gave Custer, but Feraca called it yet "another American Indian instant tradition." It may also be a romanticized rendering of the name of Arikara chief "Son-of-The-Star" who, in the spring of 1876 helped Custer recruit the contingent of some forty Arikara scouts that accompanied the 7th Cavalry to the Little Bighorn; Orin G. Libby, "The Arikara Narrative of the Campaign Against the Hostile Dakotas [sic], June 1876." *North Dakota Historical Collections*, Vol. 6., Bismarck, 1920; reprinted in W.A. Graham, *The Custer Myth*, pp. 28-29. In his *Catalogue of Stereoscopic Views of the Northwest. Including Views of Sioux Falls, Pipestone Quarries [...]. Also a Large and Complete Assortment of Indian Scenes, Representing Distinguished Chiefs and Prominent Characters [etc.]*. Published and for Sale by: J.H. Hamilton, Sioux City, Iowa [1878], Hamilton lists both, p. 4, "No. 85. Rushing Bear, Sioux Chief" and, p. 7 "No. 179. Son of a Star, Sioux Chief." A photographic portrait of the above-mentioned Arikara chief Son-of-the-Star, also known as Rushing Bear, is attributed either to W.H. Jackson, undated stereoview in NY Public Library, Catalog No., MFY Dennis Coll. 90-F81; or to Byron H. Gurnsey, 1870: *http://www.cowanauctions.com/auctions/item.aspx?Itemid=54437*

284   Evan S. Connell, *Son of the Morning Star*. North Point Press, San Francisco, 1984, p. 367.

285   W.E. Paxson, *E.S. Paxson; Frontier Artist*. Pruett Publishing Co, Boulder, Colo., 1984, pp. 7, 43.

286   On-line biography at: *http://www.bbhc.org/wgwa/paxson.cfm*

287   Paxson's "Custer's Last Stand," reproduced in W.E. Paxson, Plates 8-9.

288   Color plates on pp. 58-59 in Leslie Tillett, coll. and ed., *Wind on the Buffalo Grass*. Thomas Y. Crowell, New York, 1976, reproduced from Bad Heart Bull, *A Pictographic History*.

289   John M. Carroll, "On a Photo of Crazy Horse," in *The Eleanor Hinman Interviews on the Life and Death of Crazy Horse*. New Foreword by Eleanor H. Hinman, The Garry Owen Press, New Brunswick, N.J., 1976, p. 16.

290   M. Samuel, email.

291   Buecker, "Crazy Horse," p. 32.

292   Sprague, *Rosebud Sioux*, p. 19.

293   Hurt and Lass, *Frontier Photographer*, p. 61, Fig. 24.

294   Ibid.; sketch in *Indian Country Today*, July 2-15, 1996, p. B1. See also the article: "Crazy Horse Portrait? The Continuing Search…," *Lakota Country Times*, 2009-04-02/Front Page.

295   Sketch in Bruce Brown, "Bogus Portraits of Crazy Horse, His Wives, Black Shawl Woman and Helen 'Nellie' Laravie, and His Personal Belongins…," *http://www.astonisher.com/archives/museum/crazy_horse_bogus_pics.html*

296   Featured in the article "Crazy Horse (Tashunkewitko) (ca. 1840-1877) Oglala Lakota chief," *http://www.unitedearth.com.au/crazyhorse.html*

297   The same stamp was later issued in the series *Great American Indian Chiefs*, by the African nation of The Gambia, 2005.

298   Vine Deloria, Jr., "Introduction," p. xiii, in: Mari Sandoz, *Crazy Horse: The Strange Man of the Oglalas*. University of Nebraska Press, Lincoln, 2004.

299   The dedication, held in conjunction with the unveiling of a monument to Lieut. Levi Robinson after whom the Camp/Fort was named, was recorded on an 8mm home film by Arthur P. Howe titled *The Last Gathering of the Sioux Nation*, now at the Nebraska State Historical Society, Lincoln.

300   Various Authors, *Through Indian Eyes: The Untold Story of Native American Peoples*. Reader's Digest, New York, 1995; quotation on front cover flap. A similar quotation is attributed to Ponca Chief Standing Bear: see Hans C. Adam's "Introduction" in: *Edward S. Curtis. The North American Indian. The Complete Portfolios*. Taschen, Köln [etc.], 2003, pp. 21-22.

301   John M. Carroll, "On His Name," in *The Eleanor H. Hinman*, pp. 12-13; also, "Crazy Horse and Relatives": *http://amertribes.proboards.com/threads/107/crazy-horse relatives?*

302   White Bull in Vestal, *Warpath*, p. 207.

303   Feraca, "Crazy Horse," p. 14.

304   Ricker, "Chipps's Interview, 1907," *The Indian Interviews*, pp. 273-274.

305   Bill Donohue, "Ways and Means," *Washington Post Magazine*, June 29, 2008, pp. 8-113, 20-25.

306   Reflecting the paramount concern of treaty Indians to retain easy access to trading and the distribution of government annuities, Red Cloud Agency was originally established in 1871 on the North Platte, southeast of Fort Laramie, Wyoming Territory. It was then moved in 1873 to the upper White River (west

of the present-day town of Crawford) following the relocation of Spotted Tail and his Brule some forty miles north and east to Beaver Creek (near present-day Chadron), Nebraska. Red Cloud Agency remained on the White River until late 1877 when the government temporarily removed it to Medicine Creek on the Missouri, before it was permanently resettled the following year on White Clay Creek, Pine Ridge, South Dakota. The same year 1878 Spotted Tail Agency too was moved to its current location on Rosebud Creek, also in South Dakota. Edward Hill, *The Office of Indian Affairs, 1824-1880: Historical Sketches*. Clearwater Publishing, New York, 1979, pp. 147-148, 176.

307   Anthony R. McGinnis, *Counting Coup and Cutting Horses: Intertribal Warfare on the Northern Plains, 1738-1889*. Bison Books, 2010.

308   His photograph was taken in 1870 by B.H. Gurnsey in Sioux City, Iowa; Dickson, *Fort Robinson*, p. 10.

309   Frank Appleton, "'Out here among the infernal Red skins.' Frank Appleton's 1874 Letter from Red Cloud Agency." *Nebraska History*, Vol. 90, No. 1, 2009, pp. 2-4.

310   His photographic portrait had been taken a few years earlier at Sioux City, Iowa, by B.H. Gurnsey; Dickson, *Fort Robinson*, p. 16.

311   Ricker, "William Garnett's Interview, Jan. 10, 1907," *The Indian Interviews*, pp. 7-8; Hardorff, *The Death*, p. 43.

312   Wilhelm, *Memorandum*, p. 66.

313   Hyde, *Red Cloud's*, pp. 211-212.

314   Harry ("Sam") Young, *Hard Knocks: A Life Story of the Vanishing West*. Laird & Lee, Chicago, 1915, pp. 149-152.

315   The bearded Indian trader was an ex-confederate soldier who sought fortune out West after the war; Dickson, *Fort Robinson*, p. 15, published his photograph taken by Edric L. Eaton, ca.1875, in Omaha, Nebraska.

316   The assassination of Big Mouth is recounted and illustrated in Richard Irving Dodge, *Our Wild Indians: Thirty-three Years' Personal Experience among the Red Men of the Great West [etc.]*. With an Introduction by General Sherman. Worthington and Co., Harford, Conn., [etc.], 1883, pp. 85- 87.

317   Photographic portrait reproduced by Dickson, *Fort Robinson*, p. 14.

318   Wilhelm, *Memorandum*, p. 60.

319   Dickson, *Fort Robinson*, p. 13.

320   Wilhelm, *Memorandum*, p. 65.

321   Ibid. p. 62.

322   Ibid. p. 69.

323   Ibid. p. 67.

324   Buecker and Paul, *The Crazy Horse*, p.107; not to be confused with his contemporaneous American Horse, who was also known as Spider, as noted by Hardorff, *The Death*, p. 65.

325   Donald B. Smith, *Long Lance: The True Story of an Impostor*. MacMillan of Canada, Toronto, 1982. (Reprinted under revised title.)   ,

326   [Canon] H.W. Gibbon Stocken, *Among the Blackfoot and Sarcee*. Glenbow Alberta Institute, Calgary, Alta., 1976, p. 61.

327   Kappler, *Treaties*, p. 1003.

328   Wilhelm, *Memorandum*, p. 73.

329   Ibid. pp. 81-82.

330   Ibid. pp. 83-84.

331   Ibid. pp. 84-85.

332   Dickson, "Capturing the Lakota Spirit," p. 6.

333   Claudine Chalmers, "Jules Tavernier at Red Cloud Agency in 1874." *Antiques & Fine Arts Magazine*, Summer/Autumn 2007, pp. 163-167. Incidentally, in the article, photograph / Fig. 1 captioned "Red Cloud" should read "Jack Red Cloud," as the Indian is not the famous chief, but his son.

334   Both sketches in National Archives, RG 111-SC Box 660: No. 83152, Sioux Village, 1874; No. 83153, Camp Robinson, 1874.

335   Grange, "Fort Robinson," pp. 231-232.

336   *The New York Times*, January 1877.

337   Reproduced in Dickson, "Capturing the Lakota Spirit," p. 9.

338   D. Mark Katz, *Custer in Photographs. A Photographic Biography of America's Most Intriguing Boy General*. Custer Battlefield Museum Publishing, Garryowen, Mont., 2001, pp. 130-137.

339   Terry Clark, "email to *general@laststand.com*, May 03, 2009"; copy in authors' possession.

340   Reproduced in: *With Custer on the Little Bighorn. A Newly Discovered First-Person Account by William O. Taylor*. Foreword by Greg Martin. Viking/Penguin, New York, 1996, p. 86; in the caption only Crow King and Low Dog are identified.

341   "Private Charles Howard"; *http://amertribes.proboards.com//thread/273/ private-charles-howard*; Buecker, *Last Days,* front cover image and pp. 140-141, 142-143.

342   Larry Belitz, *The Buffalo Hide Tipi of the Sioux*. Pine Hill Press, Sioux Falls, S.Dak., 2006, p. 15. The Engagés, "Canvas Tipis." *The Museum of the Fur Trade Quarterly,* Vol. 20, No. 3, 1984, pp. 13-14; Angeline Johnson in Phillip G. Twitchell, ed., "The Camp Robinson Letters of Angeline Johnson, 1876-1879." *Nebraska History*, Vol. 77, No. 2, 1996, pp. 89-95. The wife of Lieut. Charles Johnson, Acting Agent at Red Cloud, "Angie" was least sympathetic towards Crazy Horse whom, as she wrote to her sister, "ever since his surrender [...] has never had what he deserved, a good thrashing [etc.]," p. 92.

343   Dickson, "Capturing the Lakota Spirit," p. 18; Buecker, *Last Days*, pp. 176-177.

344   Richard I. Dodge, *The Black Hills Journals of Colonel Richard Irving Dodge*. University of Oklahoma Press, Norman, 1996.

345   Paul Horsted, with Ernest Grafe and Jon Nelson, *Exploring with Custer: The 1874 Black Hills Expedition*. Golden Valley Press, Custer, S.Dak., 2002.

346   Dickson, "Capturing the Lakota Spirit," pp. 7- 9.

347   Ibid.

348   Goodyear, *Red Cloud*, p. 75 [pp. 72-80, figs. 37-39].

349   Ibid. pp. 32-33, fig. 13. See also, Wesley R. Hurt and William E. Lass, *Frontier Photographer: Stanley J. Morrow's Dakota Years*. University of Nebraska Press, Lincoln, 1956.

350   Paul L. Hedren, *With Crook in the Black Hills: Stanley J. Morrow's 1876 Photographic Legacy*. Pruett Publ. Co., Boulder, Colo., 1985.

351   Hyde, *Red Cloud's*, pp. 284-287; Jerome A. Greene, "The Surrounding of Red Cloud and Red Leaf, 1876: A Preemptive Maneuver of the Great Sioux War." *Nebraska History*, Vol. 82, No. 2, 2001, pp. 69-75.

352   Goodyear, *Red Cloud*, pp. 30-31, Fig. 12.

353   Dickson, "Capturing," p. 11, thinks that Morrow's portraits of "Spotted Tail, Two Strike, Fast Bear, and Crazy in the Lodge probably date from his visit to the Spotted Tail Agency the following year after it was removed to the Missouri River."

354   Hurt and Lass, *Frontier Photographer*, pp. 34-35, 60, Fig. 23.

355   Dickson, "Capturing," p. 11; "The Reburial Expedition," in Hurt and Lass, *Frontier Photographer,* pp. 111-118, Figs. 86-91.

356   Charles C. Hamilton, "Address of Judge Charles C. Hamilton before the Academy of Science and Letters of Sioux City, Iowa, November 27, 1928." *Annals of Iowa,* 3rd ser., Vol. 41, No. 3, 1972, pp. 809-834. A list of stereo photographers posted by the State Historical Society of Iowa provides the following information: "Hamilton, James H. – Hamilton had a studio in Sioux City, Woodbury County, in the 1870s through the 1890s. Was in partnership with Hamilton & Hoyt, Hamilton & Kodylek, and Hamilton & Co. There was also, according to Burgess, a James H. Hamilton at Spirit Lake in 1880. He had prominent series with Native Americans, 'Corn Palace Views' (1888, 1889, 1890), 'Views of the Northwest,' and 'Stereoscopic Views of the Northwest.' Census figures of 1870 indicate he was 31, born in Wayne County, Kentucky, and unable to write. The 1880 census, however, says he is 46 at the time and lives on 4th street. His wife, who is 40, is named Emilia, and was born in Pennsylvania, and his family consists of Charles C. (19) born in Missouri, James (15) born in Nebraska, Carlson (11) born in Iowa, and Harry (5) born in Iowa. He probably arrived in Iowa in 1868. He is mentioned in *A.T. Andreas Illustrated Atlas of the State of Iowa, 1875,* p. 551. [...] There are forty-five examples of the work of this photographer in the SHSI collection as Hamilton & Hoyt." *http://www.iowahistory.org/libraries/collections/iowacity*

357   Palmquist and Kailbourn, *Pioneer Photographers,* p. 301.

358   Ibid.; Dickson, "Capturing," p. 12.

359   As mentioned earlier, some of these Omaha and Winnebago images are now in British archives;A. Hopkinson, "Trail of Tears."

360   Fleming and Luskey, *Native American,* p. 195; Heriard, "Debating," pp. 20-21.

361   Buecker, "Crazy Horse," p. 33. The record in the NAA, Neg. 43584, indicates that the image is undated and the photographer not recorded, but attributed to B.H Gurnsey or Gurnsey & Illingworth; the handwritten note at bottom reads: "Chah-ur-t-kee, Pawnee chief." As noted, in 1870 Hamilton obtained some Gurnsey negatives and sold them as stereoscopic cards with the "Hamilton," "Hamilton & Kodylek," and "Hamilton & Hoyt" logos.

362   Ephriam Dickson, "Photographers at Fort Robinson," 2010, *http://www.American-Tribes.com*

363   B.H. Gurnsey, "Chak-ok-ta-kee, or, The Man That Strikes His Enemies, Pawnee Chief," albumen print, stereograph, Princeton University Library, Rare Books and Special Collections, # WA 1998:214/WC064, S0284.

364   Thomas W. Kavanagh, "Reading Historic Photographs [Pawnee]," *http://www.php.indiana.edu/-tkavanag/phothana.html* [no date].

365   Cowan's Auctions, Spring Historic Americana, June 5&6, 2008; *http://www.cowanauctions.com/auctions/item.aspex?Itemid=60352*; the cdv sold for $431.25. Cowan's Auctions had sold a "B.H. Gurnsey cdv of Rushing Bear, Hereditary Head Chief of the Arikara" in 2007 for $2,900; *http://www.cowanauctions.com/auctions/item.aspex?Itemid=54437*. A copy of the same stereo of Rushing Bear, or *Ku-Nugh-Na-Give-Nuk,* The Son of The Star, age about 56 is in the New York Public Library, Prints and Photographs, Catalog Call No. MFY Dennis Coll. 90-F81, but the record says it was taken at Fort Berthold by William Henry Jackson; possibly because Jackson lists it in his 1877 *Descriptive Catalogue*, p. 63.

366   Ryan Long, "The Battle of Little Bighorn," *History Day* 2006; *http://www.littlebighornproject.com/id21.html*

367   Dickson, "Photographers"; Dickson, "Capturing"; also Thomas R. Buecker, "A Photographic Epilogue to the Great Sioux War." *Nebraska History*, Vol. 82, No. 2, 2001, pp. 76-71.

368   C.C. Hamilton, "Address," pp. 826-827.

369   The sun dance has long been misrepresented as tribal "initiation" and "torture," a wrong popular image publicized by Elliot Silverstein's *A Man Called Horse* (1970), with Richard Harris. For an overview of the meaning of the ceremony see JoAllyn Archambault, "Sun Dance," *HNAI*, Vol. 13, Pt. 2, pp. 983-995, and references cited; see also Francis White Lance, *Why the Black Hills Are Sacred: A Unified Theory of the Lakota Sun Dance.* CreateSpace Independent Publ. Platform, 2011.

370   C.C. Hamilton, "Address," p. 827.

371   Frederick Schwatka, "The Sun-Dance of the Sioux." *Century Magazine*, Vol. 39, No. 5, Dec. 1890, pp. 739-759, December 1890; see also James R. Walker, "The Sun Dance and Other Ceremonies of the Oglala Division of the Teton Dakota." *American Museum of Natural History Anthropological Papers*, Vol. 16, No. 2, 1917, pp. 51-221, based on information provided by Little Wound, American Horse, Short Bull, and others.

372   "American Indian Photographs of the Sundance"; *http://www.cowanauctions.com/auctions/past-item.aspx?Itemid=103891*

373   C.C. Hamilton, "Address," pp. 828, 830.

374   Buecker, *Last Days*, pp. 114-115.

375   Heriard, "Debating," pp. 19-20.

376   Tom Buecker, "Telephone conversation with Pietro Abiuso, fall 2012." Buecker said that too much time had passed, but he thought seeing a copy of the photo with the same backdrop in the collections of the Nebraska State Historical Society. Our inquiries with NSHS did not help locate the image as RG0014 was still, as Buecker had originally stated, "a mess"; confirmed by Karen Keehr, "Email to Pietro Abiuso, Nov. 23, 2015."

377   Buecker, "The Search," p. 31.

378   Ephriam D. Dickson, III, "Soldier with a Camera: Private Charles Howard's Photographic Journey Through Eastern Wyoming, 1877." *Annals of Wyoming*, Vol. 77, No. 4, 2005, pp. 22-32.

379   Dickson, "Photographers," online p. 1.

380   The advertisement and some Mitchell photographs are in Dickson, "Capturing," pp. 4, 18-23; see also NAA Catalog No. 4754.

381   Dickson, "Capturing," p. 23.

382   Dickson, "Photographers," [on line.]

383   Dickson, "Capturing," p. 17.

384   Dickson, "Photographers," [on line.]

385   T.W. Wright, *The evidence*, cover page.

386   Angela Aleiss, "Is This Crazy Horse? Investigating Indian Country's Most Controversial Photo." *Indian Country*, Feb. 19, 2015, pp. 4-5.

387   Buecker, "Crazy Horse," pp. 30-31, 33.

388   "B. Garnett to Dr. V. McGillycuddy, letter dated December 14, 1927," in Friswold, *The Killing*, p. 130.

389   Editorial, "Gen. Crook. News from the Front," *Chicago Tribune*, May 3, 1877; reprinted in Hardorff, *The Death*, p. 194.

390   W.J. Bordeaux, *Custer's Conqueror*, [p. iv].

391   Chips, in Hardorff, *The Death*, p. 74; Feraca, *The Wounded Bear*, p. 10.

392   Bray, *Crazy Horse*, pp. 5-6, 18.

393   W.J. Bordeaux, *Custer's Conqueror*, p. 22.

394   "Interview with Red Feather, July 8, 1930," in Hinman, "Oglala Sources," p. 30.

395   Sprague, *Pine Ridge*, p. 15; Bray, *Crazy Horse*, p. 293; more recently, John Koster, "Plural Wives and the Plains Indians." *Wild West*, Vol. 25, No. 1, June 2012, p. 44 [pp. 44-47]; Koster also published, p. 45, the photograph of "Nellie Laravie" originally investigated by Will Robinson.

396   Bruce Brown, "Bogus Portraits of Crazy Horse, His Wives, Black Shawl Woman and Helen 'Nellie' Laravie, and His Personal Belongins...," *http://www.astonisher.com/archives/museum/crazy_horse_bogus_pics.html*

397   Hardorff, *The Death*, p. 75, footnote 4.

398   Tony Whirlwind Horse in Joan Morrison, "Crazy Horse: We may never know the truth." *Lakota Times*, Nov. 19, 1986.

399   Raymond Clown, *Amos and Julia Iron Cedar Clown*, *http://www.lbha.org* – *Crazy Horse Genealogy*, 2006. An attempt to unravel the genealogy of Crazy Horse was Richard G. Hardorff, *The Oglala Lakota Crazy Horse: A Preliminary Genealogical Study*. J.M. Carroll and Co., Mattituck, N.Y., 1985, who also published a preliminary family tree. It was followed by three articles by Joan Morrison in *Lakota Times*, Nov. 12, and Nov. 19, 1986, with an expanded but still incomplete reprint of Hardorff's "Genealogy of Crazy Horse" from pp. 270-271 in *The Death*. Another article, by Jean Hammond, also in *Lakota Times*, Nov. 12, 1986, focused on her own grandmother Victoria Conroy, granddaughter of Crazy Horse's paternal aunt Big Woman. Information on Crazy Horse's step-mothers and their kin, originally given in 1934, was later published by Gonzalez and Cook-Lynn, *The Politics*, p. 402-404. Also, the previously cited *http://www.christianforums.com*.

400   Buecker, "Crazy Horse," p. 31.

401   Trimble, "What Did Crazy Horse Look Like?"

402   "The Stories of Low Dog, Crow King, Hump, Iron Thunder (From the *Leavenworth Weekly Times* – Thursday, August 18, 1881)," in W.A. Graham, *The Custer Myth*. Stackpole Books, Mechanicsburg, Pa., 1953, p. 75 [pp. 74-79].

403   Hardorff, *The Death*, p. 29, note 6.

404   Hinman, "Oglala Sources," p. 6.

405   T. Powers, *The Killing*, p. 391.

406   Frank White Buffalo Man in E. and M. Kadlecek, *To Kill and Eagle*, p. 149.

407   Luther Standing Bear, *My People the Sioux*. Houghton Mifflin, Boston, 1928, p. 83.

408   Donovin A. Sprague, *Pine Ridge Reservation*. Arcadia Publ., Charleston, S.C., 2004, pp. 10-11, 48-49.

409   W.J. Bordeaux, *Custer's Conqueror*, p. 39.

410   Luther Standing Bear, *My People*, p. 83.

411   Hardorff, *The Oglala Lakota*, p. 56.

412   Hardorff, *The Death*, p. 18.

413   Ibid. p. 75, and sources therein.

414   Little Killer in Hinman, "Oglala Sources," p. 45.

415   Philander, "Crazy-Horse: The Death of the Indian Chieftain," *Chicago Tribune*, Sept. 11, 1877, in Hardorff, *The Death*, p. 248.

416   Editorial, "Surrender of Crazy Horse." *New York Tribune*, May 7, 1877, in ibid. p. 208.

417   Editorial, "The End of the Sioux War." *New York Sun*, May 23, 1877, in ibid. p. 209.

418   Bourke, *On the Border*, p. 414.

419   Rapherty, "Crazy Horse Sick. Special Telegram from Red Cloud, May 15," *The Cheyenne Daily Leader*, May 16, 1877, in Hardorff, *The Death*, p. 214; we purposely omitted the added remark by the *Daily* editor.

420   T. Powers, *The Killing*, p. 273.

421   Ibid., and p. 567: *Crazy Horse Gift Ledger* (No. 1986.581.9), in the Denver Art Museum.

422   Bourke, *On the Border*, p. 415.

423   "J. Irwin to Commissioner of Indian Affairs, Aug. 4, 1877," in Hardorff, *The Death*, pp. 166-167.

424   "The Death of Crazy Horse," ibid. p. 243.

425   "Frank Huston and His Comments," in W.A. Graham, *The Custer Myth*, p. 80.

426   "Portions of Letter from Dr. V.T. McGillycuddy to Eleanor H. Hinman, May 6, 1930," in Hinman, *Oglala Sources*, pp. 45-49.

427   "Henry Standing Bear Interview," in Hardorff, *The Death*, pp. 113-115.

428   W.J. Bordeaux, *Custer's Conqueror*, caption facing frontispiece.

429   Hardorff, *The Oglala Lakota*, p. 19.

430   Hardorff, *The Death*, p. 93.

431   "Major H.R. Lemly's Account of the Murder of Chief Crazy Horse, As An Eye-Witness," in Brininstool, *Crazy Horse*, pp. 49-61, quote on p. 51.

432   Victoria Conroy in Jean Hammond, "Clean-up Yields Priceless Crazy Horse Documents." *Lakota Times*, Nov. 2, 1986, p. 3.

433   Sprague, *Pine Ridge Reservation*, p. 69.

434   White Lance, *Tasunke Witko*; undated photograph by unknown, reproduced on front cover, with caption [unpaged, p. 60]: "Horn Cloud [killed at Wounded Knee] was the father of the three brothers below. They were all survivors of the Massacre. Joseph Horn Cloud is the man standing. Daniel White Lance (my great-grandfather) is seated on the left. Dewey Beard is seated on the right. He was the last living survivor and became a well-known speaker of the event and was the subject of many reports on the Massacre."

435   Laura L. Scheiber, "Skeletal Biology: Plains," in *HNAI*, Vol. 3 "Environment, Origins, and Population," Douglas H. Ubelaker, vol. ed. Smithsonian Institution, Washington, 2006, pp. 595-609.

436   Interview with Short Buffalo (Short Bull) [No location given], July 13, 1930, John Colhoff, Interpreter, in Hinman, "Oglala Sources," p. 40.

437   *Denver Daily Tribune*, May 20, 1877, in Hardorff, *The Death*, p. 217.

438   Bray, *Crazy Horse*, p. 71; J. Irwin, "Red Cloud Agency, Nebraska, August 25, 1877," in *Annual Report of the Commissioner of Indian Affairs to the Secretary of the Interior for the Year 1877*. Government Printing Office, Washington 1877, pp. 62-63.

439   J. Irwin, "Red Cloud Agency, Neb. Sept. 1, 1877, To the Hon. Commissioner of Indian Affairs," reprinted in Hardorff, *The Death*, p. 175.

440   The Eagle Elk Interview, [Pine Ridge, 1944], in Hardorff, *The Death*, p. 153.

441   Susan Bordeaux Bettelyoun, *Crazy Horse*; typescript cit., pp. 2-3; edited (incomplete) version in Bettelyoun's autobiography as dictated to Josephine Waggoner, a mixed-blood Hunkpapa, in the 1930s, *With My Own Eyes: A Lakota Woman Tells Her People's History*. University of Nebraska Press, Lincoln, 1998, pp. 107-110; see also Hardorff, *The Death*, pp. 123-129.

442   C. Eastman, *Indian Heroes*, p. 83.

443   Women occupied a generally dependent, subordinate yet central and discretely powerful position within what was otherwise a masculine and chauvinistic Lakota world. In fact, women represented the backbone of the People, carrying the heavy burdens of the nuclear and extended family, and by extension the band, figuratively and physically. Lakota women also absolved a complex, complementary function as both buffers to change and guardians

of tradition. They could marry outside their group and take up residence with their husbands, following a generalized patrilocal rule; but this, like many other features of Sioux life, was not always the case and, consistent with Lakota flexibility, the opposite also occurred. A woman would often draw her husband to her parents' camp, where the male newcomer was expected to observe strict rules of mother-in-law avoidance and father-in-law outmost respect. The dynamic tension between the sexes had a strong impact on Crazy Horse. Leaving aside – as in any other culture – the individual personality element and the sentimental aspect of relationships between men and women, Hassrick went as far as suggesting that "if Sioux men considered women as adversaries [...] to be conquered and quelled, Sioux women were no less straightforward in their opinion of men as dangerous predators." Hassrick, *The Sioux*, p. 123; see also M.N. Powers, *Oglala Women*; Beatrice (Bea) Medicine and Debra Lynn White Plume, *Cante ohitika Win (Brave-hearted Women): Images of Lakota Women from Pine Ridge Reservation*. University of South Dakota, Vermillion, 1991; and, Patricia Albers and Beatrice Medicine, eds., *The Hidden Half: Studies of Plains Indian Women*. University Press of America, Lanham, Md., 1983. Monogamy was preferred, but polygamy, particularly of the sororal type, was not uncommon, especially of older, leading headmen, as Crazy Horse's own father Worm did after the death of his first wife (*Tašunke's* mother). Divorce was an accepted solution to troubled marital relations.

444   Hassrick, *The Sioux*, p. 75.

445   W.J. Bordeaux, *Custer's Conqueror*, pp. 41-42.

446   Hardorff, *The Death*, p. 75.

447   Ibid. p. 75.

448   Interview with Red Feather, July 8, 1930, in Hinman, "Oglala Sources," p. 30.

449   Hardorff, *The Death*, p. 19.

450   Feraca, "Crazy Horse," p. 63.

451   Ricker, [Nick Ruleau's Interview, No. 20, 1906], *The Indian Interviews*, p. 312.

452   D.Brown and M.F. Schmitt, *Fighting Indians*, p. 162.

453   Theodore Stern, "Klamath and Modoc," in *HNAI*, Vol. 12, "Plateau," Deward E. Walker, Jr., vol. ed., Smithsonian Institution, Washington, 1998, p. 461, Fig.11 [pp. 446-466].

454   Sprague, *Pine Ridge*, p. 37; see also p. 59.

455   Shot in the Eye and Susan Shot in the Eye: *http://amertribes.proboards.com/thread/2173/shot-eye*

456   Buecker and Paul, *The Crazy Horse Surrender.*

457   Dickson, *The Sitting Bull Surrender*, p. 274.

458   Delaney, *Buffalo Bill's*, p. 82.

459   Richard G. Hardorff, comp. "The Nicholas Ruleau Interview," *Lakota Recollections of the Custer Fight: New Sources of Indian-Military History.* University of Nebraska Press, Lincoln, 1997, p. 39; Ricker, [Nick Ruleau Interview], *The Indian Interviews*, p. 312.

460   Pugh Young Man Afraid of His Horses, "Letter to Will G. Robinson, [dated] Oglala S.Dak Mar[ch] 26 – [19]58"; handwritten, Crazy Horse File, South Dakota State Historical Society, Pierre; copy in authors' possession.

461   Bruce Brown, "Crazy Horse Surrender Ledger"; *http://www.astonisher.com* ; see also Christina Rose, "13 Shocking and Funny Names from the Crazy Horse Surrender Ledger," *Indian Country Today*, August 5, 2015, who recently wrote: "The Nebraska Historical Society says that despite the false names the list is extremely important. [...] Deciphering who's who is an ongoing task. Doug Bissonette, Oglala, and Pine Ridge spokesman for the family of Crazy Horse, is working with the Nebraska Historical Society, the Crazy Horse Memorial in South Dakota, and Fort Robinson State Park, to honor those who surrendered with a new Crazy Horse Surrender Memorial to be built at Fort Robinson. Bissonette said several of the unusual names have been identified and she expects to be able to get to the bottom of the others." She also quoted Bruce Brown who stated: "We'll never know for sure, but I'll bet they were better known by names other than the ones they gave the gullible Americans!"

462   Dickson, *The Sitting Bull Surrender*, pp. 293, 295-296.

463   Bray, *Crazy Horse*, pp. 174, 218, 222, 276.

464   "Interview with He Dog, Oglala, South Dakota, July 13, 1930, John Colhoff, interpreter," in Hinman, "Oglala Sources," pp. 16-17.

465   Sandoz, *Crazy Horse*, p. 240.

466   W.J. Bordeaux, *Custer's Conqueror*, p. 42.

467   William J. Bordeaux, "Letter to State Historion [sic] Pierre South Dakota [dated] October 25th, 1951"; typescript, Crazy Horse File, South Dakota State Historical Society, Pierre; copy in authors' possession.

468   "The Eagle Elk Interview, Told by Eagle Elk [Pine Ridge, 1944]," in Hardorff, *The Death*, p. 152.

469   Hardorff, *The Oglala Lakota*, p. 32.

470   W.J. Bordeaux, *Custer's Conqueror*, p. 42.

471   Hardorff, *The Death*, p. 75, and sources therein.

472   In a reply letter to W.J. Bordeaux dated Oct. 26, 1951, W.G. Robinson spoke of two facial wounds: "Men who were present when No Water shot Crazy Horse say the bullet entered one cheek, was deflected by the upper jawbone, passed across his nose and made a wound in the other cheek." Robinson went on to say: "Mary Russell [a Lakota mixed-blood] tells a story, wholly unsolicited, that after Crazy Horse's death, two old women from his band who knew him well disputed about the location of the wound on his face. One of them placed it up on the cheek bone and one said it was lower down [as Chips also indicated]." Robinson eventually showed Mary Russell the picture of an Indian with two apparent facial wounds to which her comment was, "Maybe both of those women were right and he had two wounds!" Additional confusion resulted from the fact that the picture Robinson was circulating as a possible likeness of Crazy Horse, was the one featured in Wi'iyohi. As we saw, it was subsequently identified as either "Chak-ur-t-kee," a Pawnee or Arikara chief, or possibly Red Horn/Red Horned Bull/Shot in the Face, Oglala or Mnicojou, or even an unidentified Hunkpapa, though there was also a Red Horn Bull in Sitting Bull's tribe. In 1959 a copy and blow-up detail of the Wi'iyohi Indian were analyzed by a medical doctor thanks to the interest of Eugene ("Gene") L. Price of the Ohio Oil Company in Findlay. The company physician, John H. Hege, M.D., who also happened to be a lawyer, concluded, "I have closely studied the three photographs of your Indian [...] and it appears to me that he has what may well be a keloid scar under his right eye. A raised area approximately 1 millimeter in height by 3/4" long by over 1/3" wide is visible on all three photographs. It is well delineated and the outline under magnification is the same in all three pictures. Keloid scar formation tends to occur at sights of injury to the skin which may be as simple as a scratch or as severe as complete destruction of the skin tissue. It would be interesting to know if there were any observations of his body made after death to ascertain if he may have had other such scars present [...] it would add additional strength to the belief that this is a keloid scar under his right eye." J.H. Hege, M.D., "Intracompany correspondence to Mr. Eugene L. Price, [dated] July 13, 1959"; typescript, Crazy Horse File, South Dakota State Historical Society, Pierre; copy in authors' possession.

473   Mari Sandoz, "Letter to Will G. Robinson, [dated] October 19, 1947"; typescript, Crazy Horse File, South Dakota State Historical Society, Pierre; copy in authors' possession.

474   He Dog narrative as told to his son Eagle Hawk in Hardorff, *The Death*, pp. 131-150.

475   See, for example, the editorial, "Surrender of Crazy Horse," *New York Tribune*, May 7, 1877; ibid. p. 208.

476   Editorial, "The End of the Sioux War," *New York Sun*, May 23, 1877; ibid. p. 209.

477   Editorial, "The End of the Sioux War," p. 81.

478   "Chips Interview, February 14, 1907," in Hardorff, *The Death*, p. 81; in addition to the face scar, Crazy Horse had also a bullet wound scar on his arm, from the Pawnee, and one in his left calf from the Ute.

479   "Story of Gen. Jesse M. Lee," in Brininstool, "Chief Crazy Horse," pp. 31-32.

480   Trimble, "What Did Crazy Horse Look Like?"

481   Victoria Conroy in Jean Hammond, "Clean-up," p. 3.

482   Jake Herman, "Letter to J.W. Vaughn, 1956."

483   "American Horse Winter Count: 1877-78 – No. I. A soldier ran a bayonet into Crazy Horse, and killed him in the guard house, at Fort Robinson, Nebraska (September 5, 1877)," in Garrick Mallery, "Pictographs of the North American Indians – A Preliminary Paper." *Fourth Annual Report of the Bureau of [American] Ethnology, 1882-'83*. GPO, Washington, 1886, p. 146 and Plate LI; Candace S. Greene and Russell Thornton, *The Year the Stars Fell: Lakota Winter Counts at the Smithsonian*. Smithsonian Institution and University of Nebraska Press, 2007, p. 278.

484   Natalie Curtis (Burlin), *The Indians' Book. An Offering by the American Indians of Indian Lore, Musical and Narrative, [etc.]*. Harper and Brothers, New York, 1907, pp. 45-49, and photo of Arnold Short Bull.

485   Colin G. Calloway, ed., *Ledger Narratives. The Plains Indian Drawings of the Lansburgh Collection at Dartmouth College*. University of Oklahoma Press, Norman, 2012, p. 178, Plate 132, and p. 258. Although the edited caption identifies the pursuers as *Apsáalooke (Crow)*, probably from their hairstyle, the pencil notation on the original p. 37 of the Short Bull notebook identifies them as *Shoshones*.

486   Carl F. Day, *Tom Custer: Ride to Glory*. University of Oklahoma Press, Norman, 2002, pp. 74-75.

487   Ibid. p. 75.

488 Dean O'Bannon, "Letter to Will G. Robinson, [dated] 5-1-67"; handwritten, South Dakota State Historical Society, Pierre; copy in authors' possession; Lone Eagle, "Letter: The Death and Burial of Chief Crazy Horse," *Frontier Times*, July 1964, p. 39. Lone Eagle was listed among the Lakota warriors at the Little Bighorn; see also Bray, *Crazy Horse*, p. 427, note 2.

489 Pugh Young Man Afraid of His Horses, letter cited.

490 C. Walstrom, *Search for the Lost Trail*.

491 "The Chips Interview, February 14, 1907," in Hardorff, *The Death*, pp. 73-75, passim.

492 "Interview with Red Feather, July 8, 1930, Mrs. Annie Ro[w]land, interpreter," in Hinman, "Oglala Sources," p. 30.

493 Luther Standing Bear, *My People*, p. 83.

494 Little Killer in Hinman, "Oglala Sources," p. 45.

495 S. Bettelyoun, typescript cited, 1936, pp. 2-3.

496 W.J. Bordeaux, *Custer's Conqueror*, [p. ii], p. 89.

497 The Eagle Elk Interview, in Hardorff, *The Death*, pp. 153-154.

498 Ibid. p.154; also, "The Campbell Letters," ibid. p. 269.

499 Editorial, "The End of the Sioux War," *New York Sun*, May 23, 1877, in Hardorff, *The Death*, p. 209.

500 Hardorff, *The Oglala Lakota*, p. 19.

501 "Interview with Little Killer, 1930," in Eleanor Hinman, "Oglala Sources," p. 45.

502 S. Bettelyoun 1936, pp. 2-3.

503 W.J. Bordeaux, *Custer's Conqueror*, [p. ii?]

504 Thomas R. Buecker, "'I Will Pay Well for It': One Trader's Deposition." *Museum of the Fur Trade Quarterly*, Vol. 46, No. 3, Fall 2010, p. 1, 3 [pp. 1-5].

505 Robert A. Murray, "Treaty Presents at Fort Laramie, 1867-1868: Prices and Quantities from the Seth E. Ward Ledger." *The Museum of the Fur Trade Quarterly*, Vol. 13, No. 3, 1977, pp. 1-5.

506 Ibid. pp. 3-4.

507 A cabinet card of the latter sold at Cowan's Auctions for $600.

508 White Bull in Vestal, *Warpath*, pp. 157, 219.

509   "The Story of Waterman"; "The Story of Left Hand" in W.A. Graham, *The Custer Myth*, pp. 109-112.

510   W.H. Jackson, *Descriptive Catalogue*, p. 100, Nos. 40-41; John Koster, "The 'Arapaho Five' at the Little Bighorn." *Wild West*, Vol. 25, No. 1, June 2012, p. 40 [pp. 38-43]; another pose in *http://www.amertribes.proboards.com/index.cgi?board=arapaho&action=display&thread=427*

511   John Koster, "Left Hand Went from Custer Scout to Lakota Warrior at the Little Bighorn." *Wild West*, Vol. 28, No. 1, 2015, p. 24 [pp. 24-25].

512   Editorial "Incidents of the Surrender." *Denver Daily Tribune*, May 18, 1877, in Hardorff, *The Death*, p. 215.

513   Ricker, [William Garnett's Interview], *The Indian Interviews*, p. 47.

514   Ibid., p. 779.

515   DeMallie, "Scenes," pp. 58-59.

516   Hardorff, *The Death*, p. 228.

517   Charles C. Hamilton, "Address" p. 827.

518   This stereoview sold at Cowan's Auction, June 5-6, 2008 for $805.00; the caption says that the female seating next to the chief is his wife, while their son is flanked by his own wife, standing, and their young daughter, sitting: *http://www.cowanauction.com/auctions/item.aspx?Itemid=61039*

519   C. Marino, *The Long Knife: Swords and Katana of the American Indians*. Research Report submitted to Dr. Paul M. Taylor, Director, ACHP, Department of Anthropology, Smithsonian Institution, 2011. (Revised 2014).

520   "Interview with Red Feather, Pine Ridge, South Dakota, July 8, 1930," in Hinman, "Oglala Sources," p. 26.

521   Bray, *Crazy Horse*, pp. 287-289.

522   Nebraska State Historical Society, No. 103330, with erroneous identification of the Indians noted.

523   Dickson, "Photographers," pp. 7-8.

524   The Campbell Letters, in Hardorff, *The Death*, p. 269.

525   Michael Samuel, "Crazy Horse Info.," email dated Sunday, March 12, 2006; copy in authors' possession.

526   "Interview with White Calf, July 11, 1930," in Hinman, "Oglala Sources," p. 43.

527   M. Samuel, "Crazy Horse," email cit.

528   W.J. Bordeaux, *Custer's Conqueror*, p. 24.

529   M. Samuel, "Crazy Horse," email cit.

530   "Interview with White Calf," p. 43.

531   "Interview with He Dog, July 7, 1930," in Hinman, *Oglala Sources*, pp. 20-21.

532   Bray, *Crazy Horse*, pp. 382-390.

533   "Interview with He Dog, July 7, 1930," in Hinman, *Oglala Sources*, pp. 21-22.

534   Chips Interview, February 14, 1907, in Hardorff, *The Death*, pp. 73-75, passim; William K. Powers, *Yuwipi: Vision and Experience in Oglala Ritual*. University of Nebraska Press, Lincoln, 1982, pp. 8-10. James R. Walker, *Lakota Belief and Ritual*. Ed. by Raymond J. DeMallie and Elaine A. Jahner. University of Nebraska Press, Norman, 1980, 1991, p. 303, note 7. A late photograph of Horn Chips and his wife is in Sprague, *Pine Ridge*, pp. 36-37.

535   "Interview with Red Feather, July 8th ,1930," in Hinman, "Oglala Sources," p. 31.

536   "Interview with He Dog, July 13, 1930," in Hinman, ibid. p. 13.

537   "Interview with He Dog, June 30, 1931," in Hardorff, *The Death*, pp. 120-121.

538   White Lance, *Tasunke Witko*, [unpaged, p. 2].

539   Chips in Hardorff, *The Death*, p. 77, note 10.

540   Eagle Elk in Hardorff, ibid. p. 154.

541   Hardorff, "Interview with He Dog, July 30, 1931," *The Death*, pp. 120-121.

542   T. Powers, *The Killing*, p. 178.

543   Hardorff, *The Oglala Lakota*, p. 20.

544   Ibid.

545   He Dog in Hinman, "Oglala Sources," pp. 13-13.

546   Eagle Elk in Hardorff, *The Death*, p. 154.

547   Hardorff, *The Oglala Lakota*, p. 20.

548   White Lance, *Tasunke Witko*, [unpaged, p. 2].

549   Reproduced, color Plate III, in John G. Bourke, "The Medicine-Men of the Apache." *Ninth Annual Report of the Bureau of [American] Ethnology, 1887-88.* GPO, Washington, 1892 [1893], Plate III.; Hardorff, *The Death,* frontispiece (b/w).

550   "Corbusier/American Horse Winter Count" in Garrick Mallery, "Pictographs," p. 146, Plate LI; Candace S. Greene and Russell Thornton, *The Year the Stars Fell,* p. 278.

551   Ricker, "Chipps's Interview, Febr. 14, 1907," *The Indian Interviews,* p. 274.

552   Reproduction in Hedren, "The Crazy Horse Medal," p. 197.

553   Vaughn, *With Crook,* p. 42.

554   M. Samuel, email.

555   Richard Hook, in Jason Hook, *American Indian,* [facing p. 65].

556   David Shanahan, "Victory for Crazy Horse," *Little Big Horn Associates Newsletter,* Vol. XL, No. 1, Feb. 20006, frontispiece.

557   E. and M. Kadlececk, *To Kill an Eagle,* p. 149.

558   L. Standing Bear, *Land of the Spotted Eagle,* p. 209.

559   "Red Victory" by Michael Schreck, 2001, in *Research Review: The Journal of the Little Big Horn Associates,* Vol. 19, No. 2, 2005, front cover; caption on p. 1.

560   Heriard, "Debating," p. 20, Photo 3 and Photo 4.

561   John S. Bishop, "More on Crazy Horse," *Whispering Wind,* September-October, 2004.

562   David Shanahan in "Low Dog, Oglala," *http://www.American-Tribes.com/Lakota/BIO/LowDog.htm*

563   Goodyear, *Red Cloud,* pp. 36-37.

564   Ibid. p. 39.

565   John C. Ewers, "Hair Pipes in Plains Indian Adornment: A Study of Indian and White Ingenuity." *Bureau of American Ethnology Bulletin* No. 164; *Anthropological Papers* 50, 1957, pp. 60-61 [pp. 29-85, plates 13-37]. See also: Allen Chronister, "Bone Hair Pipes." *The Museum of the Fur Trade Quarterly,* Vol. 35, No. 4, 1999, pp. 13-14.

566   James A. Hanson, "Trade Goods in Some L.A. Huffman Photographs." *The Museum of the Fur Trade Quarterly,* Vol. 18, Nos. 1-2, 1982, pp. 2, 5, [pp. 1-8].

567   Angela Aleiss, "Is This Crazy Horse?" p. 3.

568   Sprague, *Pine Ridge Reservation,* p. 49.

569   Charles E. Hanson, Jr., "Oglala Hair Pipe Breastplates." *The Museum of the Fur Trade Quarterly*, Vol. 11, No. 1, 1975, p. 9 [pp. 7-10]. During a visit to the Museum of the Fur Trade, Chadron, Nebr., we were informed that the original photograph has long been lost.

570   Emil Afraid of Hawk, "Sam Little Bull." *The Indian Sentinel*, Vol. XXIII, No. 4, (April) 1943, pp. 63-64.

571   John F. Finerty, *War-Path and Bivouac: Or the Conquest of the Sioux*. M.A. Donohue and Co., Chicago, 1890, pp. 208-211; see also Richard G. Hardorff, *Hokahey! A Good Day to Die! The Indian Casualties of the Custer Fight*. University of Nebraska Press, Lincoln, 1991, p. 51.

572   Ephriam D. Dickson, III, "The Horned Horse Map of the Little Bighorn." *Little Big Horn Associates Newsletter*, Vol. XVIII, No. 7, Sept. 2009, pp. 4-5.

573   Dickson, *The Sitting Bull Surrender*, pp. 279, 295.

574   Joe De Barthe, *The Life and Adventures of Frank Grouard, Chief of Scouts, U.S.A.*, Combe Printing Co., St. Joseph, Mo., 1894, facing p. 280, name misspelled "Gaunier"; also posted by Dietmar Schulte-Möhring, "Baptiste Garnier aka Little Bat," Feb. 29, 2009, *http://amertribes.proboards.com/index*

575   "Early tintype of a Native American Indian 1860's: Lot 25387B"; Manor Auctions; *http://www.liveauctioneers.com/ item/11262543_early-tintype-of-a-native-american-indian-1860s*

576   The drawing was published by T. Powers, *The Killing*, second color inset following p. 106. For a similar breastplate in an 1870s ledger drawing see Candace Greene, "From Bison Robes to Ledgers." *European Review of Native American Studies*, Vol. 18, No. 1, 2004, p. 24, fig. 4.

577   M. Samuel, email.

578   It is not clear whether the author of the *Ledger* was the elder Red Hawk, or his son Red Hawk. Original drawings posted in the MPM website: *http://www. mpm.edu/research/collections/anthropology/online*:The Ledger Art Collection.

579   See Robert Wilson, *Mathew Brady: Portraits of a Nation*. Bloombury, New York, etc., 2013, p. 218.

580   Two Strike photo in: *http://amertribes.proboards.com/thread/327/strike*

581   Sprague, *Pine Ridge*, p. 48.

582   Bray, *Crazy Horse*, p. 290.

583   Ibid. p. 292.

584   Heriard, "Debating," p. 20, Photo 4.

585   Photo reproduced in Sprague, *Pine Ridge*, p. 61.

586   Record Portrait (Profile) of Shun-Ka Blo-Ka (He Dog) in Partial Native Dress with Headdress and Holding War Club 1875 | Collections Search Center, Smithsonian Institution: *http://collections.si.edu/search/detail/ edanmdm:siris_arc_13980?q=he+dog&record=3&hlterm=he%2Bdog&inline=true*

587   See a color-enhanced version of this photo in: *http://www.American-Tribes.com/Lakota/BIO/ThreeBears.htm*

Regarding the use of fabric dress by Indians in 1870s Sioux delegations to Washington, Herman J. Viola's excellent *Diplomats in Buckskins*, Smithsonian, 1981, should have more properly been titled "in buckskins and white shirts."

588   Feraca, "Crazy Horse," p. 62.

589   Photographic History Division, National Museum of American History: "Civil War@Smithsonian: Tintype Camera"; *http://civilwar.si.edu/life_tintype_ camera.html*

590   George Gilbert, *Photography: The Early Years. A Historical Guide for Collectors.* Harper and Row, New York, 1980; Edward M. Eastbrooke, *The Ferrotype, and How To Make It.* Gatchel and Hyatt, Cincinnati, 1872 (facsimile repr. Morgan and Morgan, New York, 1972); Janice G. Schimmelman, *The Tintype in America, 1856-1880.* American Philosophical Society, Philadelphia, 2007; Steven Kasher, *America and the Tintype.* Steidl/ICP, 2008.

591   Paula Fleming, "Crazy Horse – questions relating to the tintype," email to authors, Dec. 12, 2007.

592   Mari Sandoz, "Letter to J.W. Vaughn, [dated] New York, December 17, 1955." *Jesse Wendell Vaughn Papers, 1869-1960,* Acc. 313, Box 1, Folder 1955; American Heritage Center, University of Wyoming, Laramie.

593   Jerome A. Greene, "Faces of War: Five Soldiers of General Crook's Big Horn and Yellowstone Expedition, 1876." *Nebraska History*, Vol. 83, No. 22, 2002, pp. 98-102.

594   Hurt and Lass, *Frontier Photographer*, pp. 47-48.

595   "Garnett to McGillycuddy," letter cited in Friswold, *The Killing*, p. 130.

596   Vaughn, *With Crook*, p. 41.

597   Jesse M. Lee, "The Capture and Death of an Indian Chieftain," and, Henry R. Lemly, "The Passing of Crazy Horse." *Journal of the Military Service Institution of the United States*, Vol. 54, No. 189, May-June 1914, pp. 317-322; Buecker, "Crazy Horse," pp. 28, 30-31, 35.

598   Vaughn, *With Crook*, p. 42.

599   Sprague, *Pine Ridge*, p. 57.

600   Robert H. Ruby, *A Doctor among the Oglala Sioux Tribe: The Letters of Robert H. Ruby, 1953-1954.* Edited and with an introduction by Cary C. Collins and Charles V. Mutschler. University of Nebraska Press, Norman, 2010, pp. 29, 81.

601   Ibid. p. 135.

602   Ibid. p. 220.

603   Ibid. p. 255.

604   Robert H. Ruby, "Crazy Horse," in *The Oglala Sioux: Warriors in Transition.* Foreword by Glenn L. Emmons. New Introduction by Cary C. Collins. University of Nebraska Press, Lincoln. [1955], Bison ed., 2010, pp. 96-101.

605   The letterhead reads: State Historical Society Memorial Hall, Pierre, South Dakota, Feb. 24[,] 1953; typescript, Crazy Horse File, South Dakota State Historical Society; copy in authors' possession.

606   Ibid., pp. 43, 46.

607   Ibid. facing p.132.

608   Ellen Howard, "Letter to Fred B. Hackett, Pine Ridge, So.Dak. Dec. 30 – 57"; copy in authors' possession.

609   Friswold, *The Killing*, pp. 45-47.

610   James H. Cook, "Big Bat and Little Bat" in *Fifty Years on the Old Frontier*, Yale University Press, New Haven, Conn., 1954, pp. 161-170, and photographs.

611   John Hunton, *John Hunton's Diary, 1873-75. Volume 1: Echoes from 1875 (With a Glimpse at 1873).* L.G. (Pat) Flannery, ed., Guide-Review, Lingle, Wyo., 1956, pp. 104-106.

612   John Hunton, *John Hunton's Diary, Volume 2: 1876-1877*, L.G. (Pat) Flannery, ed., Guide-Review, Lingle, Wyo., 1958, pp. 248-249.

613   Lawrence J. Barkwell, "Garnier, Baptiste 'Little Bat,'" Louis Riel Institute, Winnipeg, Man., 2010. See also E.A. Brininstool, *Fighting Indian Warriors.* Stackpole Co., Harrisburg, Pa., 1953, pp. 271-279.

614   Hunton, *Diary*, Vol. 1, p 105.

615   White Lance, *The Genealogy.*

616   Garnier, Mousseau, Yellow Woman: *http://www.freepages.genealogy.rootsweb.com/mikestevens/SURNAME*

617   Ricker, [Louis/Louie Mousseau's Interview, Nov. 2, 1906], *The Indian Interviews*, p. 229.

618   De Barthe, *The Life*, facing p. 280.

619   Dave Alexander, "The True Legend of Dewey Beard." 3 pts. *Indian Country Today*, Sept. 12, 19, 26, 2005; according to this source Beard was born in 1858.

620   [Editorial] "Chief Iron Tail, [...] died of heart disease [etc.]." *The Indian Sentinel*, Vol. 1, No. 1, 1916, p. 28.). Iron Tail, who had fought alongside Crazy Horse, was the main character used by James Earle Frazer as the model for the Indian Head Nickel (obverse). Fred Hackett took photographs of his adopted Oglala father during Iron Tail's association with Buffalo Bill Cody's *Wild West*, from about 1898 to his death in 1916. Iron Tail's "typical Sioux" photogenic features, his veteran warrior background and elder status among the Lakota contingent in Buffalo Bill's show made him a favorite of Col. Cody. Cody featured him in colorful posters as "Iron Tail, Last of the Great Chiefs." In 1898, while the show was in New York City, Iron Tail was photographed by Gertrude Käsebier (1852-1934), a talented portrait photographer who had studied at the famed Pratt Institute and later opened her first studio in the City. Käsebier's desire to capture the inner personal character of her subjects, rather than stereo-typical portraits, was generally successful, but not without some fuss. One time Iron Tail agreed to be photographed without his spectacular war bonnet, the finished product satisfying the photographer but not her distinguished subject: "when Iron Tail saw the print, he immediately tore it in half, upset with the image. Later, the chief sat for Käsebier in full regalia." Iron Tail became a national icon and was photographed many times, including a classic profile by Delancey Gill in 1913. The buffalo nickel did the rest to memorialize Iron Tail as the 'classic' American Indian; see David W. Lange, *The Complete Guide to Buffalo Nickels*. Third Edition. DRLC Press, Virginia Beach, Va., 2006. The Indian profile on the buffalo nickel, hence the "spirit" of Iron Tail, has inspired the logo of the Washington Redskins football team, both name and mascot long at the center of heated controversy.

621   D. Alexander, "The True Legend of Dewey Beard." See also the biography by Philip Burnham, *Song of Dewey Beard: Last Survivor of the Little Bighorn*. University of Nebraska Press, Lincoln, 2014.

622   Jake Herman, "Letter to J.W. Vaughn, [dated] Pine Ridge, SD, Oct. 24, 1956." *Jesse Wendell Vaughn Papers, 1869-1960*, Acc. 313, Box 1, Folder 1956; American Heritage Center, University of Wyoming, Laramie.

623   Sprague, *Pine Ridge*, p. 110: photo of Carlisle Indian School Football Team, 1917, with Jake Herman seated in middle row.

624   "Jake Herman, Brule Sioux," in Joseph H. Cash and Herbert T. Hoover, eds., *To Be an Indian: An Oral History*. Holt, Rinehart and Winston, New York, 1971, pp. 102-103.

625   Ruby, *A Doctor*, pp. 322-323.

626   Jake Herman, "The Sacred Pole." *The Masterkey*, Vol. 37, No. 1, 1963, pp. 35-38.

627   Jake Herman – Igta-Ter Kerlia, "The Sioux in Life & in Legend: An Indian Cowboy Life." *The Indian Historian*, Vol. 2, No. 6, 1965, pp. 11-12, 14, 16.

628   "Jake Herman from Pine Ridge, SD," in 1985 Inductee Class, South Dakota Hall of Fame, Chamberlain, SD.

629   Paul B. Steinmetz, *Pipe, Bible, and Peyote among the Oglala Lakota: A Study in Religious Identity*. Syracuse University Press, Syracuse, 1998, p. 30.

630   Jake Herman, "Letter to J.W. Vaughn, [dated] October 24, 1956."

631   "Dewey Beard"; *http://amertribes.proboards.com/thread/177/dewey-beard*

632   Kappler, *Treaties*, p. 1004; the Lakota name should read *Mato-ha Shina,* Bear-skin Robe.

633   "Paul Bear Robe, Ogalla [sic]," photograph by James B. Brown, ca. 1900-1920; Denver Public Library, Western History/Genealogy Dept., call number: X-31942.

634   Indian Census Rolls, 1885-1940, Pine Ridge (Oglala Sioux Indians), Microcopy 595, The National Archives. McGregor authored *The Wounded Knee Massacre from the Viewpoint of the Sioux*. Wirth, Baltimore, 1940.

635   Omer C. Stewart, *Peyote Religion: A History*. University of Oklahoma Press, Norman, 1989; Steinmetz, *Pipe, Bible, and Peyote*.

636   Thomas H. Lewis, *The Medicine Men: Oglala Sioux Ceremony and Healing*. University of Nebraska Press, Lincoln, 1990, p. 116.

637   Ruby, *A Doctor*, pp. 179-180.

638   Ibid. p. 237.

639   Ibid. p. 68.

640   Ibid. p. 239.

641   Colin F. Taylor, *Wapa'ha: The Plains Feathered Head-dress/Die Plains-Federhaube*. Verlang für Amerikanistik, Wyk auf Foehr, Germany, 1994, pp. 13, 39 [40-43].

642   Richard Green, "'I dreamed of the elk': Iron Tail's Muslin Dance Shield." *Whispering Wind*, Vol. 38, No. 3, 2009, pp. 4-10. Leland D. Case, "The Westerners: Twenty Five Years of Riding the Range." *The Western Historical Quarterly*, Vol. 1, No. 1, 1970, pp. 63-76.

643   Don Russell, *The Lives and Legends of Buffalo Bill.* University of Oklahoma Press, Norman, 1979, pp. 128, 284, 310, 438.

644   Wildhage, *Die Winterzählungen*, pp. 37, 42, 54, 65, et seq.; James R. Walker, *Lakota Society*. Edited by Raymond J. DeMallie. University of Nebraska Press, Lincoln, 1982, p. 119.

645   Fred B. Hackett, "Letter to T.W. Wright, [dated] 8/11/58, Chicago"; Cover letter to accompany William Garnett's Report on the Death of Crazy Horse 1920; in Thomas W. Wright Papers, RG1578.AM, Nebraska State Historical Society, Lincoln; handwritten; photocopy in authors' possession.

646   Fred B. Hackett, *Calendar for Oglala Sioux Names for Years from AD. 1759 to AD. 1908.* [Based on the No Ears winter count] mimeo, ca. 1958; *Sioux*, mimeo, 1960; *Odds and Ends*, mimeo, 1962.

647   Copies of this letter and of the following one are in authors' possession.

648   T.W. Wright, *The evidence*, pp. 10-12.

649   "Interview with Short Buffalo (Short Bull) [no location given], July 13, 1930, John Colhoff, Interpreter," in Hinman, "Oglala Sources," pp. 40-41.

650   Hardorff, *The Death*, p. 136. Joseph Eagle Hawk was the son of Eagle Hawk, Četan Wamble (1832-1904), a brother of chief He Dog; Joseph Eagle Hawk, "History of Chief Crazy Horse," in Friswold, *The Killing*, pp. 46-69; Dickson, *The Sitting Bull Surrender*, p. 283.

651   Hinman, "Oglala Sources," p. 5.

652   John M. Carroll, "Editor's Introduction," in *The Eleanor H. Hinman*, p. 16.

653   Carl Rieckmann, "'Proven' Sole 1877 Photo of Crazy Horse Finds Home at Custer Battlefield Museum." *Big Horn County News*, June 19, 2003.

654   "Dean O'Bannon, Letter to Will G. Robinson [dated] Dallas, Texas, 5-1-67"; handwritten, Crazy Horse File, South Dakota State Historical Society, Pierre; copy in authors' possession.

List of Illustrations and Credits

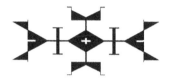

Note: The Authors made all reasonable efforts to secure permission to publish the images in the book. For images they could not determine ownership or secure permission, the Authors will gladly comply upon written notification.

Front cover: Crazy Horse, close-up, enlarged from the tintype.

The tintype, attributed to James H. Hamilton (1877). Courtesy of James "Putt" Thompson.

Crazy Horse, painting by Thom Little Moon (2014). Courtesy of the artist.

Crazy Horse's Genealogy, researched and compiled by Dr. Francis White Lance (2013). Courtesy of the author.

Crazy Horse's War Shirt (published in 1892). From original color plate in authors' possession.

A Wakinyan / Thunderbird shield given to author Cesare Marino by Randy Emery and Steve Feraca.

Crazy Horse, by Brad Holland; USA 13c stamp, Great Americans Series (1982). From original stamp in authors' American Indian Philatelic Collection.

Crazy Horse Monument, Thunder Mountain, South Dakota; the face (2017). Authors' photograph.

"The sun dancer" by Richard Emery (1970). Presented by Charles 'Chuck' Emery to author Cesare Marino.

One Horn, by George Catlin (1832). Courtesy of Smithsonian American Art Museum.

Crazy Horse's scaffold grave near Camp Sheridan, Nebraska, photographed by Pvt. Charles Howard (1877). Courtesy of U.S. Military Academy Library, West Point.

Sitting Bull the Oglala, Swift Bear, and Spotted Tail; standing: Julius Meyer and Red Cloud. Studio photograph by Frank F. Currier, Omaha, Nebraska, May 1875. From: *https://commons.wikimedia.org/wiki/File*: Indian Chiefs 1875.

Crazy Horse's Oath of Enlistment and Allegiance as a U.S. Army Scout, May 12, 1877. Courtesy of Ephriam D. Dickson; original in U.S. Army Enlistment Records, National Archives.

Crazy in the Lodge, by Stanley J. Morrow, 1876. From: *http://amertribes.proboards.com/thread/383/crazy-lodge*.

Crazy Horse, sketch by a Mormon missionary, 1934, with vague resemblance to the tintype Indian.
From: *http://www.unitedearth.com.au/crazyhorse.html*.

"Crazy Horse," by H. Soileau, is actually Crazy in the Lodge; 60c stamp, Marshall Islands, 1999. From original stamp in authors' American Indian Philatelic Collection.

Red Cloud Agency, Nebraska, by Ivan Pranishnikopf illustration in *Harper's Illustrated Weekly*, May 18, 1876. From: *https://commons.wikimedia.org/wiki/File:Red_cloud_agency.jpg*.

"165. Photographing Indians at Red Cloud" (1877), in J.H. Hamilton's *Catalogue* (1878).

"170. Learning the Use of the Stereoscope" (1877), in J.H. Hamilton's *Catalogue* (1878).

Chak-ur-t-kee (Chak-ok-ta-kee), by Byron H. Gurnsey, no date; published by J.H. Hamilton, "168. Pawnee Chief," in *Catalogue of Stereoscopic Views* (1878). Original in authors' possession.

J.H. Hamilton's *Catalogue of Stereoscopic Views of the Northwest*, Sioux City, Iowa (1878)

Composite comparison of the tintype Indian (l) and No Neck (r). Original in authors' possession.

American Horse in full regalia, studio portrait by Charles M. Bell, Washington, Oct. 1877. Courtesy of National Anthropological Archives, Smithsonian Institution BAE GN 03217 06531300.

"Crazy Horse," sketch in W.J. Bordeaux, *Custer's Conqueror* (1952). From copy in authors' possession.

Daniel White Lance, Joseph "Joe" Horn Cloud (standing), and Dewey Beard (aka Iron Hail), survivors of the Wounded Knee massacre, by unknown photographer (after 1900). Courtesy of Francis White Lance.

Composite comparison of Daniel White Lance and Crazy Horse. Courtesy of Francis White Lance.

Crazy Horse, with scar and black powder marks between the left nostril and the left ear. Enlarged detail from the tintype.

Crazy Horse, by Andrew Standing Soldier, sketched before 1940. From: *http://www.lakotacountrytimes.com/news/2009-04-02/front_page/002.html*.

Crazy Horse's light-brown eyes and 'penetrating stare.' Enlarged detail from the tintype.

Swift Bear (Mato Luzahan, 1827-1909), by A. Gardner, Washington, 1872. Courtesy of National Anthropological Archives, Smithsonian Institution, BAE GN 03134A 06516900.

The Killing of Crazy Horse (1877), by Bad Heart Bull (ca. 1890). Courtesy of Cincinnati Libraries Digital Collection.

Woman Dress, ca. 1877. Courtesy of Thomas Powers, author of *The Killing of Crazy Horse*.

Lieut. William Philo Clark and Oglala chief Little Hawk, by D.S. Mitchell, Red Cloud Agency, 1877. Courtesy of National Anthropological Archives, Smithsonian Institution, Photo Lot 24 SPC Stereo Plains Dakota 00209700.

Crazy Horse's grave, by Pvt. Charles Howard, near Camp Sheridan, Oct. 1877.

Crazy Horse's wotawe: full image and enlarged detail from the tintype.

Sam Little Bull, Jr., (b. 1861), by unknown photographer, no date, ca. late 1870s-early 1880s. Courtesy of The Museum of the Fur Trade, Chadron, Nebraska.

Baptiste "Little Bat" Garnier, by unknown photographer, no date, ca. 1880s. From: *http://amertribes.proboards.com/thread/458.*

Red Hawk shoots a Crow scout who had mortally wounded Black Whiteman (WasicuSapa). From: *http://amertribes.proboards.com/thread/992/red-hawk-ledger.*

Bad Heart Bull's drawing of Crazy Horse (body painted with dots representing hail) on his war-pony at the Little Bighorn, June 25, 1876, chasing Reno's soldiers in the valley fight. Courtesy of Cincinnati Libraries Digital Collection.

Billy Hunter Garnett (b. 1855), by unknown photographer, no date (ca. 1880-1885).

Sioux delegation, by Mathew Brady, Washington, late Sept. - Oct. 1877. Courtesy of Library of Congress, Prints and Photographs Division.

Red Cloud, shaking hands with William Blackmore, by Alexander Gardner, Washington, May1872. Courtesy of Library of Congress, Prints and Photographs Division.

"154. Family Group at Red Cloud" (1877), in J.H. Hamilton's *Catalogue* (1878).

Sioux and Arapaho delegation to Washington, late Sept. - Oct. 1877. Courtesy Princeton University Library Collection of Western Americana Photographs; 1870-1998 (mostly 1870-1915), Manuscripts Division, Department of Rare Books and Special Collections.

Three Bears (Mato Yamni), by Charles M. Bell, Washington, Oct. 1877. Courtesy of Photographs of North American Indians (WC054), Manuscripts Division, Department of Rare Books and Special Collections, Princeton University Library.

He Dog (Shunka Bloka, 1877), by Charles Bell, Washington, 1877. Courtesy of National Anthropological Archives, Smithsonian Institution, BAE GN 03229A 06533900.

Crazy Horse's protruding wrist bone. Enlarged detail from tintype.

Mrs. Ellen Howard's second affidavit, ca. 1958. From photocopy of the original in authors' possession.

Little Bat Garnier and his family, Camp Robinson, ca. 1898-1900. Royalties for permission, paid to the Nebraska State Historical Society.

Map
The Great Sioux Reservation, established by the Fort Laramie Treaty of 1868. Map in *Annual Report of the Commissioner of Indian Affairs*, 1877.

Made in the USA
Coppell, TX
14 November 2021